JOURNAL FOR THE STUDY OF THE OLD TESTAMENT
SUPPLEMENT SERIES
225

Sheffield Academic Press

A Gift of God in Due Season

Essays on Scripture and Community in Honor of James A. Sanders

edited by
Richard D. Weis and
David M. Carr

Journal for the Study of the Old Testament
Supplement Series 225

Published by Sheffield Academic Press Ltd
Mansion House
19 Kingfield Road
Sheffield S11 9AS
England

Printed on acid-free paper in Great Britain
by Bookcraft Ltd
Midsomer Norton, Bath

British Library Cataloguing in Publication Data

A catalogue record for this book is available
from the British Library

ISBN 1-85075-626-0

CONTENTS

Part II
ANCIENT AND MODERN TRANSMISSION, TRANSLATION AND APPROPRIATION OF THE CANON

FOREWORD

James M. Robinson

James A. Sanders, editor of the Psalms Scroll from Qumran Cave 11, came to Claremont to revitalize the local tradition of Dead Sea Scrolls scholarship. After all, Claremont had been one of the handful of locations within the nation to have hosted the Dead Sea Scrolls touring exhibit funded by Elizabeth Hay Bechtel a generation ago.

Under Sanders's expert guidance and counsel she established the Ancient Biblical Manuscript Center for Preservation and Research, an independent corporation housed at the School of Theology at Claremont in a wing to the library which she donated for this purpose. As the President of the foundation she was joined by Sanders as the Executive Vice-President, and later he became her successor as President. Together they organized a photographic mission to Israel to secure copies of the photographs of all the Dead Sea Scrolls in the Rockefeller Museum, to be housed in a climatized vault at the Ancient Biblical Manuscript Center itself and, for permanent safekeeping, near Lake Tahoe in what amounts to a time capsule for the rescue of our cultural heritage in a worst-case scenario.

Sanders has not let this academic treasure lie dormant, but has in two senses carried through responsibly the implications inherent in the deposit of the materials here. First of all he organized a cataloguing project, a need long sensed in Qumran studies, given the fact that there had been nowhere available an index of just what texts had been discovered and the status of their publication. He sent the cataloguer of the Ancient Biblical Manuscript Center, Stephen Reed, to Jerusalem to sort through the original texts themselves, to determine just what is extant and correlate that with the photographs, and to carry through to completion at Claremont the cataloguing begun there, now on the basis of the Center's photographic archives. The result is that the unpublished material that has only recently become available in principle to the scholarly public at large can now be identified fragment by fragment and thus be made available in practice. One need only recall the widely varying estimates of how much unpublished material there was to realize the extent of ignorance that prevailed about the extent and contents of the mass of fragments found in Cave 4. Now one can simply consult Reed's catalogue, initially published by the Ancient Biblical Manuscript Center and subsequently published in revised form by Scholars Press.[1]

The second sense in which Sanders has facilitated the use of the unpublished Dead Sea Scrolls is in fostering the ABMC's project of photographic enhancement. Not only the scroll fragments themselves, but the photographs of them made a generation ago, are deteriorating at a speed and to an extent hardly realized by a public without direct access to them. But the ABMC's Acting Director for several years, the Semitist Bruce Zuckerman, together with his brother Kenneth, a professional photographer, have combined their expertise to bring that lamentable disappearing act to a halt, in that they have developed state-of-the-art photographic techniques for rephotographing the photographic negatives at the Center so as to produce results that are actually superior to the archival copies from which their photographs are made. And with the new computer technology of the Center, photographs can be put on the screen in an infinite variety of color selection, enlargement, tone adjustment, and the like, until the last possible degree of legibility has been achieved. Indicative of the relevance of this photographic achievement is the fact that the official microfiche edition of the Dead Sea Scrolls published under the auspices of the Israel Antiquities Authority had to turn to the ABMC in a number of instances to obtain the best possible photograph of a given fragment.[2]

Scholars now seeking to obtain access to unpublished fragments from Cave 4 are best advised to turn to Sanders and his Ancient Biblical Manuscript Center to meet their needs. Here, where the material was catalogued, one can readily identify the photograph of any requested fragment; here the best-quality photographs of it can be provided; and here is available the computer facility to wring from it the last bit of information. It is thus a significant achievement of James Sanders to have made of Claremont the major American center of access to the Dead Sea Scrolls. For this we are all indebted to him.

1. S.A. Reed, *The Dead Sea Scrolls Catalogue: Documents, Photographs and Museum Inventory Numbers* (ed. M.A. Lundberg with M.B. Phelps; SBLRBS, 32; Atlanta: Scholars Press, 1994).

2. *The Dead Sea Scrolls on Microfiche* (Leiden: Brill/IDC Leiden, 1993).

ABBREVIATIONS

AASOR	Annual of the American Schools of Oriental Research
AB	Anchor Bible
ABD	D.N. Freedman (ed.), *Anchor Bible Dictionary*
AbrN	*Abr-Nahrain*
AcOr	*Acta orientalia*
ANET	J.B. Pritchard (ed.), *Ancient Near Eastern Texts*
ANQ	*Andover Newton Quarterly*
ARAB	D. Luckenbill, *Ancient Records at Assyria and Babylonia*
ArOr	*Archiv orientální*
BA	*Biblical Archaeologist*
BAGD	W. Bauer, W.F. Arndt, F.W. Gingrich and F.W. Danker, *Greek–English Lexicon of the New Testament*
BARev	*Biblical Archaeology Review*
BASOR	*Bulletin of the American Schools of Oriental Research*
BDB	F. Brown, S.R. Driver and C.A. Briggs, *Hebrew and English Lexicon of the Old Testament*
BETL	Bibliotheca ephemeridum theologicarum lovaniensium
BHS	*Biblia hebraica stuttgartensia*
BHT	Beiträge zur historischen Theologie
Bib	*Biblica*
BJS	Brown Judaic Studies
BKAT	Biblischer Kommentar: Altes Testament
BR	*Biblical Research*
BSac	*Bibliotheca Sacra*
BT	*The Bible Translator*
BTB	*Biblical Theology Bulletin*
BZAW	Beihefte zur *ZAW*
CBQ	*Catholic Biblical Quarterly*
CChr	Corpus Christianorum
DJD	Discoveries in the Judaean Desert
Ebib	Etudes bibliques
EncJud	*Encyclopaedia Judaica*
ErFor	*Erträge der Forschung*
EvT	*Evangelische Theologie*
FOTL	The Forms of the Old Testament Literature
HAR	*Hebrew Annual Review*
HAT	Handbuch zum Alten Testament
HBT	*Horizons in Biblical Theology*
HSS	Harvard Semitic Studies

HTR	*Harvard Theological Review*
HTS	Harvard Theological Studies
IB	*Interpreter's Bible*
IDB	G.A. Buttrick (ed.), *Interpreter's Dictionary of the Bible*
IDBSup	*IDB*, Supplementary Volume
IEJ	*Israel Exploration Journal*
Int	*Interpretation*
JAAR	*Journal of the American Academy of Religion*
JAC	Jahrbuch für Antike und Christentum
JANESCU	*Journal of the Ancient Near Eastern Society of Columbia University*
JAOS	*Journal of the American Oriental Society*
JBL	*Journal of Biblical Literature*
JBR	*Journal of Bible and Religion*
JBTh	Jahrbuch für Biblische Theologie
JewEnc	*The Jewish Encyclopedia*
JETS	*Journal of the Evangelical Theological Society*
JJS	*Journal of Jewish Studies*
JQR	*Jewish Quarterly Review*
JR	*Journal of Religion*
JSJ	*Journal for the Study of Judaism in the Persian, Hellenistic and Roman Period*
JSNTSup	*Journal for the Study of the New Testament*, Supplement Series
JSOT	*Journal for the Study of the Old Testament*
JSOTSup	*Journal for the Study of the Old Testament*, Supplement Series
JSPSup	*Journal for the Study of the Pseudepigrapha*, Supplement Series
JTS	*Journal of Theological Studies*
LCL	Loeb Classical Library
LD	Lectio divina
LSJ	Liddell–Scott–Jones, *Greek–English Lexicon*
McCQ	McCormick Quarterly
NCB	New Century Bible
NICOT	New International Commentary on the Old Testament
NIGTC	The New International Greek Testament Commentary
NTS	*New Testament Studies*
OBO	Orbis biblicus et orientalis
OTL	Old Testament Library
OTP	J.H. Charlesworth (ed.), *The Old Testament Pseudepigrapha*
OTS	*Oudtestamentische Studiën*
PJ	*Palästina-Jahrbuch*
PL	J. Migne (ed.), *Patrologia latina*
RB	*Revue biblique*
Rel	*Religion*
RelSRev	*Religious Studies Review*
RevQ	*Revue de Qumran*
RHR	*Revue de l'histoire des religions*
SBLDS	SBL Dissertation Series

SBLMasS	SBL Masoretic Studies
SBLMS	SBL Monograph Series
SBLRBS	SBL Resources for Biblical Study
SBT	Studies in Biblical Theology
SJLA	Studies in Judaism in Late Antiquity
SJT	*Scottish Journal of Theology*
SPB	Studia postbiblica
SR	*Studies in Religion/Sciences religieuses*
STDJ	Studies on the Texts of the Desert of Judah
TBT	*The Bible Today*
TDNT	G. Kittel and G. Friedrich (eds.), *Theological Dictionary of the New Testament*
TOTC	Tyndale Old Testament Commentaries
TS	*Theological Studies*
TT	*Teologisk Tidsskrift*
TTod	*Theology Today*
USQR	*Union Seminary Quarterly Review*
VT	*Vetus Testamentum*
VTSup	*Vetus Testamentum*, Supplements
WBC	Word Biblical Commentary
WMANT	Wissenschaftliche Monographien zum Alten und Neuen Testament
WUNT	Wissenschaftliche Untersuchungen zum Neuen Testament
ZAW	*Zeitschrift für die alttestamentliche Wissenschaft*
ZNW	*Zeitschrift für die neutestamentliche Wissenschaft*

LIST OF CONTRIBUTORS

LLOYD R. BAILEY, Methodist College, Fayetteville, NC

DOMINIQUE BARTHÉLEMY, Université de Fribourg (retired)

ROBERT A. BASCOM, United Bible Societies

NANCY R. BOWEN, Earlham School of Religion

MARY CHILTON CALLAWAY, Fordham University

DAVID M. CARR, Methodist Theological School in Ohio

PETER W. FLINT, Trinity Western University

GEORGE M. LANDES, Union Theological Seminary, New York (retired)

MERRILL P. MILLER, Pembroke State University

EUGENE A. NIDA, American Bible Society (retired)

JAMES M. ROBINSON, Claremont Graduate School and the Institute for Antiquity and Christianity

MARVIN A. SWEENEY, School of Theology at Claremont and Claremont Graduate School

SAMUEL TERRIEN, Union Theological Seminary, New York (retired)

RICHARD D. WEIS, New Brunswick Theological Seminary

INTRODUCTION

> I have often claimed that biblical criticism was a gift of God in due season, and that canonical criticism is a supplement and a logical sequel to the earlier disciplines.

'A gift of God in due season.' With these words James A. Sanders has characterized the historical-critical method.[1] With those same words we wish to characterize the life and work of Sanders himself, as we honor his achievements and mark his retirement with this collection of essays. The gift that we celebrate is, of course, a long and distinguished career. We mark a significant legacy that we trust is not yet finished.

The character of that career and legacy can be marked in a variety of ways. It is a journey that can be traced by positions at first Colgate Rochester Divinity School (1954–1965), then Union Seminary in New York (1965–1977), and finally the School of Theology at Claremont, Claremont Graduate School and the Ancient Biblical Manuscript Center (1977–1997). It is a life of great productivity marked by generations of students, a considerable list of publications, and countless sermons and lectures in churches and synagogues. It is a voice in the scholarly conversation that has had significant and timely things to say. It is this last characterization of the career and legacy of James A. Sanders that we wish to elaborate in this introduction, and in so doing set this collection of essays in the context of his work on Scripture and community.

A reviewer of the bibliography of James A. Sanders would notice three or four broad, recurring emphases: canonical criticism, the Second Temple appropriation of Scripture, textual criticism, and the editing and making available of the Dead Sea Scrolls and other manuscripts. Within and across these four emphases two foci stand out. First, Sanders's work on 11QPs[a] played a significant role in all these emphases. Secondly,

1. J.A. Sanders, 'Canonical Context and Canonical Criticism', in *From Sacred Story to Sacred Text* (Philadelphia: Fortress Press, 1987), p. 171. Again, and most recently in J.A. Sanders, 'Scripture as Canon for Post-Modern Times', *BTB* 25 (1995), p. 61.

from beginning to end, Sanders's work has been preoccupied by a set of issues and themes that have come to be associated with the term 'canonical criticism'. The other emphases of his work all find place in relation to this central one.

At the core of canonical criticism as developed by Sanders is the perception that to call a tradition, text or collection of texts canonical or authoritative is to recognize that it is enmeshed in a symbiotic relationship with communities of believers to whom the tradition, text or collection 'gives life', and who at the same time 'give life' to it. Canonical or authoritative materials give such communities life by providing a source for a communal identity that enables the establishment or maintenance of communal integrity in a particular historical context. The believing communities give life to such traditional materials as each new generation grants them authority to name the community's life, thus selecting, transmitting and elaborating them for succeeding generations.

In particular, Sanders has pointed out that this relationship between authoritative traditions or texts and the communities that grant them that authority has been present at every stage in the life of the materials now contained within the various canonical collections of Judaism and Christianity. It was at work in the period before the appearance of the forms in which the texts now come to us, just as it was at work in the transmission of those extant textual forms. The recognition of the canonical process in the period after the appearance of the extant forms of the canonical texts led to his conclusion that the history of the texts' transmission is also inescapably a history of appropriation which takes its place in the broader history of continuing communal appropriation of canonical texts. Thus the object of study for textual criticism is not simply a mechanical copying process, but a process of ongoing adaptation of the text, a transmission of meaning far more than a transmission of marks on the page. The recognition of the canonical process in the period leading up to the appearance of the extant textual forms led to the conclusion that the relics of the canonical process can be found within Scripture itself.

Within the canonical process Sanders identifies three key characteristics of authoritative materials: adaptability, stability and ideological pluralism. Adaptability and stability are characteristics he finds in canonical materials at all stages in the process from the emergence of the first oral tradition to the functioning of canonical texts in present believing communities. Ideological pluralism emerges as a characteristic of canonical materials as those begin to take the form of extended texts, and especially collections of texts.

Within the life of the communities that have recourse to these traditions and texts the canonical process is seen as a process of negotiating the adaptability, stability and ideological pluralism of those materials in order to provide a coherent interpretation of the context in which the community finds itself, and a viable identity for the community in the midst of that context. Sanders has pressed the investigation of this process of negotiating meaning principally in terms of the twin questions of function and hermeneutics. Canonical criticism in Sanders's conception of it as an exegetical method is particularly concerned to ask how texts functioned within believing communities in particular moments of interpretation, and what were the hermeneutical principles, assumptions and criteria used in the adaptation of the text to address communal needs. In investigating these questions himself, Sanders has argued for the identification of cases in the development of Scripture where traditions or texts functioned to confirm, and particularly critique, the established ethos of the believing audience. Moreover, he has proposed that those communities who developed texts now regarded as canonical tended to highlight the potential of their texts to help them theologically to understand their world (rather than moralize) and—in particular—to grasp the whole of reality in an understanding of it as under the control of one God. To use Sanders's terms, communities forming the Jewish and Christian Scriptures used a 'theocentric' and 'monotheizing' 'hermeneutic'. Sanders further maintains that these and other precedents within the process of formation of the canon can serve as a guide for creative, yet faithful, interaction with Scripture now.

Scholars have and will disagree about the extent to which such trends can actually be observed in the development of Scripture, and their significance even where they can be observed. Nevertheless, Sanders's contribution is hardly confined to any specific set of observations about function and hermeneutics within the canonical process. Instead, his has been one of the major voices calling for us to consider the dynamics of the process of Scripture's development as one key in determining how we appropriate it. Indeed, in this way his own method militates against any overly unilinear conception of exegesis or hermeneutics, canonical or otherwise. Citing as warrant the realization that the process of negotiating new meanings from old traditions is found in Scripture itself, Sanders has argued for an approach to interpretation that recognizes the text's capacity to generate multiple meanings. In this way, he denies the claim of any single method or construction of meaning to be the only correct adaptation of the text.

Here consideration of the context of Sanders's work can illuminate the particular character of the questions he was trying to answer. Canonical criticism arose as a response to a crisis of meaning in the churches, resulting from a historicizing application of the historical-critical method. At the time that Sanders published *Torah and Canon* (1972), the first full statement of canonical criticism, the crisis had already been joined in which modern believing communities had begun to feel that the Scriptures were being locked in the past by the efforts of modern scholarship pursuing the historical-critical method. In effect, the critics had so emphasized the need for the adaptation of the canonical texts that they had over-stressed the distance between the text and the modern believing communities to the point that a relation between Scripture and community seemed increasingly difficult to construct. At the same time there was (and still is) a contrasting interest in naive readings of the text that went to the other extreme of collapsing the distance between text and community, ignoring the necessity of adaptation. Sanders, in proposing canonical criticism, attempted to steer a middle way that affirmed (1) *both* the possibility *and* the necessity of adapting anew the canonical text to the life of the ever-changing communities of belief, and (2) the need to preserve some sort of claim of the text over against those communities' preexisting beliefs and values. His key has been to use the process of the development of canonical texts and the canon as a whole as the paradigm for both freeing up the canon for adaptation and for governing that adaptation.

This response to a theological and ecclesiastical expression of the crisis of modernity anticipated and resonates in striking ways with significant aspects of postmodernist approaches to Scripture, but largely from within the modernist approach and without recourse to the concepts and approaches introduced from postmodern literary theory, which in 1972 were only beginning to impact biblical studies. The most easily discernible resonance is the emphasis in his work on influence and intertextuality, long before such terms had gained currency in biblical studies. This emphasis was inherent in his focus on the inner- and post-biblical appropriation of Scripture, an appropriation he often dealt with under the rubric of 'comparative midrash'. To be sure, comparative midrash studies of Sanders and others often had a focus on sequential genetic relationships between intertexts that would be foreign to many of the literary theorists who first coined and popularized the term 'intertextuality'. Moreover, he has consistently stressed a certain stability of the text that clashes with some postmodern arguments for the text's non-existence or almost total indeterminacy. Nevertheless, Sanders shares with much recent literary scholarship an interest in the intensely intertextual character of a community's construal and construction of their world.

Perhaps even more significant is the way that the community emphasis in Sanders's canonical criticism anticipated a shift in biblical scholarship from meanings intended by authors and editors to those constructed by readers. Although never stressed in quite those terms by Sanders, his emphasis on the role of believing communities in relation to canon is an emphasis on readers, rather than authors. The examination in comparative midrash of the codifications of meaning produced by those readers (thus treating them as authors of a new text) has made it easy to overlook this emphasis, but the producer of an adaptation of an authoritative tradition or text is first of all a reader of that tradition or text. The act of applying hermeneutics is an act of reading, and the believing communities are communities of believing readers. Thus canonical criticism differs from tradition history by emphasizing the believing community's reception and reading of tradition, rather than the individual tradent's 'authorial' intention. As a complement to this emphasis on the reader, canonical criticism's emphasis on the adaptability of Scripture moves, at least in broad terms, toward the notion of indeterminacy common to some reader-response approaches.

Finally, canonical criticism has been at pains both to affirm the value of the historical-critical method, and at the same time to relativize and define the limits of its claims. There is a degree of development on this point that can be observed in Sanders's writing. In *Text and Canon* canonical criticism is the next step within the advancing phases of the historical-critical method.[2] Six years later, in his presidential address to the Society of Biblical Literature Sanders argues instead that a canonical approach recognizes the historical-critical method as an Enlightenment contribution to a long list of modes of adapting Scripture, each appropriate in its time and culture. As he put it in the concluding sentence of that address, 'We are heirs of a very long line of tradents and not neces-

2. J.A. Sanders, *Torah and Canon* (Philadelphia: Fortress Press, 1972), pp. xi-xix.

sarily more worthy of the traditions than they.'[3]

On the other hand, we would not do justice to Sanders to conclude that canonical criticism is simply postmodern interpretation in other language. In addition to the points of difference noted earlier, we would add that for Sanders canonical criticism's concern for the modern adaptation of canonical materials is founded on the observation of the prior history of their adaptation in the communities that formed Scripture. If to the modernists Sanders would say that we are 'not necessarily more worthy of the traditions' than our predecessors, to the postmodernists he would say, 'We are heirs of a very long line of tradents'.

So we end this all too brief survey of Sanders's contribution to the ongoing study of the life of Scripture amid the communities that prize it where we began, with the opening quotation from his own words. Whether one regards this *oeuvre* as a gift *from God* will depend on one's theology, but surely the contribution of James A. Sanders to our common enterprise in the field of biblical studies has been a great gift. It most certainly has been 'in due season', and indeed is worthy of honor.

The essays in this volume address from a variety of vantage points the relation of Scripture and community that has been so central in Sanders's work. They are linked by their connections to the canonical-critical emphasis on the appropriation of Scripture by the believing communities, even as they mirror the multivalency of Scripture in their diverging explorations of this theme. David Carr ('Canonization in the Context of Community') attends to the historical specificity behind the concept of 'believing communities', and argues that the shifting and often multiform character of Jewish and early Christian communities must be treated as a major factor in any history of the formation of the Jewish and Christian canons. Peter Flint ('Of Psalms and Psalters'), on the basis of an examination of the totality of Psalms fragments from Qumran, confirms Sanders's position concerning the lack of closure in the canon of the Psalter in the late Second Temple period. Lloyd Bailey ('Biblical Math as *Heilsgeschichte*?') and Marvin Sweeney ('Jesse's New Shoot in Isaiah 11') explore the function of specific texts in their particular communities of origin. Samuel Terrien ('Ezekiel's Dance of the Sword and Prophetic Theonomy') pursues an early theme in the work of Sanders, human and divine suffering, as a locus for a theocentric, monotheizing hermeneutic. George Landes ('Jonah in Luke')

3. J.A. Sanders, 'Text and Canon: Concepts and Method', in *From Sacred Story to Sacred Text*, pp. 145-47. The quotation is found on p. 147.

examines Luke's use of canonical materials in the creation of a new text that also achieved canonical status. Robert Bascom ('Adaptable for Translation'), and Dominique Barthélemy ('L'appropriation juive et chrétienne du Psautier') explore particular historic adaptations and appropriations of canonical materials. Merrill Miller ('The Authority and Intelligibility of Torah') analyzes a rabbinic reflection on the tension between the authority and intelligibility of Scripture, a dichotomy reminiscent of Sanders's discussions of 'stability' and 'adaptability' in Scripture. Beginning with a rabbinic metaphor for the interpretive process, Mary Callaway ('Exegesis as Banquet') presses further the examination of the plurality of perspectives inscribed in canonical texts and the effect of that pluralism on the adaptation and appropriation of texts. Eugene Nida ('Canonicity and Bibles Today') examines the variety of bases on which canonical authority has been ascribed to new translations of Scripture, and thus extends the factors to be considered in examining why believing communities come to regard specific texts as canonical. Nancy Bowen ('Canon and the Community of Women') and Richard Weis ('Stained Glass Window, Kaleidoscope, or Catalyst') venture in various ways into territory identified, but not intensively explored by Sanders, namely, the socio-political dimensions of the contemporary Bible-reading process, as these are rooted in the complex social reality behind the construct 'believing community'.

The essays are organized according to a two-part structure. This is grounded in Sanders's contention that the canonical process extends from the origins of the canonical literature through to the present day, and yet displays a degree of periodicity. Thus the first section includes those essays concerned with the canonical process leading up to and including the formation of fixed collections of canonical texts. Within this section essays dealing with the formation of the canon as a whole or portions thereof come first, followed by essays on specific passages in canonical order. The second section begins at the point where collections of canonical texts have largely come into existence and contains essays that examine the appropriation of those texts by believing communities up to and including the modern period. In this section the essays are arranged in the approximate chronological order of the communities whose appropriation they consider. The volume concludes with a complete bibliography of the works of James A. Sanders.

In drawing this introduction to a close, we wish to acknowledge persons and institutions without whom there would have been no book. Of course, we are deeply appreciative to each of the authors for their individual contributions to the volume. We are also grateful for their patience with the volume's long gestation, and for the wonderfully cooperative spirit with which they responded to editorial suggestions and queries. Ms Jean Hanson of New Brunswick Theological Seminary turned half a dozen of the submissions into word processing files with admirable skill and grace, Ms Olga Morales of the School of Theology at Claremont did the same for Sanders's bibliography on very short notice, and Ms Datha Meyers of the Methodist Theological School in Ohio kept materials flowing smoothly among editors and contributors. We are deeply grateful for their help. We also wish to register our appreciation for the support rendered by our institutions, the Methodist Theological School in Ohio, and the New Brunswick Theological Seminary. We are most grateful to Professor David J.A. Clines and Sheffield Academic Press for accepting this volume into the Journal for the Study of the Old Testament Supplement Series. We express profound appreciation to Barbara, and to Sharon, Talia and Jeremy for their patient endurance of all the vicissitudes that editing a volume like this can lead its editors to inflict on their families. And last of all, we tender our great thanks to Jim for all his generosity and care for students and colleagues over the years, offering a spirit of love for Scripture and its tradents that this book celebrates.

David Carr
Richard Weis

Part I
The Creation of the Jewish and Christian Canons and Texts in Them

Canonization in the Context of Community: An Outline of the Formation of the Tanakh and the Christian Bible

David M. Carr

One of James Sanders's greatest contributions to biblical studies has been his insistence on the role of community in all stages of the process of canonization. In particular, he has insisted that canonization is not a phenomenon restricted to the identification of a single list of 'scriptural' books, whether in the church councils of the third and fourth centuries CE, or a purported 'council' at Yavneh. Instead, he has argued that any such closure, any such agreement on what texts were in or out, necessarily followed a larger and in some ways more significant community process: the process by which certain traditions were affirmed through repetition and adaptation as 'adaptable for life'. Only after such traditions had proven to be life-giving in a variety of communities over time could they even be considered for inclusion in an authoritative list.[1]

Just such considerations raise a caution to those who would insist that the word 'canon' be applied only to clearly defined, exclusive bodies of literature, bodies such as the early Christian 'canons' of the third and fourth centuries. Sanders's work suggests that we must be careful not to draw too sharp a distinction between the late formation of such 'canons' and the process that led up to them.[2] Indeed contemporary comparative

1. A citation for this paragraph would encompass most of Sanders's work, but see in particular, 'Adaptable for Life: The Nature and Function of Canon', in F.M. Cross, W.E. Lemke and P.D. Miller (eds.), *Magnalia Dei: The Mighty Acts of God. Essays on the Bible and Archaeology in Memory of G. Ernest Wright* (Garden City, NY: Doubleday, 1976), pp. 531-60 (reprinted with an illuminating foreword in J.A. Sanders, *From Sacred Story to Sacred Text* [Philadelphia: Fortress Press, 1987], pp. 9-39); and *Canon and Community: A Guide to Canonical Criticism* (Guides to Biblical Scholarship; Philadelphia: Fortress Press, 1984).

2. Cf. J. Barr, *Holy Scripture: Canon, Authority, Criticism* (Philadelphia: Westminster Press, 1983), pp. 50-51; J. Barton, *Oracles of God: Perceptions of Ancient Prophecy in Israel after the Exile* (London: Darton, Longman & Todd,

study of religious literature confirms and extends Sanders's suggestion of a broad 'canonical continuum', with the intense Scriptural consciousness of Islam at one end, and institutionally authorized, context-specific oral utterances at the other.[3] In between, there is a wide variety of types of Scripture and canon, sometimes even within the same tradition, and a variety of modes of reading such religious texts.[4] Such data suggest that we must be careful in too sharply defining the point where 'text' ends, and 'canon' begins.

Indeed, even given a narrow definition of 'canon' as a clearly defined, exclusive body of literature, there are important ways in which this kind of 'canon' is directly anticipated by developments quite close to canon, but for which such a word did not yet exist. Early instances of recognition of what we might term the 'special authority of texts' constitute important preliminary stages along the trajectory leading to 'canonization' more narrowly conceived. The mention of the authority of the 'Torah', 'Prophets', or even a book like *Enoch* reflects an implicit recognition

1986), pp. 55-75; and J. Maier, 'Zur Frage des biblischen Kanons im Frühjudentum im Licht der Qumranfunde', in I. Baldermann *et al.* (eds.), *Zum Problem des biblischen Kanons* (JBTh, 3; Neukirchen–Vluyn: Neukirchener Verlag, 1988), p. 137, among others who do argue for such a sharp distinction. Cf. also the somewhat different reflections along these lines in G. Veltri, 'Zur traditionsgeschichtlichen Entwicklung des Bewußtseins von einem Kanon: Die Yavneh-Frage', *JSJ* 21 (1990), pp. 210-15.

3. Sanders, *Canon and Community*, p. 28. For comparative studies of canons see in particular the following: J. Smith, 'Sacred Persistence: Towards a Redescription of Canon', in W.S. Green (ed.), *Approaches to Ancient Judaism: Theory and Practice* (BJS, 1; Missoula, MT: Scholars Press, 1978), pp. 11-28; essays in F.M. Denny and R.L. Taylor (eds.), *The Holy Book in Comparative Perspective* (Studies in Comparative Religion; Columbia, SC: University of South Carolina Press, 1985); W.A. Graham, *Beyond the Written Word: Oral Aspects of Scripture in the History of Religion* (Cambridge: Cambridge University Press, 1987); W.C. Smith, 'Scripture as Form and Concept', in M. Levering (ed.), *Rethinking Scripture: Essays from a Comparative Perspective* (Albany, NY: State University of New York, 1989), pp. 29-55; K. Folkert, 'The "Canons" of "Scripture"', in Levering (ed.), *Rethinking Scripture*, pp. 170-79; H. Coward, *Sacred Word and Sacred Text: Scripture in World Religions* (Maryknoll, NY: Orbis Books, 1988); *idem*, 'The Role of Scripture in the Self-Definition of Hinduism and Buddhism in India', *SR* 21 (1992), pp. 129-44; and W.C. Smith, *What is Scripture? A Comparative Approach* (Minneapolis: Fortress Press, 1993).

4. M. Levering, 'Scripture and its Reception: A Buddhist Case', in *idem* (ed.), *Rethinking Scripture*, pp. 58-101; T. Coburn, 'Scripture in India', in Levering (ed.), *Rethinking Scripture*, pp. 102-28.

that there are other writings which are not as noteworthy. For these reasons, we may distinguish between narrow usage of the term 'canon' to refer to the recognition of a closed, clearly defined body of Scriptures, and broad usage of the term to refer to the process leading up to this recognition, a process which might be more precisely termed 'proto-canonical'.[5] The two halves of this latter term recognize both truths about the process leading to canonization: 'proto' indicates the distinction of such preliminary recognition of authority from the later official codification of a clearly defined, exclusive canon in church or synagogue decisions; 'canonical' indicates the extent to which such preliminary recognition is not only an indispensable precondition for later inclusion of such writings in an official 'canon', but is also already implicitly exclusive, implying that the recognized writings enjoy a certain noteworthy authority beyond that of others.

Whereas much of Sanders's work on canon has focused on the early, 'proto-canonical' process of repetition and particularly adaptation, this essay is an attempt to extend Sanders's community-focused approach into a reexamination of a broader canon clarification process: the move *from* such proto-canonical recognition of writings *to* the later stages of canonization. Its contribution will consist not so much in bringing new evidence to bear on the question, but in using new models to interpret the evidence. This community-centered approach is important for the following reason: although most treatments of the canonization process have tended to be unilinear, our growing knowledge of Judaism of the time indicates that it was highly multiform.

Most studies of the canonization process have looked to early Jewish texts for the earliest analogy to part (Torah, Prophets, Writings) or all of

5. E. Blum uses a German equivalent to this term ('proto-kanonischen' put between quotation marks) when referring to the late tradition history of the Pentateuch in his *Studien zur Komposition des Pentateuch* (BZAW, 189; Berlin: de Gruyter, 1991), p. 357.

On the distinction in uses of the term 'canon' cf. in particular Sanders's similar distinction between use of the word 'canon' to refer to 'the shape of a limited body of sacred literature' and to 'its function'; 'Canon', *ABD*, I, p. 839. Along similar lines, Sundberg and others have suggested distinguishing between affirmation of the particular authority of a text, that is a recognition of it as 'Scripture', and the later inclusion of such a text in a collection excluding other writings, inclusion in a 'canon'; A.C. Sundberg, 'The "Old Testament": A Christian Canon', *CBQ* 30 (1968), pp. 147-48.

a present-day canon,[6] and when such a text has been identified, such studies have tended to conclude that the given text testifies to the canon (singular!) recognized by Judaism of that time. For example, from the late eighteenth century onward most such studies have depended heavily on (1) Nehemiah 8 to establish canonization of Torah around 400 BCE, (2) Ben Sira (or the Prologue to Ben Sira) to establish a second-century BCE canonization of the prophets and (a preliminary) third category, and then (3) Josephus and 2 Esdras to establish the finalization of this third category in the second half of the first century CE.[7] Despite excellent critiques of such a unilinear approach by Sanders (in 1976) and Lightstone (in 1979), most subsequent treatments have not adopted alternative models.[8] Whether maintaining the traditional model of canonization of Hebrew Scriptures (Sundberg, McDonald, Steck, Schiffman), dating the process earlier (Leiman, Beckwith), or substantially reconceiving the process (Barton), most recent studies of canonization share a presupposition of a basically unitary Judaism, where texts are used to establish a canon shared by the whole.[9] To be sure, some focused studies of canon,

6. It is important in any discussion of the formation of canon to recognize the ongoing diversity of contemporary canons of Christian Scripture. For a helpful overview of the major variations see H.P. Rüger, 'Der Umfang des alttestamentlichen Kanons in den verschiedenen kirchlichen Traditionen', in S. Meuer (ed.), *Die Apokryphenfrage im ökumenischen Horizont: Die Stellung der Spätschriften des Alten Testaments im biblischen Schrifttum und ihre Bedeutung in den kirchlichen Traditionen des Ostens und Westens* (Die Bibel in der Welt, 22; Stuttgart: Deutsche Bibelgesellschaft, 1990), pp. 137-45.

7. H.E. Ryle, *The Canon of the Old Testament* (London: Macmillan, 1892) is a classic, often cited, statement.

8. Sanders, 'Adaptable for Life', p. 533; J.N. Lightstone, 'The Formation of the Biblical Canon in Judaism of Late Antiquity: Prolegomena to a General Reassessment', *SR* 8 (1979), pp. 135-42. T. Swanson's unpublished dissertation is another important exception to the overall consensus: 'The Closing of Holy Scripture: A Study in the History of the Canonization of the Old Testament' (PhD dissertation, Vanderbilt University, 1970).

9. A.C. Sundberg, *The Old Testament of the Early Church* (HTS, 20; Cambridge, MA: Harvard University Press, 1964), pp. 46-47, 67-79 and 113-28 [Note: this comment pertains specifically to Sundberg's history of the Hebrew canon, not his brilliant repudiation of the Alexandrian canon hypothesis]; L.M. McDonald, *The Formation of the Biblical Canon* (Nashville: Abingdon Press, 1988); O.H. Steck, 'Der Kanon des hebräischen Alten Testaments: Historische Materialien für eine ökumenische Perspektive', in J. Rohls and G. Wenz (eds.), *Vernunft des Glaubens: Wissenschaftliche Theologie und kirchliche Lehre. Festschrift*

such as discussions by Sanders,[10] and a series of studies of canon at Qumran,[11] are beginning to provide more nuanced pictures of the problem. Nevertheless, the bulk of scholarship has not yet moved from a fundamentally unilinear conceptualization of the canonization process.

Such a unilinear approach contrasts with our picture of a highly pluralistic Judaism during the Second Temple period. By now it has

zum 60. Geburtstag von Wolfhart Pannenberg (Göttingen: Vandenhoeck & Ruprecht, 1988), pp. 231-52; L. Schiffman, *Reclaiming the Dead Sea Scrolls: The History of Judaism, the Background of Christianity, the Lost Library of Qumran* (Philadelphia: Jewish Publication Society, 1994), pp. 161-69; cf. also D.F. Morgan, *Between Text and Community: The 'Writings' in Canonical Interpretation* (Minneapolis: Fortress Press, 1990), pp. 34-40, and G.M. Hahneman, *The Muratorian Fragment and the Development of the Canon* (Oxford: Clarendon Press, 1992), pp. 71-83.

S.Z. Leiman, *The Canonization of Hebrew Scripture: The Talmudic and Midrashic Evidence* (Transactions of the Connecticut Academy of Arts and Sciences, 47; Hamden, CT: Archon Books, 1976); R. Beckwith, *The Old Testament Canon of the New Testament Church and its Background in Early Judaism* (London: SPCK, 1985).

Barton (*Oracles of God*, pp. 35-55), argues for an overall bipartite rather than tripartite canon during the 'age of the New Testament'. Here he is similar to a less systematic proposal by Barr (*Holy Scripture*, pp. 52-56); cf. also Barton's earlier treatment in '"The Law and the Prophets": Who Are the Prophets?', *OTS* 23 (1984), pp. 1-18.

10. See most recently Sanders, 'Canon', pp. 837-52; *idem*, 'Understanding the Development of the Biblical Text', in H. Shanks *et al.* (eds.), *The Dead Sea Scrolls After Forty Years* (Washington, DC: Biblical Archaeology Society, 1991), pp. 57-73.

11. H.-J. Fabry, '11QPs[a] und die Kanonizität des Psalters', in E. Haag and F.L. Hossfeld (eds.), *Freude an der Weisung des Herrn: Beiträge zur Theologie der Psalmen* (Festschrift Heinrich Gross; Stuttgart: Katholisches Bibelwerk, 1986), pp. 45-53; Maier, 'Zur Frage des biblischen Kanons', pp. 135-46; J. VanderKam, *The Dead Sea Scrolls Today* (Grand Rapids: Eerdmans, 1994), pp. 149-57; E. Ulrich, 'Pluriformity in the Biblical Text, Text Groups and Questions of Canon', in J. Trebolle Barrera and L. Vegas Montaner (eds.), *The Madrid Qumran Congress: Proceedings of the International Congress on the Dead Sea Scrolls, Madrid 18–21 March, 1991* (STDJ, 12.1; Leiden: Brill, 1992), pp. 23-42; *idem*, 'The Bible in the Making: The Scriptures at Qumran', in *idem* and J. VanderKam (eds.), *The Community of the Renewed Covenant: The Notre Dame Symposium on the Dead Sea Scrolls* (Christianity and Judaism in Antiquity, 10; Notre Dame: University of Notre Dame Press, 1994), pp. 77-93. The body of this essay was complete before the contributions by VanderKam and Ulrich appeared, so their reflections on these questions could not be fully incorporated although they often parallel reflections in this essay.

become a commonplace to recognize that Judaism of this time was diverse. By the early Roman period there were a wide array of competing forms of Judaism: establishment, populist, dissident (of various types), 'gnostic', and so on.[12] To be sure, such an emphasis on diversity can be taken too far. We cannot ignore lines of continuity in the Judaisms of the period, nor should we overlook the diversity also present before and after the Second Temple period. Nevertheless, Qumran, Nag Hammadi, and other findings have helped emphasize the irreducible plurality of Judaism of the Second Temple period. Moreover, Judaism was not as pluralistic before and after this time. Prior to the period there seems to have been enough cohesion that the Pentateuch became a common inheritance to the varieties of Judaism that developed later. After the period, two groups gradually emerge from the pluralism that was Second Temple Judaism: the ancestor communities to our present day 'Judaism' and 'Christianity'. In sum, the particular pluralism of Second Temple Judaism contrasts with the frequent assumption by scholars that there was a unitary Jewish canon in this period, and raises the possibility of a multilinear process of canonization.

Furthermore, the evidence for various stages of canonization does not support the picture of a unilinear canonization process. General mention of three types of data relating to the canonization of the Jewish Scriptures will suffice for now. The details will be discussed in a later section.

1. Although there are scattered references to a tripartite organization of the canon (4QMMT C10; Lk. 24.44),[13] there is continuing evidence for many Second Temple Jewish groups working with a bipartite (2 Maccabees, Qumran, New Testament) or even a one-part (Samaritans, Sadducees) canon. Indeed, even in the bodies of literature where these references to a tripartite division occur, they occur alongside references to a bipartite canon, and the designations for the third part vary widely.

2. Neither Ben Sira nor other Second Temple texts testify to a

12. On this see M. Stone, *Scriptures, Sects and Visions: A Profile of Judaism from Ezra to the Jewish Revolts* (New York: Collins, 1980); G.G. Porton's helpful overview, 'Diversity in Postbiblical Judaism', in R.A. Kraft and G.W.E. Nickelsburg (eds.), *Early Judaism and its Modern Interpreters* (Atlanta: Scholars Press, 1986), pp. 57-80; and more recently, S. Talmon, 'The Internal Diversification of Judaism in the Early Second Temple Period', in *idem* (ed.), *Jewish Civilization in the Hellenistic-Roman Period* (Philadelphia: Trinity Press International, 1991), pp. 16-43.

13. Other texts whose testimony to this are less clear include the Prologue to Ben Sira; Josephus, *Apion* 1.38-41; and Philo, *Vit. Cont.* 25. These texts are discussed below, pp. 42-45.

closed collection of 'Prophets'. Although Ben Sira seems familiar in his 'Praise to the Fathers' with the books making up the present Prophets division of the Tanakh, he also knows many books in the present Writings category, and he does not seem to distinguish these Prophetic and Writings books from one another. Moreover, a number of other early Jewish sources cite the Psalms and other present-day Writings as 'Prophets'.[14]

3. Citations in early Jewish documents suggest diverging patterns of what was recognized as uniquely authoritative. To be sure, certain texts, particularly the Torah, seem to have enjoyed almost universal recognition across early Judaism. Nevertheless, other texts now included in the canon—Esther is a prime example[15]—seem to have enjoyed less recognition in certain contexts. Moreover, several texts now excluded—such as *Jubilees* and *Enoch*—are cited in certain communities as Scripture. Indeed, as Sanders has suggested, in cases such as 11QPs[a] we have evidence that some groups seem to have seen the form of now canonical books as still open to modification or substitution.[16]

In each case, scholars working with a unilinear model of canonization have tended to attempt to explain away such evidence as inconclusive, drawn from 'sectarian' groups, or in some way anomalous. In each case, a multilinear model linking canon and community can account for the evidence. Let us look in more detail now at what such a model might look like.

14. On this see foremost Barton's discussions in 'Law and Prophets', *passim*, and *Oracles of God*, pp. 35-55.

15. Leiman, *The Canonization of Hebrew Scripture*, provides a helpful survey of the relevant texts in n. 301 on p. 171.

16. J.A. Sanders, 'Cave 11 Surprises and the Question of Canon', *McCQ* 21 (1968), pp. 284-98. For references to more recent discussion of the issue and an endorsement of Sanders's evaluation of the data see Barton, *Oracles of God*, pp. 85-86, 285 (nn. 107-111); Fabry, '11QPsa und die Kanonizität des Psalters', pp. 45-67, particularly 55-66.

On the Temple Scroll cf. Y. Yadin, *The Temple Scroll* (English edn; Jerusalem: Israel Exploration Society, 1983), pp. 390-92; *idem*, *The Temple Scroll: The Hidden Law of the Dead Sea Sect* (New York: Random House, 1985), pp. 222-24; B.Z. Wachholder, *The Dawn of Qumran: The Sectarian Torah and the Teacher of Righteousness* (Cincinnati: Hebrew Union College Press, 1983), pp. 1-21; and (in contrast) H. Stegemann, 'The Literary Composition of the Temple Scroll and its Status at Qumran', in G.J. Brooke (ed.), *Temple Scroll Studies: Papers Presented at the International Symposium on the Temple Scroll, December, 1987* (JSPSup, 7; Sheffield: JSOT Press, 1989), pp. 127-31, 142-45.

An Outline of the Canon Clarification Process

From the Seventh Century to the Time of Ezra

Perhaps the earliest clear evidence for such preliminary recognition of an authoritative text are the frequent references to an authoritative ספר התורה ('book of the Torah') in the Deuteronomistic History. As is generally recognized, up to this point the word 'Torah' had been applied to authoritative instruction given by priests, sages and prophets.[17] Yet it seems that when the first edition of the Deuteronomistic History is written—probably some time around Josiah's reform[18]—the word 'Torah' is reappropriated to refer to an early form of the book of Deuteronomy. Notably, the innovation represented by use of the word 'Torah' to refer to such an extensive authoritative *text* is recognized through the constant use of modifiers to specify which Torah is meant: whether near demonstratives referring to the overall context of a passage (התורה הזאת ['this Torah']),[19] references to the Torah 'scroll',[20] or references to the Torah which God (or Moses) commanded.[21] We do not see frequent references to simply 'the Torah' until the post-exilic period.[22]

17. G. Liedke and C. Petersen, 'Tôrah, Weisung', in E. Jenni and C. Westermann (eds.), *Theologisches Handwörterbuch zum Alten Testament* (Munich: Chr. Kaiser Verlag, 1971), pp. 1032-40 and references therein.

18. On this see particularly F.M. Cross, 'The Themes of the Book of Kings and the Structure of the Deuteronomistic History', in *Canaanite Myth and Hebrew Epic: Essays in the History of the Religion of Israel* (Cambridge, MA: Harvard University Press, 1973), pp. 274-89; R. Nelson, *The Double Redaction of the Deuteronomistic History* (JSOTSup, 18; Sheffield: JSOT Press, 1981); S.L. McKenzie, *The Trouble With Kings: The Composition of the Book of Kings in the Deuteronomistic History* (VTSup, 42; Leiden: Brill, 1991); and (for a somewhat different concept of the contents of this seventh-century edition) I. Provan, *Hezekiah and the Books of Kings: A Contribution to the Debate about the Composition of the Deuteronomistic History* (BZAW, 172; Berlin: de Gruyter, 1988).

19. Deut. 1.5; 4.8, 44; 27.3, 8, 26; 28.58, 61; 29.20, 28; 31.9, 11, 12, 24, 26; 32.46; Josh. 1.8. Cf. הספר הזה ('this scroll') in Deut. 29.19, 26.

20. Josh. 8.34; 2 Kgs 22.8, 11. See also the Torah in the scroll in Deut. 28.58; 31.24; 2 Kgs 23.24. Cf. ספר הברית ('scroll of the covenant') in 2 Kgs 23.2, 21.

21. Josh. 1.7; 8.31, 32; 23.6; 24.26; 1 Kgs 2.3; 2 Kgs 10.31; 14.6; 21.8; 23.25. Cf. 2 Kgs 17.13: התורה אשר צויתי את־אבתיכם ואשר שלחתי אליכם ביד עבדי הנביאים ('The Torah which I commanded your fathers and which I sent to you by way of my servants, the prophets').

22. Ezra 10.3; Neh. 8.2, 7, 9, 13, 14; 10.35, 37; 13.3; 2 Chron. 34.19 ('the Torah' versus 'the book of the Torah' in 2 Kgs 22.11). Note that such a simple

Thus, in the period surrounding Josiah's reform we see a significant development. Prior to this point, authority in ancient Israel seems to have been almost exclusively localized in institutions, whether in the monarchy, priesthood, prophecy or other offices. In addition, such authority seems to have been at least as much orally mediated as textually, with texts authorized by way of institutional authority. But now the mode of authorization begins to reverse significantly, so that new prophecy, for example, is measured in Deuteronomy by its adherence to the law, rather than the law by prophecy (Deut. 13.2-6).[23] On a broader level, a reform from within one of Israel's traditional authorizing institutions, the monarchy, is itself authorized through frequent reference to a central authorizing text, (an early form of) Deuteronomy. In these and other ways, a critical transformation has begun to occur: from institutional authorization of a text, to textual authorization of an institution.[24] Moreover, terminology adapted from the early institutional loci of authority, 'Torah', seems to have been consciously adapted to assert this text's authority.

reference to Torah does occur in the Deuteronomistic History, but in a late insertion into it, the blessing of Moses (Deut. 33.4). Also, even when modifiers from the Deuteronomistic History are used in later documents, the simplest ones are selected, often just 'the book of the Torah' or the 'Torah of Moses' or 'Torah of God' (Mal. 3.22; Pss. 1.2; 19.8; 119.1; Dan. 9.13; Ezra 3.2; 7.6; Neh. 8.1, 3, 8, 18; 13.1; 1 Chron. 16.40; 2 Chron. 23.18; 31.3, 4; 34.15 [//2 Kgs 22.8], 30 [//2 Kgs 23.2]; 35.26). Slight variations on Deuteronomistic patterns occur in Exod. 13.9; Ps. 119.72; 2 Chron. 17.9; 25.4 [diverges from 2 Kgs 14.6]; 30.16; 34.14; 35.12; Neh. 9.3; 10.29, 30. Modification of the word 'Torah' through use of simple possessive suffixes referring to God also occurs in Deut. 33.10 (see above); Pss. 1.2; 78.10; 89.31; 94.12; 119.18, 29, 34, 44, 51, 53, 55, 61, 70, 77, 85, 92, 97, 109, 113, 126, 136, 142, 150, 153, 163, 165, 174; Neh. 9.26, 29, 34 and 2 Chron. 6.16. In many of these latter references, particularly the Psalms, it is not clear that the Pentateuch is meant.

23. J.N. Lightstone, *Society, the Sacred, and Scripture in Ancient Judaism* (Studies in Christianity and Judaism, 3; Waterloo, Ontario: Wilfrid Laurier University Press, 1988), pp. 27-28. For some stimulating reflections on the taming of prophecy in the Deuteronomistic History and later traditions see G.L. Bruns, 'Canon and Power in the Hebrew Scriptures', *Critical Inquiry* 10 (1984), pp. 462-80.

24. Here I adapt Folkert's useful conceptual apparatus developed from a cross-cultural study of religious canons: 'The "Canons" of "Scripture"'. Folkert proposes distinguishing between 'Canon I'—that is, normative texts present in tradition by force of a certain limited institutional 'vector'—and 'Canon II'—texts which move independently of such vectors and indeed themselves function as 'vectors'. Clearly, with the Deuteronomic law, this transformation from 'Canon I' to 'Canon II' is at an embryonic stage with the Josiah reform.

The next major move in this direction, the beginnings of the establishment of a 'Torah of Moses' in post-exilic Judah, is likewise probably connected with the community struggles and politics of the time. In this case, as recent studies have persuasively argued, the establishment of an authoritative 'Torah' was probably part of a larger program by which the Persians solidified control of their western frontier through sponsoring local Egyptian and Palestinian elites in collecting and establishing their peoples' indigenous laws.[25] Moreover, it seems as if, by the time of Ezra, this Torah is no longer confined to the Deuteronomic Torah which was prominent in our earlier discussions. Instead, it is probable that both inner-Israelite and external (particularly Persian) political forces encouraged a linking of the Deuteronomi(sti)c Torah with Priestly and other traditions, producing a Torah closer to the highly varied Pentateuch we now know.[26] Even as it was in an ongoing process of development, this expanded 'Torah' then became the official, Persian-recognized, local law of the newly established city state of Jerusalem.[27] In some texts of the period—such as the traditions surrounding Ezra (Ezra 7.6 [cf. 25-26];

25. See now the excellent discussion and review of literature by K.G. Hoglund, *Achaemenid Imperial Administration in Syria-Palestine and the Missions of Ezra and Nehemiah* (SBLDS, 125; Atlanta: Scholars Press, 1992), *passim* and particularly pp. 228-36.

26. For persuasive arguments against recent theories that there is no direct connection between Ezra's law and the present Pentateuch, see H.G.M. Williamson, *Ezra, Nehemiah* (WBC, 16; Waco, TX: Word Books, 1985), pp. xxxvii-xxxix. See also F. Crüsemann's helpful formulation in 'Israel in der Perserzeit: Eine Skizze in Auseinandersetzung mit Max Weber', in W. Schluchter (ed.), *Max Webers Sicht des antiken Christentums: Interpretation und Kritik* (Frankfurt am Main: Suhrkamp, 1985), pp. 216-17 (and n. 89 on p. 229). On the linkage of different tradition streams cf. O.H. Steck, 'Strömungen theologischer Tradition im Alten Israel', in *idem* (ed.), *Zu Tradition und Theologie im Alten Testament* (Biblische-Theologische Studien, 2; Neukirchen–Vluyn: Neukirchener Verlag, 1978), pp. 50-51; and M. Smith, *Palestinian Parties and Politics that Shaped the Old Testament* (New York: Columbia University Press, 1971), pp. 170-82. For an excellent, brief survey of the significance of Torah terms in the final form of Ezra–Nehemiah see T.C. Eskenazi, *In an Age of Prose* (SBLMS, 36; Atlanta: Scholars Press, 1988), n. 93 pp. 75-76.

27. For discussion with references see Blum, *Studien zur Komposition des Pentateuch*, pp. 345-60; D. Carr, *Reading the Fractures of Genesis: Historical and Literary Approaches* (Louisville, KY: Westminster/John Knox Press, 1996), pp. 324-33.

Neh. 8.1-18 *passim*; 9.3, 14, 29; 10.29, 35, 37)—the focus is almost exclusively on this Torah.[28]

Nevertheless, the authority represented by the prophets is never fully supplanted throughout this period. Thus, not only does prophetic activity continue (Haggai, Zechariah), but oracles of these and other figures are collected, adapted and extended to fit new situations. Particularly interesting in this respect are the texts in Isaiah 40–55 regarding the 'former things' and the 'latter/coming/new things' (Isa. 41.22-23; 42.9; 43.9; 46.9; 48.3-8; cf. 43.19; 44.6-8; 45.21-22). If recent studies of these references are correct, the relevant texts are to be read (at least in their present context in the book) as founding a new prophetic message to exiles on the fulfillment of previous prophetic texts in the Isaianic tradition.[29] In other words, the exilic audience is being told that they can believe God's new word of comfort because God's earlier message of judgment through Isaiah came true. Although somewhat less precise than the above discussed references to the Torah, these 'former things' texts of Isaiah 40–55 do seem to represent an early proto-canonical recognition of the special authority of certain prophetic texts.

In the later post-exilic period we see further developments in recognition of the unique authority of prophetic texts, developments not always consistent with one another. On the one hand, in certain late passages in Zechariah we see references to God's previous words through 'former prophets' (Zech. 1.4; 7.7), and even a text which asserts an equivalence

28. Note that Ezra 9.10-12 does refer to the 'commandments which you commanded by your servants the prophets', but then quotes what are clearly Pentateuchal regulations. Later, Neh. 9.26 briefly refers to the prophets as warning the people to turn back to the Torah.

Two important texts introducing Nehemiah's two governerships also refer exclusively to legal authority, Neh. 1.7 and 13.1, 3 (cf. anti-prophetic traditions in 6.7, 10-14), but both seem to refer to Deuteronomistic regulations, and are probably best seen as predecessors to the later veneration of the complete Pentateuch during Ezra's time.

29. See in particular B.S. Childs, *Introduction to the Old Testament as Scripture* (Philadelphia: Fortress Press, 1979), pp. 328-30; R.E. Clements, 'The Unity of the Book of Isaiah', *Int* 36 (1982), p. 125; D.G. Meade, *Pseudonymity and Canon* (WUNT, 39; Tübingen: Mohr [Paul Siebeck], 1986), pp. 35-36; and C. Seitz, 'The Divine Council: Temporal Transition and New Prophecy in the Book of Isaiah', *JBL* 109 (1990), p. 244; *idem*, *Zion's Final Destiny: The Development of the Book of Isaiah—A Reassessment of Isaiah 36–39* (Minneapolis: Fortress Press, 1991), pp. 199-202.

between God's warning through these 'former prophets' and through 'the Torah': 'They made their hearts adamant in order not to hear the Torah and the words that the Lord of hosts had sent by God's spirit through the former prophets' (Zech. 7.12).[30] Similarly, the one positive general reference to prophecy in Ezra–Nehemiah asserts a similar equivalence:

> Nevertheless, they were disobedient and rebelled against you and cast your Torah behind their backs and killed your prophets who had warned them in order to turn them back to you, and they committed great blasphemies (Neh. 9.26).

On the other hand, certain other late prophetic texts include no such explicit coordination of authority between the various types of literature. For example, even as the Pentateuch was being established as part of a larger Persian-sponsored program, a program which involved an attempt to purge Jerusalem of foreign elements (Neh. 10; 13.1-3, 23-27; Ezra 9–10), so at the same time divine prophetic authority is claimed by authors opposing that very program (most prominently anonymous authors of parts of Isa. 56–66).[31] For example, Isa. 56.1-8, a divine oracle asserting God's intent to include foreigners in the cult, concludes with:

> Thus says the Lord God,
> who gathers the outcasts of Israel,
> I will gather yet others to them
> besides those already gathered.
> (Isa. 56.8)

Not only does this text directly invoke divine authority for inclusion of foreigners in Israel, but its emphasis on such inclusion *as an extension of God's gathering in of the Israelite Diaspora* is a distinctive feature, one which apparently alludes to and builds upon an earlier prophetic text in the Isaiah tradition:

30. Throughout this essay, translations of extended biblical passages like this one are adapted from the NRSV unless otherwise noted.

31. For similar exploration of diversity in post-exilic Judaism see A. Rofé, 'The Onset of Sects in Postexilic Judaism: Neglected Evidence from the Septuagint, Trito-Isaiah, Ben Sira, and Malachi', in J. Neusner *et al.* (eds.), *The Social World of Formative Christianity and Judaism: Essays in Tribute to Howard Clark Kee* (Philadelphia: Fortress Press, 1988), pp. 41-42.

God says:
'It is too light a thing that you should be my servant
to raise up the tribes of Jacob
and to restore the survivors of Israel;
I will give you as a light to the nations,
that my salvation may reach to the end of the earth'
(Isa. 49.6)

Thus, in post-exilic texts, we sometimes see different forms of authority being invoked for the various sides of a post-exilic community dispute. On the one side is God's Torah. On the other side lies a progression of oracles of YHWH within the Isaianic tradition.

The above texts constitute only the barest survey of the evidence for preliminary recognition of the authority of certain texts in post-exilic Judaism, texts which would eventually form the heart of the Jewish and Christian 'canons'. Yet already at this point it is clear that such recognition of authority is community based, and as such involves significant debate around issues such as the authority of different types of texts, coordination of the authority of these different types, and the bearing of these texts on issues of central community concern. Though debate in Israel is hardly new, nor is debate on authority, this kind of growing disagreement about the authority of given texts is relatively new. Such controversy regarding texts has become another 'front' on which early Jewish communal conflict is waged.

In sum, prior to this period, ancient Israel seems to have been dominated by institutional loci of authority, but particularly with Josiah's reform we see a growing focus on certain central textual authorities (alongside institutional ones): first the Deuteronomic Torah under Josiah, and then the proto-Pentateuch probably established during Persian-sponsored consolidation of the community of Judah. Moreover, we have found alongside this process an evolving recognition of the authority of prophetic *texts* in certain groups, an authority occasionally implicitly opposed to, but usually coordinated with the claims and aims of 'the Torah'. We turn now to consider data from the rest of the Second Temple period.

From Alexander to the Destruction of the Second Temple

With the possible exception of the groups responsible for producing the Temple Scroll and *Jubilees*, Second Temple Judaism seems to have had at least one thing in common: recognition of the authority of 'the

Torah'.[32] This is the common element in all the evidence testifying to proto-canonical consciousness in the Second Temple period, and the textual tradition for the Torah is markedly less fluid than that for other books.[33] At the same time certain groups within the Second Temple Jewish matrix seem to have recognized little more than the Torah as Scripture. The prime example is that of the Samaritans. As is well known, the Samaritans' Scripture includes only the Samaritan Pentateuch. Although in earlier studies such evidence from Samaria was usually dismissed out of hand as non-Jewish, it now seems that the Samaritan–Jewish split probably occurred fairly late in the Second Temple period.[34] Thus, with the Samaritans, we have evidence for at least one Jewish group, in effect, 'closing' their canon already toward the middle of the Second Temple period. Their Torah-only Scripture is already a 'canon' in the narrower sense of the word discussed above.

The Samaritans, however, probably were not alone in working with such a canon. Another group outside Judah, the Alexandrians, seems to have had a propensity to focus on Torah alone, or almost exclusively on Torah. The *Letter of Aristeas* promotes an Alexandrian translation of Torah, without ever mentioning other books.[35] Similarly, Philo mentions a festival celebrating this translation in Pharos (*Vit. Mos*. 41-43), and again does not refer to the prophets or other books.[36] Even Philo himself, who does occasionally cite non-Torah texts as Scripture, cites Torah approximately 40 times as often as texts outside it.[37]

Finally, this tendency to focus completely or almost completely on Torah as Scripture seems to have been present within certain priestly and/or other establishment groups in Palestine. First, Swanson has persuasively argued that evidence in Ben Sira suggests that though he knows non-Torah Jewish writings and ascribes a possible 'secondary'

32. For an excellent, brief survey of what diversity did exist in types of recognition of Torah see Steck, 'Der Kanon des hebräischen Alten Testaments', pp. 236-37.

33. Sanders, 'Understanding the Development of the Biblical Text', p. 61.

34. On this see the literature survey by J.D. Purvis, 'The Samaritans and Judaism', in Kraft and Nickelsburg (eds.), *Early Judaism and its Modern Interpreters*, pp. 81-98.

35. Swanson, 'The Closing of Holy Scripture', pp. 131-34.

36. M. Goodman, 'Sacred Scripture and "Defiling the Hands"', *JTS* 41 (1990), pp. 104-105.

37. W.L. Knox, 'A Note on Philo's Use of the Old Testament', *JTS* (o.s.) 41 (1940), p. 30.

authority to them, he recognizes only the Torah as having an authority beyond that of his own words.[38] Secondly, data from several early Church Fathers suggests that the Sadducees maintained a Torah-only canon.[39] These data should not be dismissed on the mistaken presumption that the Sadducees must have shared the canon of other groups during this period.[40] Thirdly, in a fascinating study, Maier has argued

38. Swanson, 'The Closing of Holy Scripture', pp. 114-21.

39. Hippolytus (*Refutation*, 9.29), Origen (*Against Celsus* 1.49; *Commentary on Matthew* 17.35-36), Tertullian (*Praescr. Haeret.* 45) and Jerome (*ad Matt.* 22.31-32). Fuller references can be found in J. Le Moyne, *Les Sadducéens* (Paris: Gabalda, 1972), pp. 150-51 referring to a text list on pp. 142-45. The discussions in Josephus, *Ant.* 13.10.6 and 18.1.4 focus on the divergence between Pharisees and Sadducees regarding regulations in oral law. Though these texts testify to a focus among the Sadducees on written law, they do not establish the existence of any kind of dispute between Sadducees and Pharisees regarding Prophets or other written Scriptures. On this see now S. Mason's very compelling treatment of these issues in his *Flavius Josephus on the Pharisees: A Composition-Critical Study* (SPB, 39; Leiden: Brill, 1991), pp. 230-45, 288-93.

Josephus's silence on a distinctive Sadducean canon is conspicuous, particularly given his willingness to talk about numerous other differences between Jewish groups. Moreover, in one context, *Apion* 1.38-41, Josephus explicitly asserts that Jews do not differ on canon. Notably, however, in this latter text he is primarily arguing that Jews do not add to their canon in the way that Gentiles do. Thus, although he extends the traditional 'neither add nor subtract' legal formula to the scope of canon as a whole to support his argument, it is the former part of the formula (concerning addition) with which he is most concerned, and the latter (concerning subtraction) which would pertain to the Sadducees. Moreover, Josephus may be maintaining somewhat the Pharisean party line at this point, or perhaps reflecting his sympathies with Essene-like groups, both of which recognize both Torah and non-Torah books. In any case, Josephus's silence on the Sadducees' canon is important, but it is not decisive evidence against a Sadducean Torah-only canon.

For further discussion of possible additional evidence on the Sadducees see D. Barthélemy, 'L'Etat de la Bible juive depuis le début de notre ère jusqu'à la deuxième révolte contre Rome (131–135)', in J.-D. Kaestli and O. Wermelinger (eds.), *Le Canon de l'Ancien Testament: Sa formation et son histoire* (Geneva: Labor & Fides, 1984), pp. 10-11. Later (p. 13), Barthélemy mentions the Ebionites as another Second Temple group which is described as rejecting the inspiration of the prophets.

40. Swanson, 'The Closing of Holy Scripture', p. 124, n. 3. For critique of the idea that the Sadducees had a Torah-only canon cf. Sundberg, *The Old Testament of the Early Church*, pp. 77-78 and references there. Perhaps the most important concern raised about the Church Fathers' testimony regarding the Sadducean canon is the question of whether they are confusing the Sadducees with the Samaritans on this

persuasively that early priestly regulations preserved in Mishnah (*m. Zab.* 5.12) and reflected in Heb. 9.19 ascribe a special holiness to the Torah scroll alone (appearing as הספר, 'the scroll'). This degree of holiness renders heave offerings invalid, places the Torah scroll on the same level of purity as Temple vessels, and thus restricts the handling of the Torah text to the priestly class.[41] This latter point then becomes confirming evidence for the supposition that the Sadducees revered the Torah alone. For in *m. Yad.* 4.6 the Sadducees are described as opposing the Pharisaic position that the 'holy writings' (כתבי הקדש) in general 'render the hands unclean' (מטמאין את הידים).[42] By this point, the rabbis as heirs of the Pharisees have shifted the issue from a specifically priestly concern (rendering offerings invalid) to an issue of more potential relevance to the laity.[43] Nevertheless, just as the earlier priestly regulation

point. Examples of early Christian confusion of Sadducees and Samaritans are listed in Le Moyne, *Les Sadducéens*, p. 151.

Another theory bearing on this question is Schiffman's proposal that the Qumran community had Sadducean roots. If this were the case, then recognition of the Scriptural status of non-Torah material at Qumran might imply similar Sadducean recognition of that material. On this see especially Schiffman's *Reclaiming the Dead Sea Scrolls*, pp. 167-68, with his theory regarding the origins of the Qumran community presented in *idem*, 'The New Halakhic Letter (4QMMT) and the Origins of the Dead Sea Sect', *BA* 53 (1990), pp. 64-73; *idem*, 'The Law of the Temple Scroll and its Provenance', in J. Kapera (ed.), *The First International Colloquium on the Dead Sea Scrolls* (Folia Orientalia, 25; Kraków: Polskiej Akademii Nauk, 1989), pp. 93-94; and *idem*, *Reclaiming the Dead Sea Scrolls*, pp. 86-89; and agreement with this view in E. Qimron and J. Strugnell, *Qumran Cave 4*, V (DJD, 10; Oxford: Clarendon Press, 1994), pp. 117-21. But see the important questions regarding this theory raised by J. VanderKam in 'The People of the Dead Sea Scrolls: Essenes or Sadducees?', *BR* 7 (1991), pp. 42-47, and *idem*, *The Dead Sea Scrolls Today*, pp. 93-95. Although Schiffman—among others—is probably right about the Zadokite origins of the Dead Sea community, and although the Sadducees probably also had Zadokite origins, the use of the term 'Sadducean' to describe the origins of the Qumran community implies a misleading degree of closeness between that community and the group known in other sources as the Sadducees.

41. J. Maier, *Jüdische Auseinandersetzung mit dem Christentum in der Antike* (ErFor, 177; Darmstadt: Wissenschaftliche Buchgesellschaft, 1982), pp. 10-19. He also discusses *y. Šab.* 1.5-6; *b. Šab.* 13b/14a and notes similar textual arguments for special priestly access to legal texts in Deut. 17.18 and the Qumran Temple Scroll (56.20-21).

42. For analysis of early and late strata in this passage see Maier, *Jüdische Auseinandersetzung*, pp. 33-38.

43. Maier, *Jüdische Auseinandersetzung*, pp. 12-14.

(*m. Zab*. 5.12) focused on the holiness of just הספר ('the [Torah] scroll'), so also the Sadducees are described here (*m. Yad*. 4.6) as opposing the assertion of a particular holiness of a group of writings, כתבי הקדש ('the holy writings'), which goes beyond just the Torah. In sum, although the exact establishment connections of Ben Sira, the Sadducees and these early priestly regulations are not easy to ascertain, each seems to have some special connection to the priestly establishment[44] and each seems to accord a special holiness or authority to the Torah alone.

Other Jewish groups seem to have seen the Torah collection as closed,[45] but also recognized the authority of additional non-Torah documents, usually termed 'the prophets'. Thus Dan. 9.2 cites Jer. 25.11-12; 29.10 as authoritative, and later talks of the people's disobedience of the laws set before them by 'the prophets' and of their violation of 'God's Torah', bringing upon themselves 'the curse and oath which are written in the Torah of Moses, the servant of God' (Dan. 9.10-13). Similarly, Dead Sea Scrolls from as early as the mid-second century BCE contain numerous references to 'the Torah' and 'the Prophets' (see 1QS 1.2-3;[46] 8.12-16; CD 7.15-17; 4QDibHam[a] 3.12-13; 4Q381[4QapPs] 69.4-5;[47] 4QMMT C17 [as reconstructed, cf. C10]), and similar references also occur in 2 Macc. 15.9 and throughout most early Christian literature (in rough chronological order): Rom. 3.21; Q 16.16 (Lk. 16.16//Mt.

44. With regard to Ben Sira, his connections to the priestly establishment are indicated by his conclusion of his praise to the fathers with an extended praise of the high priest Simon (Sir. 50.1-24), along with some other indicators. With regard to the Sadducees, a number of texts link the Sadducees with the Jerusalem aristocracy in some way (see Porton, 'Diversity in Postbiblical Judaism', p. 66, for texts and references to secondary literature). On the early Mishnaic traditions, see Maier's arguments that they—in contrast with later Pharisaic inversions of them—make sense within the Temple purity system: Maier, *Jüdische Auseinandersetzung*, pp. 10-19.

45. Again, the communities that produced and/or revered the Temple Scroll may be an important exception.

46. The expression '[God's] servants, the prophets' which is coordinated here and in 4QDibHam[a] 3.13 with the Torah of Moses, also appears by itself in 1QpHab 2.9; 7.5; 4QpHos[a] 2.5.

47. E.M. Schuller (*Non-Canonical Psalms from Qumran: A Pseudepigraphic Collection* [HSS, 28; Atlanta: Scholars Press, 1986], p. 206) notes that instruction by the prophets appears here in line 4 before the giving of the law through Moses is mentioned in line 5. She notes that, if a historical sequence is intended here, this text is tracing the prophets back to the pre-Mosaic period. Yet there is no indication in the text that the sequence is meant to be chronological, and the context is too broken to determine the logic of the text at this point.

11.13); Lukan material (Lk. 16.29-31; 24.27; Acts 13.15; 24.14; 26.22; 28.23; cf. 3.22-24); Matthew (5.17; 7.12; 22.40); and Jn 1.45. Even Philo, who was mentioned above as among the Alexandrians who focus almost exclusively on Torah, seems to work with a corresponding concept of two sources of Scripture, 'Moses'—for the Torah—and the 'disciples of Moses' (ἑταῖροι/γνώριμοι τῶν Μωυσέως) for other books (Psalms, Proverbs, Zechariah).[48]

Despite this recognition in many groups of a category of Scripture alongside Torah, they do not appear to have agreed on what books this category contained. To be sure, as noted above, Ben Sira's praise to the fathers (Sir. 44–50) seems to know many of the books in the present Prophets section of the Tanakh, including the Book of the Twelve Prophets (Sir. 49.10). Nevertheless, Ben Sira's praise is thoroughly informed by texts such as Chronicles, which are now in the Writings section of the Tanakh. Moreover, Ben Sira's review goes on beyond the Book of the Twelve Prophets (Sir. 49.10) to review figures such as Zerubbabel and Nehemiah (Sir. 49.11-13) before jumping back to the beginning of the epic story in mentioning Enoch, Joseph, Shem, Seth and Adam (Sir. 49.14-16). To be sure, Ben Sira never uses the term 'prophet' for Nehemiah or Zerubbabel, but neither does he consistently use the term 'prophet' for other figures now found in the Prophets section of the Jewish canon (Sir. 46.11-12; 47.2-25; 48.17-22a; 49.1-3). Rather than focusing exclusively on what he understood to be prophetic figures or material from a defined 'prophetic' corpus, Ben Sira in chs. 44–49 gives a historical overview extending from the creation to Nehemiah, an overview which draws freely on a number of non-Torah authoritative writings, writings now found both inside and outside the Prophets section of the later Jewish canon. Such data militate against an assumption that Ben Sira had before him any circumscribed, 'canonical' collection of prophets.[49]

48. Barton (*Oracles of God*, p. 49 and nn. 34-36 on p. 280) cites three cases where non-Torah Scriptures are cited as from the disciples of Moses: *Conf. Ling.* 39 (Psalmist), 62 (Zechariah); and *Congr.* 177 (Solomon).

49. Barton, *Oracles of God*, p. 48. Cf. O.H. Steck, *Der Abschluss der Prophetie im Alten Testament: Ein Versuch zur Frage der Vorgeschichte des Kanons* (Biblisch-Theologische Studien, 17; Neukirchen–Vluyn: Neukirchener Verlag, 1991), pp. 136-43. Steck marshals two other types of argument to support his thesis of a closed prophetic corpus by the time of Ben Sira. First, he argues for a complex process of successive redactions focused alternately on the end of the book of Isaiah and the end of the Book of the Twelve. Steck takes this process to imply a

Furthermore, as Swanson, Barr and Barton have been foremost in pointing out, other Second Temple Jewish texts seem to have used the title 'prophet' to designate the authors of authoritative books in general, particularly books outside the Torah.[50] A prime example is *4 Macc.* 18.10-19, where texts from Daniel, Psalms and Proverbs are mentioned as coming from 'the prophets'. Likewise, toward the end of the Second Temple period, many early Jewish texts, such as those by Josephus[51]

consciousness of a defined corpus extending from Isaiah to the Book of the Twelve (pp. 22-120). Secondly, he argues for an *inclusio* between the divine call in Joshua for Israel 'to act according to the entire Torah which I commanded Moses my servant' and the divine call in Mal. 3.22 to 'remember the Torah of Moses, my servant, which I commanded him'. While I cannot do justice to Steck's redactional analysis here, I will note that it is not self-evident how these redactional theories—even if true—would bear on the problem of corpus definition, particularly because the first set of modifications are successive additions to the end of Isaiah rather than the beginning. Regarding the *inclusio*, it is clear that Mal. 3.22 aims to coordinate the conclusion of the Book of the Tweve Prophets with the Torah of Moses, and this verse links especially closely with the last book of the Torah, Deuteronomy. It may even be that Mal. 3.22 was modeled in part on Josh. 1.7, though most of the individual components of Mal. 3.22 are paralleled by other texts as well. Be that as it may, it is not at all clear that an *inclusio* binding up a prophetic canon is meant here, especially given the vast distance that separates these texts and the probable oral context in which they were read and for which they were written. Finally, as Steck himself notes in an appendix on Psalms (pp. 157-63), Jews after the time of Ben Sira seem to have worked with a broader concept of prophecy and broader concept of what was included in the 'Prophets' than what is now included in the Prophets section of the Jewish Tanakh.

50. Barr, *Holy Scripture*, pp. 54-56; Swanson, 'The Closing of Holy Scripture', p. 198; Barton, 'Law and Prophets', *passim*; *idem*, *Oracles of God*, pp. 35-55. Also see Leiman's suggestive discussion in *Canonization of Hebrew Bible*, pp. 59, 64-72 and nn. 287 and 288 on pp. 167-68; and Ulrich, 'The Bible in the Making', pp. 81-82.

In the past, a prominent argument for early closure of the 'Prophets' collection has been that Daniel would have been included in it if it had still been 'open' in the second century (cf. for example, Leiman, *The Canonization of Hebrew Scripture*, p. 28). Much of this argument depends on our lack of knowledge of why some books were eventually included in the Prophets section while others were put in the writings. Certainly, there are other possible explanations of why Daniel was included in the Writings. It may be that Daniel's distinctive apocalyptic character played a role, or its (lack of) liturgical usage may have been a factor (Barton, *Oracles of God*, pp. 75-79).

51. *Ant.* 8.109-10 (David); 10.266-69 (Daniel).

and Philo,[52] along with Qumran texts[53] and early Christian materials,[54] use the term 'prophet' for David, Daniel and any other author of a purportedly Scriptural book.[55] Thus texts of the Second Temple period using the term 'Torah and Prophets' are not necessarily referring to the Torah and a collection like that of the Prophets now in the tripartite Jewish Bible. Instead, they are probably referring to the Torah and a significantly wider collection of non-Torah authoritative works.

To be sure, this categorization of all non-Torah Scriptural books as prophets does not always seem to have appeared fully adequate, even to groups maintaining an overall bipartite canon. Instead, we find in at least a couple of settings the mention of an additional category, or categories, for Scriptural writings. Lk. 24.44 refers to fulfillment of the 'Law of Moses, the prophets, and the psalms', and 4QMMT C10 says '[We have wr]itten to you so that you might understand the book of Moses, [the words of the pro]phets, and Da[vid and the words of the days of every] succeeding generation'. Both of these quotes occur in the context of documents (Luke) or bodies of writings (Dead Sea Community Texts) which otherwise exclusively use the 'Torah' and 'Prophets' categories. Indeed, in both cases, these references to a third category of Scripture occur in close literary proximity to passages which mention just two categories of Scripture, 'Torah and Prophets'. The original editors of 4QMMT reconstructed with the help of other manuscripts a reference to '[the book of] Moses and bo[oks of the Prophet]s' on line 17 of column C, just after the reference to three categories of Scripture in line 10,[56]

52. *Agr.* 50 (Psalm); *Rer. Div. Her.* 290 (Psalm); cf. *De Ebr.* 31 (Proverbs). Swanson, *The Closing of Holy Scripture*, p. 246.

53. 4QFlor 2.3 (Daniel); 11QPs^a 27.(3-)11 (David). Regarding 11QPs^a, see J. Sanders, *The Psalms Scroll of Qumran Cave 11 (11QPs^a)* (DJD, 4; Oxford: Clarendon Press, 1965), pp. 48, 91-93.

54. Mt. 24.15 (Daniel); Acts 2.30 (David). Swanson, *The Closing of Holy Scripture*, p. 256.

55. Josephus, *Apion* 1.37; cf. *War* 1.18. On Josephus's link between prophecy and inspiration see L. Feldman, 'Prophets and Prophecy in Josephus', *JTS* 41 (1990), pp. 397-99. Cf. also *Sifre Deut.* 1.1 which talks about David and Solomon as prophesying.

56. Qimron and Strugnell, *Qumran Cave 4*, p. 60. The relevant reading in the composite text is underlined, thus indicating that the lacuna here was filled 'with the help of text preserved in one or more of the other manuscripts' (p. 1). I was not able, however, to locate the other manuscript on which Qimron and Strugnell based their reading.

and Lk. 24.44 follows closely on a mention of 'Moses and all of the prophets' in Lk. 24.27. Moreover, the special mention of certain non-Torah writings in both Lk. 24.44 and 4QMMT C10 can be explained by the literary function of each text: (1) the mention of Psalms in Lk. 24.44 seems a reflex of the focus at this point on messianic predictions in Scripture[57] and (2) the mention of David in 4QMMT C10 serves as a prelude to the discussion in C12-28 of David as a model of royal repentance and resulting blessing. Nevertheless, Lk. 24.44 and 4QMMT C10 may also represent the nascent recognition in certain groups of the possibilities opened up by characterizing Scripture in terms of a tripartite structure.

Yet at this point some additional qualifications are in order. Given the propensity of earlier studies to read later canonical constructs—especially the Jewish three-part Tanakh—back into early Jewish texts, we must be quite careful at this point in how we use these texts and like evidence. For example, the following text from 2 Maccabees has been repeatedly used to support a dating of the Jewish canon to the mid-second century BCE:

> The same things are reported in the records and in the memoirs of Nehemiah, and also that he founded a library and collected the books about the kings and prophets, and the writings of David and letters of kings about votive offerings. In the same way Judas also collected all the books that had been lost on account of the war that had come upon us, and they are in our possession. So if you have any need of them, send people to get them from you. (2 Macc. 2.13-14)

As Barton points out, this text is no testimony to the creation of a canon. Instead, it focuses exclusively on the salvaging of a library in the wake of the Maccabean war, a library probably including, but not exclusively made up of, scrolls which later became part of the present Tanakh and Old Testament.[58] Note the lack of typical Second Temple terminology for the Scriptures (no reference to Torah) and inclusion of documents which clearly do not now belong to any present canonical collection (such as 'letters of kings about votive offerings'). Similar

57. Swanson, *The Closing of Holy Scripture*, p. 256.

58. Barton, *Oracles of God*, p. 57. Cf. Leiman, *The Canonization of Hebrew Scripture*, pp. 28-30 (and n. 132 on p. 149); Beckwith, *Old Testament Canon*, pp. 150-52. Similar comments could be made about Beckwith's arguments in support of the idea of an early Temple Archive consisting of the Jewish Bible. See his *Old Testament Canon*, pp. 80-86.

objections can be raised to the use of Philo's description of the library of the Theraputae (*Vit. Cont.* 25) to determine either his canon or the Theraputae's canon. The terminology used in this text is similar, but not identical, to that used in other early Jewish texts for Scripture, and there is no claim in this text to be describing a body of authoritative texts.

Finally, even the often cited Prologue to Ben Sira is not a sure guide to early Jewish concepts of Scripture. In this Prologue to the translation of his grandfather's book, Ben Sira's grandson describes the importance of his translation enterprise in the following way:

> The Law (τοῦ νόμου), the Prophets (τῶν προφητῶν), and the other writers succeeding them (τῶν ἄλλων τῶν κατ' αὐτὺς ἠκολουθηκότων) have passed on to us great lessons, in consequence of which Israel must be commended for learning and wisdom. Furthermore, it is a duty, not only to acquire learning by reading, but also, once having acquired it, to make oneself of use to people outside by what one can say or write. My grandfather Jesus, having long devoted himself to the reading of the Law, the Prophets, and other books of the Fathers (τῶν ἄλλων πατρίων βιβλίων) and having become very learned in them, himself decided to write something on the subjects of learning and wisdom, so that people who wanted to learn might, by themselves accepting these disciplines, learn how better to live according to the Law.[59]

A little later the grandson describes the difficulties of translation, saying:

> The fact is, that there is no equivalent for things originally written in Hebrew when it is a question of translating them into another language; what is more, the Law itself, the Prophets and the other books (τὰ λοιπὰ τῶν βιβλίων) differ considerably in translation from what appears in the original text.

As others have pointed out, the Torah (referred to with ὁ νόμος), is the only common term in the three descriptions of Israelite literature, and it is the Torah which is singled out in the list of documents which suffer in translation. The 'Prophets' category is somewhat stable, and since it is mentioned in other Jewish writings as a category of Scripture, Ben Sira's grandson is probably using the term to refer to a category of Scripture. But there is little indication that Ben Sira's grandson meant to describe a specifically Scriptural category in mentioning the 'other

59. Here the *New Jerusalem Bible* translation (Garden City, NY: Doubleday, 1985) is followed. The NRSV translates the second clause with an explanatory 'those who read the Scriptures', clearly prejudging interpretation of this passage as referring to Scripture.

writers succeeding them'. Instead, the sense of this text clearly indicates that Ben Sira's grandson is talking here of a category for post-Prophetic books like his grandfather's own writing.[60] Although such teachings are clearly worthy and worth translating, there is no special Scriptural authority being attached to them here, and the wide variation in terminology to refer to the works and/or their authors is a key to this.[61]

Even in the texts where some reference to a third category of authoritative writings may be intended, the full contents, title and ordering of any such category are still not standardized. Regarding contents and terminology, we see references to 'Psalms' in Lk. 24.44 and '[words of] David' in 4QMMT C10. The book of Psalms is the probable referent of both texts.[62] Nevertheless, the terminology is different. This variety is even more evident when we survey all references to a category of non-Torah, non-Prophetic books, including those from Philo and Ben Sira: 'Psalms', '[words of] David', 'Psalms and other books which foster and perfect knowledge and piety', and 'other writers'/'other books of the Fathers'/'other books'.

As to ordering, from the 'Torah' and 'Prophet' references discussed earlier we know that the Torah and non-Torah writings were separated, and almost certainly understood in historical sequence. Otherwise, we have no more evidence for the arrangement of the contents of early Jewish Scriptures than we do for the contents themselves. Q 11.(49-)51 (Lk. 11.51//Mt. 23.35) does not solve this problem:

> Therefore also the Wisdom of God said, 'I will send them prophets and apostles, some of whom they will kill and persecute, so that this generation may be charged with the blood of all the prophets shed since the foundation of the would, from the blood of Abel to the blood of Zechariah, who perished between the altar and the sanctuary' (Lk. 11.49-51).

60. Swanson, 'The Closing of Holy Scripture', pp. 125-30, 248-50; Barton, *Oracles of God*, pp. 47, 50.

61. Swanson, 'The Closing of Holy Scripture', p. 129.

62. Sanders, 'Canon', p. 839. Cf. Schiffman, 'The New Halakhic Letter', p. 66, who suggests that Chronicles may be intended in 4QMMT C10, 'the primary subject of which is David'. He bases this suggestion on the focus here in 4QMMT on the history of the monarchy. Other early Jewish documents such as 11QPs[a] 27.(3-)11 seem to think of the book of Psalms as the uniquely Davidic book. If 4QMMT is referring to Psalms here, it is closely parallel to Lk. 24.44 in separating Psalms out from Torah and Prophets.

This text is evidence for one early conceptualization of the scope of biblical history, one drawn from the biblical histories: from Genesis (Gen. 4.1-16; Abel) to Chronicles (2 Chron. 24.20-22; Zechariah).[63] Since such a historical range could be established irrespective of the ordering of biblical scrolls, such a conceptualization of biblical history has no necessary connection to any standard ordering of the scrolls. Indeed, as Barr and Barton have argued, it is difficult to project what kind of purpose or context such a standard ordering might have had. Through the first few centuries CE there were no codices containing the whole Bible, but instead biblical books, or small groups of them, were transmitted on individual scrolls or (later) relatively small codices. Even when larger codices covering the entire Bible appear, no universally established ordering of the Tanakh was adopted until the modern standardization of printed editions of the Hebrew Bible.[64]

In sum, there is no evidence for Jewish consensus on the overall structure of the canon during the Second Temple period, whether tripartite or bipartite. Instead, just as there was a plurality of Jewish groups during this time, there seems to have been an plurality in conceptions of Scripture. Some groups, such as the Samaritans, Alexandrians, and certain establishment groups in Palestine seem to have focused exclusively or almost exclusively on Torah alone. Others seem to have worked with

63. Beckwith (*Old Testament Canon*, p. 220) objects that this reference could not be to a historical range because the last martyr recorded in the Bible is Shemaiah of Kiriath-Jearim (Jer. 26.20-23), not Zechariah. In this case, however, it seems as if the author of this saying in Q chose not Beckwith's historical range, but a historical range based on the limits of the biblical histories.

64. N. Sarna, 'Bible', *EncJud*, IV, pp. 827-30; I. Yeivin, *Introduction to the Tiberian Massorah* (trans. E.J. Revell; SBLMasS, 5; Missoula, MT: Scholars Press, 1980), pp. 38-39; Sanders, 'Canon', pp. 840-41. See also Swanson, 'The Closing of Holy Scripture', pp. 260-61; Barr, *Holy Scripture*, p. 57; Ulrich, 'The Bible in the Making', pp. 80-81; and particularly Barton, *Oracles of God*, pp. 83-86. Cf. Steck, *Abschluss der Prophetie*, p. 24, who argues against Barton on the basis of the existence of redactional layers extending across books in the Pentateuch, Deuteronomistic History, Chronistic History, and Prophetic corpus. Certainly there are cases where biblical books appear to have been subjected to similar redactions by the same group of tradents. Nevertheless, biblical scholars have probably been a bit too quick to assume continuity of redactors across books in cases such as the redaction of the Deuteronomistic History, and common redaction may tell us nothing more than that a given group of books was transmitted by the same group of tradents for a period. It is not necessarily an indicator of the existence of a consciousness of a set of books as a closed or clearly ordered corpus.

the Torah and a group of non-Torah, authoritative books termed 'Prophets'. And finally, we have seen—particularly in certain groups more generally working with a bipartite canon—at least a couple of texts draw an occasional distinction between the 'prophets' and a variously described collection of other non-Torah authoritative books, although the contents of such a collection and terminology for it are not standardized. The lines of continuity between these varying conceptions are twofold: Torah is present in all of them, and if there is an additional category, the next one is usually termed 'Prophets'. Otherwise, variety reigns.

This diversity regarding the structure of Scripture also extends to its contents. Not only did Second Temple Jews diverge in whether and how much they used non-Torah books, but also in which non-Torah books they used. Certain books—such as Isaiah for example—were used quite frequently by most early Jewish groups, while other books—such as Esther, *Jubilees*, *Testament of Levi*, and a number of now unknown works—were used by some groups and not by others.[65] Although most books later included in the present (Jewish and Christian) canons seem to have been used more consistently than books later excluded from those canons, this is not always true and there does not seem to have been any widely established, sharp line (corresponding to present canonical boundaries) demarcating canonical and non-canonical books during the period.[66] For example, Esther does not seem to have been used by the Qumran community, but the Damascus Document does cite *Jubilees* (CD 16.2-4) and (possibly) *Testament of Levi* (CD 4.15) and a now unknown 'book of meditation' (CD 10.6; 13.2; 14.7-8; see also

65. Both Qumran and New Testament writings cite a number of works no longer extant, including: the 'book of meditation' (CD 10.6; 13.2; 14.7-8; 1QS 1.6), perhaps a work entitled the 'Wisdom of God' (Lk. 11.49) and a number of unnamed texts not found in present Bibles (Jn 7.38; 1 Cor. 2.9; see also Mt. 27.9 and Jas 4.5). On Qumran see now VanderKam, *The Dead Sea Scrolls Today*, pp. 153-57. Cf. G. Maier, 'Der Abschluß des jüdischen Kanons und das Lehrhaus von Jabne', in *idem* (ed.), *Der Kanon der Bibel* (Giessen: Brunnen Verlag, 1991), p. 6.

66. Therefore, it can be misleading to organize discussions of this question into separate sections surveying how (now) canonical and (now) non-canonical books were treated by early Jewish groups. Beckwith's discussion in *Old Testament Canon* (pp. 274-433), divided as it is into two parts—'Books Included as Canonical' (pp. 274-337) and 'Books Excluded as Uncanonical' (pp. 338-433)—is a prime example of this phenomenon.

1QS 1.6).[67] Similarly, Song of Songs, Ecclesiastes, Esther and Ezra do not seem to be alluded to or cited in the New Testament,[68] but Jude 14-15 does cite *Enoch* as a special source of authority.[69]

In sum, *if we do not presuppose that use in one group is evidence for Second Temple usage in general*, it seems that different Jewish groups during this period worked with varying and relatively fluid assortments of authoritative writings, with no such assortment yet exactly matching the later Christian or Jewish canons.[70] To be sure, to some extent, the above discussed data (particularly the lack of attestation of certain books in certain communities) can be attributed to our patchy evidence on the Scriptural usage of various Second Temple Jewish groups. Nevertheless, the above described phenomenon of varying assortments of non-Torah Scriptures probably also reflects the lack of a closed canon and the intense diversity which characterized Judaism of the time.

So far this survey has not focused much on community correlates to

67. I.H. Eybers, 'Some Light on the Canon of the Qumran Sect', (reprinted) in S.Z. Leiman (ed.), *The Canon and Masorah of the Hebrew Bible: An Introductory Reader* (New York: Ktav, 1974), pp. 32-33, discusses the Jubilees citation and some problems in the purported citation of the *Testament of Levi*. On the 'book of meditation' see Maier, 'Zur Frage des biblischen Kanons', pp. 142-43.

Beckwith (*Old Testament Canon*, p. 364) argues that the citation formulae in these two cases 'does not imply canonicity'. Yet both formulae seem to stress the sources of information, thus implying recognition of the special authority of those sources. Beckwith's criteria for implication of canonicity seem conveniently strict to exclude evidence contradicting his early dating of the canon.

68. R.H. Pfeiffer, 'Canon of the Old Testament', *IDB*, I, p. 512.

69. Cf. Maier, 'Der Abschluß des jüdischen Kanons', p. 5.

The above comments regarding the inclusive concept of Scripture at Qumran and in the New Testament still do not even to begin to reckon with the less easily delimited, but nevertheless extremely important group of reminiscences of and allusions to various texts (whether now canonical or non-canonical) in Second Temple Jewish literature. For fuller discussion of this phenomenon in the New Testament see Sundberg, *Old Testament of the Early Church*, pp. 52-55. Nevertheless see the important cautions regarding Sundberg's collation of New Testament allusions to Apocrypha in F. Stuhlhofer, 'Der Ertrag von Bibelstellenregistern für die Kanongeschichte', *ZAW* 100 (1988), pp. 251-54.

70. In general, treatments such as Beckwith's (*Old Testament Canon*, pp. 274-433) have tended to work with a double standard for (now) canonical and non-canonical texts. Second Temple usage of a canonical text is taken as evidence of widespread canonicity, while usage (or non-usage) of a (now) non-canonical text is interpreted as 'sectarian'. Cf. also Leiman, *Canonization of Hebrew Scripture*, pp. 34-37 and n. 167 on p. 153.

the proto-canonical structures discussed above. To some extent, we simply do not have much knowledge of what was going on with each group during large portions of the period in question. Nevertheless, at this point we can briefly note one pattern which seems to emerge out of the diversity of Scriptural structures present in this period: the Torah-only canon seems to have been common primarily among groups associated with an ongoing Temple cult (the Sadducees, and certain Priestly circles in Jerusalem, the Samaritans at Mt Gerizim).[71] In contrast, the broader Torah and Prophets canon seems to have been favored by groups whose base of activity lay primarily outside Temple circles (the Pharisees, Qumran community, and early Christians).[72]

This fundamental difference in types of canons at least occasionally played a role in the positioning of these groups in relation to each other. In at least the case of the early Christians and the Qumran community, Jews outside the Temple cult used texts from the 'Prophets' section of the canon to condemn the existing Temple cult. Moreover, the permeability of the boundaries of this 'Prophets' portion of their canon allowed them to include (and even produce) new authoritative writings which could support their opposition to the status quo. In response, the more Temple-based groups could reject such writings as less authoritative and present themselves as living out the emphasis in the Pentateuch on the cultic sanctuary and regulations for it.

This pattern suggests that we have an arrangement in the later Second Temple period much like that found in the earlier Second Temple period regarding 'the Torah' and prophetic traditions. At that point, prophetic materials seem to have been particularly favored by groups (such as that behind Isa. 56.1-8) occupying a marginal position vis-à-vis the Torah-centered groups in power. Likewise, during the later Second Temple period, it is the opposition groups which can be depended upon to refer

71. One might add to this the correspondence of the probable Torah-focus of Alexandrians with a possible connection between them and the Temple cult at Leontopolis. Nevertheless, the Torah-focus of the Alexandrians is not as sharply defined as in the case of the Samaritans, Sadduccees and Priestly groups reflected in the Mishnah, and the Alexandrians have a less clear relation to Leontopolis than the Palestinian groups listed above. Therefore, it is just as likely that other factors, such as distance from innovation in Palestine, explain the predominant focus on the Torah in certain traditions associated with Alexandria.

72. Here I am indebted to Richard Weis, personal communication, for insights into the way relations of Second Temple Jewish groups to a Temple cult correspond to the types of canon each recognized.

frequently to their tradition as 'Torah' and 'Prophets', apparently including in the latter category some now non-canonical apocalyptic texts.[73]

Whereas a case can be made that the flexibility of a bipartite canon may have been particularly utilized by opposition groups (among others), it is much more difficult to establish a similar community–canon connection with regard to the scattered references to a tripartite division of scriptural books. These references, through their very isolation (occurring [with the exception of the Prologue to Ben Sira] only once in a given text and often in literatures otherwise dominated by a bipartite concept of the canon: Lk. 24.44 in the New Testament and 4QMMT at Qumran), do not seem to have been rooted in community processes. Instead, these references to a tripartite structure may have been prompted by problems in categorizing certain non-Torah books as 'prophets', lack of historical focus in certain non-Torah books, or other factors not easy to determine because of the meager evidence. In any case, two things seem clear: (1) there is no demonstrable differentiation during this period between the status of these two groups of non-Torah books in our few references to them, and (2) such a tripartite categorization did not achieve universal recognition across the full range of Second Temple Jewish groups.

After the Destruction of the Second Temple

Formation of the Tanakh in Judaism

It is only in the first century CE that we see the beginnings of the formation of a closed, well-established canon much like the present Tanakh. The germ of this development toward a more formal concept of Scripture is already reflected in the gradual standardization of Hebrew texts and revision of Greek texts to reflect them more closely. Already by this point some of the most often cited Scriptural books—Torah, Isaiah and Psalms—appear in proto-Masoretic form at Qumran, Masada and Naḥal Ḥever.[74] Moreover, the Naḥal Ḥever Minor Prophets scroll

73. Exploration of a similar prophecy-narrative dynamic across the pre-exilic to Second Temple periods is the focus of J. Blenkinsopp's *Prophecy and Canon: A Contribution to the Study of Jewish Origins* (University of Notre Dame Center for the Study of Judaism and Christianity in Antiquity, 3; Notre Dame: University of Notre Dame Press, 1977).

74. On this question see in particular E. Tov, 'Groups of Biblical Texts Found

(8ḤevXIIgr) already testifies to a growing tendency around 0 CE to revise Greek translations to conform with a proto-Masoretic *Vorlage*.[75] Sanders has been foremost in insisting on the connection between such textual developments and developments in concepts of canon.[76] Following him, this move toward standardization of Hebrew texts and revision of Greek texts to conform to them suggests a growing canon consciousness—at least among certain scribal circles in Palestine.

Josephus provides both a clue to which circles may have been most prominent in this development and a suggestion as to their connection with the canon of later rabbinic Judaism. His discussion of canon occurs in the context of an argument for the superiority of Jewish sacred books over against those of the Greeks:

> We do not possess myriads of inconsistent books, conflicting with one another; but our books, those which are justly believed, are only twenty-two, and contain the record of all time. Of these, five are the books of Moses... From the death of Moses down to Artaxerxes who followed Xerxes as king of Persia, the prophets after Moses wrote the events of their own times in thirteen books. The remaining four books contain hymns to God and precepts for the conduct of human life...
>
> We have given practical proof of our reverence for our own Scriptures. For, although such long ages have now passed, no one has ventured to add, or to remove, or to alter anything, and it is an instinct with every Jew, from the day of his birth, to regard them as the decrees of God, to abide by them, and (if need be) cheerfully to die for them. Time and again ere

at Qumran', in D. Dimant and L.H. Schiffman (eds.), *Time to Prepare the Way in the Wilderness: Papers on the Qumran Scrolls by Fellows of the Institute for Advanced Studies of Hebrew University, Jerusalem* (STDJ, 16; Leiden: Brill, 1995), pp. 85-102. My deep thanks to Professor Tov for allowing me to read and benefit from an early version of this article. Working from the charts in the article and the publications available to me, I am initially impressed by the early dates of non-proto-Masoretic texts on the one hand, and the predominantly late dates of clearly proto-Masoretic texts on the other. Hence the suggestion here that *by this point* proto-Masoretic texts were appearing at Qumran.

75. E. Tov, *The Greek Minor Prophets Scroll from Naḥal Ḥever (8ḤevXIIgr)* (DJD, 8; Oxford: Clarendon Press, 1990), pp. 145-53 surveys the textual affinities of the Prophets Scroll *Vorlage* and finds a clear leaning of the scroll toward proto-Masoretic readings. On dating see the discussion in the same volume by P.J. Parsons, 'The Scripts and their Date', pp. 19-26. He concludes that the scroll dates 'in the later i B.C.'

76. J.A. Sanders, 'Text and Canon: Concepts and Method', *JBL* 98 (1979), pp. 5-29.

> now the sight has been witnessed of prisoners enduring tortures and death in every form in the theaters, rather than utter a single word against the laws and the allied document. (LCL *Apion* 1.38-41)

As Swanson has suggested, Josephus's claims at this point for the antiquity of a certain form of the Jewish canon—22 books—may have a broader background. Particularly given the prominence of Pharisaism during the time of his later writings and his statement that he followed them in public life (*Life* 12), Josephus's testimony here may be evidence for the Pharisaic concept of canon and claims regarding it.[77] Certainly, it was this concept of a 22-book canon which won out along with many parts of the Pharisaic program in the post-Second Temple consolidation of Judaism. Indeed, his 22-book numbering and his use of the reign of Artaxerxes as a chronological limit-point for continuous prophetic succession from Moses—and thus the limit for canon—both correspond remarkably closely with concepts of canon limits which are testified to in later rabbinic Jewish texts.[78]

77. Swanson, 'The Closing of Holy Scripture', pp. 267-68, and F.M. Cross, 'The Text Behind the Text of the Hebrew Bible', *BR* 1.2 (1985), pp. 23-25. For correction of the traditional view that Josephus identified fully with Pharisaic beliefs and for detailed discussion of *Life* 12, see Mason, *Flavius Josephus on the Pharisees*, *passim*, particularly pp. 342-56.

78. Cf. Josephus, *War* 1.18 (Barton, *Oracles of God*, p. 48). As W.C. van Unnik points out, Josephus here is not claiming an end to prophecy, but to a continuous succession of prophets: *Flavius Josephus als historischer Schriftsteller* (Heidelberg: Verlag Lambert Schneider, 1978), pp. 47-49. For rabbinic texts reflecting the concept of an end to prophecy at the time of Artaxerxes, see in particular *t. Soṭ.* 13.3, which is cited in *b. Soṭ.* 48b and reflected in *b. Yom.* 9b and *b. Sanh.* 11a. Cf. also *b. Yom.* 21b and *S. 'Ol. R.* 30. A similar chronological limit-point for canon is mentioned as an issue in exclusion of Ben Sira in *t. Yad.* 2.13.

Notably, earlier comments in 1 Maccabees regarding the ceasing of prophecy of Israel (e.g. 1 Macc. 4.46; 9.27) do not indicate any analogous proto-canonical consciousness. Instead, they are isolated early testimony to an idea that prophecy had ceased by the time of the Maccabean revolt. The cessation of prophecy is not more exactly located in 1 Maccabees. Most importantly, 1 Macc. 4.46 seems to keep open the possibility that prophecy would resume. For discussion of the wider cultural and historical context of these passages see Blenkinsopp, *Prophecy and Canon*, p. 111.

Fabry ('11QPs[a] und die Kanonizität des Psalters', p. 56) suggests that the chronological canon criterion found in Josephus is already implicit in 4Q380/381 because the Psalms in this text are given superscriptions which assign them to ancient figures. Such attribution to early figures, however, seems to long predate any overall concept of a chronologically limited canon. For example, such attribution is

Notably, the polemical focus of the text means that it is not necessarily sound evidence for the antiquity of a 22-book 'canon' or for any divisions within it.[79] As we have already seen in our previous discussion of other Second Temple witnesses to canon, Josephus's claim for long-time Jewish unanimity on canon is not borne out by the evidence in the Second Temple period. Therefore, rather than being read as an accurate reflection of the history of the Jewish canon, Josephus's comments should more appropriately be read in relation to his overall aim: convincing Gentile readers of the superiority and legitimacy of the Jewish canon.

Similarly, Josephus's description of the contours of that canon must be read in context. Although he claims a great antiquity for a 22-book Jewish canon, a close examination of the text indicates that he makes no such claim regarding divisions within that canon. The relevant units in the passage can be outlined as follows:

Argument for the legitimacy of a 22-book Jewish canon

1. Initial contrast of the limited number (22) of Jewish books with the myriad of Greek books
2. Rough definition (for Gentile audience) of the contents of the limited canon
3. Concluding claim for the antiquity of the Jewish 22-book limit

As indicated, the middle section describing the contents of the Jewish canon plays a subservient role vis-à-vis the preceding and following sections, merely clarifying in general terms the nature of the books which are included in the limited, 22-book Jewish canon being advocated. In this general description, Josephus does not seem intent here on reporting the exact organization and terminology of an existing Jewish canon. Instead, both his simple distribution of non-Torah books into historical and non-historical categories and his explanatory terminology for the non-historical books—'hymns to God and precepts for the conduct of human life'—are best understood as reflections of an aim to clarify the contents of these 22 books to Gentiles, who were unfamiliar with them.[80] Indeed, having thus clarified the contents of the books, he concludes his discussion with a statement about how Jews have been willing to suffer

already occuring in the early stages of the traditio-historical development of the Psalter and Prophetic works in general.

79. Hahneman, *The Muratorian Fragment*, p. 75.

80. Barton, *Oracles of God*, p. 48. See also Swanson, 'The Closing of Holy Scripture', pp. 272-74.

all rather than speak a word against 'the laws and the allied documents' (τοὺς νόμους καὶ τὰς μετὰ τούτων ἀναγραφάς), an apparent reflection of a bipartite concept of the canon. In sum, Josephus is not so much an accurate testimony to the antiquity of any 22-book limit for the Jewish canon or tripartite division of it. Instead, he is a probable witness to the Pharisaic canon already taking shape in the first century, a canon perhaps reflected in the gradual manuscript standardization in the first century and then finalized in later rabbinic Judaism.

Lest we assume that the Pharisaic concept of canon has already triumphed in Josephus's time, 2 Esd. 14.44-48 indicates both the increasing dominance of this idea of a limited canon, and resistance to it:

> So during the forty days, ninety-four books were written. And when the forty days were ended, the Most High spoke to me, saying, 'Make public the twenty-four books that you wrote first, and let the worthy and the unworthy read them; but keep the seventy that were written last, in order to give them to the wise among your people. For in them is the spring of understanding, the fountain of wisdom, and the river of knowledge.' And I did so.

This saying, which concludes the older version of 2 Esdras, occurs in the context of a redescription of Ezra's reception of the Scriptures. The number 24 corresponds to the numbering of the books in the Tanakh which becomes dominant in the Amoraic period and afterward.[81] In this text, the authority of such a grouping of books is acknowledged through describing them as read by worthy and unworthy among the people. Yet this passage goes on to claim a yet higher authority for the 70 scrolls containing more perfect wisdom to be kept only for the 'wise among your [Ezra's] people' (2 Esd. 14.46). Thus, on the one hand, we have a block of books now recognized as generally accepted Scripture. On the other hand, we have a claim for yet higher revelation in certain apocalyptic works. In other words, a late first-century push to establish the exclusive authority of a 24-book canon seems to be counteracted in this text by an attempt to claim yet higher authority for certain books outside that canon. Thus, 2 Esd. 14.44-48 is an important testimony not only to the emergence of a 24-book canon but also to continuing resistance at the end of the first century to the recognition of just such a closed canon.

Thus far in Josephus and 2 Esdras we see only the apparent final results of various efforts to define explicitly a canon which excludes certain

81. Cf. Swanson, 'The Closing of Holy Scripture', pp. 278-79, who argues against relying on 2 Esd. 14.44-48 for early testimony to a 24-book canon.

books, but in early rabbinic literature we find some ongoing internal arguments bearing on such a proto-canonical definitional process.[82] Thus, for example, *ARN* 1.4 suggests that Proverbs along with Ecclesiastes and Song of Songs were once 'withdrawn' (גנז) because they were long ago thought to be '[mere] parables and not from the Scriptures' (משלות ואינן מן הכתובים; cf. *b. Šab.* 30b on Ecclesiastes and *b. Sanh.* 100b on Ben Sira).[83] Along similar lines, we see rabbinic discussion of whether or not certain books 'defile the hands' (מטמא את הידים). One consideration in deciding whether a book 'defiled the hands' seems to have been whether or not it was inspired (*m. Yad.* 3.5; *t. Yad.* 2.14; *b. Meg.* 7a; *b. Sanh.* 100a; cf. also *m. Yad.* 4.6),[84] and early rabbinic texts suggest that questions were raised on this issue regarding Ecclesiastes,[85] Song of Songs,[86] Esther,[87] and Ben Sira.[88]

82. See Barthélemy, 'L'Etat de la Bible juive', pp. 26-30.

83. As Leiman stresses (*The Canonization of Hebrew Scriptures*, pp. 79-81), such discussions usually presuppose the holiness of the objects being considered for withdrawal, and thus they do not pertain to the inclusion or exclusion of a given writing from an emerging canon. For these reasons he argues persuasively that the discussions of storing Ezekiel in *b. Šab.* 13b and *b. Ḥag* 13a presuppose the canonical status of that book, and pertain only to its possibly misleading contradictions of Torah. Nevertheless, Leiman also recognizes that the wording of the *ʾAbot de Rabbi Nathan* reference indicates the presence of proto-canonical concerns, and suggests that *b. Sanh.* 100b on the storing of Ben Sira may imply like concerns because Ben Sira's status was questionable.

84. As the discussions in *m. Yad.* 3.4-5 and 4.5 indicate, these arguments pertain to the holiness of the scrolls on which biblical books were written, and thus the participants are described as considering other issues besides whether or not a book is thought to be inspired, issues such as the numbers of letters written on the scroll (*m. Yad.* 3.5), types of letters (4.5), type of writing material and writing substance (4.5), holiness of unwritten parts of the scroll (3.4), and holiness of texts where only portions or quotations of biblical texts are written (*t. Yad.* 2.12). Thus, although proto-canonical concerns such as inspiration play a role in these discussions, 'defiling the hands' is not an exactly equivalent concept to canonicity. Cf. Barr, *Holy Scripture*, pp. 50-51; Barton, *Oracles of God*, pp. 68-71, who make a stronger distinction between the issue of 'defiling the hands' and any considerations of canonicity. Cf. also the more recent discussion of this issue in Veltri, 'Zur traditionsgeschichtlichen Entwicklung des Bewußtseins von einem Kanon', pp. 215-26.

85. *m. Yad.* 3.5; *t. Yad.* 2.14; cf. *m. 'Ed.* 5.3; *b. Meg.* 7a.

86. *m. Yad.* 3.5; cf. *m. 'Ed.* 5.3; *b. Meg.* 7a.

87. *b. Sanh.* 100a; *b. Yom.* 29a; cf. *b. Meg.* 7a.

88. *t. Yad.* 2.13. This text has also previously been read as denying the canonicity of Christian 'gospels' (גליונין) and 'books of the heretics' (ספרי מינים). This reading,

By the time of the redaction of these rabbinic texts (200 CE and following), the inspired character of all of the above mentioned marginal works had been accepted, with the exception of Ben Sira.[89] Thus, on the one hand, during the early Tannaitic period we first see Greek translations of these marginal works begin to appear, translations which are part of the larger Jewish effort of the time to produce a set of Greek translations which better match the increasingly defined, proto-Masoretic Hebrew Bible.[90] On the other hand, although Ben Sira is still quoted by some rabbinic authorities, the relevant rabbinic discussions agree that Ben Sira does not 'defile the hands'.[91] Indeed, Ben Sira is mentioned in

however, has been seriously questioned. Early in this century, Ginzberg argued that these discussions related not to whether or not such sectarian works were holy on their own merits, but whether such writings might be holy by virtue of long Scripture quotes contained in them: L. Ginzberg, 'Some Observations on the Attitude of the Synagogue Towards the Apocalyptic-Eschatological Writings', *JBL* 41 (1922), pp. 122-23 (n. 19). In support of this latter interpretation, Ginsberg argued that *t. Yad.* 2.13 is a reflection not on the inherent holiness of books (which he sees in *m. Yad.* 4.6), but on whether a scroll is still holy if it contains only a few letters of Scripture (the first part of *m. Yad.* 3.5). Thus, *t. Yad.* 2.13 would parallel discussions elsewhere in Tosefta about what to do about sectarian documents that contain the name of God (*t. Šab.* 13.5; *y. Šab.* 16.1; *b. Šab.* 116a).

Subsequent studies have gone even further, concluding that what is at issue here is not 'gospels' and 'sectarian works of heretics', but '[Bible scroll] margins' and '[Bible] scrolls of the heretics': K.G. Kuhn, 'Giljonim und sifre minim', in W. Eltester (ed.), *Judentum, Urchristentum, Kirche* (BZNW, 26; Berlin: Töpelmann, 1964), pp. 24-61; Sundberg, *The Old Testament of the Early Church*, pp. 121-24; Swanson, 'The Closing of Holy Scripture', pp. 297-99; G. Stemberger, 'Yabneh und der Kanon', in Baldermann *et al.* (eds.), *Zum Problem des biblischen Kanons*, pp. 168-69; cf. Maier, *Jüdische Auseinandersetzung*, pp. 28-74. Such usage would better conform with early rabbinic usage of the word גליונין to mean 'margins'. Only later do Amoraic rabbinic documents make a wordplay on גליונין ('margin') and εὐαγγέλιον (gospel; cf. *b. Šab.* 116a). As Sundberg points out, such a wordplay would be unlikely in the Tosefta, since contemporary Christians were only just beginning to refer to their own Gospels as τὰ εὐαγγέλια; Sundberg, *The Old Testament of the Early Church*, p. 124.

89. Leiman, *Canonization of Hebrew Scripture*, pp. 86-120.

90. Barthélemy, 'L'Etat de la Bible juive', pp. 19-22.

91. Leiman, *The Canonization of Hebrew Scripture*, pp. 92-102 gives most of the relevant texts, references to previous discussion, and analysis. In an unpublished paper presented at the 1990 SBL Annual Meeting, B.W. Wright raises some important cautions regarding determination of where the rabbis actually used the/a book of Ben Sira and in which form: 'The Use of the Wisdom of Ben Sira in

the Jerusalem and Babylonian Talmuds as among the 'outside books' prohibited by Akiba in *m. Sanh.* 10.1.[92]

Taken together, these late first-century and second-century passages suggest three things. First, in formative Judaism there is an emerging widespread concern to define with greater clarity not only which books are authoritative, but also which books are not. Secondly, there appears to be increasing consensus on the basic contents of the Jewish canon: a collection variously numbered as 22 or 24 scrolls. Notably, second- and third-century testimony from Church Fathers regarding the Jewish canon confirms this impression.[93] Thirdly, in each case, the passages in question make clear that the concern to define this collection (or another larger one in the case of 2 Esdras) as uniquely authoritative occurs in the context of polemic against other groups: whether between formative Judaism and its opponents (2 Esd. 14.44-48) or Jews and Gentiles (Josephus, *Apion* 1.38-41).

Such concern for increasing definition of a canon over and above other texts fits well with the focus of Judaism during this time of consolidation in the wake of the destruction of the Second Temple. Whereas the preceding period was characterized by an intense diversity in types of Judaism, the period after 70 CE sees the gradual emergence of a relatively coherent and dominant form of post-destruction Judaism. This newly dominant form is reflected in the Mishnah (and other formative Jewish documents) and the increasing dominance of the rabbinic schools. While other forms of Judaism seem to have coexisted with rabbinic Judaism, ultimately no form of Judaism seems to have survived and flourished which did not accommodate itself in some way to the new rabbinic structures and texts which became dominant at this point.[94]

Rabbinic Literature'. This paper was obtained by the author via the IOUDAIOS computer discussion group archive and is cited with permission.

92. *y. Sanh.* 28a and *b. Sanh.* 100b. For translation of ספרים החיצונים as 'outside books' (rather than 'books of the heretics') see Ginzberg, 'Attitude of the Synagogue', pp. 125-26. As Stemberger ('Jabne und der Kanon', pp. 172-73) points out, the Jerusalem Talmud discussion is less germane to questions of canon than the Babylonian Talmud text.

93. Sundberg (*Old Testament of the Early Church*, pp. 133-40) discusses several Eastern theologians' reports of Jewish practice. His references include Melito's letter cited in Eusebius, *Eccl. Hist.* 4.26.13; Origen's list in Eusebius, *Eccl. Hist.* 6.25; and Athanasius's *Festal Letter* 39.3-4.

94. The Karaite movement of the eighth and following centuries CE is a possible exception to this statement.

Only well into the midst of this consolidation process do we finally see the definitive numbering and particular organization of biblical books presently found in the Tanakh.[95] Thus, most Tannaitic passages still testify to (1) a bipartite canon, 'Torah' and 'Prophets'[96] and (2) continuing disputes about the status of certain books.[97] It is only during the late Tannaitic and early Amoraic periods that we begin to see the widespread establishment of the Tanakh as we know it: the traditional numbering of 24 books, division of them into three parts, and terminology for these three parts.[98] The most often cited text in this connection is the *baraita*

95. Sanders, 'Canon', p. 839 cites an unpublished major paper by P. Pettit as arguing this case in more detail: 'Comparative Study of Torah Citations and Other Scripture in the Mishnah', 1988.

96. *Sifre Deut.* 21.18 (see also 1.1); *m. Roš Haš.* 4.6; *m. Meg.* 4.1, 3, 4; and *t. Ter.* 1.10 and *t. B. Meṣ.* 5.8; 11.23. These references are from Leiman, *Canonization of Hebrew Scripture*, pp. 58-59. The mention of all three present divisions in *t. Roš Haš.* 4.6 is the main exception. Nevertheless, this reference is somewhat isolated and, occuring in the Tosefta, probably testifies to developments toward the end of the Tannaitic period. The discussion of which scrolls are to be saved in *m. Šab.* 16.1 is often mentioned as another Tannaitic testimony to the tripartite canon, but the text itself only mentions texts which are read versus texts which are not. From the Babylonian Talmud onward (*b. Šab.* 15a) this has been interpreted to refer to a distinction between Torah and Prophets (which are read) and Writings (which are not). On the other hand, *y. Šab.* 16.1 suggests that the issue is whether scrolls with too many mistakes to be read from should still be saved from a fire. Given the prevelance elsewhere in the Mishnah of a bipartite classification and lack of explicit terminology at this point, this text is not a secure basis for postulation of a tripartite canon in the Mishnah.

97. See again Leiman, *Canonization of Hebrew Scripture*, pp. 86-120, for texts and discussion. As Leiman stresses, some kind of authority of these books is presupposed in many of these discussions. The issue is whether now to exclude them from a closed collection of Scriptural books.

98. On the 24-book numbering see Leiman, *Canonization of Hebrew Scripture*, pp. 53-56.

At another point, n. 297 on p. 170, Leiman argues that the widespread presence of the tripartite division can be established on the basis of the following passages: *t. Roš Haš.* 4.6; *y. Meg.* 73d-74a; *b. B. Bat.* 13b; and *ARN* [version B] ch. 1, p. 2a in Schechter. Yet the reference in *'Abot de Rabbi Nathan* does not in fact clearly testify to a tripartite canon, and the references in the Yerušalmi and Bavli are later than the period under discussion. This leaves the Tosefta passage, a text which is somewhat isolated when compared with the bulk of Tannaitic discussions of the problem and, moreover, occurs in a document, the Tosefta, which was redacted toward the end of the Tannaitic period.

in the Babylonian Talmud, *b. B. Bat.* 14b-15a. In addition, Jerome's testimony to the tripartite Jewish canon also belongs to this period (*Pref. SamKg*). Additional texts testifying to a tripartite division include: *t. Roš Haš.* 4.6; *y. Meg.* 70d, 73d-74a; *y. Ḥag.* 77b; *b. Ta'an.* 8a; *b. B. Bat.* 13b; *b. Sanh.* 90b; *Lev. R.* 16.4; *Cant. R.* 1.11; and *Tanḥuma* on Deut. 11.26.[99] As Leiman points out, the above texts from the Tosefta and Yerušalmi are particularly significant because they add the 'Writings' category to supplement earlier Tannaitic discussions which mention only Torah and Prophets.[100]

In sum, at the beginning of this period, in Josephus, 2 Esdras and several Tannaitic passages, we see our first evidence for what will become a consensus in rabbinic Judaism on the basic contents of the Jewish canon and an emerging concern to define explicitly the importance of a canon including non-Torah books over against the texts of opposition groups. These developments seem to have been parts of the initial consolidation of Judaism in the wake of the destruction of the Second Temple. They represent the first steps toward Tanakh 'canonization' narrowly conceived: a process of explicit exclusion as well as inclusion. The final steps toward such 'canonization' occur only when the Jewish community is more fully consolidated, during the Amoraic period. This is the point at which we first see full-fledged attestation of the present three-part Tanakh.

Formation of the Two-Testament Bible in Christianity

Clearly, long before the final emergence of the Jewish Tanakh, the bulk of the early Christian movement had departed from Jerusalem and was

99. Although many of the texts in this latter list cite Tannaitic authorities as maintaining a tripartite canon (*y. Meg.* 73d-74a; *y. Ḥag* 77b; *b. Sanh.* 90b; *Lev. R.* 16.4), such attributions are unreliable in this period (for references and discussion see H.L. Strack and G. Stemberger, *Introduction to the Talmud and Midrash* [trans. M. Bockmuehl; Edinburgh: T. & T. Clark, 1991], pp. 63-66). Particularly given the sharp shift in concept of canon from Tannaitic to Amoraic documents (*t. Roš Haš-Šanah* being the main exception), it is likely that these Amoraic texts are a poor source for investigation of Tannaitic concepts of canon.

100. Leiman, *Canonization of Hebrew Scripture*, p. 63. The parallels are as follows: *t. Roš Haš.* 4.6//*m. Roš Haš.* 4.6; *y. Meg.* 73d//*t. Meg.* 4.20. Leiman (*Canonization of Hebrew Scripture*, p. 64 and n. 291, pp. 168-69) argues that the reference to just Torah and Prophets in *Sop.* 3.1 is an abbreviation of an earlier tradition regarding Torah, Prophets and Writings in *y. Meg.* 73d-74a and *b. B. Bat.* 13b. Cf. Barton, *Oracles of God*, pp. 52-54.

defining itself increasingly over against its Jewish roots. As indicated by numerous references to the 'Torah and Prophets', the early church took with it a bipartite conception of Jewish Scriptures, thus following one of the options for structuring of Scripture present in Judaism during the Second Temple period.[101] Aside from this, however, the church did not take an exactly delimited set of Hebrew or Greek Scriptures. Here again, it is important to remember that during this period biblical books, and translations of them, circulated separately.[102] Although certain Greek translations of individual books and groups of books (Torah, Isaiah, *Jubilees*, *Enoch*) seem to have been circulated, there is no clear evidence for the existence of a clearly defined 'Greek Bible', a 'LXX', which predated the early Christian process of defining an 'Old Testament'.[103] A full text of a standard 'LXX'—one including the books to be found in modern editions of the LXX—does not appear until the Christian canonical lists and large codices of the late fourth century. In sum, although the early Christian movement took with it a bipartite set of Jewish Scriptures, largely used in Greek translation, its full 'Old Testament' does not emerge until the development of a full two-Testament Greek Bible, in the second to fourth centuries.[104]

At first, the Christian church seems to have worked with this some-

101. See for example Ignatius (*Smyrn.* 5.1) and Melito (Eusebius, *Eccl. Hist.* 4.26.13).

102. On this see above, p. 46.

103. To be sure, early Jewish texts (such as the Prologue to Ben Sira) and Christian texts do talk about Greek translations of Scripture as a group. Moreover, particularly in the late first century and following, some Jewish revisions (Aquila, Theodotian, etc.) seem to have been made across large swathes of the present Jewish canon. Nevertheless, even as late as the middle of the first century CE, several books presently in the Jewish and Christian canons—Qohelet, and possibly Song of Songs, Ruth and Lamentations—may not yet have been translated into Greek. In addition, multiple Greek translations of several others (Esther, Tobit, Ben Sira) seem to have been in circulation. Barthélemy, 'L'Etat de la Bible juive', pp. 20-21.

104. Interestingly, though Sundberg persuasively demolishes the 'Alexandrian canon' hypothesis, he nevertheless maintains the idea of a pre-Christian LXX. See his *Old Testament of the Early Church*, pp. 46-47. His primary data are (1) the Prologue to Ben Sira, which refers to Greek translations of the Torah, Prophets and other books and (2) evidence of connections between the Greek translation of Ben Sira and Greek translations included in the present LXX. This evidence does not, however, establish the existence of a set of Greek translations identical to our present LXX. Instead, this is testimony to the early use of certain individual translations of books into Greek, translations later included in the Christian Greek Old Testament.

what undefined, bipartite set of Jewish Scriptures (including occasional references to *Enoch*, *4 Ezra* and other now non-canonical works[105]) along with a variety of non-Scriptural early Christian traditions, whether oral or (increasingly) written. In some contexts, such early Christian traditions seem to have been quoted alongside Jewish Scriptural texts without differentiation, often using citation formulae for both.[106] Yet, at least during the first century and a half of the Christian movement, no universally accepted distinction of Jewish Scriptures from early Christian traditions seems to have emerged. Some seem to have worked with little or no such distinction. Thus, for example, early Christians continue to refer to the Scriptures as simply the 'law and the prophets' (Ignatius, *Smyrn.* 5.1; Melito in Eusebius, *Eccl. Hist.* 4.26.13), and Theophilus refers to Rom. 2.7-9 and 1 Cor. 2.9 when calling Autolycus to hear and reverence 'the prophetic Scriptures' (*Ad Autolycum* 1.14).[107] In other writings, however, early Christians are already developing some initial categories for distinguishing the Jewish heritage from early Christian Scriptures, whether the 'Prophets' as distinguished from the command of 'the Lord' and 'Apostles' (Polycarp, *Phil.* 6.3), or 'the books' versus the 'Apostles' (*2 Clem.* 14.2), or the 'Prophets' as read alongside the 'Apostles' (Justin, *Apol.* 1.67.3). Throughout it is clear that many factors—such as liturgical usage and the gradual shift from oral to written Christian traditions—contributed to the veneration of a class of Christian writings in the early church *as part of/alongside* its Jewish heritage.[108]

Nevertheless, the decisive impetus for definition of a widespread, clearly defined *two-Testament* Christian canon seems to have been the struggle with heresy, particularly Marcion's mid-second-century pro-

105. For discussion of the relative frequency of such citations see Stuhlhofer, 'Der Ertrag von Bibelstellenregistern für die Kanonsgeschichte', pp. 249-50.

106. H. Camphausen, *Die Entstehung der christlichen Bibel* (BHT, 39; Tübingen: Mohr, 1968), pp. 80-86. The following texts are often cited in this connection: *Barn.* 4.14; Polycarp, *Phil.* 7.1, 2; 12.1; *2 Clem.* 2.4; 14.2; 2 Pet. 3.15-16.

107. Note also Tertullian's comment that Valentinus uses the 'entire volume' of Scriptures, contrasting his usage with that of Marcion. This may imply a concept of New Testament writings as part of a unitary Scripture including Jewish Scriptures as well; Tertullian, *Praescript.* 38.4ff.

108. On the importance of internal factors in the canonization of Christian writings see the summary of problems with Camphausen's approach in H. Gamble, 'The Canon of the New Testament', in *The New Testament and its Modern Interpreters* (Atlanta: Scholars Press, 1989), pp. 214-19, and U. Swarat, 'Das Werden des neutestamentlichen Kanons', in Maier (ed.), *Der Kanon der Bible*, pp. 35-44.

posal to substitute a Christian Gospel and Apostle (abbreviated Luke and Paul) for the Jewish Torah and Prophets. It is only during the period following Marcion's proposal that a two-covenant periodization of salvation history becomes prominent in the anti-Gnostic church: the new covenant through Jesus and old covenant through Moses. This then gradually becomes a framework for coordination of Jewish and Christian Scriptures. From the late second century to the early third century, early Church Fathers begin to refer to the Jewish Scriptures as the 'Old Covenant', and specifically Christian Scriptures as the 'New Covenant'. As Camphausen has argued forcefully, this two-Testament coordination of Scriptures allowed the anti-Gnostics to relegate to the past those parts of the Old Testament which were problematic to Christians, while defending their anti-Gnostic position from the standpoint of a (now) more normative set of early Christian writings.[109] Indeed, Trobisch in a provocative recent study of the final redaction of the New Testament goes further. He argues persuasively that various editorial elements of the New Testament point to its being a late-second-century answer to issues traditionally associated with Marcion: particularly the rejection of the Jewish Scriptures and the preference for Paul the apostle. In response, the canonical edition of the New Testament that emerges at this point carefully balances Paul and Peter, and coordinates the whole of the apostolic witness with the Jewish Scriptures. As a result, we see in this period the emergence of a cohesive New Testament alongside Jewish Scriptures conceived of as an 'Old Testament'.[110]

This does not mean, however, that the canon issue was settled. For unanimity does not seem to have reigned at first in recognition of a canonical Old or New Testament. Instead, from Marcion (160) to the Councils of Hippo (393) and Carthage (397, 418) early Church Fathers produced varying lists of authoritative books, diverging in both the ordering and number of scrolls included. Generally the Eastern Fathers stayed closer to the contents of the Scriptures as defined in Judaism since the end of the first century (2 Esdras and Josephus). In contrast, the Western Fathers (Jerome being an important exception) included more books.[111]

109. Camphausen, *Die Entstehung der christlichen Bibel*, pp. 306-11.

110. D. Trobisch, 'Die Endredaktion des Neuen Testaments: Eine Untersuchung zur Entstehung der christlichen Bibel' (Habilitationsschrift, Heidelberg Universität, 1994), *passim*, particularly pp. 86-152.

111. Sundberg, *Old Testament of the Early Church*, pp. 55-60, 129-59.

By the end of the fourth century, the bulk of the church seems to have settled on the fairly broad Old Testament of the Western church.[112] This inclusive policy regarding the Old Testament may have been enabled in part by the development of a sharp distinction of the Jewish Scriptures from the now more normative New Testament. In contrast, perhaps because of the controversy with the Montanists,[113] or because the production of an authoritative edition of the New Testament stood toward the beginning of the process,[114] there was considerable dispute over the canonical status of certain problematic early Christian writings. In the end, the exclusion process characteristic of the closing of a canon seems to have focused in the Christian instance on these problematic early Christian writings. Whereas the church eventually included most disputed Old Testament writings in its canon, it ended up excluding some Christian writings, such as the *Apocalypse of Peter* or *Shepherd of Hermas*, which were revered and occasionally cited as Scripture at the outset of the canon clarification process.[115]

The important point for our purposes is that the Christian Old Testament was developed as part of a process encompassing the definition of an entire two-Testament Bible. To be sure, once the Testaments were distinguished, they were often discussed separately.[116] Nevertheless, the canonization of each Testament proceeded simultaneously, in response

112. On the continuing diversity regarding the contents of the canon, see K. Aland, *The Problem of the New Testament Canon* (London: Mowbrays, 1962), pp. 11-13.

113. Camphausen, *Die Entstehung der christlichen Bibel*, pp. 245-82. For studies raising questions about the importance of this factor see the references in the following discussions: Gamble, 'The Canon of the New Testament', pp. 216-17 and B.S. Childs, *The New Testament as Canon: An Introduction* (Philadelphia: Fortress Press, 1984), pp. 16-21.

114. Trobisch, 'Endredaktion'.

115. W.G. Kümmel, *Einleitung in das Neue Testament* (Heidelberg: Quelle & Meyer, 17th edn, 1973), pp. 434-41.

116. See, for example, Eusebius's own discussion of New Testament books in *Eccl. Hist.* 3.25.1-7; his list of books Melito found were included in the Old Testament (*Eccl. Hist.* 4.26.12-14); or his lists of books Origen put in each Testament, a list of Old Testament books said to be from Origen's commentary on Psalms, and a list of New Testament books said to be from his commentary on Matthew (*Eccl. Hist.* 4.25.1-14). Similarly, Jerome lists only books in the Jewish canon in his preface to the books of Samuel and Kings, while the Muratorian fragment may concern itself exclusively with the New Testament canon. But on the latter cf. Hahneman, *The Muratorian Fragment*, pp. 180-81.

to similar forces, and the final rulings regarding the Christian canon encompassed both.[117] At the outset, the push toward definition and consolidation of the Christian canon—both Old and New Testaments—was an outgrowth of church controversies. In the end, the push under Constantine toward uniformity may also have been a factor encouraging standardization of canonical lists.[118] A formal list of New Testament Scriptures first appears in Eusebius at the outset of the fourth century. Athanasius of Alexandria a few decades later is the first to produce a list of both Old and New Testament books similar to those which are adopted by later church councils, also applying for the first time the term 'canon' to this body of Scripture.

Concluding Reflections

All of the above is not to suggest that we can form an exact picture of the canonization process. The data is admittedly sketchy at points, and too much must not be made of silence in many instances. Instead, the proposal being made here is the following: that rather than assuming a unitary canon along with a unitary Judaism during the Second Temple period and then seeing if the evidence disproves it, instead—prompted by the evidence for pluralism in Second Temple Judaism—we should explore the possibility that there was diversity of Scriptural structures in Second Temple Judaism. The purpose of the preceding sketch is to show that in fact the evidence for proto-canonical consciousness is most plausibly interpreted in just this way. More specifically, the evidence, such as it is, suggests that there was quite a variety in the Scriptures of Second Temple Judaism, not just a variety regarding the terminology and contents of the 'Writings' category, but in more fundamental issues such as the following: whether non-Torah books were recognized as Scripture, determination of which books were included in the 'Prophets', and whether any kind of additional category of non-Torah, non-Prophetic books was recognized. Standardization was not achieved until well after

117. Thus, for example, Athanasius's thirty-ninth *Festal Letter* covers the contents of both Old and New Testaments, as does Cyril of Jerusalem in his catechetical lectures (4.33-36). For excellent discussion of this phenomenon see Hahneman, *The Muratorian Fragment*, pp. 77-83, 174-75.

118. McDonald, *Formation of the Christian Biblical Canon*, pp. 110-16. See also D. Groh, 'Hans von Campenhausen on Canon: Positions and Problems', *Int* 28 (1974), pp. 342-43 on the broader move toward collection and codification of writings in the Roman world already around 200 CE.

the Second Temple period, with (1) the Tanakh being defined in the process of the development and consolidation of post-destruction rabbinic Judaism and (2) both Testaments of the two-Testament Christian Bible being defined during the period between the initial struggle with Marcion and the final drift toward centralization under Constantine and his successors.

Whatever the fortunes of the details of this tentative survey, the overall methodological point must be reckoned with. Anachronistic presumption of an early unified Scriptural 'canon' in Second Temple Judaism will no longer do. To be sure, most Jews (excepting those with a closed Torah-only canon) seem to have recognized a similar core of books as 'Scripture', a group of books now dominating the present Jewish and Christian ('Old Testament') canons. Nevertheless, the evidence suggests that many of the distinctive elements of our present canons—both contents and structure—did not emerge until well after the split between Judaism and Christianity. In sum, for both Judaism and Christianity, canon and community formation seem to have been inextricably connected to one another.[119]

119. I wish to thank the following scholars who read and commented on earlier drafts of this article; Drs David Reimer, Steve Mason, Marvin Sweeney, Erhard Blum, and Richard Weis. Their help was invaluable. Of course, I bear full responsibility for the final product. Thanks also go to the Association of Theological Schools and Alexander von Humboldt foundation for financial support during a sabbatical during which the final version of this article was completed.

OF PSALMS AND PSALTERS: JAMES SANDERS'S INVESTIGATION OF THE PSALMS SCROLLS

Peter W. Flint

Among the hundreds of manuscripts that have been discovered in the Judaean desert, no book, whether biblical or otherwise, is represented as frequently as the Psalter. This article discusses how research into the Psalms scrolls—and the debate surrounding them—began with the publication of 11QPsa[a] by James Sanders in 1965. Sanders has accomplished two notable feats with respect to the Psalms manuscripts: editing the largest of all these documents and being the first to articulate their implications for our understanding of the book of Psalms. After spending several years completing a dissertation and a book on the Psalms scrolls[1] and also preparing editions for the DJD series,[2] I am particularly pleased to contribute to this volume in honor of a great pioneer in the field. In the pages that follow I shall present a brief overview of all the Psalms manuscripts, comment on Sanders's two editions of 11QPs[a], and assess one component of what may be termed his 'Qumran Psalms Hypothesis'.

1. *Psalms Scrolls from the Judaean Desert*

Between 1947 and 1956, eleven caves were discovered in the region of Khirbet Qumran, about 1.6 km inland from the western shore of the Dead Sea and some 13 km south of Jericho. These caves yielded almost 900 manuscripts, of which more than 200 are classified as 'biblical scrolls', since they contain material found in the canonical Hebrew Bible, and constitute our earliest witnesses to the text of Scripture. In addition

1. P.W. Flint, 'The Psalters at Qumran and the Book of Psalms' (PhD dissertation, University of Notre Dame, IN, 1993); *The Dead Sea Psalms Scrolls and the Book of Psalms* (STDJ, 17; Leiden: Brill, 1996).

2. P. Skehan, E. Ulrich and P. Flint, *Edition of the Cave 4 Psalms Scrolls*; and P. Flint, *Edition of the Biblical Scrolls from Naḥal Ḥever (Wadi Seiyal)*. All in preparation for the series Discoveries in the Judaean Desert (Oxford University Press).

to the Qumran finds, several more manuscripts were discovered at locations in the vicinity of the Dead Sea, including Wadi Murabbaʿât (1951–52), Naḥal Ḥever (1960–61),[3] and Masada (1963–65). Portions of 39 Psalms scrolls or manuscripts incorporating Psalms have been found: 36 at Qumran, two at Masada, and different portions of the same manuscript at Naḥal Ḥever and Wadi Seiyal. No other book is represented in as many of the Dead Sea Scrolls, which is indicative of the importance of the Psalms for the Qumran community. The full listing of manuscripts is as follows:

Psalms Scrolls Found at Qumran

1Q10. 1QPs^{a}	1Q11. 1QPs^{b}	1Q12. 1QPs^{c}		
2Q14. 2QPs				
3Q2. 3QPs				
4Q83. 4QPs^{a}	4Q84. 4QPs^{b}	4Q85, 4QPs^{c}	4Q86. 4QPs^{d}	
	4Q87. 4QPs^{e}	4Q88. 4QPs^{f}	4Q89. 4QPs^{g}	4Q90. 4QPs^{h}
4Q91. 4QPs^{j}	4Q92. 4QPs^{k}	4Q93. 4QPs^{l}	4Q94. 4QPs^{m}	
4Q95. 4QPs^{n}	4Q96. 4QPs^{o}	4Q97. 4QPs^{p}	4Q98. 4QPs^{q}	
4Q98a. 4QPs^{r}	4Q98b. 4QPs^{s}	4Q98c. 4QPs^{t}	4Q98d. 4QPs^{u}	
4Q236. 4QPs89	4Q522. 4QPs122			
5Q5. 5QPs				
pap6Q5. pap6QPs				
8Q2. 8QPs				
11Q5. 11QPs^{a}	11Q6. 11QPs^{b}	11Q7. 11QPs^{c}	11Q8. 11QPs^{d}	
11Q9. 11QPs^{e}	11Q11.11QPsAp^{a}			

Psalms Scrolls From Other Locations

Masada (2 scrolls):	MasPs^{a} (M1039–160), MasPs^{b} (M1103–1742)
Naḥal Ḥever (1 scroll):	Hev/SePs

2. *James Sanders's Two Editions of 11QPs^{a}*

On November 10, 1961, James Sanders began unrolling the large Psalms scroll from Cave 11 (11QPs^{a}), which he published four years later in the official series Discoveries in the Judaean Desert.[4] This care-

3. Naḥal Ḥever is also known as Wadi Khabra. It was previously thought that parts of this manuscript were found at Naḥal Se'elim (Wadi Seiyal), but it now seems certain that the entire scroll comes from Naḥal Ḥever.

4. *The Psalms Scroll of Qumrân Cave 11 (11QPs^{a})* (DJD, 4; Oxford: Clarendon Press, 1965).

fully executed work constitutes the critical edition of the largest of all the Psalms manuscripts. Two years later he produced a companion volume, often termed the 'Cornell Edition', with a more general audience in view.[5] Omitting most of the technical data and copious footnotes found in the *editio princeps*, the later edition presents the Hebrew text with facing English translations. Details are also furnished concerning the discovery of 11QPs[a] by the Bedouin in 1956, and how the fragile scroll was unrolled, all of which makes fascinating reading. Furthermore, Sanders reports that—after the DJD edition had appeared and when the more popular edition was already in the publisher's hands—a telegram from the Israeli scholar Yigael Yadin arrived in December 1965, announcing that he had gained possession of a missing section of 11QPs[a].[6] Designating this piece as 'Fragment E', Yadin was to publish a preliminary edition soon afterwards (1966).[7] Although it was now too late to incorporate this important new material in the appropriate place in the Cornell volume, Sanders was fortunately able to append a *Postscriptum*, which includes a photograph, transcription and English translation of the new fragment.[8]

With the publication of these two editions, Sanders's achievement was threefold. First, he made available to scholarship the largest and most important of the Psalms manuscripts in a timely fashion. Secondly, by also producing a more popular edition, Sanders enabled a wider audience to read and appreciate the contents of 11QPs[a]. Thirdly, he started to investigate the significance and implications of this important document. Especially in the introduction and conclusion to the Cornell volume, Sanders began articulating his views regarding the 'Qumran Psalter', which were to give rise to intense debate.

3. *The 'Qumran Psalms Hypothesis'*

Copied sometime between 30 and 50 CE, 11QPs[a] is particularly interesting because it diverges radically from the Masoretic Psalter (or 'MT-150 Psalter') in view of the number of Psalms it contains. Not only

5. *The Dead Sea Psalms Scroll* (Ithaca, NY: Cornell University Press, 1967).

6. The large fragment contains parts of Pss. 118, 104, 147 and 105 in that order, joining frg. D and col. I of the larger manuscript.

7. Y. Yadin, 'Another Fragment (E) of the Psalms Scroll from Qumran Cave 11 (11QPs[a])', *Textus* 5 (1966), pp. 1-10 + pls. i-v. The fragment is quite substantial, containing parts of three columns.

8. Sanders, *Dead Sea Psalms Scroll*, pp. 155-65.

does 11QPs[a] preserve many Psalms in a different order, it also includes several compositions that are not present in the MT-150 collection. Consequently, this scroll questions traditional ideas concerning the shape and the finalization of the book of Psalms. In a series of publications commencing in 1966,[9] Sanders arrived at several conclusions that pose a serious challenge to traditional views of the text and canonization of the book of Psalms. One such proposal is that 11QPs[a] is part of the 'Qumran Psalter', an earlier form of the Hebrew Psalter prior to its finalization and viewed by the community at Qumran as a true Davidic Psalter. According to Sanders, the Qumran Psalter was regarded by those who used it as 'canonical' (since it incorporated Pss. 1–89, which had been finalized), yet also as 'open' (being able to admit additional contents or arrangements, since Pss. 90 onwards were still fluid). He went on to say that the process of stabilization was arrested when the founders of the Qumran community left Jerusalem, at a time when Psalms 1–89 had reached finalization. Psalms 90 onwards then developed independently in two directions, resulting in two collections, which had Psalms 1–89 in common but differed from Psalms 90 onwards. These are the 'Qumran Psalter', of which almost all the second half is represented by 11QPs[a], and the Psalter found in the Masoretic Text, whose second half comprises Psalms 90–150. If Sanders's proposals are correct, the evidence from Qumran attests not to a single, finalized Psalter, but to more than one edition; this would mean that there was no closed and generally accepted form of the Psalter among Jews in the first half of the first century CE, when the manuscript was copied.

When James Sanders's proposals are considered together, they comprise what I shall term the 'Qumran Psalms Hypothesis', which contains four main theses:

1. Concerning *Gradual Stabilization*: 11QPs[a] witnesses to a Psalter that was being gradually stabilized, from beginning to end.
2. Concerning *Textual Affiliations*: Two or more Psalters are represented among the scrolls from the Judaean desert.

9. For example, 'Variorum in the Psalms Scroll (11QPs[a])', *HTR* 59 (1966), pp. 83-94; 'Cave 11 Surprises and the Question of Canon', *McCQ* 21 (1968), pp. 1-15 (reprinted in S. Leiman [ed.], *The Canon and Masorah of the Hebrew Bible: An Introductory Reader* [New York: Ktav, 1974], pp. 37-51); 'The Qumran Psalms Scroll (11QPs[a]) Reviewed', in M. Black and W.A. Smalley (eds.), *On Language, Culture, and Religion: In Honor of Eugene A. Nida* (The Hague and Paris: Mouton, 1974), pp. 79-99.

3. Concerning *Provenance*: 11QPs[a] was compiled at Qumran, and thus may be termed the 'Qumran Psalter'.
4. Concerning *Status*: 11QPs[a] contains the latter part of a true scriptural Psalter. It is not a secondary collection that is dependent upon Psalms 1–150 as found in the received Masoretic Text.

The remainder of this *Festschrift* article is devoted to an examination of the first of Sanders's theses: that the scrolls attest to gradual stabilization of the Psalter. This also affords an opportunity to respond to Gerald H. Wilson's treatment of this topic,[10] and to refine somewhat the methodology he has employed. Although all four elements of the Qumran Psalms Hypothesis cannot be discussed here due to the constraints of time and space, I have examined them in detail elsewhere.[11]

4. *The Theory of Gradual Stabilization*

According to Sanders, 11QPs[a] contains the latter part of a Psalter which was regarded by the Qumran community as both 'canonical' and 'by no means closed'.[12] This terminology sums up his view that 11QPs[a] is part of a Psalter that in the early first century CE could admit additional compositions, although Psalms 1–89 had already been stabilized. Sanders's position has in fact evolved as to precisely which Psalms were regarded as fixed and which were viewed as fluid at Qumran.[13] After initially describing Psalms 1–72 as stabilized and 73 onwards as fluid in the Cornell edition of 11QPs[a], he subsequently observed in the *Postscriptum* that 'the last third' of the collection indicates a still open-ended Psalter in the first century CE.[14] Sanders's viewpoint is clearly expressed in a 1969 article, where he refers to 'the last third (or slightly more)' of the Qumran Psalter as unstable, and explicitly states: 'The fluidity in the Qumran Psalter...is in the last two Psalter books, IV and

10. G.H. Wilson, 'The Qumran Psalms Manuscripts and the Consecutive Arrangement of Psalms in the Hebrew Psalter', *CBQ* 45 (1983), pp. 377-88; and *The Editing of the Hebrew Psalter* (SBLDS, 78; Chico, CA: Scholars Press, 1985).

11. See nn. 1 and 33.

12. 'Psalms Scroll Reviewed', p. 98.

13. Cf. P.W. Skehan, 'Qumran and Old Testament Criticism', in M. Delcor (ed.), *Qumrân: Sa piéte, sa théologie et son milieu* (BETL, 46; Paris: Duculot; Leuven: Leuven University Press, 1978), pp. 163-82, esp. p. 165.

14. Sanders, *Dead Sea Psalms Scroll*, pp. 13 and 158.

V, Psalms 90 and following'.[15] This formulation takes into account the data provided by 11QPs[a], where the earliest Psalm (in Masoretic terms) is Psalm 93 in col. xxii. For Sanders, the scroll thus has important implications for our understanding of the canonical process, and should be regarded 'as a signpost in the multi-faceted history of the canonization of the Psalter',[16] for which a gradual process of stabilization from beginning to end is to be assumed.

In the present article, I shall first assess the degree of stability evident in the scrolls for Psalms 1–89, and secondly for Psalms 90 onwards. This will be done with recourse to two main types of evidence: order (i.e., differences in arrangement of adjoining Psalms), and content (i.e., the linkage of Psalms with compositions absent from the Masoretic Psalter). Despite the fragmentary state of many scrolls, the statistics that emerge should provide two bases for comparison between Psalms 1–89 and Psalms 90–150: (1) the proportion of conflicts and agreements with the order of the MT; and (2) the overall number of times that specific Psalms are joined to non-Masoretic compositions. When viewed together, these results should provide a firm basis for comparing the stability and fluidity of Psalms 1–89 and 90–150 in relation to each other.

5. *Adjoining Psalms in the 39 Manuscripts*

The criteria of order and content involve the various groupings of Psalms in 11QPs[a], the other Psalms scrolls, and the Masoretic Psalter. Agreements between the MT and the scrolls may be regarded as indicative of stability: for example, Psalm 5 followed by Psalm 6 in 4QPs[a]. In contrast, disagreements in order or content provide evidence of fluidity. An example of fluidity in order is Psalm 38 followed by Psalm 71 in 4QPs[a], while fluidity in content is illustrated in 11QPs[a] where Psalm 150 is followed by the Hymn to the Creator.[17]

With recourse to the method for comparison that was pioneered by Gerald Wilson,[18] Table 1 below contains two columns of adjoining

15. 'Cave 11 Surprises', pp. 109-10.

16. *Psalms Scroll*, p. 13; 'Variorum', pp. 90-91; 'Cave 11 Surprises', p. 288.

17. The first two examples show how the same manuscript (in this case, 4QPs[a]) may contain individual instances of support for, and conflict with, the Received Psalter.

18. Wilson, *Editing of the Hebrew Psalter*, pp. 116-21. Examining the consecutive arrangement of material in the Psalms manuscripts, Wilson correlated the instances of support of, and conflict with, the MT-150 Psalter. He did not examine

Psalms, concerning which the following points may be noted. (1) The first column indicates agreements between the Masoretic Psalter and specific scrolls, while the second indicates disagreements. (2) This listing is exhaustive, specifying every instance where a Psalm is joined to another Psalm or composition in the 39 manuscripts under discussion.[19] (3) The sign → indicates that a Psalm is continuous with the one preceding it. (4) In several instances, a particular sequence of Psalms is very likely, although not physically verifiable by the manuscript evidence. Such cases are accordingly indicated by the use of parentheses.[20] (5) The asterisk * denotes those manuscripts which do not physically preserve the points of transition between the designated Psalms, but nevertheless appear to support the arrangement that is indicated.

Table 1: *Adjoining Psalms and Other Compositions*

Book I (Psalms 1–41)

	Supports Masoretic Order		*Contradicts Masoretic Order*
Psalm 5→6	4QPs^{a}	4QPs^{S}	
Psalm 7→8	Seiyal 4		
Psalm 9→10	Seiyal 4		
Psalm 10→11	Seiyal 4		
Psalm 12→13	11QPs^{c}	Seiyal 4	
Psalm 13→14	11QPs^{c}		
Psalm 15→16	5/6 Hev Ps		
Psalm 17→18	11QPs^{c}		

specific variants, but only whether Psalms that are consecutively joined agree with their order in the Masoretic book of Psalms.

19. Comparisons in arrangement can be made only when at least one of the 150 Psalms from the Received Psalter is included. (Nevertheless, the sequence Ps. 151B→Blank col. in 11QPs^{a} will be included because it signifies the end of the Psalter involved. Compare Ps. 150→Blank col. in the MT, also denoting the end of the collection.) Consequently, the following sequences do not feature in Table 1:

Psalm 154→Plea	11QPs^{a}
Sir. 51→Apostrophe	11QPs^{a}
Apostrophe→Hymn	4QPs^{f}
Hymn→Last Words	11QPs^{a}
Hymn→Judah	4QPs^{f}
Last Words→Dav Comp	11QPs^{a}

20. The full list is: Pss. 28[→29]→30 in 4QPs^{r}; 63[→64→65]→66→67[→68]→69 in 4QPs^{a}; 107[→108?]→109 in 4QPs^{f}; 116[→117]→118 in 4QPs^{b}; and 148[→120]→121 in 11QPs^{a}.

Psalm 23→24	Seiyal 4				
Psalm 26→27	4QPsr^{r}				
Psalm 27→28	4QPs^{c}	*4QPsr			
Psalm [28→29]	*4QPs^{r}				
Psalm [29]→30	*4QPs^{r}				
			Psalm 31→33	4QPs^{a}	4QPs^{q}
Psalm 33→34	4QPs^{a}	*4QPs^{q}			
Psalm 34→35	4QPs^{a}	*4QPs^{q}			
Psalm 35→36	4QPs^{a}				
Psalm 36→37	11QPs^{e}				
			Psalm 38→71	4QPs^{a}	
Psalm 39→40	11QPs^{d}				

Book II (Psalms 42–72)

Supports Masoretic Order		*Contradicts Masoretic Order*	
Psalm 49→50	4QPs^{c}		
Psalm 50→51	4QPs^{c}		
Psalm 51→52	4QPs^{c}		
Psalm 52→53	4QPs^{c}		
Psalm 53→54	4QPs^{a}		
Psalm 62→63	4QPs^{a}		
Psalm 63→[64]	*4QPs^{a}		
Psalm [64→65]	*4QPs^{a}		
Psalm [65]→66	*4QPs^{a}		
Psalm 66→67	4QPs^{a}		
Psalm 67→[68]	*4QPs^{a}		
Psalm [68]→69	*4QPs^{a}		
		Psalm 38→71	4QPs^{a}

Book III (Psalms 73–89)

Supports Masoretic Order		*Contradicts Masoretic Order*
Psalm 76→77	4QPs^{e}	
Psalm 77→78	11QPs^{c}	
Psalm 81→82	MasPs^{a}	
Psalm 82→83	MasPs^{a}	
Psalm 83→84	MasPs^{a}	
Psalm 84→85	MasPs^{a}	

Book IV (Psalms 90–106)

Supports Masoretic Order			*Contradicts Masoretic Order*		
			ApocrPs III→Psalm 91	11QPsAp^{a}	
			Psalm 91→Blank col.	11QPsAp^{a}	
Psalm 91→92	4QPs^{b}				
Psalm 92→93	4QPs^{b}				
			Apostrophe→Psalm 93	11QPs^{a}	
Psalm 93→94	4QPs^{b}				
			Psalm 93→141	11QPs^{a}	
Psalm 95→96	1QPs^{a}				
Psalm 99→100	4QPs^{b}				
Psalm 101→102	11QPs^{a}				
Psalm 102→103	4Q4QPs^{b}	HQPs^{a}			
Psalm 103→112	4QPs^{b}				
Psalm 118→104	4QPs^{e}	11QPs^{a}			
Psalm 147→104	4QPs^{d}				
Psalm 104→147	*4QPs^{e}	11QPs^{a}			
Psalm 147→105	*4QPs^{e}	11QPs^{a}			
Psalm 105→146	4QPs^{e}	11QPs^{a}			
Psalm 106→147	4QPs^{d}				

Book V (Psalms 107–150)

Supports Masoretic Order		*Contradicts Masoretic Order*		
Psalm 107→[108]	4QPs^{f}			
Psalm [108]→109	4QPs^{f}			
		Psalm 109→Apostr.	4QPs^{f}	
		Psalm 103→112	4QPs^{b}	
Psalm 112→113	4QPs^{b}			
Psalm 114→115	4QPs^{o}			
Psalm 115→116	4QPs^{e}			
Psalm 116→[117]	*4QPs^{b}			
Psalm [117]→118	*4QPs^{b}	Psalm 118→104	4QPs^{e}	11QPs^{a}
		Psalm 132→119	11QPs^{a}	
		Psalm 119→135	11QPs^{a}	
		Psalm 148→[120]	*11QPs^{a}	
Psalm [120]→121	*11QPs^{a}			
Psalm 121→122	11QPs^{a}			
Psalm 122→123	11QPs^{a}			
Psalm 123→124	11QPs^{a}			
Psalm 124→125	11QPs^{a}			

Psalm 125→126	4QPs^{e}	11QPs^{a}			
Psalm 126→127	*4QPs^{e}	11QPs^{a}			
Psalm 127→128	*4QPs^{e}	11QPs^{a}			
Psalm 128→129	*4QPs^{e}	11QPs^{a}			
Psalm 129→130	4QPs^{e}	11QPs^{a}			
Psalm 130→131	11QPs^{a}				
Psalm 131→132	11QPs^{a}		Psalm 132→119	11QPs^{a}	
			Psalm 141→133	11QPs^{a}	11QPs^{b}
			Psalm 133→144	11QPs^{a}	11QPs^{b}
			Psalm 140→134	11QPs^{a}	
			Psalm 134→151A	11QPs^{a}	
			Psalm 119→135	11QPs^{a}	
Psalm 135→136	11QPs^{a}				
			Psalm 135.12→136.22	4QPs^{n}	
			Psalm 136→Catena	11QPs^{a}	
			Psalm 139→137	11QPs^{a}	
Psalm 137→138	11QPs^{a}				
			Psalm 138→Sirach 51	11QPs^{a}	
			Plea→Psalm 139	11QPs^{a}	
			Psalm 139→137	11QPs^{a}	
			Dav Comp→Ps. 140	11QPs^{a}	
			Psalm 140→134	11QPs^{a}	
			Psalm 93→141	11QPs^{a}	
			Psalm 141→133	11QPs^{a}	11QPs^{b}
			Psalm 155→142	11QPs^{a}	
Psalm 142→143	11QPs^{a}				
			Psalm 143→149	11QPs^{a}	
			Psalm 133→144	11QPs^{a}	11QPs^{b}
			Psalm 144→155	11QPs^{a}	
			Catena→Ps 145	11QPs^{a}	
			Psalm 105→146	4QPs^{e}	11QPs^{a}
			Psalm 146→148	11QPs^{a}	
			Psalm 104→147	*4QPs^{e}	11QPs^{a}
			Psalm 106→147	4QPs^{d}	
			Psalm 147→104	4QPs^{d}	
			Psalm 147→105	*4QPs^{e}	11QPs^{a}
			Psalm 146→148	11QPs^{a}	
			Psalm 148→[120]	*11QPs^{a}	
			Psalm 143→149	11QPs^{a}	
Psalm 149→150	11QPs^{a}				
Ps 150→Blank col.	MasPs^{b}				
			Psalm 150→Hymn	11QPs^{a}	
			Ps 151B→Blank col.	11QPs^{a}	

6. *The Psalms Scrolls and Progressive Stabilization of the Psalter*

The information presented in Table 1 indicates that eleven scrolls sometimes differ from the Masoretic Text with respect to contents or order or both: 4QPs^{a}, 4QPs^{b}, 4QPs^{d}, 4QPs^{e}, 4QPs^{f}, 4QPs^{k}, 4QPs^{n}, 4QPs^{q}, 11QPs^{a}, 11QPs^{b}, and 11QPsAp^{a}. The list of adjoining Psalms has direct bearing on Sanders's thesis of gradual fixation for the Hebrew Psalter, according to which Psalms 1–89 were stabilized first and Psalms 90 onwards remained fluid. When all 39 Psalms scrolls are taken in to consideration, the following picture emerges. For Psalms 1–89, no deviations in *content* are evident in the scrolls, since no compositions absent from the Received Psalter are found joined to any of these Psalms.[21] With respect to *order*, only two deviations emerge prior to Psalm 90:

Conflict with MT	*Manuscript(s)*
Psalms 31→33	4QPs^{a}, 4QPs^{q}
Psalms 38→71	4QPs^{a}

However, for Psalms 90 onwards disagreements with the Masoretic Psalter are far more extensive, both in terms of the ordering of material and the presence of compositions not found in the MT-150 Psalter. Variations in content are frequent, as is illustrated by the following 'apocryphal' pieces joined directly to 'biblical' Psalms:

Conflict with MT	*Manuscript(s)*
'Apocryphal' Psalms→Psalm 91	11QPsAp^{a}
Plea for Deliverance→Psalm 139	11QPs^{a}, 11QPs^{b}
David's Compositions→Psalm 140	11QPs^{a}

Numerous divergences in arrangement also occur, of which three examples may be listed:

Conflict with MT	*Manuscript(s)*
Psalms 118→147	4QPs^{d}
Psalms 103→112	4QPs^{b}
Psalms 133→144	11QPs^{a}, 11QPs^{b}

21. The only possible exception may be Ps. 22 in 4QPs^{f}, which also contains parts of Pss. 107 and 109 and several 'apocryphal' Psalms. However, since this Psalm is not joined here with any other composition, it does not necessarily follow that it was linked with an apocryphal Psalm. Ps. 22 may have appeared far earlier in the manuscript, or could even belong to another scroll written in the same hand.

From these statistics two correlations emerge, which indicate support or disagreement with the Received Psalter. The first correlation below (Table 2) is in terms of the order (or arrangement) of adjoining Psalms, concerning which a precautionary note is necessary with regard to the earlier treatment by Gerald Wilson.[22] Simply to compare the number of disagreements between the scrolls and the Masoretic Psalter for Psalms 1–89 and 90–150, as Wilson did, can be misleading. This is because less of Psalms 1–89 has survived than of Psalms 90 onwards, since the beginnings of scrolls are usually on the outside and are thus more prone to deterioration.[23] A higher total of discrepancies vis-à-vis the Masoretic arrangement is thus to be expected for Psalms 90–150 than for Psalms 1–89. A more accurate estimate of stability versus fluidity is obtained by calculating the *proportion* of agreements and disagreements between the scrolls and the Masoretic arrangement. This more nuanced correlation of the primary data yields the following results:

Books (Psalms)	*Consecutive Joins*	*Agreements with MT*	*Conflicts with MT*
I (1–41)	20	18 (90%)	2 (10%)
II (42–72)	13	12 (92%)	1 (8%)
III (73–89)	6	6 (100%)	0
IV (90–106)	18	7 (39%)	11 (61%)
V (107–150)	62	24 (39%)	38 (61%)

Table 2: *Agreements and Conflicts with the Masoretic Text in Arrangement*

When the cumulative evidence for Books I–III (Pss. 1–89) is compared with that for Books IV–V (Pss. 90–150), the small number of disagreements with the MT-150 Psalter for Psalms 1–89 contrasts markedly with the high incidence of variation for Psalms 90–150. For Books I–III, 36 Psalms are found in the same arrangement as in the MT, which represents 92% of the total, as opposed to only 3 Psalms in a conflicting

22. Wilson, *Editing of the Hebrew Psalter*, pp. 120-21; and 'Qumran Psalms Manuscripts', pp. 386-87.

23. See R.T. Beckwith, 'The Courses of the Levites and the Eccentric Psalms Scrolls from Qumran', *RevQ* 44 (1984), pp. 499-524. Beckwith estimates that only five Psalms from 90–150 are not found among the scrolls, while 29 Psalms are totally missing from 1–89. With recourse to additional manuscripts, my own analysis confirms his observation with respect to Pss. 90–150, with 90, 108(?), 110, 111, and 117 not represented. However, for Pss. 1–89 only 21 Psalms are lacking: 3–4, 19–21, 29, 32, 41, 46, 55, 58, 61, 64–65, 70, 72–75, 80, and 87.

order (8%). For Books IV–V only 31 joins support the Masoretic arrangement (39%), while 49 are in a conflicting order (61%).

The second correlation involves content, i.e., the presence or absence of compositions not included in the Masoretic Psalter. While Gerald Wilson did not incorporate this correlation in his discussion, its inclusion is necessary to provide a more complete analysis of the data. For the purpose of situating a particular work within the earlier and later sections of the Psalter, only those compositions which directly precede or follow a 'biblical' Psalm are considered.[24] The figures in Table 3 show that these additional pieces are never joined with any of Psalms 1–89, but are linked 13 times with compositions that appear in Psalms 90–150 of the Received Psalter.

Books (Psalms)	*'Apocryphal' Psalms*
I (1–41)	0
II (42–72)	0
III (73–89)	0
IV (90–106)	2
V (107–150)	11

Table 3: *Conflicts with the Masoretic Text in Content*

These two correlations indicate that for Psalms 1–89 (or thereabouts) the order and content of Psalms in the scrolls varies very little from that of the Received Psalter, but for Psalms 90 and beyond such divergences are strongly evident. These data strongly support Sanders's proposal that Books I–III were stabilized, but Books IV–V remained fluid, during the Qumran period.

7. *The Criterion of Chronological Age*

In addition to differences in arrangement and content, a chronological schema has been proposed as indicative of stability or fluidity in a collection of Psalms. According to Gerald Wilson,[25] when the relative ages of manuscripts that either support or contradict the Received Psalter are considered, the following pattern emerges:

24. See the list of excluded sequences in n. 19.

25. *Editing of the Hebrew Psalter*, pp. 121-22; 'Qumran Psalms Manuscripts', pp. 387-88.

Manuscript	*Date*	*Relationship to MT*
4QPs[a]	Mid-2nd century BCE	Contradictory
4QPs[f]	c. 50 BCE	Contradictory
4QPs[d]	Mid-1st century BCE	Contradictory
4QPs[b]	2nd half of 1st century BCE	Contradictory
4QPs[e]	1st half of 1st century CE	Contradictory
11QPs[a]	30–50 CE	Contradictory
11QPs[b]	1st half of 1st century CE	Contradictory
MasPs[a]	1st half of 1st century CE	Supportive
4QPs[q]	Mid-1st century CE	Contradictory
4QPs[s]	50 CE	Supportive
4QPs[c]	50–68 BCE	Supportive
Hev/SePs	2nd half of 1st century CE	Supportive

Table 4: *Wilson's View of the Age of Manuscripts and their Relationship to the Masoretic Text*

In Wilson's view, this evidence indicates that there is no manuscript at Qumran dated before the first century CE that supports the consecutive arrangement of the Masoretic Psalter. This correlation, he observes, affirms a 'certain looseness' in arrangement of Psalms manuscripts, followed by gradual conformity to the Received Psalter which reached its height about the mid-first century CE and prevailed thereafter. He concludes that the theory of gradual stabilization is thus further supported when the age of supportive and contradictory manuscripts is considered.

However, this criterion is problematic, since for Psalms 1–89 the primary evidence does not consistently confirm Wilson's evaluation of certain manuscripts as 'contradictory' and others as 'supportive' in relation to the Masoretic Psalter. For instance, the classification of 4QPs[a] and 4QPs[q] as contradictory (on the one hand) and 4QPs[c], 4QPs[s] and MasPs[a] as supportive (on the other) is unsatisfactory, at least on the criteria of content and the ordering of material. As will be shown below,[26] there is a high degree of correlation between the Psalms manuscripts and the Masoretic Text with respect to the order of Psalms 1–89, with deviation seemingly possible for only four Psalms: 10, 33, 43 and 71. It is evident from Table 1 that 4QPs[a] and 4QPs[q] follow this pattern, deviating from the Masoretic order at Psalms 31→33 (4QPs[a] and 4QPs[q]) and 38→71 (4QPs[a]). Since the extant parts of 4QPs[c], 4QPs[s] and MasPs[a] include no material from Psalms 10, 33, 43 and 71, nor from Psalm 90 onwards, it is only to be expected that these manuscripts

26. See section 8: 'Superscriptions and Different Arrangements of Psalms'.

will conform closely to the Masoretic arrangement. Furthermore, it cannot be assumed that these three scrolls originally contained the sequences 31→32 and 38→39 rather than 31→33 and 38→71, since they are no longer extant at these junctures. To regard 4QPs[a] and 4QPs[q] as 'contradictory' to the Masoretic Text and the other three manuscripts as 'supportive' is thus not valid, since different quantities are being compared: scrolls that contain material at the crucial junctures, and others that do not. While it is *possible* that 4QPs[c], 4QPs[s] and MasPs[a] were originally more similar to the Masoretic Psalter than were 4QPs[a] and 4QPs[q], this cannot be demonstrated on the basis of arrangement as Wilson has tried to do. The physical evidence permits us to conclude only that during the Qumran period Psalms 1–89 were stabilized except at a few specific junctures. Allowing for the two stipulated exceptions, it may be stated that all five of the manuscripts discussed here are in general agreement with the Masoretic arrangement of Psalms 1–89. In fact, the real points of disagreement in order and content between the Psalms scrolls and the MT are located in Books IV and V of the Psalter. The following table presents a modified and more cautious summary of the evidence:

Manuscript	*Date*	*Relationship to MT*
4QPs[a]	Mid-2nd century BCE	Supportive
4QPs[f]	c. 50 BCE	Contradictory
4QPs[d]	Mid-1st century BCE	Contradictory
4QPs[b]	2nd half of 1st century BCE	Contradictory
4QPs[e]	1st half of 1st century CE	Contradictory
11QPs[a]	30–50 CE	Contradictory
11QPs[b]	1st half of 1st century CE	Contradictory
MasPs[a]	1st half of 1st century CE	Supportive
4QPs[q]	Mid-1st century CE	Supportive
4QPs[s]	50 CE	Supportive
4QPs[c]	50–68 BCE	Supportive
Hev/SePs	2nd half of 1st century CE	Supportive

Table 5: *The Age of Manuscripts and their Relationship to the Masoretic Text*

These data do not support the thesis of *gradual* stabilization of the Psalter with recourse to the age of individual manuscripts. Despite their fragmentary state, the manuscripts instead bear witness to the fixation of Psalms 1–89 (as in 4QPs[a.c.q.s] MasPs[a], and Hev/SePs) and to the ongoing fluidity of Psalms 90 and beyond (as in 4QPs[b.d-f] and 11QPs[a-b]). The scrolls thus strongly suggest that the book of Psalms was finalized in two definite stages, with the first part virtually stabilized by the beginning of the Qumran period in c. 150 CE, while the second remained fluid well into the first century CE.

8. *Superscriptions and Different Arrangements of Psalms*

The preceding section shows that the extant portions of the Judaean Psalms scrolls contain only two instances of deviation from the Masoretic ordering of Psalms 1–89: Psalms 31→33 in 4QPs^{a} and 4QPs^{q}, and Psalms 38→71 in 4QPs^{a}. Both deviations coincide with the rare absence of superscriptions in Books I to III of the Masoretic Psalter, which indicates a correlation between stabilization and the presence of titles for Psalms 1–89. The absence of superscriptions in the MT appears to identify those Psalms whose positions were not yet finalized as late as the first century CE (cf. 4QPs^{q}), thus rendering them prone to varying combinations with other Psalms. For Psalms 1–89, only six lack superscriptions in the MT, namely Psalms 1, 2, 10, 33, 43, and 71; the first two of these are special cases, as will presently become clear. That the only instances of deviation exhibited by the Dead Sea Scrolls for Books I–III are found among the remaining four 'orphan' Psalms is surely more than mere coincidence. It would be helpful at this point to discuss briefly the six untitled Psalms and the different arrangements in which they occur at Qumran and elsewhere.

Psalm 10 was arranged in at least two different ways in the ancient sources. (1) In Codex L (Leningradensis) and most other Masoretic manuscripts it follows Psalm 9 after a break, but without any superscription. (2) In the Septuagint and in a few Masoretic manuscripts it is combined directly with Psalm 9. As is noted in *BHS*,[27] this combination is obviously preferable to the separation attested in Codex L, since Psalms 9 and 10 together form one acrostic poem. (3) Unfortunately, of these two Psalms only 9.3-7 is extant among the scrolls from the Judaean desert (in 11QPs^{c}). Thus we do not know whether Psalm 10 had a superscription in 11QPs^{c}, whether it was untitled, or if Psalms 9 and 10 were combined as a single acrostic poem.

Psalm 33 features in several arrangements and sometimes has a superscription. The following table is provided for purposes of clarity:

27. 'Recte', see n. 10:1^{a} in *BHS*.

Arrangement	*Tradition or MSS*	*Superscription*
Psalm 32→33	L and most 𝔐^MSS	No
32 and 33 joined	A few 𝔐^MSS	No
Psalm 32[31]→33[32]	𝔊 and έ	τῷ Δαυιδ
Psalm 31→33	4QPs[q]	לדויד שיר יר מזמור
Psalm 31→33	4QPs[a]	No[28]

Table 6: *Arrangements of Psalm 33*

Due to the fragmentary nature of 4QPs[a] and 4QPs[q], which are the only scrolls from Qumran containing portions of Psalms 31 and 33, it is not possible to decide whether Psalm 32 occupied another place in these manuscripts. We are not even certain that this Psalm was known at Qumran.

Psalm 43 was arranged in at least three different ways. (1) In Codex L and the majority of Masoretic manuscripts Psalm 43 follows 42 with a break, but with no superscription. This also appears to be the case in 11QPs[d], the only scroll from Qumran that contains part of Psalm 43.[29] (2) In many Masoretic manuscripts Psalm 43 is joined with 42, which is preferable since the two form a single lament.[30] (3) A superscription is provided in a few Masoretic manuscripts (לדוד), as well as in the Septuagint tradition (𝔊 θ′ ψαλμὸς τῷ Δαυιδ [Ps. 42]).

Psalm 71 features in four different types of arrangement. (1) In Codex L and most other Masoretic manuscripts Psalm 71 follows 70 with a break, but without any superscription. (2) In many Masoretic manuscripts Psalms 70 and 71 are directly joined. (3) In the Septuagint tradition, Psalm 71[70] follows 70[69] and has a superscription (τῷ Δαυιδ· υἱῶν Ιωναδαβ καὶ τῶν πρώτων αἰχμαλωτισθέντων). (4) At Qumran, Psalm 71 follows directly on 38 (without even a break) in 4QPs[a]. There is a logical explanation for this combination: of the 150 Psalms that are collected in the MT, only 70 and 38 have a superscription indicating that each Psalm is 'For the memorial offering' (cf. מזמור לדוד להזכיר, Ps. 38; and למנצח לדוד להזכיר, Ps. 70). The tendency for the untitled Psalm 71 to be linked with a להזכיר Psalm is indicated in the Masoretic Psalter

28. Ps. 33 begins a new line; spacing indicates that no superscript was written (Wilson, *Editing of the Hebrew Psalter*, p. 96).

29. Dr F. García Martínez (editor of several scrolls from Cave 11) indicates by letter that 43.1-3 is found only in 11QPs[d], and that the superscript appears to be 'definitely excluded as in MT'. His assistance in this matter is appreciated.

30. 'Recte', according to n. 43:1[a] in *BHS*.

(Codex L), where it follows Psalm 70, and in 4QPs[a], where it is joined directly with Psalm 38.

Psalms 1 and 2 are the two remaining untitled Psalms, which perform a special introductory function (at least in the Masoretic collection), and thus do not feature among the 'moveable Psalms'. It seems either that both Psalms were prefixed to the rest of the Psalter,[31] or that Psalm 1 originally served as an introduction or preamble to the collection, while Psalm 2 was originally counted as the first Psalm.[32] The only occurrence of these two Psalms among the Qumran scrolls is in the Florilegium (4Q174), where Ps. 2.1 + *pesher* follows quotations of Ps. 1.1, Isa. 8.11 and Ezek. 37.23(?). Here the order of quotations seems to suggest that the compiler of the Florilegium was using a Psalter in which Psalm 2 followed Psalm 1.

When the absence of superscriptions and deviations from the Masoretic arrangement are correlated with respect to Psalms 1–89, the extant manuscript evidence strongly indicates that 4QPs[a] and 4QPs[q] are no less 'supportive' of the received order than are 4QPs[c], 4QPs[s] and MasPs[a]. The first two of these scrolls 'deviate' only at expected junctures: Psalms 31→33 in 4QPs[a] and 4QPs[q], and Psalms 38→71 in 4QPs[a]. The other three scrolls preserve no material from Psalms 10, 33, 43 and 71, which renders it by no means certain that they originally contained the exact arrangement found in the Masoretic Psalter. While all five of these manuscripts are fragmentary and incomplete, the evidence that we do have supports their classification as generally supportive of the received order.

9. *Results and Conclusions*

The greater part of this *Festschrift* article has dealt with the first component of James Sanders's 'Qumran Psalms Hypothesis', that the Dead Sea Scrolls attest to gradual stabilization of the book of Psalms. Four

31. Cf. E.S. Gerstenberger, *Psalms, Part I with an Introduction to Cultic Poetry* (FOTL, 14; Grand Rapids: Eerdmans, 1988), p. 37.

32. See A. Weiser, *The Psalms: A Commentary* (OTL; Philadelphia: Westminster Press, 1962), p. 102; H.-J. Kraus, *Psalms 1–59: A Commentary* (Minneapolis: Augsburg, 1988), pp. 113 and 125. Note also the reading of some Western texts (D 1175 gig) in Acts 13.33, where Ps. 2 is quoted and referred to as the first Psalm (ἐν τῷ πρώτῳ...ψαλμῷ), rather than the second Psalm (ἐν τῷ ψαλμῷ...τῷ δευτέρῳ) as in the most widely accepted text (*Novum Testamentum Graece* [4th edn]).

main results have emerged. (1) On the criteria of consecutive ordering, the inclusion of 'apocryphal' compositions, and the relative age of manuscripts, the proposal that the Hebrew Psalter was stabilized over time is supported by the scrolls from the Judaean desert. (2) This stabilization seems to have taken place in two distinct stages: Psalms 1–89 prior to the first century BCE, and Psalms 90 onwards towards the end of the first century CE. Although the manuscript evidence is not complete, the scrolls strongly suggest that during the entire Qumran period Psalms 1–89 were largely finalized as a collection, while Psalms 90 and beyond remained much more fluid. (3) For Psalms 1–89, the order of contiguous Psalms almost always corresponds with that of the MT-150 Psalter (92% supportive, 8% contradictory), with the only two clear exceptions involving Psalms that lack superscriptions in the Received Text. This overall stability is in marked contrast to Psalms 90 and beyond, where the divergences are far more extensive (39% supportive, 61% contradictory), and are generally indicated by the lack of such superscriptions. (4) It is not exactly clear where the cut-off point between the largely stabilized collection and the fluid part of the Psalter should be. Psalm 89 was selected in this study because it concludes Book III of the Masoretic Psalter, and Psalms 91 and 93 appear in arrangements that conflict with that of the MT (in 11QPsAp[a] and 11QPs[a], respectively). However, since one cannot be certain that the Psalter had been divided into five constituent books in the Second Temple period, it is possible that the stabilized collection concluded with the Davidic series at Psalm 72, or with a different Psalm.

The results of this investigation confirm James Sanders's thesis concerning the stabilization of the Psalter over time. However, the evidence also suggests that this thesis can be further nuanced by dividing the process of stabilization into two distinct stages. It now seems abundantly clear that two or more editions incorporating the latter part of the Psalter were in circulation in the Second Temple period.[33] The (Hebrew) book of Psalms was only to reach finalization in a universally accepted form towards the end of the first century CE, when all other editions were eclipsed and the proto-Masoretic Psalter survived.

33. See P.W. Flint, 'The Psalms Scrolls from the Judaean Desert: Relationships and Textual Affiliations', in G.J. Brooke (ed.), *New Texts and Studies: Proceedings of the First Meeting of the International Organization for Qumran Studies* (STDJ, 15; Leiden: Brill, 1994), pp. 31-52.

BIBLICAL MATH AS *HEILSGESCHICHTE*?

Lloyd R. Bailey

Even the most casual reader of the Bible will be astonished by the ages of the pre-diluvians as reported in Genesis 5, and to a lesser extent by those of the post-diluvians as found in ch. 11. The particulars are exhibited in Table 1.

Table 1: *Early Biblical Ages*

The Pre-Diluvians (Genesis 5)

Name	*Age at marriage*	*Age at time of first-born*	*Remaining years*	*Lifespan*
Adam	–	130	800	930
Seth	–	105	807	912
Enosh	–	90	815	905
Kenan	–	70	840	910
Mahalalel	–	65	830	895
Jared	–	162	800	962
Enoch	–	65	300	365
Methuselah	–	187	782	969
Lamech	–	182	595	777
Noah	–	500	450	950

(The flood began in Noah's 600th year = Shem's 100th year)

The Early Post-Diluvians (Genesis 11)

Name	*Age at marriage*	*Age at time of first-born*	*Remaining years*	*Lifespan*
Shem	–	100	500	600
Arpachshad	–	35	403	438
Shelah	–	30	403	433
Eber	–	34	430	464
Peleg	–	30	209	239
Reu	–	32	207	239
Serug	–	30	200	230
Nahor	–	29	119	148
Terah	–	70	135	205

The Patriarchal Figures (Genesis–Deuteronomy)

Name	*Age at marriage*	*Age at time of first-born*	*Remaining years*	*Lifespan*
Abraham	–	100	–	175
Sarah	–	90	–	127
Isaac	40	60	–	180
Ishmael	–	–	–	137
Jacob	–	–	–	147
Esau	40	–	–	–
Joseph	–	–	–	110
Moses	–	–	–	120
Joshua	–	–	–	110

The ages of the pre-flood generations at the time of death range from a mere 365 years to a maximum of 969 with the average at 858 years. No less surprising are the ages at which these individuals are presented as having fathered their first child. They range from 65 to 500 with the average being 156 years.

How does one account for such depictions of longevity? Those interpreters who have assumed that the text intended to relate literal biological history have labored long and hard to find a believable explanation. Among the suggestions have been the following.

1. Perhaps names have been accidentally lost from the list. Such a possibility has been suggested for genealogies elsewhere in the Bible. That of Jesus in Matthew 1, for example, omits several generations from the supposed master-list in 1 Chronicles 1–3.[1]

Alternatively, could it be that the list intended to include only the more illustrious ancestors? This conclusion results from the following interesting accommodation of biblical data to modern scientific estimates of the age of the earth.

> The assumption is that this genealogy...(is) consecutive and without omission...If the ages data are added together...the flood is seen to occur 1,656 years after the creation of Adam...(and) a date of creation of 4004

1. R.E. Brown, *The Birth of the Messiah* (AB Reference Library; Garden City, NY: Doubleday, 1979), pp. 74-95. For the contrasting argument that the manipulation of the genealogy into three groups of 14 generations each has necessitated deliberate omissions, see L. Bailey, *Genesis, Creation, and Creationism* (Mahwah, NJ: Paulist Press, 1993), pp. 71-73, 76. Grouping of generations by groups of 14 (2 × 7) is otherwise attested in Scripture (p. 74).

> B.C. is obtained. This date is no longer tenable in the light of present knowledge of antiquity...another view regarding the structure of the dates of chapter 5 must be found...One can, in general, hold that there are gaps between the ten names, that these were actual people, that they did live certain years, and that others followed them at indeterminate lengths.[2]

In such a view, corresponding perhaps to a list of dynastic heads, the lifespan figure for an individual would actually be the total for all of the missing generations. As for the more problematic age at time of first-born, 'it may well be that those are the actual dates at which a son was born, or a grandson even, who is not actually the one named but who was an actual link and from whom came, in the latter's descendants, the son who is the next-named person'.[3]

2. Perhaps a 'year' in the calendar of Genesis 5 was not as long as in our present one. If the term indicated, for example, only a lunar month, then the ages of the pre-diluvians would be reduced to ones comparable to our own. Thus Methuselah's record-breaking 969 would become a reasonable 81 years!

The problem here, of course, is evident within the surrounding biblical material. In the story of the flood, for example, we read not merely of years, but of divisions within them called 'months' (twelve in a year) and within those of 'days' (29 or 30 each). All indications are that the calculation of duration of the biblical year was little different from modern ones.

3. Perhaps the environment was cleaner then and one could lead a healthier (and presumably longer) life? Martin Luther cites this approach as well worn, even in his day, and then finds it unnecessary.

> ...compared with our own lifetime, they lived incredibly long. This, as explained by some, was because at that time the nature of man was stronger, the food more salubrious, and man more moderate in eating and drinking...Today our bodies are more weakened by our food and drink than they are nourished. For me this one explanation suffices, namely, that God during that best age of the world wanted people to live that long.[4]

2. H.G. Stigers, *A Commentary On Genesis* (Grand Rapids: Zondervan, 1976), pp. 93-94.

3. Stigers, *A Commentary On Genesis*, pp. 93-94. For details, he cites W.H. Green, 'Primeval Chronology', *BSac* 186 (1890), pp. 285-303.

4. *Commentary on Genesis* (trans. J.T. Mueller; Grand Rapids: Zondervan, 1958), p. 121.

Modern Creationists have their own variation on this explanation for pre-diluvian longevity.[5] They usually propose that, prior to the biblical flood, the earth was surrounded by a massive canopy of water vapor (the condensation of which produced that great catastrophe). The implications for human longevity have been expressed as follows:

> Perhaps the most important effect of the canopy was the shielding action provided against the intense radiations impinging upon the earth from space. Short wave-length radiation, as well as bombardment of elementary particles of all kinds, is known to have diminishing effects—both somatic and genetic effects—on organisms...But to return to the question of antediluvian longevity, it surely is quite reasonable...to infer that, over the centuries since the Flood, the accumulation of these effects in man in particular has resulted in gradual deterioration and decreasing life-span.[6]

Such explanations have not been compelling save to a small number of persons. To 'old line' fundamentalists, they are transparent and unnecessary attempts to make the Bible acceptable to the modern rational mind. By contrast, ought one not simply to accept Scripture at face value? ('It says what it means, and means what it says! God is capable of this minor feat, so what is the problem?')

Modern historical-critical scholarship, by contrast, has centered on the suspicion that some sort of sophisticated symbolic 'number game' is being presented in the ages. 'Cracking the code', however, has been exceedingly difficult. Thus an able modern interpreter has put it this way.

5. These so-called 'young earthers', biblical fundamentalists who often have a graduate degree in one of the physical sciences, propose that the sciences, when properly understood, affirm the cosmology and cosmogony of the Bible and establish that the earth (indeed the universe) is perhaps no more than 10,000 years old. Such a position is put forward by H.M. Morris and G.E. Parker, *What Is Creation Science?* (San Diego: Creation-Life Publishers, 1982). For an evaluation and rejection from the standpoint of 'main-line' scientists, see A.N. Strahler, *Science and Earth History: The Evolution/Creation Controversy* (Buffalo: Prometheus Books, 1987). For an evaluation and rejection by 'main-line' biblical scholarship, see C. Hyers, *The Meaning of Creation: Genesis and Modern Science* (Atlanta: John Knox Press, 1984). For an evaluation and rejection from a standpoint that is largely devoid of the assumptions of modern critical ('liberal') scholarship, see Bailey, *Genesis, Creation, and Creationism.*

6. J.C. Whitcomb, Jr, and H.M. Morris, *The Genesis Flood* (Philadelphia: The Presbyterian and Reformed Publishing Company, 1961), pp. 299, 404.

> Every commentator on Genesis, including the present writer, has spent hours over pencil and paper, and recently with pocket calculator, trying to wrest some sense or pattern out of the figures with which the MT supplies us. The best conclusion drawn from this effort is that there are other pursuits more rewarding. There undoubtedly is, or was, a key to these numbers...but whether it has disappeared in transmission or simply now eludes us is impossible to determine.[7]

The state of affairs is not quite so bleak, however. The text contains clues, if not clear indications, not only to the likelihood that biological 'facts' are not intended but also to the nature and origin of the numerical scheme. The present article will outline what has been or can be said about the origin of these expressions of longevity, and conclude with reflections upon how the genealogies may have been understood when they were first heard within the larger narrative context.

Divisibility by Five

The first fundamental observation to be made is that the ages are not randomly distributed. One might reasonably expect them to end in each integer from zero to nine, were they actual expressions of biological duration. Instead, the vast majority of them are divisible by five (i.e., they end in a zero or a five). Among the pre-diluvians, 21 of the 30 ages end in this fashion. Useful contrast can now be made with the true randomness of the length of reigns of the kings of Israel and Judah (as recorded in the books of Kings, beginning with Rehoboam): 17, 3, 41, 2, 24, 2, 7 days, 12, 22, 25, 2, 8, 1, 28, 40, 17, 16, 29, 52, 41, 6 months, 1 month, 10, 2, 20, 16, 16, 9, 29, 55, 2, 21, 3 months, 11, 3 months, and 11. Note that these end in every available number of the 0–9 sequence, and that only five of them (from a total of 36) are divisible by five (about what one would expect from random distribution). It is quite unlikely, therefore, that the ages in Genesis 5 represent biological reality.

A concern for units of five years (which the Romans called a *lustrum*) is also evident in the focus of the lifespan on the number 900 (the two deviations, Enoch and Methuselah, will be discussed below). This number may be composed of five units of (60 + 60 + 60),[8] or alternatively as 30^2 or as (60 × 15). For the symbolic role of the number 60, see below.

7. B. Vawter, *On Genesis: A New Reading* (Garden City, NY: Doubleday, 1977), p. 108.

8. U. Cassuto, *A Commentary on the Book of Genesis*. I. *From Adam to Noah* (Jerusalem: Magnes Press, 1961), p. 278.

The Addition of a Seven

Notice, furthermore, that eight of the remaining nine pre-diluvian ages end either in seven or two, a percentage far too high to represent historicity. There is a relationship between this series and the previous one in that the addition of seven to a number divisible by five yields either two or seven (5 + 7 = [1]2; 0 + 7 = 7).[9] The consequence is that 29 of the 30 ages in the list belong in a divisible-by-five category. Even the one deviation, Methuselah, may fit the scheme, since his 969 years may be 955 + 7 + 7. That is, his age at time of first-born is 180 + 7, and his remaining years are 775 + 7.[10]

Is there evidence elsewhere in ancient Near Eastern literature of the deliberate addition of a seven to numbers? It is conspicuously present in the lists of pre-diluvian rulers known as the Sumerian King List. In two of the three editions that have been preserved, the ancient scribe expressed the total of reigns in terms of a standard symbolic number plus an additional number seven (see Table 2, below).

As for biblical literature, consider the case of the number of provinces in the Persian Empire. Internal records list from 20 to 30 of them at the time of Darius, whereas the Bible states that there were 120 (Dan. 6.1).[11] However, at the time of his successor (Ahasuerus), there were 127 of them (Est. 1.1). Nothing prevents an empire from expansion, but why precisely by seven?

Then, consider the ages of the patriarchal figures (Table 1). Keep in mind that the 'ideal' age among the Egyptians was variously stated to be 110 or 120,[12] and that the maximum lifespan allowable by the Bible is also 120 (Gen. 6.3). Curiously, only those persons who attain precisely those ages have been residents of Egypt (Joseph and Joshua at 110 and Moses at 120). One might be astonished, therefore, to notice that Sarah attains the age of 127!

9. The symbolic nature of the number 7 in ancient Near Eastern literature hardly needs comment. See the relevant entry, with bibliography, in the standard dictionaries. In all likelihood it derives from worship of the major astral deities (the five visible planets plus the sun and moon).

10. As proposed by Cassuto, *Genesis*, I, p. 260.

11. The symbolic significance of this figure (a multiple of 60) will be discussed below.

12. See V. Wessetzki, 'Alter', *Lexikon der Ägyptologie* I, 1 (Weisbaden: Otto Harrassowitz, 1972), p. 156 (for discussion of evidence from a coffin text).

These concerns apply to the ages of the post-diluvians as well, although less conspicuously so (Table 1):15 cases out of 27. It is also evident in most of the other numbers in the early chapters of Genesis, among them the following: the dimensions of Noah's ship (300 × 50 × 30), rain for 40 days and 40 nights, water covers the tops of the mountains to a depth of 15 cubits and endures for 150 days.

Calculation in Base-60

The second fundamental observation to be made is that a substantial number of the ages involve the number 60. For example: Enoch's 300 years is 60 × 5, Kenan's 840 years is 60 × 14, Moses' 120 years is 60 × 2, Methuselah's 187 years is (60 × 3) + 7, Sarah's 127 years is (60 × 2) + 7, Enosh and Sarah's 90 years is 60 + 60/2, and Shelah, Peleg and Serug's 30 years is 60/2. Fixation with this same number is evident in many other places in the early chapters of Genesis and conspicuously so in the dimensions of Noah's ark. Its volume is 450,000 cubic units, which can be expressed as 602 × [(60 × 2) + 5] cubic units.

That this focus on the number 60 represents a common ancient Near Eastern convention, rather than biological reality, becomes clear from a comparison with the Sumerian King List (Table 2).

Table 2: *The Sumerian King List*

Name		*Length of Reign*	
	W-B 62[13]	*W-B 444*	*Berossos*[14]
Alulim	67,200 (to be corrected[15] to 68,400) ($60^2 \times 19$)	28,800 ($60^2 \times 8$)	36,000 ($60^2 \times 10$)

13. W-B 62 and W-B 444 are cuneiform texts in the Weld-Blundel Collection of the Ashmolean Museum at Oxford University. For detailed analysis, see T. Jacobsen, *The Sumerian King List* (Assyriological Studies, 11; Chicago: University of Chicago Press, 1939).

14. Berossos (Latin: Berossus) was a Babylonian priest who lived in the third century BCE, and wrote a history of his country. His work survives only in partial form, in extensive quotations by such early historians as Josephus and Eusebius (the latter getting them from Alexander Polyhistor and Apollodorus). The list given here is dependent upon Polyhistor (who has spelled the names with much variation).

15. Since the total of the reigns is given in the text itself (in *šar*-units), and does not agree with the total of the reigns actually given, one must conclude that one or

Alalgar	72,000 ($60^2 \times 20$)	36,000 ($60^2 \times 10$)	10,800 ($60^2 \times 3$)
Emmenluanna	21,600 ($60^2 \times 6$)	43,200 ($60^2 \times 12$)	46,800 ($60^2 \times 13$)
Emmengalanna	not listed	28,800 ($60^2 \times 8$)	64,800 ($60^2 \times 18$)
...kidunnu	72,000 ($60^2 \times 20$)	not listed	not listed
...alimma	21,600 ($60^2 \times 6$)	not listed	not listed
Evedoragxos	not listed	not listed	64,800 ($60^2 \times 18$)
Ammemon	not listed	not listed	43,200 ($60^2 \times 12$)
Dumuzi	28,800 ($60^2 \times 8$)	36,000 ($60^2 \times 10$)	36,000 ($60^2 \times 10$)
Ensipazianna	36,000 ($60^2 \times 10$)	28,800 ($60^2 \times 8$)	36,000 ($60^2 \times 10$)
Enmenduranna	72,000 ($60^2 \times 20$)	21,000 ($60^2 \times 5$) + (60×50)	not listed
Ubartutu	28,800 ($60^2 \times 8$)	18,600 ($60^2 \times 5$) + (60×10)	28,800 ($60^2 \times 8$)
Ziusudra	36,000 ($60^2 \times 10$)	not listed	64,800 ($60^2 \times 18$)
TOTALS	457,200 (corrected)	241,200	432,000

more of the individual reigns has been erroneously copied at some time in the process of transmission. Since the initial one (for Alulim) alone is not a multiple of 60^2, it becomes the candidate. The small 'correction' shown then brings the column into line with the stated total.

or:	$60^2 \times [120 + 7]$	$60^2 \times [60 + 7]$	$60^2 \times 120$
or:	$(60^2 \times 120) +$ (7×60^2)	$60^3 + (7 \times 60^2)$	$60^3 \times 2$
or:	120 *šar** + 7 *šar*	1 great *šar* + 7 *šar*	120 *šar*

*The Sumerian numerical unit *šar* (given in the text itself) is 60^2 and a 'great' *šar* is 60^3.

The names are those of kings who reigned in Sumer before a great flood. Each of the ages is multiple of 60 × 60 (60^2), a reflection of calculation in the so-called sexagesimal system (base-60, as opposed to the Western system in base-10).[16]

The intention is to idealize kingship by expressing the duration of each reign in terms of multiples of the 'fundamental' number. Especially conspicuous is the total of elapsed time from the beginning of kingship to the flood as derived from Berossos's list: the cube of the ideal number! Note also that two of the totals can be expressed by the addition of a seven.

The same concept is at work in the expression of the dimensions of the 'Babylonian Noah's' boat: it is a cube, each side being 120 (60 × 2) cubits in length, for a volume of $60^3 \times 8$ units.[17] Little wonder, then, that it survived the waters of the great deluge!

The parallel between Genesis 5 and the King List is more than a common concern with pre-diluvian generations. There are five other considerations which make the comparison a valid one.

1. Both are concerned with divine activity which set a chronological period into motion. In the case of the Bible, it is the creation of the world to be followed quickly by that of human generations. In the case of the King List, it is divine intervention into the created order by means of instituting human monarchy based upon a heavenly paradigm. Hence the List begins: 'When kingship was [first] lowered from heaven, the kingship resided in [the city of] Eridu'. That is, meaningful history only begins with this gift of a divine order.

16. O. Neugebauer, *The Exact Sciences in Antiquity* (New York: Harper & Brothers/Torch Books, 1962), pp. 17-23. The system is still used when we divide an hour into 60 minutes, a minute into 60 seconds, a circle into 6 × 60 degrees, etc.

17. *Gilgamesh Epic*, Tablet XI, line 58.

2. The list of pre-diluvian generations is the same. W-B 62 and Genesis 5 have ten each. W-B 444 and Genesis 4 have eight each, although the latter does not conclude with the flood. Curiously, if one begins in Genesis 5 with Enosh ('human being') instead of with Adam ('human being'), the result is eight as well.[18]

3. The King List states that, after the great flood, kingship was again lowered from heaven, initially to the city of Kish. It then lists 23 kings, giving the duration of reign for 21 of them. The ages are drastically reduced from multiples of 60^2 to multiples of 60. It is clear that there is a fascination with a duration of 900 years, which can be understood either as $5(60 + 60 + 60)$, or as $(60 \times 10) + (60 \times 10)/2$. Specifically, five of the reigns are 900 years exactly, two are 960 (900 + 60), and three are 840 (900 – 60).[19] The list of lifespans in Genesis 5 is quite similar: eight of the ten are very close to 900 years.

4. Both W-B 444 and Genesis 5 have, as the seventh generation, a character with an unusual and identical fate: both Enmenduranna and Enoch are summoned to heaven (see below).[20]

5. Elapsed time between generations drops without exception from Adam through Mahalalel: 130, 105, 90, 70, and 65 years. Then, at the time of Jared, the trend is reversed: 162 years pass before the birth of Enoch. This is an all-time high. The figure goes higher still for Methuselah, then drops off again. These fluctuations may indicate that, in a lost narrative about these patriarchs, there were 'happenings' of some sort: a new situation or condition of humanity which affected the birth rate. Awareness of the possibility of a correlation with the King List at this point must await the mathematics to be outlined below (under the heading 'Derivation of Elapsed Time').

Such analysis and comparison does not suggest that the biblical figures are not 'true'. Rather, it raises the possibility that they depict a mode of 'truth' that differs from modern concern with chronological accuracy. The expressions are a translation of narrative hyperbole into mathematics. In the case of the Persian Empire, it is a way of expressing admiration, regardless of the true number of provinces ('There's a real

18. See the comparative chart in Bailey, *Genesis, Creation, and Creationism*, p. 237.

19. As pointed out by Cassuto, *Genesis*, I, p. 278.

20. On the special role assigned to the seventh generation in biblical genealogies, see J. Sasson, 'Generation, Seventh', in *IDBSup*, pp. 354-56; for rabbinic recognition of this, see Cassuto, *Genesis*, I, p. 282.

government for you!'). In the instance of Sarah, this is a way of saying that she attained the ideal age and then some: 'She lived life to the full; the perfect paradigm of the Israelite woman'. In the case of the pre-diluvians, it is unclear why certain persons have had their age garnished with the mathematical complement 'seven' whereas others have not.

The Relationship between 5 and 60

The fundamental question now becomes: Why should there be a concern to express ages that are divisible by five? The answer, apparently, resides in the fact that our two fundamental observations are related. The common ground between 5 and 60 is that 5 years contain 60 months.[21] The ages of the pre-diluvians, thus converted, are shown in Table 3.

Table 3: *Ages of the Pre-Diluvians in Months (Multiples of 60)*

Name	*Age at time of first-born*	*Remaining lifetime*
Adam	60×26 or: 2(60) years + 2(60) months	$2(60^2) + (60 \times 40)$
Seth	60×21	$2(60^2) + (60 \times 40)$ + 7 years
Enosh	60×18	$2(60^2) + (60 \times 43)$
Kenan	60×14	$2(60^2) + (60 \times 48)$
Mahalalel	60×13 or: 60 years + 60 months	$2(60^2) + (60 \times 46)$
Jared	(60×31) + 7 years	$2(60^2) + (60 \times 40)$
Enoch	60×13	60^2
Methuselah	(60×36) + 7 years	$2(60^2) + (60 \times 35)$ + 7 years
Lamech	(60×35) + 7 years	$60^2 + (60 \times 59)$
Noah	$60^2 + (60 \times 40)$ at flood: $2(60^2)$	$60^2 + (60 \times 30)$

The formulators of the biblical list, apparently aware of the Mesopotamian literature (most likely in Berossos's edition[22]), sought to depart from it in their own mathematical idealism in two ways: (1) by using multiples of 60 rather than of 60^2, and (2) by computing in multiples of 60 months (converted to years) rather than of 60 years.

This does not mean that the persons who formulated Genesis 5 took the King List and modified it line by line by a standard formula. In fact,

21. Having come to this conclusion, I was rather disappointed to find that Umberto Cassuto had already made it (*Genesis*, I, pp. 259-64).

22. He is not far removed, chronologically, from the so-called Priestly writers who apparently finalized the Pentateuch in Babylon and incorporated Gen. 5 therein.

in only one case does there seem to be a clear connection, that of the hero of the flood story.

Derivation of Individual Ages

Only in a few cases can the origin of the individual ages be plausibly conjectured.

1. In the Sumerian version (W-B 62), Ziusudra reigns for 36,000 years ($60^2 \times 10$), whereas his biblical equivalent (Noah) was aged 600 when the flood began (60×10).[23]

2. It has often been pointed out that Enoch's lifespan of 365 years equals the number of days in the solar year. The connection between the two lies in the identity of his counterpart in the W-B 444 King List (both in the seventh position), named Enmenduranna. Another text tells us that he was summoned to heaven to be instructed in the lore of the *baru*-priesthood.[24] His cult city, according to the King List, is Sippar, well known as a seat of solar worship. Further connection between the two persons (Enoch and Enmenduranna) may be found at Gen. 5.24 where the former is likewise taken to heaven ('Enoch walked with God; and he was not, for God took him').

3. The lifespan of Lamech, the seventh-born in the list in Genesis 4, is 777 years. As a mighty man, boasting of his power of revenge, it is perhaps appropriate that he be considered a 'perfect seven' (7-7-7). Another factor may be at work, however. He is listed as the son of Methuselah (the seventh successor of Adam), the gematria of whose name is exactly 777.

4. Elapsed time from creation to the birth of Methuselah is 687 years. He then lives a total of 969 years which brings one to the year of the great flood (*Anno Mundi* 1656). Why the biblical genealogists wanted him to die at that time, and why him as opposed to some other pre-diluvian, is unclear.[25] Either they want him to perish in the flood as

23. For the attempt to relate the two names linguistically, see L. Bailey, *Noah: The Person and the Story in History and Tradition* (Columbia: University of South Carolina Press, 1989), pp. 165-67.

24. From the Kuyunjik Collection in the British Museum, Text No. 2486. See, briefly, Jacobsen, *The Sumerian King List*, p. 74 n. 28, and the literature cited there.

25. This may be compared with the chronology in the Samaritan Pentateuch where three of the pre-diluvians met their demise in the year of the flood: Jared, Methuselah and Lamech. In the LXX traditions, Methuselah either dies a few years

a means of punishment (hence setting his date deliberately in that year), or they want him to die just before and thus escape its judgmental effects. In the latter case, his age might have been derived (as aforementioned) by the double-complement of seven: 955 + 7 + 7.

Mention should here be made of a highly original approach to the problem taken by Dwight Wayne Young.[26] He suggests that the formulas and solutions to foundational problems in Babylonian mathematics have been utilized by those who set the biblical lifespans (who presumably were trained in that mathematical tradition). Take, for example, the Old Babylonian text which expresses the relationship between the squares of certain numbers.[27] It is concerned with those cases where $a^2 + b^2 = c^2$, a formula later to be appropriated by the so-called Pythagorean Theorem. The first entry of the tablet, presumably known to any mathematician at the time, is 120. The initial line says, in effect: if a = 120 and b = 119, then c = 169. Concerning this Young remarks:

> The author of the patriarchal life spans seems to have been familiar with at least the initial computation...since two of the numbers show up in the biblical material...Twice in the Pentateuch this same number [120] is mentioned...the delimitation of human lifetime [Gen. 6.3]...(and) as the number of years that Moses lived [Deut. 34.7]...[The number] 119...is the final segment of Nahor's lifetime [Gen. 11.25].

As for the remaining member of this 'Pythagorean triple' (169), it can be understood as a component of the lifespan of Methuselah: 800 + 169 (where 800 seems to be a fundamental number in other age calculations).[28]

Such an explanation would be quite compelling, of course, if all of the equations which Young employs had come from a single text, or if all of the solutions (yielding biblical ages) were sequentially from a single equation (or even a single cuneiform text), or if the data from a single equation explained all of the data for a given individual in Genesis 5. When, instead, many equations are called upon, and when the data from

before the flood or lives through it! See Bailey, *Genesis, Creation, and Creationism*, Appendix XII.

26. 'On the Application of Numbers from Babylonian Mathematics to Biblical Life Spans and Epochs', *ZAW* 100 (1988), pp. 331-61; 'The Influence of Babylonian Algebra on Longevity among the Antediluvians', *ZAW* 102 (1990), pp. 321-35.

27. No. 322 in the Plimpton Collection at Columbia University Library. For a photograph and discussion, see Neugebauer, *The Exact Sciences in Antiquity*, pp. 36-40 and Plate 7.

28. Young, 'Application of Numbers', p. 346.

a single solution must range for applicability over Moses, Nahor and Methuselah, considerable doubt is cast upon it.

Derivation of Elapsed Time

Since there is no obvious reason for the other individual ages (within the confines of each being a multiple of 60 months), the possibility arises that such ages are secondary to the accumulated total. That is, perhaps the basic datum is elapsed time from Adam to the flood (1,656 years), with the individual ages then tailored to produce the total. How this figure might have been derived has given rise to much speculation.

1. Jules Oppert begins with Berossos's total of 432,000 years (Table 2), dividing it into groups of five (comparable to the Roman *lustrum*), which yields 86,400 units.[29] In the Bible, however, the fundamental liturgical time-unit (for the Priestly writers of Gen. 5) is the week. How many weeks are contained in the 1656 years from Adam to the flood? The answer is 86,407, in close agreement with the number of *lustra* in Berossos's total.[30] Expressed in other ways: (1) Berossos's total is 72 × 6,000 years (72 × 1,200 *lustra*), while the MT total is 72 × 1,200 weeks; (2) 6,000 years in the King List is the equivalent of 23 years in Genesis 5; (3) Genesis 5 years are the equivalent of .0038333 King List years.

This formula now enables us to discover the fifth correlation between Genesis 5 and the King List (for anticipation of which see above under the heading, 'Calculation in Base-60'). Ages at time of first-born decrease from Adam through Mahalalel, for a span of 460 years. This is not an intelligible unit in biblical terms (i.e. it is not divisible by 60, 40, 12 or 7, the standard 'symbolic' numbers). When converted to their Mesopotamian 'equivalent', however, the result is 120,000 years ($60 \times 2 \times 10^3$, or 20 periods of 6,000 years each). One is alerted to the possibility of such 'equivalency' by noting that 460 is a multiple of 23 (23 × 20).

One then looks for other blocks of elapsed time in Genesis 5 that are divisible by 23. The next three patriarchs then emerge as candidates, just as they should, given the downward plunge after Methuselah. The total for Jared, Enoch and Methuselah is 414 years (23 × 18), yielding a Mesopotamian figure of 108,000 years ($60^2 \times 30$).

The remaining pre-flood persons in Genesis 5 (Lamech, Noah and

29. J. Oppert, 'Chronology', *JewEnc*, IV, pp. 64-68.

30. That is: 2,656 (years) × 365.25 (days/year) ÷ 7 (days/week), assuming the awareness of the fractional day.

Shem, who is aged 100 at the time of the flood) yield a total elapsed time of 782 years (23 × 34), for a Mesopotamian equivalent of 204,000 years.

There may be, then, three distinct time periods for the biblical pre-diluvians, discoverable only if the figures were dependent in some way upon a Mesopotamian prototype. Oppert is possibly right when he remarks: 'The three periods correspond to legends now altogether lost'.[31]

2. Umberto Cassuto, finding Oppert's calculations too complicated to be acceptable, initially sought to explain the common figure (86,400) as

> a characteristic figure of the sexagesimal system in use among the Sumerians (60 × 60 × 24, which is the number of seconds in a day), and to conjecture, on this basis, that there was a common tradition in the ancient near east concerning 86,400 units of time that elapsed before the flood.

He subsequently became convinced that this was not the case, primarily because Genesis 5 'contains not the slightest allusion to a hebdomadal unit'.[32] I do not find his skepticism compelling at this point since the week is, after all, the fundamental chronological and liturgical unit of the Priestly source to which modern scholars have assigned the chapter.

Cassuto then opts for beginning with a hypothetical biblical total of 600,000 days from creation to the flood. This yields 1,643 solar years of 365 days each.[33] To this he would add 7 + 7 ('as was done in the case of Methuselah's years'), obtaining 'exactly 1657' (1,656 plus the year of the flood).

It is amusing to note that Cassuto, having objected to Oppert's solution on the basis that the unit 'week' plays no role in Genesis 5, introduces the unit 'day' about which it is likewise silent! Perhaps this incongruity struck him as well, since he remarks, 'The fact that the total of 600,000 days is not expressly mentioned is not a valid objection. The omission is characteristic of the Torah.'[34] He seeks to bolster his approach by pointing to the accumulated total of lifespans of the pre-diluvians: 8,226 years. This can be understood, he says, as 8,219 years (3,000,000 days) + 7 years. He might have made his figure more in line with others in the chapter by factoring it into $5(60 \times 10^4)$ days + 7 years.

The likelihood of a relationship between Berossos's total for the pre-

31. Oppert, 'Chronology', p. 66.

32. Cassuto, *Genesis*, I, p. 256.

33. Cassuto, *Genesis*, I, p. 261. The figure is actually 365.8 days.

34. Cassuto, *Genesis*, I, p. 261. He neglects to mention that this might apply to Oppert's approach as well.

diluvian monarchs and that of Genesis 5 (in MT), and thus that Oppert's approach cannot be ruled out as easily as Cassuto prefers, is supported by the LXX total of elapsed time (*Anno Mundi* date for the flood). It is 2,242 years, which may be related (in a different way) to the account of ancient divine rulers in Egypt as reported by the Egyptian historian Manetho (a contemporary of Berossos). These two historians, whose countries were rival fragments of the empire of Alexander the Great, each extolled the glory of his particular realm by pointing to the great antiquity of its kingship. Presumably, at a time when the text of Genesis 5 was still fluid and consisted only of a list of names, editors sought to determine a total of elapsed time. Those in Babylonia (in the proto-MT textual tradition) appealed to the indigenous King List tradition, whereas editors in Egypt appealed to local traditions as reported in Manetho and others. Details of the latter calculation need not detain us here.[35]

For that minority of 'conservative' interpreters who have concluded that elapsed time is actual history and is to be measured, not by the accumulated total of ages at time of first-born, but rather by the accumulated total of lifespans as indicators of generation gaps (see above at n. 2), then the span from creation to the flood becomes 8,225 years and creation may be set at 11,465 BCE.[36] It is much more likely, however, that this figure is part of the symbolism of the base-60 computations outlined above: 8,226 years (adding one for the duration of the flood itself) = $5(60 \times 10^4)$ days + 7 years.

The Purpose(s) of the Chapter

1. *The Chapter in Isolation from its Literary Context*

Since parallels with the Sumerian King List tradition are too numerous to be ignored, it is plausible to suggest that the departures therefrom in Genesis 5 (outlined above) are deliberate and didactic. Cassuto has put the matter clearly.

> The Babylonian tradition was essentially...of a mythological epic character. It told of ancient kings, the representatives of the monarchy that 'descended from heaven'...who were in part divinities...To these kings was attributed an excessively exaggerated longevity...The Torah sets itself in opposition to all this. Scripture did not consider it right to invalidate completely all the existing traditions on the subject, or to pass over

35. Bailey, *Genesis, Creation, and Creationism*, Appendix XII.

36. Stigers, *A Commentary on Genesis*, p. 95.

> them in silence, since they could be of value for its didactic purpose. However, it sought to purify and refine them, and to harmonize them with its own spirit... It is correct—the Bible comes to tell us—that there lived before the flood ten generations of notable personages; but they were only ordinary mortals, not gods, or demi-gods, or even men transformed into divinities, and they had no mythological associations whatsoever. They were born, they begot sons and daughters, and in the end they died; that is all...There is no reference here to *kingship that descended from heaven...* Neither monarchy nor might is important in the eyes of the Torah, for God's pleasure is not in the power of man.[37]

Whereas the Sumerian King List merely concludes its description of each reign with the statement that X ruled for so many years, Genesis 5 not only observes that each person lived for so many years but also adds 'and he died'. These concluding words 'represent that recognition of the inevitability of death which sounds through all history like the strokes of an iron bell'.[38]

2. *Is Genesis 5 Part of a Larger Chronological Framework?*

Computation of elapsed time since creation (*Anno Mundi* dating) easily proceeds through the early post-diluvians with the aid of Genesis 11 (which continues the seriatim listing of age of parent at time of first-born). Beyond that point, things get increasingly difficult.[39] The most famous projection, of course, is that of Archbishop James Ussher.[40] He dated the initial act of creation to 'the entrance of the night preceding the twenty third of *Octob.* in the year of the Julian Calendar, 710', which a marginal notation fixes as 4004 BC.[41]

Most modern interpreters, having grown wary of the many uncertainties in constructing such an absolute chronology (be it 'historical' or

37. Cassuto, *Genesis*, I, pp. 262-63.

38. C. Simpson and W.R. Baker, 'The Book of Genesis', in *IB*, I, p. 528.

39. According to K. Wieseler, 'Era', in the *Schaff-Herzog Encyclopedia of Religious Knowledge* (New York: Funk & Wagnalls, 1882), I, p. 753, an eighteenth-century series of volumes entitled *L'art de vérifier les dates* (by C. Clémencet and U. Durand) 'gives no less than a hundred and eight different views; and the two extremes differ no less than two thousand years from each other'.

40. *The Annals of the World* (London: E. Tyler, 1658).

41. This he did by working downward until he reached an event which he could date in terms of the Julian Calendar (assigning it a BC date), then working backward. That pivotal event, for him, was the death of King Nebuchadnezzar of Babylon, which he set at 562 BC (see his 'Epistle to the Reader'). See Bailey, *Genesis, Creation, and Creationism*, Appendix XIII.

not), have settled for a more modest goal. Is there a pivotal event within the Hebrew Bible itself, the *Anno Mundi* date for which the pre-diluvian ages are merely the introduction? Many such interpreters have been fond of setting the exodus from Egypt at 2666 *Anno Mundi*, conceived as 'two thirds of a world era of four thousand years' (100 generations of 40 years each).[42] However, I know of no value placed upon the fraction 2/3 in ancient Near Eastern chronology, and in any case the proposed date is not a factor of 60.

It seems more likely to me that the real goal of the chronology of the Priestly writer is the founding of the contemporary Second Temple. That date may, with some difficulty, be set at 3600 *Anno Mundi*. If so, it would have been made to fall on the conspicuous and highly symbolic number, 60^2.[43]

3. *The Chapter in Literary Context*

Presuming the Pentateuch to have taken its final and present form at the hands of the Priestly writers during and after the exile to Babylonia, the question may be asked as to how the intended audience 'heard' Genesis 5. What significance, intended or otherwise, might they have perceived for their difficult historical circumstance? Perhaps at least the following themes will have occurred to them.

1. The focus upon computation in base-60 conveys an element of regularity and control. The events depicted are thus not mere random 'happenings': they evidence a marvelous divine oversight. Even if the ages are not 'historically' correct, they nonetheless attest a divine providence that incorporates an otherwise enigmatic period of exile.

2. The extended ages of the pre-diluvians suggest that the 'primeval' world was an ideal one. God intended continuity, tranquillity and longevity for humans, in keeping with the 'paradise' story in Genesis 2–3. Otherwise put: The world as it now appeared to the exiles was not the ideal that God had in mind. Genesis 5 supplies no explanation for a departure from the ideal, but the larger context does. Neither does the chapter provide a remedy for the emerging human problem. That

42. T. Nöldeke, 'Die sogenannte Grundschrift des Pentateuchs', in *Untersuchungen zur Kritik des Alten Testaments* (Kiel: Schwers, 1869), pp. 1-144, and widely followed by others.

43. A. Jepsen, 'Zur Chronologie des Priesterkodex', *ZAW* 47 (1929), pp. 251-55; Bailey, *Genesis, Creation, and Creationism*, Appendix XIII.

remains for subsequent materials in the context, primarily the story of the flood and the 'call' of Abraham.

3. In Genesis 1 humans are blessed and told to 'be fruitful, and multiply, and fill the earth' (v. 28). That narrative source continues in ch. 5 where God's blessing begins to materialize: one generation follows another with mathematical regularity. Despite the human rebellion to which chs. 2–4 attest, God's blessing continues unabated. This must have been a comforting realization to the initial audience, amidst the negativism of the surrounding Babylonian and Canaanite cultures.

4. When the so-called 'Primeval Story' (Gen. 1–11) was prefaced to that of the history of the patriarchs, the call of Abraham and Sarah became the goal toward which the entire story seemed to move. The purpose of their call became God's response to the condition to which humanity has descended. They are to become the beginning of a community through which 'all the families of the earth will be blessed'.[44] Even so, that blessing was a long time in coming, as the genealogy in ch. 5 makes clear. Repeatedly we read, 'X lived so many years, and he died...his son Y lived so many years and he died'. How things will ultimately turn out is not yet clear in transit. The generations rise and pass away. Only at some future date does God's sovereignty, God's saving activity in history, become clear.

44. Reading the ambiguous verb as a passive, in keeping with the understanding of the LXX and the New Testament (Acts 3.25; Gal. 3.8). For discussion of the options, see C. Westermann, *Genesis 12–26* (Minneapolis: Augsburg, 1985), pp. 151-52. He understands the verb in a reflexive sense but with a meaning equivalent to the passive: 'When one blesses oneself with the name of Abraham, blessing is actually bestowed and received'.

JESSE'S NEW SHOOT IN ISAIAH 11: A JOSIANIC READING OF THE PROPHET ISAIAH

Marvin A. Sweeney

I

When compared to its sister text in Isa. 9.1-6, Isa. 11.1-16 presents major theological and literary problems. Although both passages contribute to the messianic aspects of the book by speaking of a coming Davidic monarch, Isaiah 11 takes a much more militant stance than that of its counterpart in that it projects Israelite domination of various nations together with the return of the exiles and the restoration of Israel. Consequently, scholars are reluctant to assign much of the chapter to Isaiah, who is generally regarded as a prophet of peace. Large portions of the chapter, particularly vv. 10-16, are usually assigned to the post-exilic period because of their emphasis on the restoration of Israel. Scholars are divided over vv. 1-5 or 1-9; many maintain that this material reflects Isaiah's language and vision of a future monarch whereas others maintain that such idealism must also be the product of post-exilic hopes for restoration.[1]

This situation is anomalous in that various factors militate against dividing Isaiah 11 or separating it from its present literary context. The image of the new 'shoot' in v. 1 clearly ties into that of the dismembered Assyrian tree in Isa. 10.5-34; likewise, references to the 'rod' (שבט) by which the righteous monarch rules in v. 4 and the 'remnant' (שאר) that will be gathered from Assyria and Egypt in v. 11 contrast with the

1. For a review of research on Isa 11.1-9, see R. Kilian, *Jesaja 1–39* (ErFor, 200; Darmstadt: Wissenschaftliche Buchgesellschaft, 1983), pp. 10-12; H. Wildberger, *Jesaja 1–12* (BKAT, 10.1; Neukirchen–Vluyn: Neukirchener Verlag, 1972), pp. 442-43; J. Vermeylen, *Du prophète Isaïe à l'apocalyptique* (EBib; Paris: Gabalda, 1977), pp. 269-70. Verses 10, 11-16 are almost universally regarded as post-exilic (see for example Vermeylen, *Du prophète Isaïe*, p. 279; Wildberger, *Jesaja 1–12*, pp. 439, 466-67)

oppressive 'rod' of Assyria in Isa. 10.5 and the projection that Assyria will become a 'remnant' of a withered forest in 10.18-19. There are also obstacles to placing Isaiah 11 either in the time of the prophet or in the post-exilic era. The explicit references to the return of exiles from punished Assyria and Egypt (vv. 11, 15-16) are difficult to understand either in relation to the time of Isaiah, when Egypt was a potential Judean ally, or in the post-exilic period when the return of exiles from Babylonia would be the object of greater concern. Furthermore, it seems unlikely that Isaiah would think about the domination of the Philistines, Moabites, Edomites and Ammonites at a time when Judah's very existence was at stake, and by the post-exilic period, these nations had virtually ceased to exist. Finally, the image of the recovery of a disrupted Davidic dynasty hardly applies to the eighth century when no Davidic monarch was removed from the throne, and the image of a 'small youth' (נער קטן, v. 6) as monarch hardly applies to the post-exilic period.

A resolution to this dilemma appears in relation to recent research concerning the presence of a seventh-century 'Josianic' or 'Assyrian' redaction within Isaiah 1–39. According to this hypothesis, substantial amounts of material in chs. 1–39, and especially in chs. 5–12, are the product of a seventh-century redaction that presents the downfall of Assyria and the rise of Judah under King Josiah (639–609 BCE) as the objects and ultimate fulfillments of the prophecies of Isaiah ben Amoz.[2] This paper will argue that Isa. 11.1-16 is the product of this seventh-century redaction and that it represents an attempt to reinterpret Isaiah's prophecies in relation to the rise of Josiah's Judah.[3] First, it will establish

2. On the 'Josianic' redaction of Isa. 1–39, see H. Barth, *Die Jesaja-Worte in der Josiazeit: Israel und Assur als Thema einer produktiven Neuinterpretation der Jesajaüberlieferung* (WMANT, 48; Neukirchen–Vluyn: Neukirchener Verlag, 1977); Vermeylen, *Du prophète Isaïe*; R.E. Clements, *Isaiah 1–39* (NCB; Grand Rapids: Eerdmans; London: Marshall, Morgan & Scott, 1980); G.T. Sheppard, 'The Anti-Assyrian Redaction and the Canonical Context of Isaiah 1–39', *JBL* 104 (1985), pp. 193-216. On the 'Josianic' redaction of Isa. 5.1–10.4, see C.E. L'Heureux, 'The Redactional History of Isaiah 5.1–10.4', in W.B. Barrick and J.R. Spencer (eds.), *In the Shelter of Elyon: Essays on Ancient Palestinian Life and Literature in Honor of G.W. Ahlström* (JSOTSup, 31; Sheffield: JSOT Press, 1984), pp. 99-119; cf. B.W. Anderson, '"God with Us"—In Judgment and Mercy: The Editorial Structure of Isaiah 5–10(11)', in G.M. Tucker, D.L. Petersen and R.R. Wilson (eds.), *Canon, Theology and Old Testament Interpretation: Essays in Honor of Brevard S. Childs* (Philadelphia: Fortress Press, 1988), pp. 230-45.

3. Although Vermeylen argues that Isa. 11.1-5 stems from the seventh-century

the relationship of Isaiah 11 to its literary context, particularly Isa. 10.5-34. Secondly, it will examine internal references in Isaiah 11 that demonstrate the Josianic origin of Isaiah 11. Thirdly, it will consider the hermeneutical perspective by which Isaiah 11 reinterprets Isaiah's prophecies, particularly the anti-Assyrian oracle in Isa. 10.5-34.

II

Although Isa. 11.1-16 is generally treated as a distinct textual unit, a number of syntactical and thematic features indicate that it constitutes several components of a larger textual unit in Isa. 10.5–12.6. Isa. 10.5–12.6 in turn constitutes the concluding sub-unit of the textual block Isaiah 5–12.[4]

Isa. 10.5–12.6 begins with an introductory הוי against Assyria in Isa. 10.5 that distinguishes the following material from the 'outstretched hand' oracles of Isa. 9.7–10.4 which are directed against Israel. Various syntactical features of the passage bind its sub-units together. These include the conjunctive *waw*, 'and', in 10.12; 11.1; and 12.1, the conjunctive לכן, 'therefore', in 10.16, 24, and the conjunctive formula והיה ביום ההוא, 'and it shall come to pass in that day', in 10.20, 27; 11.10, 11 (cf. 12.1, 4). The introductory והיה, 'and it shall come to pass', indicates that each of the ביום ההוא formulas refer back to the statement concerning YHWH's work on Mt Zion and the intention to punish Assyria introduced by the statement, והיה כי יבצע אדני, 'and it shall come to pass when my Lord accomplishes...' (10.12). The superscription in Isa. 13.1 introduces an entirely new section of oracles against the nations in the book of Isaiah.

Thematic features, including the use of tree-trimming imagery[5] and the contrast of the oppressive Assyrian monarch with the righteous Davidic monarch also indicate the unity of Isa. 10.5–12.6 in its present form. Because of the Assyrian monarch's boasts, Isa. 10.12 portrays him

redaction in the time of Josiah, he assigns the balance of the chapter to post-exilic rereadings of Isaiah (*Du prophète Isaïe*, pp. 269-80).

4. On the definition of the textual block Isa. 5–12, see M.A. Sweeney, *Isaiah 1–4 and the Post-Exilic Understanding of the Isaianic Tradition* (BZAW, 171: Berlin and New York: de Gruyter, 1988), pp. 37-44.

5. On the use of tree imagery in Isa. 1–39 in general and in Isa. 10.5–12.6 in particular, see K. Nielsen, *There is Hope for a Tree: The Tree as Metaphor in Isaiah* (JSOTSup, 65; Sheffield: JSOT Press, 1989), esp. pp. 123-44, 187-201.

as a large overgrown tree in need of trimming. Isa. 10.15-19 employs similar imagery to portray Assyria as a rebellious ax or saw as well as a forest that will suffer YHWH's burning. Isa. 10.27 points to Assyria's fullness or fatness as a basis for the statement that Assyria will be trimmed or cut down in Isa. 10.33-34. The phrase וחבל על מפני שמן in Isa. 10.27b is problematic in that the reference to שמן, 'oil' or 'fatness', seems to make little sense to scholars, who attempt to identify it as the first of a series of place names in Isa. 10.27b-32.[6] But שמן makes perfect sense when it is considered in relation to the tree imagery employed throughout the larger context of Isa. 10.5–12.6. The noun שֶׁמֶן derived from the root שמן, 'to make fat', generally indicates fertility or abundance and is frequently employed in reference to olive oil and trees.[7] This is particularly important in that Isa. 10.33-34 employs the imagery of a large tree that is to be pruned by beating its high branches and thicket with iron. Beating an olive tree with rods was apparently one means of recovering the olive harvest in antiquity, although this procedure often resulted in the loss of many upper branches.[8] Thus שמן in Isa. 10.27 appears to refer to the 'oil' or 'fatness' of an olive tree that is ripe for harvest. Verses 33-34 merely describe the punishment of the Assyrian monarch by employing the imagery of an overripe olive tree that will be beaten, harvested and trimmed back.[9] Isa. 11.1-9 then presents the new

6. Based upon the belief that מפני שמן here refers to a place name, scholars have attempted to emend the text to מפני רמון עלה, 'he has gone up from Rimmon', or other place names such Samaria, Beth-El, Yeshimon and so on, in an attempt to reconstruct the beginning of the invader's itinerary portrayed in Isa. 10.27b-32. But the versions contain no readings that might suggest an alternate text, and the text must stand according to the MT. For a full discussion of the problem, see D. Barthélemy *et al.*, *Critique textuelle de l'ancien testament.* II. *Isaïe, Jérémie, Lamentations* (OBO, 50.2; Freiburg: Editions universitaires; Göttingen: Vandenhoeck & Ruprecht, 1986), pp. 77-78; S. Irvine, *Isaiah, Ahaz, and the Syro-Ephraimitic Crisis* (SBLDS, 123; Atlanta: Scholars Press, 1990), pp. 276-77.

7. See Deut. 8.8; 1 Kgs 6.23, 31, 32, 33; Isa. 41.19; Neh. 8.15.

8. See 'Olive', *EncJud*, XII, cols. 1364-66 for a description of the olive harvest in antiquity. Note also that the term for beating in Isa. 10.34 is ונקף, which stems from the same root used in Isa. 17.6 (נקף, cf. Isa. 24.13) for the beating of olive trees at harvest time. The use of the terms שבט, 'rod', and מטה, 'staff', to describe the beating of Assyria in Isa. 10.24-26 (cf. Isa. 10.5) likewise relates to the olive harvest in that such rods were employed to beat the olive trees. Cf. Isa. 28.27 which refers to the 'rod' (שבט) and 'staff' (מטה) used to harvest cumin.

9. Note the reference to the 'fruit of the arrogance of the heart' attributed to the Assyrian monarch in Isa. 10.12 which YHWH promises to punish. This statement

shoot of the house of David that will result from the pruning of the Assyrian, and thereby contrasts the peace and absence of destruction on Mt Zion under the Davidic monarch (cf. esp. 11.9) with the destructive purpose of the Assyrian monarch and his threats against Zion (cf. esp. 10.7, 10-11, 32). The passage concludes with a portrayal of the restoration of Israel and a hymn of thanksgiving.

The structure of Isa. 10.5–12.6 is determined by an interest in announcing the punishment of the Assyrians and the future consequences of that punishment, including the fall of the Assyrian monarch and the rise of the Davidic monarch. Consequently, the passage comprises two major sections: the woe oracle in Isa. 10.5-11 announces Assyria's punishment, and Isa. 10.12–12.6, characterized by its future-oriented language in Isa. 10.12, 20, 27; 11.10, 11; 12.1, 4, announces the consequences of that punishment for both Assyria and Israel. Each of the above-mentioned examples of the ביום ההוא formula serves as a major structural marker within the larger framework of Isa. 10.12–12.6. The announcement of punishment against the Assyrian monarch in Isa. 10.12-19 is followed by four sub-units which elaborate upon the consequences of the Assyrian king's fall. Isa. 10.20-26 describes the future relief of the remnant of Israel from Assyrian oppression; Isa. 10.27–11.9 describes the future fall of the Assyrian monarch in contrast to the rise of the Davidic king;[10] Isa. 11.10 describes the nations' future recognition of the Davidic monarch; Isa. 11.11-16 describes the future restoration of Israel; Isa. 12.1-6 comprises a concluding hymn of thanksgiving.[11]

Although Isa. 10.5–12.6 includes a number of generic elements, including the woe oracle against Assyria in 10.5-11, the announcement of judgment against Assyria in 10.12-19, and the hymn of thanksgiving in 12.1-6, the overarching genre of the entire passage appears to be based in the announcement of a royal savior. This is evident from the basic structure of the passage with its future-oriented language which presents the emergence of the new Davidic monarch in 11.1-9 and the

apparently contributes to the analogy between the Assyrian monarch and the harvested olive tree in this passage.

10. For the relationship between Isa. 10 and 11, see Barth, *Die Jesaja-Worte*, pp. 57-76; Nielsen, *There is Hope for a Tree*, pp. 123-40. Note that the converted perfect verbs of the *waw*-consecutive verbal chain in Isa. 11.1 (ויצא), 2 (ונחה), 3 (והריחו), 4 (ושפט), 5 (והיה), and 6 (וגר) presuppose the imperfect verbal forms ישפלו and יפול in Isa. 10.33-34. They thereby present the rise of the righteous Davidic monarch as the direct result of the fall of the oppressive Assyrian monarch.

11. Cf. Wildberger, *Jesaja 1–12*, pp. 478-79.

consequent recognition by the nations and restoration of Israel in 11.10, 11-16 as the climax of the passage. The announcement of a royal savior is a typical form used throughout the ancient Near East to announce the inauguration of the reign of a new king.[12] It is generally set in the royal court, and it focuses on a description of the positive attributes of the new king's rule with special emphasis on the justice of the new king's decisions and the peace that will result from his rule. Naturally, a description of the prior ills of the land frequently precedes the idyllic picture of the new monarch's regime.[13]

Although the preceding arguments do not require that Isa. 11.1-16 was composed together with Isa. 10.5-34, they clearly demonstrate that the chapter is closely related to its present literary context. This is particularly important in that Isa. 11.1-16 constitutes the climactic passage not only within the immediate context of Isa. 10.5-34, but within the larger context of chs. 5–12. Obviously, this has important implications for the overall interpretation of the passage.

III

Although Isa. 11.1-16 clearly relates to its present literary context in Isa. 10.5–12.6, particularly to Isa. 10.5-34, there is evidence of historical tension within 10.5–12.6 that suggests its composite nature. Whereas Isa. 11.1-16 focuses especially on the rise of the Davidic monarchy in the overall context of the restoration of Israel, Isa. 10.5-34 focuses on YHWH's defense of Zion and the punishment of Assyria. Both sections share an interest in the restoration of Israel and the centrality of Zion, but Isa. 10.5-34 shows no interest whatsoever in the Davidic monarchy. It focuses instead on YHWH's authority as the essential antithesis to Assyrian claims of hegemony. These considerations in and of themselves do not demonstrate that Isa. 10.5-34 and 11.1-16 (+12.1-6) were composed in different historical settings, but a number of other factors indicate that Isa. 11.1-16 was composed during the reign of King Josiah and that Isa. 10.5-34 is based on a composition by Isaiah ben Amoz.

Vermeylen has already argued that Isa. 11.1-5 stems from the late-seventh-century redaction of Isaiah,[14] but the following considerations

12. For example, 'The Prophecy of Neferti', *ANET*, pp. 444-46.

13. For a full discussion of the announcement of a royal savior, see Wildberger, *Jesaja 1–12*, pp. 440-41.

14. See Vermeylen, *Du prophète Isaïe*, pp. 269-75.

demonstrate that the whole of Isa. 11.1-16 must be attributed to the Josianic redaction.

First, many scholars note that the passage presupposes a threat to the Davidic dynasty as indicated by its reference to a 'stump' (גזע) or 'root' (שרש) from which a new 'shoot' (חטר) or 'sprout' (נצר) must grow.[15] Such imagery presupposes that the threat very nearly succeeded in that it portrays a tree that has been nearly destroyed but is still capable of rejuvenating itself. Although the Davidic dynasty was certainly threatened by the Syro-Ephraimitic coalition in 735–732 BCE, the threat never reached a point at which a ruling Davidic monarch was killed or removed from the throne. Instead, the threat to the dynasty was averted when the Syro-Ephraimitic coalition failed to install a certain ben Tabeel on the Judean throne (cf. Isa. 7.6). Furthermore, the literary context of Isa. 11.1-16 indicates that the threat to the dynasty comes from Assyria, not from the Syro-Ephraimitic coalition. The Assyrian invasion of Judah in 701 BCE may well have threatened the Davidic dynasty, but neither Sennacherib's annals nor the biblical tradition give any indication that he attempted to remove Hezekiah from the throne.[16] On the other hand, such a scenario corresponds well to the reign of Josiah. His father Amon was assassinated in a coup by his 'servants' which was apparently motivated by an interest in reversing Manasseh's policy of subservience to the weakening Assyrian empire (2 Kgs 22.19-26; 2 Chron. 33.21-25). Nevertheless, 'the people of the land' defeated the coup attempt and restored the eight-year-old Josiah to the throne. Josiah's age at the time and the fact that no brother, uncle or other Davidic figure exercised authority during his minority suggests that Josiah was the only Davidic heir to survive the attempted coup.[17] The imagery of new growth in Isaiah 11 signified by a 'shoot' or 'sprout' corresponds well to the circumstances that brought Josiah to the throne.

15. For example, Clements, *Isaiah 1–39*, pp. 121-22.

16. Sennacherib's annals indicate that Hezekiah delivered greater tribute to the Assyrian monarch and even his own daughters and concubines, but there is no suggestion that Hezekiah's position as monarch, or that of the Davidic dynasty, was threatened. For Sennacherib's annals and building inscriptions, see *ANET*, pp. 287-88; *ARAB* II, sec. 239-40, 284, 347. For the biblical accounts of this campaign, see Isa. 36–39; 2 Kgs 18.13–20.19; 2 Chron. 32.

17. Cf. Athaliah's attempted coup against the Davidic dynasty as narrated in 2 Kgs 11. All of the Davidic house perished in the coup attempt with the exception of the seven-year-old Jehoash who was hidden by his aunt Jehosheba and later restored to the throne.

Secondly, the passage makes specific mention of a 'small youth (נער קטן) leading them' in v. 6b (cf. v. 8). The imagery of normally antagonistic wild animals resting harmlessly together is commonly employed in the announcement of a royal savior genre to depict the new king's reign.[18] Although references to the birth of a child are not unknown to the genre, the portrayal of a small boy and his leading role is striking in this context. Again, it suggests an allusion to the boy-king Josiah.

Thirdly, the emphasis on the new king's justice and wisdom is certainly not remarkable in a text concerned with the reign of a new Near Eastern monarch; kings promulgate law codes.[19] But it is noteworthy that one of the major features of Josiah's reform was the establishment of a newly found book of law as its basis (2 Kgs 22.8-20; 2 Chron. 34.8-33).

Fourthly, Isa. 11.11-16 emphasizes the cessation of enmity between Ephraim and Judah, their reunification, and the re-establishment of Davidic authority over Philistia to the west and Edom, Moab and Ammon to the east. These verses further emphasize the punishment of Egypt and Assyria in the context of the return of the exiles from these countries. This scenario corresponds precisely to Josiah's attempt to rebuild the Davidic empire in the face of opposition from Egypt and Assyria in the late seventh century.[20] His dismantling of the altar at Beth-El indicates his interest in reclaiming the territory and population of the former northern kingdom of Israel (2 Kgs 23.15-20). His marriage to Hamutal of Libnah (2 Kgs 23.31; 24.18) indicates an interest in securing the Shephelah and Philistine regions and his marriage to Zebidah of Rumah (2 Kgs 23.36) indicates his interest in securing the north and the Trans-

18. Wildberger, *Jesaja 1–12*, pp. 378, 440-41.

19. Cf. the prologue to the law code of Hammurabi, *ANET*, pp. 164-65.

20. The same scenario appears in Zeph. 2.4-15 with mention of the same nations (with the exception of Edom). Zephaniah likewise appears to support Josiah's reform and political ambitions (see D.L. Christensen, 'Zephaniah 2:4-15: A Theological Basis for Josiah's Program of Political Expansion', *CBQ* 46 [1984], pp. 669-82; M.A. Sweeney, 'A Form Critical Reassessment of the Book of Zephaniah', *CBQ* 53 [1991], pp. 388-408). Recent arguments by N. Na'aman ('The Kingdom of Judah under Josiah', *Tel Aviv* 18 [1991], pp. 3-71) and J.M. Miller and J.H. Hayes (*A History of Ancient Israel and Judah* [Philadelphia: Fortress Press, 1986], pp. 388-90) that Josiah did not attempt to resurrect the Davidic empire correctly note that Josiah did not succeed in this ambition, but they fail to demonstrate that this was not his intention. The evidence cited here indicates that such political ambitions were indeed among the goals of Josiah's program, even if he failed to realize them.

Jordan.[21] Furthermore, as Assyrian power weakened during the course of the late seventh century, Egypt emerged as the major obstacle to Josiah's ambitions and eventually caused his death at Megiddo (2 Kgs 23.28-30).[22]

Finally, the interest in traditions pertaining to the exodus is apparent in both Isa. 11.11-16 and Isa. 12.1-6. Isa. 11.11-16 refers to YHWH's smiting of Egypt and Assyria in order to recover Israelite and Judean exiles and to restore Israelite hegemony over the former Davidic empire. Several motifs from the exodus tradition appear in this context. The smiting of 'the tongue of the sea of Egypt' (v. 15aα) calls to mind the division of the sea in Exodus 14. The reference to the 'burning wind' that YHWH will employ against the Euphrates River of Assyria (v. 15aβ) recalls the east wind that divided the sea and defeated the Egyptians in Exod. 14.21; 15.8. Likewise, the 'waving' of YHWH's hand in a context that refers to the 'ensign' (נס; vv. 10, 12; cf. Isa. 5.26) to the nations calls to mind Moses' outstretched hand that resulted in the defeat of the Amalekites in Exod. 17.8-16. The altar erected to commemorate Israel's victory over the Amalekites was called 'YHWH is my ensign' (ה" נסי). The 'highway' for the return of the remnant of the people from Egypt and Assyria (v. 16a) recalls the King's Highway used by Israel in the wilderness traditions to journey to the land of Canaan (Exod. 15.13-18; Num. 20.17-19; 21.22). Isa. 11.16b makes the analogy explicit by noting that the return of the exiles will take place 'just as it was for Israel on the day of its going up from the land of Egypt'. Likewise, Isa. 12.1-6 quotes an altered version of Exod. 15.2a (cf. Ps. 118.14) in v. 2b and v. 5a corresponds to Exod. 15.1b. Verse 4a quotes Ps. 105.1 which praises YHWH for leading Israel out from Egypt at the exodus. This interest in the exodus tradition is particularly noteworthy in relation to the reign of King Josiah. As 2 Kgs 23.21-23 and 2 Chron. 35.1-19 indicate, the celebration of Passover served as the festival basis for Josiah's reform. Insofar as Passover celebrates the exodus of Jews from Egypt and their return to the land of Israel, this holiday would be particularly important to the ideology of Josiah's program of religious reform and national restoration.

21. On the political significance of Josiah's marriages, see J.A. Wilcoxen, 'The Political Background of Jeremiah's Temple Sermon', in A. Merrill and T. Overholt (eds.), *Scripture in History and Theology* (FS J.C. Rylaarsdam; Pittsburgh: Pickwick, 1977), pp. 151-66.

22. On Egyptian influence in Syro-Palestine during the reign of Josiah, see A. Malamat, 'Josiah's Bid for Armageddon', *JANESCU* 5 (1973), pp. 267-78.

These considerations establish quite a parallel between the major concerns of Isa. 11.1-16 (+ 12.1-6) and those of King Josiah's program of reform and restoration. When taken together with the objections to Isaianic and post-exilic composition of the passage mentioned above, one must conclude that Isa. 11.1-16 (+ 12.1-6) were composed during the reign of King Josiah in order to support his program of religious reform and national restoration.

Although many scholars consider Isa. 10.20-26 to be redactional additions,[23] several factors indicate that Isa. 10.5-34 is based on a composition by Isaiah ben Amoz.

The speeches by the Assyrian monarch quoted in Isa. 10.8-11 and 10.13-14 make reference to a number of cities that were taken by the Assyrian army during the late eighth century. With the exception of Jerusalem, the cities referred to were taken by 717 BCE at the latest. Thus, the Hittite city of Carchemish was taken by Sargon II in 717, and the north Syrian city of Calno was taken by Tiglath-Pileser III in 738. Hamath, on the Orontes River in Syria, was taken by Sargon in 720 and Arpad, in north Syria, fell to Tiglath-Pileser in 738 and again to Sargon in 720. Damascus fell to Tiglath-Pileser in 734, and Samaria was taken by Tiglath-Pileser or Sargon in 722–721. A clear pattern emerges in which the conquests of Sargon II are grouped with those of Tiglath-Pileser III. Of course, we cannot be certain that the Isaiah text represents a quotation of the words of an Assyrian monarch,[24] but it is well known that Sargon was a usurper of the Assyrian throne who strove to strengthen the Assyrian empire and thereby to legitimate his position as monarch.[25] A comparison by Sargon of his achievements with those of Tiglath-Pileser III, who initiated the rise of the neo-Assyrian empire in the late eighth century, would certainly correspond with his interest to secure his throne. Although Sargon never mounted a full assault against Jerusalem, he passed through the region on various occasions from 720

23. For example, Barth, *Die Jesaja-Worte*, pp. 43-49, 287-88, 292-94; Clements, *Isaiah 1–39*, pp. 114-17; Vermeylen, *Du prophète Isaïe*, pp. 262-65; Wildberger, *Jesaja 1–12*, pp. 412-22.

24. See P. Machinist, 'Assyria and its Image in the First Isaiah', *JAOS* 103 (1983), pp. 719-37, who argues that the language employed here reflects that of neo-Assyrian royal inscriptions.

25. On the reign of Sargon II, see W.W. Hallo and W.K. Simpson, *The Ancient Near East: A History* (New York: Harcourt, Brace, Jovanovich, 1971), pp. 55 (n. 46), 138-43; P. Machinist, 'Sargon II', in P. Achtemeier *et al.* (eds.), *Harper's Bible Dictionary* (San Francisco: Harper & Row, 1985), pp. 907-908.

to 711 in order to secure his borders and trade relations with Egypt and to put down revolts by the Philistines. It is likely that the statements referred to in Isa. 10.5-19 reflect an actual attempt by Sargon to intimidate Jerusalem in order to prevent potential resistance or support for a Philistine revolt.[26]

The itinerary of terrified cities mentioned in Isa. 10.28-32 reinforces this view. Although these verses have often been related to Sennacherib's campaign of 701, the fact that he conducted his campaign from Lachish and the Philistine plain militates against the march of an army from the north along the Shechem/Beth-El highway to Jerusalem as depicted here.[27] Attempts to claim that this text represents the invasion route of the Syro-Ephraimitic coalition against Jerusalem in 735 must also be rejected as the context clearly indicates an Assyrian invader.[28] It seems best to view this route in relation to Sargon's western campaign of 720 in which he suppressed revolt in upper Syria, Damascus and Samaria, prior to moving against the Philistines in the south. A pass by Jerusalem would present the opportunity to display his army at Nob (present-day Mt Scopus) with its commanding view of Jerusalem. Such a move would demonstrate to the Judean monarch the folly of attempting to resist the new Assyrian monarch. It would likewise secure Sargon's rear prior to his advance against Philistia. Such a strategy is consistent with the route outlined in Isa. 10.28-32, which bypasses the Judean stronghold at Mizpah. A protracted siege of Mizpah or Jerusalem would only delay Sargon and allow the Egyptians to move their forces in support of Philistia.[29]

In its present form, Isa. 10.5-34 may well be the product of the Josianic redaction. But the preceding arguments indicate that this text, particularly vv. 5-19 and 27-34, stems originally from Isaiah ben Amoz.

IV

Although Isa. 10.5–12.6 contains several distinct textual sub-units that derive from different historical settings, the present form of this text

26. Cf. Clements, *Isaiah 1–39*, pp. 109-10.

27. For the details of this route, see G. Dalman, 'Palästinische Wege und die Bedrohung Jerusalems nach Jesaja 10', *PJ* 12 (1916), pp. 37-57.

28. See H. Donner, *Israel unter den Völkern* (VTSup, 11; Leiden: Brill, 1964), pp. 30-38; Irvine, *Isaiah, Ahaz, and the Syro-Ephraimitic Crisis*, pp. 274-79.

29. For a detailed presentation of this position, see M.A. Sweeney, 'Sargon's Threat against Jerusalem in Isaiah 10,27-32', *Bib* 75 (1994), pp. 457-70.

constitutes a structurally and generically coherent text that was composed as a part of the seventh-century Josianic redaction of the prophecies of Isaiah ben Amoz. This has certain implications for the reading of this text, both in and of itself and in relation to its literary context.

First, it is quite clear that by composing Isa. 11.1–12.6 as the conclusion for Isa. 10.5-34, the Josianic redactors intended to present King Josiah and his planned restoration of Israel as the fulfillment of the prophecies of Isaiah ben Amoz. This is evident from the juxtaposition of Isaiah's prophecies concerning YHWH's planned judgment against Assyria and the Assyrian monarch for hubris with the Josianic announcement of the coming of a royal savior who would restore Israel and Judah. The rise of Josiah's kingdom coincides with the fall of the Assyrian empire in the latter part of the seventh century. Although Isaiah ben Amoz spoke in the late eighth century, the Josianic redaction presents him as anticipating events of the late seventh century. According to the Josianic redaction, Isaiah prophesied Josiah's reign and his program for national restoration.

This is accomplished not only by the juxtaposition of textual sub-units, but by thematic development pertaining to the harvest and pruning of an olive tree as well. The use of tree imagery to depict the fall of Assyria in Isa. 10.5-34 is well known, but scholars have noted some tension in the transition of this image from ch. 10 to ch. 11. Whereas ch. 10 portrays the fall of Assyria in relation to the felling of a forest of cedars of Lebanon (esp. vv. 15-19, 33-34), ch. 11 portrays the growth of the new Davidic monarch from a single shoot or stump. This discrepancy provides evidence for scholars who wish to assert the presence of a redactional link between chs. 10 and 11.[30] Sargon II was well known for his logging operations in Lebanon and Armenia to supply wood for his palace at Dur Sharrukin, and this imagery apparently explains the use of the tree-felling metaphor by Isaiah in ch. 10 to depict the punishment of the Assyrian monarch.[31] But when read in relation to the lopping off of

30. For example, Barth, *Die Jesaja-Worte*, pp. 57-76; Vermeylen, *Du prophète Isaïe*, pp. 265-75. Contra Nielsen, *There is Hope for a Tree*, pp. 123-40, who argues that the imagery is consistent and that it stems from Isaiah, but that it lends itself to reinterpretation in later historical contexts.

31. See A.T. Olmstead, *A History of Assyria* (Chicago and London: University of Chicago Press, 1951), pp. 272-74. Cf. Isa. 14.8 in which the cedars of Lebanon rejoice at the fall of the Babylonian monarch because no hewer will come against them. According to H.L. Ginsberg ('Reflexes of Sargon in Isaiah after 715 B.C.E.', in W.W. Hallo [ed.], *Essays in Memory of E.A. Speiser* [New Haven: American

upper boughs (10.33-34), the 'fatness' or 'oil' of the 'Assyrian' tree (10.27), and the motif of the beating 'rod' or 'staff' (10.5, 20-26), the new shoot in Isa. 11.1 presents the image of an olive tree renewing its growth after it has been harvested by beating (and lopping off) its boughs. Such imagery is particularly striking in relation to Assyria's use of the Shephelah and the former Philistine regions as a major olive oil production center during the seventh century BCE.[32] The fact that a significant portion of the population of the former northern kingdom of Israel was shifted to this region in order to support olive oil production only adds to the significance of this image in relation to the Josianic redaction of Isaiah. Just as Assyria had employed the 'rod' against displaced Israelites to reap the olive harvest of the land, so Assyria's downfall in the late seventh century was portrayed as YHWH's beating of a fat olive tree with a rod at harvest time. The aftermath of the beating/ harvest was the new growth of a renewed Davidic kingdom.

Secondly, by juxtaposing Isa. 10.5-34 and 11.1–12.6, the Josianic redactors of Isaiah have dehistoricized the Assyrian monarch portrayed in Isaiah's prophecy. Although the monarch is never named in the passage, various considerations discussed above indicate that the object of this passage is Sargon II. The narratives concerning Sennacherib's 701 BCE invasion of Judah and siege of Jerusalem in Isaiah 36–37

Oriental Society, 1968], pp. 47-53), Isa. 14.4b-21 was originally written in reference to the death of Sargon II in 705 BCE.

32. Recent excavations at Tel Miqne (Ekron) demonstrate the presence of sufficient olive presses to support olive oil production for the entire Assyrian empire. Furthermore, the presence of horned altars at the site demonstrates that Israelites were employed in this industry. On the excavations at Tel Miqne and the significance of these finds, see S. Gitin, 'Tel Miqne-Ekron: A Type-Site for the Inner Coastal Plain in the Iron Age II Period', in S. Gitin and W.G. Dever (eds.), *Recent Excavations in Israel: Studies in Iron Age Archaeology* (AASOR, 49; Winona Lake, IN: Eisenbrauns, 1989), pp. 23-58; *idem*, 'Ekron of the Philistines, Part II: Olive-Oil Suppliers to the World', *BARev* 16.2 (March–April 1990), pp. 32-42, 59; *idem*, 'Last Days of the Philistines', *Archaeology* (May–June 1992), pp. 26-31; *idem*, 'Incense Altars from Ekron, Israel and Judah', *Eretz Israel* 20 (1989), pp. 52*-67*; *idem*, 'New Incense Altars from Ekron: Context, Typology and Function', *Eretz Israel* 23 (1992), pp. 43*-49*; *idem*, 'Seventh Century BCE Cultic Elements at Ekron', in *Proceedings of the IInd International Congress on Biblical Archaeology, June 1990* (Jerusalem: Israel Exploration Society, forthcoming); T. Dothan and S. Gitin, 'Tel Miqne, 1986', *IEJ* 37 (1987), pp. 63-68; *idem*, 'The Rise and Fall of Ekron of the Philistines: Recent Excavations at an Urban Border Site', *BA* 50 (1987), pp. 197-222.

suggest that Sennacherib is the object of ch. 10 in that many of the statements concerning the gods of Hamath, Arpad, Samaria and so on correspond to those of Isa. 10.9-11. Some have argued that Isaiah 36–37 is the product of a seventh-century edition of Isaiah.[33] If this is the case, it indicates that the Josianic redaction of Isaiah was not interested in an accurate historical portrayal of the Assyrian monarch or the prophecies of Isaiah; rather the redaction employed elements from Isaiah's speech concerning Sargon to construct a portrayal of Sennacherib in order to serve its theological and literary aims. Sennacherib's invasion symbolizes the oppression of Judah and Jerusalem by the Assyrians in general and YHWH's defeat of the Assyrians in this narrative symbolizes YHWH's guarantees of protection. The presentation of the Assyrian monarch in Isaiah 10 thereby becomes the basis for a typological presentation of Assyrian oppression in the Josianic edition of Isaiah. It does not matter that Sargon II was the object of Isaiah's speech; it only matters that Isaiah foretold the downfall of Assyrian rule over Jerusalem.

The same might be said concerning the promises of a righteous monarch in Isaiah. Although Isa. 9.1-6 likely refers to Hezekiah as the righteous monarch promised by Isaiah,[34] the Josianic edition of Isaiah presupposes that Josiah will fulfill this promise. Hezekiah does indeed serve as a righteous model in Isaiah 36–37 insofar as he turns to YHWH in a time of crisis and thereby saves Jerusalem from the Assyrians. But ultimately, Josiah is the one who will reunite Israel and Judah after the downfall of Assyrian power. The placement of Isa. 11.12-16 at the conclusion of the major textual block in Isaiah 5–12 ensures that the presentation of punishment against Israel and Judah, as well as the subsequent punishment of Assyria once judgment against Israel and Judah is realized, will culminate in the righteous reign of Josiah over a restored Israel and Judah. Again, Isaianic statements from the eighth century are dehistoricized to serve the interests of the Josianic redaction.

Finally, the Josianic redaction's dehistoricization of the Assyrian monarch has implications for the subsequent growth of the book of Isaiah as well in that the image of this figure becomes adaptable to later

33. For example, R.E. Clements, *Isaiah and the Deliverance of Jerusalem: A Study of the Interpretation of Prophecy in the Old Testament* (JSOTSup, 13; Sheffield: JSOT Press, 1980).

34. For a full discussion of this passage and its context, see my study, 'A Philological and Form-Critical Reevaluation of Isaiah 8:16–9:6', *HAR* 14 (1994), pp. 215-31.

historical contexts and theological agendas. The Assyrian monarch becomes a type of oppressor in the book of Isaiah that can be identified later with the Babylonians; the figure thereby serves as a means to link Isaiah 40–66, which presupposes Babylonia as the major oppressor of Judah and object of YHWH's wrath, to the first part of the book.[35] Likewise, the Davidic monarch also becomes a type in that neither 11.1-16 nor the other royal prophecies in 9.1-6 and 32.1-20 ever identify the king by name. In later parts of the book, Cyrus is identified as the messiah (Isa. 44.28; 45.1), the people of Israel are granted the royal promises of David (Isa. 55.3), and even YHWH is identified as the king in Jerusalem (Isa. 66.1-2). Clearly, the Josianic redaction of Isaiah set the pattern by which the referents of the book could be reread and reinterpreted in relation to later historical situations.[36] It was this capacity for shifting referents and adapting them to new situations and theological concerns that ensured the continued relevance of the book of Isaiah through the centuries that followed.[37]

35. Note the juxtaposition of the oracle against Babylon and the Babylonian monarch in Isa. 13.1–14.23 with YHWH's promise to destroy Assyria in Isa. 14.24-27. The presentation of these passages together indicates an interest in identifying the Babylonians as the successors to the Assyrians in the book of Isaiah (cf. R.E. Clements, 'Isaiah 14,22-27: A Central Passage Reconsidered', in J. Vermeylen [ed.], *The Book of Isaiah/Le Livre d'Isaïe: Les oracles et leurs relectures unité et complexité de l'ouvrage* [BETL, 81; Leuven: Peeters, 1989], pp. 253-62). Note also Isa. 39.1-8 which anticipates the Babylonian exile (cf. P. Ackroyd, 'An Interpretation of the Babylonian Exile: A Study of II Kings 20 and Isaiah 38–39', *SJT* 27 [1974], pp. 329-52; reprinted in *Studies in the Religious Tradition of the Old Testament* [London: SCM Press, 1987], pp. 152-71, 282-85). On the links between First and Second Isaiah, see R.E. Clements, 'Beyond Tradition History: Deutero-Isaianic Development of First Isaiah's Themes', *JSOT* 31 (1985), pp. 95-113.

36. Cf. J.A. Sanders, 'Adaptable for Life: The Nature and Function of Canon', in F.M. Cross, W.E. Lemke and P.D. Miller (eds.), *Magnalia Dei: The Mighty Acts of God* (FS G.E. Wright; Garden City, NY: Doubleday, 1976), pp. 531-60.

37. I am indebted to Prof. Yair Zakovitch who invited me to present some of the initial ideas for this paper to his seminar on 'The Exodus Tradition in the Bible' at the Hebrew University of Jerusalem, April 24, 1990. Postscript: H.G.M. Williamson's recent studies, 'Isaiah xi 11-16 and the Redaction of Isaiah i-xii', in J.A. Emerton (ed.), *Congress Volume: Paris 1992* (VTSup, 61; Leiden: Brill, 1995), pp. 343-57, and *The Book Called Isaiah: Deutero-Isaiah's Role in Composition and Redaction* (Oxford: Clarendon Press, 1994), came into my hands only during the final editing of this essay for publication. Although there is much to commend in Williamson's hypothesis of a sixth-century Isaiah redaction, his analysis of Isa. 11.1-16 does not take sufficient account of the identities of the nations in vv. 11-16

APPENDIX

Structure Diagram: Isaiah 10.5–12.6

Prophetic announcement of a royal savior		Isa. 10.5-11
I.	Woe oracle against Assyria	10.12–12.6
II.	Announcement of judgment against Assyria and of a royal savior for Judah	10.12-19
	A. Announcement of judgment against Assyria	10.20-26
	B. Elaboration #1: concerning the future relief of the remnant of Israel from Assyrian oppression	10.27–11.9
	C. Elaboration #2: concerning the fall of the Assyrian monarch and the rise of a righteous Davidic monarch	10.5–12.6
	D. Elaboration #3: concerning the nations' future recognition of the Davidic monarch	11.10
	E. Elaboration #4: concerning the future restoration of Israel	11.11-16
	F. Concluding Hymn of Thanksgiving	12.1-6

and the overall scenario of Israel's and Judah's reunification and domination of these nations. Likewise, his views on Isa. 8.21-23a must be weighed against my arguments as presented in 'A Reevaluation of Isaiah 8:16–9:6'.

EZEKIEL'S DANCE OF THE SWORD AND PROPHETIC THEONOMY

Samuel Terrien

Early in his career, Jim Sanders wrote a book on *Suffering as Divine Discipline in the Old Testament and Post-Biblical Judaism* (1955). A few years later he published *The Old Testament in the Cross* (1961), where he pursued a related theme that embraced both Jewish and Christian Scriptures. Here he anticipated his later concern for canonical theology and the interaction between Gospel and Torah.

In the present essay I propose to investigate some aspects of Ezek. 21.14-22 [Eng. 9-17] as a contribution to the theme of human and divine suffering in the light of prophetic theonomy. Although commentators have generally called this poem 'The Song of the Sword', several of its features suggest that the prophet not only sang an oracle but also danced and juggled with the naked blade of a sword. He was performing a prophetic act. Different from the symbolic gestures which Isaiah, Jeremiah and Ezekiel himself enacted, and not unlike Hosea's account of mating with a harlot, this prophetic deed involved both a prediction of divine judgment and a portrayal of divine self-immolation. To those Judahites who hoped that Yahweh, the Holy Warrior, would appear from heaven to win his battle against Babylon, Ezekiel said in effect, 'No! God just broke his heart.'[1]

I

The form of this poem approximates that of an oracular ballad.[2] Its structure comprehends three strophes crowned by an *envoi* which is

1. J.A. Sanders, *The Old Testament in the Cross* (New York: Harper, 1961), p. 121.

2. The word 'ballad' designates a late medieval form, but it may be applied to a mixed structure that participates in oracular lyrical poetry, especially when it ends with an *envoi* of distinct rhythm. The literary form of the 'Song of the Sword' differs

couched in another rhythm.[3] Each strophe begins with a command addressed to the prophet as 'son of man', and it develops three distinctly purposive movements of the dance: (1) the sharpening of the sword; (2) its striking; (3) its juggling and falling.

The text is sometimes obscure and possibly, but not obviously,

from those which have been analyzed among the many prophetic oracles. It is not similar to the cries of woe or the announcement of judgment. See C. Westermann, *Basic Forms of Prophetic Speech* (trans. H.C. White; Philadelphia: Westminster Press, 1967), pp. 169-76, 190-94.

3. The oral cadence reveals a structure in two mirror-like parts with alternate sequences of imperative and indicative verbal modes, articulated upon a pivot-center.

A.	v. 14ab [Eng. 9]	imperative	
B.	vv. 14c-16 [Eng. 10-11]	indicative	
C.	v. 17 [Eng. 12]	imperative	
D.	v. 18 [Eng. 13]		PIVOT-CENTER
C′.	v. 19 [Eng. 14]	imperative	
B′.	v. 20 [Eng. 15]	indicative	
A′.	vv. 21-22 [Eng. 16]	imperative and indicative	

See B. Tidiman, *Le livre d'Ezéchiel*, I (Commentaires évangeliques de la Bible, 4; Vaux-sur-Seine: EDIFAC, 1985), p. 262.

The composition of the poem was predicated by oracular psychology, but it may have received the influence of literary expressions of earlier dates. Cf. F. Delitzsch, 'Assyriologische Notizen zum Alten Testament, IV: Das Schwertlied Ezech. 21, 13-22', *Zeitschrift für Keilschriftforschung* 2 (1855), pp. 385-98; B. Maarsingh, 'Das Schwertlied in Ez 21, 13-22 and das Erra-Gedicht', in J. Lust, *et al.* (eds.), *Ezekiel and his Book: Textual and Literary Criticism and their Interrelation* (BETL, 74; Leuven: Leuven University Press, 1986), pp. 350-58; *idem*, *Ezechiël*, II (Nijkerk: Uitgeverij G.F. Callenbach, 1988), pp. 98-103; 271-73; D. Bodi, *The Book of Ezekiel and the Poem of Erra* (OBO, 104; Fribourg: Editions universitaires; Göttingen: Vandenhoeck & Ruprecht, 1991), pp. 231-57.

The symmetrical structure discerned by Tidiman favors the thesis of compositional unity. It argues against the validity of the many conjectures of literary additions, or even compilations, introduced by Ezekielian disciples and scribes (see Bodi, *Ezekiel*, p. 232 n. 9 and pp. 233, 237-57). The hypothesis of additions is not without merit, but must be viewed with caution (cf. R.J. Tournay, 'Le Poème de l'épée, Ezéchiel 21: 13-22 et ses relectures', in A. Rofé, *et al.* [eds.], *Essays on the Bible and the Ancient World*, II [I.L. Seeligmann Volume; Jerusalem: Elhanan Rubinshtayn, 1983], pp. 249-62).

While twentieth-century criticism has tended to stress the literary aspects of the prophetic oracles and to underplay the ecstatic psychology of their origins, contemporary exegesis implies an equilibrium between the two trends (see S. Terrien, *The Elusive Presence: Toward a New Biblical Theology* [San Francisco: Harper & Row, 1978], pp. 261-68).

corrupt, even in its notoriously cryptic sentences (especially v. 15cd [Eng. 10cd]. This tentative translation and its prosodic arrangement are proposed only as a preface to the discussion that follows.

First Strophe (vv. 14-16 [Eng. 9-11])
The Sharpening of the Sword
14 Son of man! Prophesy and say,
Thus speaks Adonay Yahweh!
Sword, sword! sharpened and polished,
15 sharpened for the slaughter,
polished to flash like a lightning bolt!
(Or shall we make mirth?)[4]
The scepter of my son despises [me]
with every wooden [idol].
16 He has given it to be polished
for the palm of the hand to grasp it.
The sword is verily to be sharpened
and polished for the slayer's hand.

The words of the first strophe in themselves do not compel the exegete to affirm that the song is also a prophetic act. However, the LXX has understood as a vocative the twice-repeated noun חרב, 'sword'. It has also construed the verbs as imperatives. In the Greek version, which likewise considers the verbs to be imperatives in v. 15, the singer still addresses the sword,

Be thou sharp enough to catch the gleam!
Be prepared for the slaying,
Slay thou! Bring to nought!
Reject every tree!

4. Many commentators consider this line (v. 15b) to be a scribal addition. See W. Zimmerli, *Ezekiel 1: A Commentary on the Book of the Prophet Ezekiel, Chapters 1–24* (trans. R.E. Clements; Hermeneia; Philadelphia: Fortress Press, 1979), p. 435. It is not necessary to view it in an eschatological and messianic context (A. van den Born, *Ezechiel, de profeet van de babylonische gevangenschap* [Roermond-Maasiek: J.J. Romen & Zonen, 1934], p. 135). The question, 'Or shall we have mirth?' might well be an 'aside' of ironical and even satirical intent. See the history of the text and interpretation in D. Barthélemy, *et al.*, *Critique textuelle de l'Ancien Testament*, III (OBO, 50.3; Fribourg: Editions universitaires; Göttingen: Vandenhoeck & Ruprecht, 1992), pp. 161-64. 'My son' and 'his scepter' (v. 15c) probably alluded likewise with biting criticism to one of the last kings of Judah before the final defeat.

If the sword is the object to which the words are directed, the blade is being readied for the bloody deed. It is being honed to razor-edged refinement for the sake of a faultless efficiency, and furbished to gleam in the dark like a flash of lightning.

The imagery of the Divine Warrior evokes the terminology of the Northwest Semitic theophany.[5] The Ugaritic profile of a helmeted Baal in the Louvre brings together the thunderbolt and a club.[6] It is no accident that the sword is being polished to gleam like a lightning bolt, for the two motifs are also brought together in the Song of Moses with 'the lightning bolt of the sword' (Deut. 32.41), an expression which is followed by the image of the devouring sword (v. 42; cf. Isa. 31.8) that is soon sated with blood (cf. Isa. 34.6; Jer. 12.12; 47.6; cf. Isa. 26.21; 66.16; Zeph. 2.12).

The motif of an avenging sword associated with fire is found at the conclusion of the myth of the garden (Gen. 3.24), and the exclamative address to the sword belongs to the pattern of the Holy War, 'A word for Yahweh and for Gideon!' (Judg. 7.20).

The link between the sword and the lightning flash presides over the juxtaposition of the three preceding poems in Ezekiel 21, although they appear to have been independent before they were collected in the final form of the book. The first of these poems deals with the fire that will devour the forest land (21.1-4); the second calls for the sword of Yahweh against Jerusalem (21.7-10); the third actually summons the prophet to act out bodily his horror at the incoming news of the disaster (21.11-12). This third unit, which immediately precedes the Song of the Sword, demands the realistic interpretation of the poem as descriptive of an actual performance, for it implies the enactment of a symbolic gesture. It also intimates the prophet's physiological reactions in a realistically clinical style. Ezekiel is ordered to groan heavily; his loins weaken and refuse to support him; a bitter sensation seizes him in the stomach; out of breath, he pants; and his knees melt like water. Before the Song of

5. G. von Rad, *Der heilige Krieg im alten Israel* (Zürich: Zwingli Verlag, 1951); P.C. Craigie, 'Yahweh is a Man of War', *SJT* 22 (1967), pp. 185-86; F.M. Cross, 'The Divine Warrior in Israel's Early Cult', in A. Altmann (ed.), *Biblical Motifs* (Cambridge, MA: Harvard University Press, 1969), pp. 11-30; *idem*, *Canaanite Myth and Hebrew Epic* (Cambridge, MA: Harvard University Press, 1973), pp. 105-11, 226-29; P.D. Miller, *The Divine Warrior in Early Israel* (Cambridge, MA: Harvard University Press, 1973).

6. *ANET*, fig. 491 (pp. 168, 307).

the Sword is intoned, we witness a hint of the acrobatic leaps and changes of posture which have already raised the tension of the performer, strained his muscles, and intensified the acuity of all his senses.

That the first strophe should be viewed as initiating a prophetic act is confirmed by the dramatic handling of a dangerous weapon (cf. the specific features in the second and third strophes).

Second Strophe (vv. 17-18 [Eng. 12-13])
The Striking of the Sword

17 Scream and howl, son of man!
For it has indeed fallen upon my people;
The terrors of the sword's piercing force
Have fallen within my people;
Therefore, smite thy thigh!
18 For it is the ultimate test! What [is to happen],
If even the scepter that despises [me]
Is no more? Oracle of Yahweh.

The meaning of v. 18 is uncertain. What precedes v. 17, however, shows that the prophet no longer addresses the sword as a dance partner. He had done so in the first strophe (vv. 14-16), and he will do this again in the *envoi* (v. 21), but in the second strophe Yahweh himself once more apostrophizes the prophet in order to explain the significance of his symbolic act.

The third person feminine singular perfect *qal*, היתה, should be read הותה, from the verb הוה, 'to fall'.[7] The prophet Hosea had already spoken, in a context of judgment, of a personified sword that rages, consumes and devours like fire (11.6; cf. Gen. 49.27; Isa. 34.5).

Because the second strophe begins with a double admonition, 'Scream and howl, son of man!' (v. 17a), it prepares for the third strophe, where the prophet actually juggles with the sword as he dances. The blade falls upon him and strikes his thigh, thereby eliciting a shriek of pain at the impacting wound. The cutting of the prophet's flesh initiates a sympathetic rapport with the falling of the sword upon the people and especially upon the princes.

The personification of the sword as a living partner is further evidenced by the use of the word אל as a noun in the construct state, bringing the 'terrors' and the sword into a complex of power, the force of a paradivine, animistic reality. Juggling with the blade is a feature of the art of

7. The letters *waw* and *yôd* are practically identical in many MSS and thus interchangeable. Verbal suggestion of T.H. Gaster in a private conversation.

the sword dance. This interpretation may also help us to grasp the emotional intensity which is suggested in the third strophe.

Third Strophe (vv. 19-20 [Eng. 14-15])

The Juggling with the Blade

19 And thou, son of man, prophesy!
And clap thy hands!
Let the sword double over! Let it [fall] a third time!
It is the sword of the slain,
The sword of the Great One [who is] pierced,
The [sword] that encompasses them in the dark,
20 In order to melt their hearts
And to multiply their stumbling.
On all their gates I have set the point of the sword;
It is sharp! It turns into a flash of lightning
To be grasped for the slaughter.

The command for the prophet to clap his hands reinforces the interpretation of a juggling act. One cannot strike the hands together while holding a sword. The chanting of the song is punctuated by a dancing posture, and the hand-clapping necessitates a juggling interruption. As the sword is hurled high into the air, the performer strikes his palms together before he makes ready to catch the falling blade. The 'doubling over of the sword' does not yield an obvious meaning, although the 'trebling' implies that the gesture is twice repeated. The Targum has understood that the repetition 'sword, sword' in the first strophe (v. 9 [14]) refers to two distinct weapons. If this interpretation is correct, the strange verb ותכפל (v. 14 [19]), followed by the even more cryptic feminine form שלישתה, 'a third', might refer to two or three different blades used in the juggling act.

The verb כפל appears in the Priestly description of the Tabernacle, referring to the double curtains and the double breast-pieces (Exod. 26.9; 28.16; 39.9). Its cognate, כֶּפֶל, also describes the double jaw of the cosmic monster in Job (41.5), or it may designate a sort of superlative quality, as a 'double wisdom' (Job 11.6) or the double retribution of Jerusalem (Isa. 40.2).

When these features are viewed together, the preliminary impression gains validity. An act is being performed involving the throwing upward of two or even three swords, or at least the repeated juggling of a single weapon. Already in 1889, Oort had observed that the clapping of the hands should be likened to para-logical activity.[8] At a time when

8. H. Oort, 'Ezechiël XXI:18-19', *TT* 23 (1889), pp. 510-13.

exegetes appeared to be reluctant to take realistically the descriptions of symbolic gestures found in the prophetic literature, Oort was reminded of the story of King Joash striking the ground three times with arrows in answer to Elisha's prediction of a victory over Damascus (2 Kgs 13.18). It is generally admitted today that such gestures were believed to carry within themselves a hidden power capable of compelling the occurrence of the event which they portrayed.

With the balance of the third strophe (v. 20 [Eng. 15]), the climactic moment is approaching. The poet turns his attention, and most likely also the juggler centers the focus of his vision, and indeed his dancing posture and the articulation of his arms and hands, upon the very point of the blade. It is possible that the *hapax legomenon* אבחת־חרב, 'the torment of the sword' (cf. the Akkadian *'abahu*) supports this exegesis. Be that as it may, the sword will penetrate 'all the gates of the people'. We may here have a *double entendre*, since the word שער, 'gate', originally suggested a split orifice in the human body.

Instead of the monosyllabic word אח in v. 20, Symmachus, Theodotion and Jerome appear to have read the dissyllabic חדה, 'sharp', which recalls the beginning of the first strophe (v. 14), as does also the reference to the flash of lightning. The structure of the Song thus presents a double *inclusio poetica*. There is a subtle difference, however, between the opening motif and the closing one. Through the use of a consonantal alliteration, the poet abandons the word מרוטה, 'polished', and substitutes the word מעטה, 'grasped by the hand', a participle *pu'al* of the root עטה II (cf. Isa. 22.17), rather than the commonly used עטה, 'to conceal'.[9] It so happens that Near Eastern sword-jugglers were trained, until a few years ago, to seize blades by the cutting edges or even by the points, with which they 'played' in an elegant gesture of daring recklessness.

The final apostrophe to the sword brings out graphically the three-dimensional aspect of the performance. The words imply both the use of an actual sword and also the physical concreteness of a choreographic movement.

9. Some scholars derive this participle *pu'al* from עטה I, and they construe its meaning as the privative of 'to envelop', hence 'to uncover' or 'to unsheathe' (M. Dahood, *Proverbs and Northern Semitic Philology* [Rome: Pontifical Biblical Institute, 1963], p. 19). Such an act would be superfluous since the sword had been drawn from its scabbard all along (cf. 21.11).

Envoi (vv. 21-22 [Eng. 16-17])
21 [Sword!] Go either way to the right!
Set thyself to the left!
Wherever thy edge is facing!
22 And I, even I, will clap my palm against my palm,
[And] will wreak my fury!
I, myself, Yahweh, I have spoken.

Once more, the sword is addressed directly, as a living force. It will swat in all directions of the compass again. The blade is not continually held; to the contrary, it is rhythmically thrown up in the air, since the clapping of palm against palm would otherwise free the weapon to fall on the ground.

It may even be surmised that the alternation of clapping and juggling provokes an accelerating rhythm, more ample and more terrifying as the sword rises higher and higher, thus to descend upon the hands of the performer with a harder impact, and risking eventually hitting the shoulders and the thighs. The identification between the prophet and his God is brought out ever more forcefully as the dancer apparently sways or even turns around to catch the falling blade. It is Yahweh himself who dances the Dance of the Sword.[10]

II

This poem is usually called 'The Song of the Sword', not 'The Sword Dance', although many commentators recognize the dramatic realism of its oracular commands to act or to perform.[11] Some scholars note 'the

10. Primitive dance has often been associated with the dance of the god (G. van der Leeuw, *Sacred and Profane Beauty* [trans. D.E. Greene; New York: Holt, Rinehart & Winston, 1963], pp. 29, 265), but the dance of death has not apparently been viewed as the dance of the god (p. 44).

If the prophet performed a symbolic act, the blade he handled must be understood not in the figurative style but in the visible and cruel sense of 'the sword of Yahweh' (Lev. 26.33; Deut. 32.41; Job 40.19-20; Ps. 7.12; 17.13; Isa. 66.16; Ezek. 5.2, 12; 12.14; 32.10; Zeph. 2.12; also Gen. 3.24; Josh. 5.13-14; 1 Chron. 21.27, 30; cf. 2 Sam. 24.16).

The weapon of Ezek. 21.14-22 [Eng. 9-17] is nearly personified, but it scarcely corresponds to a 'hypostasization.' Some scholars hesitate between the interpretation of a prophetic act and that of a vision (Bodi, *Ezekiel*, p. 240 nn. 41-42).

11. Today, symbolic acts are taken realistically as gestures which the prophets performed as integral elements of the oracles they delivered. See D. Buzy, *Les symboles de l'Ancien Testament* (Paris: Gabalda, 1923); A. Regnier, 'Le réalisme dans

symbolic action' described in the preceding oracles (21.1-12 [Eng. 20.45–21.12]), but they still maintain that the pericope of vv. 14-22 [Eng. 9-17] is supposed not to command gestures but simply to narrate a vision.[12] It has also been suggested on the basis of an earlier oracle in which the Lord God orders, 'Clap your hands and stamp your foot' (6.11) that the prophet had borrowed a kind of *gigue* traditionally

les symboles des prophètes', *RB* 22 (1923), pp. 383-408; H. Wheeler Robinson, 'Prophetic Symbolism', in *Old Testament Essays* (London: n.p., 1927), pp. 1-17; A. Lods, 'Recherches récentes sur le prophétisme israélite', *RHR* 104 (1931), pp. 279-316; F. Häussermann, *Wortempfang und Symbol in der alttestamentlichen Prophetie: Eine Untersuchung zur Psychologie des prophetischen Erlebnisses* (BZAW, 58; Giessen: Töpelmann, 1932); A. van der Born, *De symbolische handelingen der oud-testamentische profeten* (Utrecht-Nijmegen: Dekker & Van de Vegt, 1935); S. Mowinckel, 'Ecstatic Experience and Rational Elaboration in Old Testament Prophecy', *AcOr* 13 (1935), pp. 264-91; E.C. Broome, 'Ezekiel's Abnormal Personality', *JBL* 65 (1946), pp. 277-92; G. Fohrer, 'Die Gattung der Berichte über symbolischen Handlungen der Propheten', *ZAW* 64 (1952), pp. 101-20; G. Fohrer and K. Galling, 'Das Schwertlied', in *Ezechiel* (HAT, 1.13; Tübingen: Mohr, 1955), pp. 120-22; H.H. Guthrie, 'Ezekiel 21', *ZAW* 74 (1962), pp. 268-81; W. Eichrodt, *Ezekiel: A Commentary* (trans. C. Quin; OTL; London: SCM Press, 1970), pp. 292-97; E.R. Fraser, 'Symbolic Acts of the Prophets', *Studia Biblica et Theologica* 4 (1974), pp. 45-53; G. Stroete, 'Ezekiel 24 15-27: The Meaning of a Symbolic Act', *Bijdragen* 38 (1977), pp. 163-73; Zimmerli, *Ezekiel 1*, pp. 28-33, 432-35; S. Amsler, 'Les prophètes et la communication par les actes', in R. Albertz, *et al.* (eds.), *Werden und Wirken des Alten Testaments: Festschrift für C. Westermann* (Göttingen: Vandenhoeck & Ruprecht; Neukirchen–Vluyn: Neukirchener Verlag, 1980), pp. 194-201; J.B. Blenkinsopp, *Ezekiel* (Interpretation; Louisville, KY: Westminster/John Knox Press, 1990), pp. 92-95.

12. K.F. Keil, *Biblical Commentary on the Prophecies of Ezekiel*, I (trans. J. Martin; Grand Rapids: Eerdmans, 1950 [1882]), pp. 293-95; D.H. Müller, 'Das Schwertlied', in *Die Propheten in ihrer ursprünglichen Form*, I (Vienna: A. Hölder, 1896), pp. 147-53; J. Skinner, *The Book of Ezekiel* (Expositor's Bible; New York: Armstrong, 1907), pp. 165-67; S.M. Margolies, 'Das "Schwertlied" Ezechiels', in *Scripta universitatis atque bibliothecae Hierosolymitanarum* (Jerusalem: Hebrew University, 1923), pp. 1-2; D.J. Hermann, *Ezechiel übersetzt und erklärt* (Leipzig and Erlangen: A. Deichert, 1924), p. 132; G.A. Cooke, *The Book of Ezekiel: A Critical and Exegetical Commentary on the book of Ezekiel* (Edinburgh: T. & T. Clark, 1936), pp. 229-31; J.B. Taylor, *Ezekiel: An Introduction and Commentary* (TOTC; Downers Grove: Inter-Varsity Press, 1969), p. 162; J. Wevers, *Ezekiel* (The Century Bible; London: Nelson, 1969), pp. 164-66 (is a dance implied?); K.W. Carley, *The Book of the Prophet Ezekiel* (Cambridge Bible Commentary; London and New York: Cambridge University Press, 1974), pp. 139-41; R.H. Hals, *Ezekiel* (FOTL, 19; Grand Rapids: Eerdmans, 1989), p. 150.

danced at weddings and on feast days, with hand-clapping and heel-tapping.[13] Such a dance was, however, to be twisted into a horrible parody of gaiety, perhaps fitting the ironic question, 'Or shall we make mirth?' (v. 15).

One critic even calls the poem of 6.11-13 'La danse de la mort', but he still entitles the pericope of 21.9-17 [Heb. 14-22] 'Le chant de glaive'. Yet, the same commentator observes, 'This barbarous poem is really composed in order to be danced'.[14]

There seems to be no documentary mention of sword dances in the ancient Near East.[15] Iconographic evidence reveals, however, that dancing and juggling with swords was not unknown.[16] A cylinder seal of the Old Babylon period shows two figures dancing with one leg raised and bent, while holding in their hands throw-sticks, which may have been used as clubs or clappers.[17] These figures affect the same posture as the *Mww* dancers.[18] There may also be Mesopotamian representations of dancers and jugglers playing with circular objects and surrounding a god with a mace.[19] Jugglers and a man who swallows a sword are seen on a Hittite relief from Alaca Hüyük.[20] According to Edith Porada[21] the

13. J. Steinmann, *Le Prophète Ezéchiel et les débuts de l'exil* (LD, 13; Paris: Cerf, 1953), p. 40.

14. Steinmann, *Ezéchiel*, p. 46.

15. Sword dances and dances of death, however, have been performed in many cultures. See K. Meschke, *Schwerttanz und Schwerttanzspiel im germanischen Kulturekreis* (Leipzig and Berlin: B.G. Teubner, 1931); R. Cirilli, *Les prêtres danseurs de Rome: étude sur la corporation sacerdotale des Saliens* (Paris: P. Geuthner, 1913); C. Sachs, 'Sword Dances', in *World History of the Dance* (trans. B. Schönberg; New York: W.W. Norton, 1963), pp. 115, 119-23.

16. M.-G. Wosien, *Sacred Dance: Encounter with the Gods* (London: Thames & Hudson, 1974), 'Panel of the chair of Sitamun, tomb of Juia and Thuin, Egypt, *ca.* 1400 B.C.' (Plate 25); 'Wall painting, tomb of Mehu, Saqqara, ca. 2500–2350 B.C.' (Plate 35).

17. E. Porada, *Mesopotamian Art in Cylinder Seals of the Pierpont Morgan Library* (New York: Pierpont Morgan Library, 1947), no. 52. See also publication no. 63 of the Musée Guimet in Paris.

18. H. Junker, 'Der Tanz der Mww', *Mitteilungen des deutschen Instituts für ägyptische Altertumskunde* 9 (1940), pp. 1-39.

19. M. Matuša, 'Quelques remarques sur la danse en Mésopotamie', *ArOr* 38 (1970), pp. 140-47.

20. A. Akurgal, *The Art of the Hittites* (New York: H.N. Abrams, 1962), Plate 93.

21. In a personal communication.

running gods from Yazilikaya are probably deities of the Netherworld, who dance while holding a curved weapon or sickle-shaped sword similar to a scimitar.[22]

Ancient Egyptian war dances include three Libyan soldiers who beat time with curved weapons while two others fight with daggers.[23] The dwarf god Bes is often represented with swords in his hands.[24]

Before World War II, sword dances were practiced by members of various Islamic sects, especially in Egypt and Lebanon.[25] A sword dancer not only engaged in choreographic figures, postures and acrobatic leaps but also sang an Arabic *mélopée*. Eventually he would drop his few garments and juggle naked with small daggers, and his body would soon be covered with self-inflicted wounds. At the climactic finale of the performance, he would switch to a single sword, which he then threw many times into the air, until he offered himself to its ultimate fall, in a symbolic emasculation, before he vanished in the darkness with a shriek.

Mimetic dances of death have been observed by travelers and cultural anthropologists.[26] The late medieval *danse macabre*, picturing social equality, from pope to beggar, with the partnership of 'Sir Death', had its origin in classical and oriental antiquity.

If we admit for a moment that Ezekiel danced with a sword, we may entertain the hypothesis that he simulated or even actually inflicted upon himself an act of mutilation. The prophets of Baal on Mount Carmel 'cried aloud and cut themselves after their custom with swords and lances, until the blood gushed out of them' (1 Kgs 18.28).[27]

The book of Jeremiah mentions the eight men from Shechem, Shiloh

22. Akurgal, *Art of the Hittites*, Plates 86, 87.

23. I. Lexona, *Ancient Egyptian Dances* (trans. K. Haltmar; Prague: Oriental Institute, 1935), Fig. 61 (pp. 30-35).

24. J.E. Quibell, *The Tomb of Yuaa and Thuiu* (Cairo: Institut français d'archéologie orientale, 1908), Plates XXXIX and XLI.

25. In the company of several anthropologists and medical psychologists, I observed such 'sword dances', also called 'dances of death' in a suburb of Cairo (May, 1934), as well as in Beirut and north of Aleppo. The claim that the performers were Shiite 'separatists' was later doubted.

26. L. Spence, in 'Dancing and Primitive Religion', states without reference that a pigmy who knew the dance of the god was presented to a pharaoh of the Fourth Dynasty (*Myth and Ritual in Dance, Game and Rhyme* [London: Watts, 1947], p. 99).

27. The priests of Baal danced (lit., 'skipped'), probably in a state of ecstatic frenzy, and they may have practiced self-mutilation.

and Samaria who came 'with their bodies gashed' (41.5). We may assume that Ezekiel, like them, and also like other sword dancers across the ages, to this day, survived his self-inflicted wounds through psychophysiological phenomena of hemato-vascular constriction.

Through numerous monographs on comparative religion, anthropology and cultural psychology, one has obtained a new awareness of the significance of gesture interacting with rhythmic speech, especially in the art of dancing song. With due caution, it may be appropriate to draw possible implications from Ezekiel's 'Dancing-Song of the Sword' on the prophetic theonomy of pathos.[28]

III

Kinesthetic activity permits exegetical hypotheses about meanings that are not explicitly supported by a verbal text.[29] The various elements of the oracle indicate that God himself sang, danced and juggled. The rhetorical, artistic and acrobatic act induces a form of identification between the Invisible Actor and his prophetic 'stand-in'. The words illuminate the gestures, which, in turn, prolong the resonance of the words.[30] The prophet becomes a quasi-incarnation of Yahweh. He juggles with the sword blade and lets it fall over his own body. The slaying of Israel means the self-immolation of Yahweh.

28. 'The theology of pathos is...a reaction to human history, an attitude called forth by man's conduct; a response, not a cause'; A. Heschel, *The Prophets* (New York: Harper & Row, 1962), I, p. 225; see II, pp. 1-11, 269-72.

29. Hypothetical interpretations are legitimate provided that cryptic features are placed within the Ezekielian context and, eventually, in the canonical corpus. The role of imagination is being rediscovered in 'postmodern' hermeneutics, but must be viewed with constrained discipline. Cf. W. Brueggemann, *Texts under Negotiation: The Bible and Post-Modern Imagination* (Minneapolis: Fortress Press, 1993), pp. 12-25.

30. 'Gesture is the means through which the movements of the dance complete themselves'; R.P. Blackmur, *Language as Gesture* (London: Allen & Unwin, 1954), p. 9. See M. Jousse, *Le style oral rythmique et mnémotechnique chez les verbomoteurs* (Paris: Gallimard, 1935); *idem*, in 'La manducation de la parole', *L'anthologie du geste*, II (Paris: Fondation Marcel Jousse, 1975), pp. 45, 48; L. Lévy-Brühl, *L'expérience mystique et les symboles chez les primitifs* (Paris: Gallimard, 1938); P. Watzlawick, J. Beavin and D. Jackson, *The Pragmatics of Human Communication: A Study of Interactional Patterns, Pathologies and Paradoxes* (New York: Norton, 1967); H.-G. Gadamer, *Truth and Method* (New York: Crossroad, 1982), pp. 235-74.

If the Deity and the prophet have entered into a rapport of mystical empathy through the emotional complex of intensity in the singing, dancing and juggling, the words reveal that not only that God is the judge and the executioner of his people but also that he participates in that people's agony. He wounds himself by exercising his justice. His slaughter hurts him in the core of his being.

In Hosea's sexual union with 'a woman who is beloved of a paramour and is an adulteress' (Hos. 3.1), Yahweh is unmistakably presented as a deceived and mocked husband. Likewise, and even more scandalously than in the eighth-century prophet, the God who is dramatically enacted by Ezekiel's dance of death takes upon himself the suffering and even the immolation of Israel.

The word 'theonomy' has been used as indicative of the theocentricity of the prophets' worldview. Israel cannot live apart from its divine Center. Humanistic autonomy is a manifestation of self-destructive heteronomy.[31] Prophetic theonomy, on the contrary, points to the peculiarity—indeed, the uniqueness—of the Hebrew faith, which radically altered the anthropocentric concerns of the ancient Semitic rituals. Perhaps Abraham Heschel should have included Ezekiel 21 in his study of the prophets. He might thereby have lent further support to the truth encapsulated in his well-known aphorism, also attributed to Karl Barth, 'The Bible is not man's theology, but God's anthropology.'[32]

The early Christians, facing the scandal of the crucifixion of Jesus, 'a just man', developed the theme of the Suffering God. This theme emerged not from foreign mythology but from the Hebraic theology of pathos. Like the themes of the Suffering Servant in Isaiah 53 or of the pierced figure in Zechariah 12, the Song of the Sword foreshadows kenotic theology (Phil. 2.7). The Dance of the Sword is, in effect, a mimetic portrait of the Deity. The oracle is couched in the first person singular (v. 22 [Heb. 17]): God himself is dancing and juggling with death.

The fury of God, as Zimmerli so well expressed it,[33] not only reveals divine righteousness but also brings life out of death. 'God is great

31. P. Tillich, *Systematic Theology* (Chicago: University of Chicago Press, 1951–1961), I, pp. 148-50; III pp. 249-68, 415.

32. A. Heschel, *Man is Not Alone* (New York: Jewish Publication Society of America, 1951), p. 129.

33. Zimmerli, *Ezekiel 1*, p. 435.

because His thought is action, because with Him to think is to create.'[34] Ezekiel, in his prophetic act, reaches the larger context of canonical theology—Old and New Testament—a biblical theonomy not of death but of life-proclamation 'to a generation yet to be born', when it will be said, 'you cannot...pierce with scimitar'.[35]

Prophetic theonomy—this intimate communion, this closeness, this mystical concourse of near-identity between divine and human—allows the interpretation of God's absence in history as a sign of his presence in judgment. He wounds himself as he destroys. 'He delivered his power into captivity' (Ps. 78.61). Divine servitude amplifies even divine magnitude.

34. G. Mazzini, quoted by Miguel de Unamuno, *Tragic Sense of Life* (trans. J.E. Crawford Flitch; New York: Dover, 1921), p. 153.

35. E. Dickinson, *The Complete Poems of Emily Dickinson* (ed. T.H. Johnson; Boston: Little, Brown, 1970), No. 384.

JONAH IN LUKE: THE HEBREW BIBLE BACKGROUND TO THE INTERPRETATION OF THE 'SIGN OF JONAH' PERICOPE IN LUKE 11.29-32

George M. Landes

My long-standing research interest in the book of Jonah has led me to give some attention to its New Testament appropriation, especially in the so-called 'sign of Jonah' texts in Mt. 12.38-42 and Lk. 11.29-32.[1] In the early 1970s, when Professor Sanders was still my colleague at Union Theological Seminary in New York, I recall discussing with him my interest in the 'sign of Jonah' text in Luke. Among other things, he suggested that in my investigation of this passage I not overlook the thesis of C.F. Evans[2] that Luke may have been influenced by the ordering of the book of Deuteronomy in his arrangement of the material he included in the Central Section of his Gospel (within which the 'sign of Jonah' pericope appears). After several unavoidable interruptions, I have now

1. Because of the very obvious connection between Jon. 2.1 and Mt. 12.40, I was drawn to study the Matthew pericope first. I published the results in 1983 in a *Festschrift* honoring David Noel Freedman. See G.M. Landes, 'Matthew 12:40 as an Interpretation of "The Sign of Jonah" Against its Biblical Background', in C.L. Meyers and M. O'Connor (eds.), *The Word of the Lord Shall Go Forth: Essays in Honor of David Noel Freedman in Celebration of his Sixtieth Birthday* (Winona Lake, IN: Eisenbrauns, 1983), pp. 665-84.

2. C.F. Evans, 'The Central Section of St. Luke's Gospel', in D.E. Nineham (ed.), *Studies in the Gospels: Essays in Memory of R.H. Lightfoot* (Oxford: Basil Blackwell, 1957), pp. 37-53. For Professor Sanders's early favorable reception of this thesis, see his study, 'The Ethic of Election in Luke's Great Banquet Parable', in J.L. Crenshaw and J.T. Willis (eds.), *Essays in Old Testament Ethics* (*J. Philip Hyatt, in Memoriam*) (New York: Ktav, 1974), pp. 247-71, esp. pp. 254-56, republished in revised form in C.A. Evans and J.A. Sanders (eds.), *Luke and Scripture: The Function of Sacred Tradition in Luke–Acts* (Minneapolis: Fortress Press, 1993), pp. 106-20, esp. pp. 108-10; also more extensively in his *Canon and Community: A Guide to Canonical Criticism* (Guides to Biblical Scholarship, OT Series; Philadelphia: Fortress Press, 1984), pp. 63-66.

been able to follow through this suggestion, and will be presenting my conclusions toward the end of this study, after first investigating other aspects of my interest in Lk. 11.29-32. The whole I am happy to dedicate to Professor Sanders as a part of this celebratory volume honoring his distinguished contributions to biblical scholarship.

I

Luke, like most of the other New Testament writers, did not hesitate either to quote from or allude to many passages from a rather wide variety of places in the Hebrew Bible. As might be expected, he was rather selective in the books from which he directly quoted,[3] but much more inclusive when it was just a matter of making allusions or drawing upon verbal parallels.[4] It is to the latter category that we must classify Luke's use of the book of Jonah, since he does not quote directly from it (as Matthew comes close to doing in 12.40). Altogether he mentions Jonah four times, all in ch. 11 (vv. 29, 30, and 32 [twice]),[5] though all may derive from but a single incident in the book. That, however, is a matter of debate, and I shall return to it below.

But while Luke does not make extensive use of Jonah, and focuses all his references in a single pericope, the interpretive problems it raises are immense. Solutions that have been proposed are sometimes quite divergent, and few elicit a wide consensus. The main purpose in this study is to see whether a fresh look at the background to Luke's 'sign of Jonah' pericope in the Hebrew Bible might not provide a helpful way of reassessing the plausibility of the more important solutions that have

3. On the basis of the Scripture index in the 26th edition of the Nestle–Aland text of the Greek New Testament (Stuttgart: United Bible Societies, third edn [corrected], 1983), he included direct citations from only seven books of the Hebrew Bible (Exodus, Leviticus, Deuteronomy, Psalms, Isaiah, Daniel and Malachi), with the heaviest concentrations from Exodus (5), Deuteronomy (6), Psalms (6), and Isaiah (5).

4. Again, using the scriptural index mentioned in the previous note, we learn that Luke made allusions to or cited verbal parallels from 27 different writings in the Hebrew Bible (counting the books of Samuel, Kings and Chronicles as one each), with the most coming from five: Genesis (27), Exodus (21), Kings (19), Psalms (37), and Isaiah (35).

5. Here the Scripture index in *The Greek New Testament* would appear to be misleading, since it records only two allusions to Jonah in Luke, viz., those in 11.32. It is puzzling why those equally obvious in vv. 29 and 30 have been overlooked.

been offered, even though other factors will doubtless also have to be brought into the picture.

The phrase 'the sign of Jonah', of course, is nowhere attested in the book of Jonah,[6] nor anywhere else in early Jewish literature. Its three occurrences in the New Testament are confined to the Synoptic Gospels of Matthew (12.39; 16.4) and Luke (11.29), with some effort to explain what it might mean only in Mt. 12.40 and Lk. 11.30. But while these verses formally correspond to each other in semantic structure, both being what Richard Edwards has designated 'eschatological correlatives',[7] in which something in relation to Jonah is compared with something in relation to the Son of Man, they also manifest striking differences in wording, especially in the analogue indicating the relationship between Jonah and the Son of Man. There seems no reason to doubt that Mt. 12.40a is quite clearly derived from Jon. 2.1 (Eng. 1.17). Nevertheless, Lk. 11.30 seems less obviously dependent upon this portion of Jonah, even though such a connection has been stoutly defended. What part of Jonah, then, did inspire Lk. 11.30: Jon. 2.1? Verses in Jonah 3? Or even Jonah 4? To this issue we now turn.

II

Lk. 11.30 on its own is not self-explanatory. One must therefore investigate extrinsic data in an effort to ascertain its meaning: how it relates to its basis in the book of Jonah; what light its narrower and larger context in Luke may cast upon it; and finally, what possible illumination may come from other New Testament writings, early Jewish and early Christian works, and possibly even from Greco-Roman traditions. My interest at this point is in the first of these: the portion of the Jonah story that seems to have inspired Lk. 11.30a.

A number of interpreters have thought that Lk. 11.30a must have had the same textual basis in Jonah as Mt. 12.40, viz., Jon. 2.1, even though

6. Nonetheless, there are still Bible readers who will seek for it in the text of Jonah. I recall a former faculty colleague at Union Seminary (not in the biblical field) who once commented that he had carefully read through the whole book of Jonah in search of 'the sign of Jonah', but had not been able to find it, though he felt somehow it ought to be there!

7. First in his article, 'The Eschatological Correlative as a Gattung in the New Testament', *ZNW* 60 (1969), pp. 9-20, then more extensively in his monograph, *The Sign of Jonah in the Theology of the Evangelists and Q* (SBT, 2.18; London: SCM Press, 1971), pp. 49-58.

Matthew and Luke appear to have different ways of expressing how this verse explains 'the sign of Jonah'. Luke says nothing about Jonah being in the belly of the sea monster for three days and three nights, but rather simply affirms that 'Jonah was a sign to the Ninevites'.[8] But how in the book of Jonah was the prophet a sign to the Ninevites? What does this mean?

For many the most obvious answer is that Jonah was a sign to the Ninevites as one miraculously delivered from almost certain death in the sea and/or the great fish.[9] This was the sign that authenticated Jonah to them as a genuine prophet for his God. Why else would the Ninevites—both instantaneously and unanimously (Jon. 3.5)—believe Jonah when he predicted their demise within forty days? It must be because they had some clear evidence that he had been divinely sent, viz. his rescue-from-death experience, which plausibly suggested a deity's action. Moreover, it is especially this experience that is mentioned when Jonah is alluded to in extra-biblical written sources extant at the time Luke was writing his Gospel (cf. the pseudepigraphical works *3 Macc*. 6.8 and *Liv. Proph*. 10.2; note also Josephus, *Ant*. 9.10.2 §213). Further, this understanding of Jonah's sign coheres well with a common usage of the word 'sign' in the New Testament as indicating some kind of wonder or miracle that serves to verify one's divine power and authority. In the context of Lk. 11.29-32, this is surely the meaning that must be understood when, according to Lk. 11.16, 'others, to test him [Jesus], kept demanding

8. Since there is a general scholarly consensus that both Matthew and Luke derived their tradition about 'the sign of Jonah' from the so-called 'sayings source', Q, it is puzzling that they differ so strikingly when giving their interpretation of the meaning of this expression. We do not have sufficient evidence to reach a firm conclusion about this, so that attempts to explain the difference in content between Mt. 12.40 and Lk. 11.30 must remain conjectural. On the general issue, see J.A. Fitzmyer, *The Gospel according to Luke X–XXIV: A New Translation with Introduction and Commentary* (AB, 28A; Garden City, NY: Doubleday, 1985), p. 931.

9. Some of those who support this view are J. Jeremias, ''Ιωνᾶς', *TDNT*, III, p. 409; I.H. Marshall, *The Gospel of Luke: A Commentary on the Greek Text* (NIGTC; Exeter: Paternoster Press, 1978), p. 485; E.H. Merrill, 'The Sign of Jonah', *JETS* 21 (1980), p. 29; and A. Vögtle, 'Der Spruch vom Jonaszeichen', in J. Schmid and A. Vögtle (eds.), *Synoptische Studien: Festschrift für Alfred Wikenhauser* (Munich: Karl Zink Verlag, 1953), p. 269. Though it is not often pointed out, the textual basis in the book of Jonah for the prophet's deliverance should not be limited to 2.1, but expanded to include the following psalm (where Jonah describes his rescue from drowning in the sea) and also v. 11 (where Jonah is expelled from the fish), hence the whole of Jon. 2.

from him a sign from heaven'. Finally, the comparison between the Son of Man and Jonah in Lk. 11.30b makes good sense if Jonah's sign to the Ninevites referred to his deliverance from death. For then the sign the Son of Man will be to this generation would indicate Jesus' corresponding triumph over death.[10] In short, the 'sign of Jonah' is the sign of resurrection.[11]

But there are some weighty arguments against construing Jon. 2.1 (or all of Jon. 2) as the portion of the book of Jonah that Luke (and Q)[12] had in mind. First, within the text of Jonah, where the prophet gives his only speech to the Ninevites, he drops not the slightest hint at what happened to him at sea or in the great fish.[13] When the Ninevites respond to Jonah's terse announcement threatening doom (Jon. 3.5), the reader is not guided by the text to think that the Ninevites' reaction is motivated by anything Jonah said about himself. Rather it is what he says about their future, not his past, that moves them to acts of contrition and change of conduct. True, this is not made explicit by the text, but in 3.6-9 the narrative at least offers the hint that the Ninevites'

10. Here Luke seems clearly to be equating the Son of Man with the risen Jesus.

11. So J. Swetnam, 'No Sign of Jonah', *Bib* 66 (1985), pp. 126, 129. To judge from the Jonah iconography in early Christian art, there is no doubt that in the post-apostolic church the regurgitation of Jonah from the fish was interpreted as a symbol of resurrection. See for example F. Gerke, *Die christlichen Sarkophage der vorkonstantinischen Zeit* (Berlin: de Gruyter, 1940), esp. p. 133, Pl. 1, nos. 1-3; Pl. 16, no. 3; O. Mitius, *Jonas auf den Denkmälern des christlichen Altertums* (Archäologische Studien zum christlichen Altertum und Mittelalter, 4; Tübingen: Mohr, 1897); L. Réau, *Iconographie de l'art chrétien* (Paris: Presses universitaires de France, 1956), II/1, pp. 412-13, 416-17; H. Schmidt, *Jona: Eine Untersuchung zur vergleichenden Religionsgeschichte* (Göttingen: Vandenhoeck & Ruprecht, 1907), pp. 144-55. But also note E. Stömmel, 'Zum Problem der frühchristlichen Jonasdarstellungen', *JAC* 1 (1958), pp. 112-15.

12. In this paper, it will be generally assumed that what is attributed to Luke in 11.29-32 probably had its original form in Q (unless there is some good reason for doubt), and I will not hereafter append the parenthetical '(and Q)'.

13. This of course is acknowledged by some of those who think that it is Jonah's restoration to life from the realm of death that best explains why the Ninevites took his prophecy so seriously. See, for example, Jeremias, ''Ιωνᾶς', *TDNT*, III, p. 409 n. 26; and Marshall, *The Gospel of Luke*, p. 485. But they discount the significance of this information gap by conjecturing that Jesus' contemporaries would not have understood the meaning of the word 'sign',when linked to Jonah, in any other way than as a reference to Jonah's miraculous deliverance. This ignores the multivalency of the word 'sign', and its implications, as we shall see below.

response is triggered by a sudden conviction—sparked by Jonah's prophecy—that their 'evil ways' will have dire consequences unless they rather quickly ('yet forty days') amend their lifestyle. It is thus their experience, not Jonah's, that seems better to explain why they act the way they do. Moreover, they are inclined to accept the veracity of Jonah's words because they detect a divine authority behind them ('the people of Nineveh believed God', 3.5), and because they realize that the pronouncement of their doom indicates a legitimate consequence to their sinful situation.

Secondly, if Luke had Jonah 2 in mind as the scriptural ground for understanding what the 'sign of Jonah' meant, it would indicate that for this expression, at least, he had limited the definition of 'sign' to some kind of prodigious act or event. But aside from the fact that Luke both understood and could use the word 'sign' to mean something other than a miraculous wonder (cf. 2.12, 34, and probably also 21.7), in 11.30 it seems very unlikely that he sees in the 'sign' something quite similar to what the people are after when they ply Jesus for a 'sign from heaven' (11.16). If that were the case, Jesus' initial response to the people's demand in v. 29 would not seem to make good sense, when he says, 'but no sign will be given to it', unless he means that no sign will be given of the same type and definition for which they are asking. So by adding the words 'except the sign of Jonah', Jesus is not conceding a partial acquiescence to the people's request, but giving a different definition to 'the sign of Jonah' from what 'this generation' wanted in a 'sign from heaven'.[14]

Thirdly, an insistence that Luke found the biblical basis for the understanding of 'the sign of Jonah' in the miraculous saving of Jonah from death, as described in Jonah 2, encounters a further difficulty. Because of the analogue with the Son of Man in 11.30b, the wondrous deliverance of Jonah would most likely be interpreted as a resurrection experience. Thus, the sign that Jonah and the Son of Man would represent to the Ninevites and 'this generation', respectively, would be a sign of

14. The words 'except the sign of Jonah' thus do not constitute a genuine exception to Jesus' categorical refusal to grant what the sign-seekers wanted, most starkly represented in Mark (8.12), where 'the sign of Jonah' is never mentioned. The reason for Mark's omission of the expression is uncertain, though it may have something to do with some unclarity about how the phrase was to be understood, particularly in relation to Jesus' unwillingness to perform signs in accordance with popular demand.

resurrection. But not only does Luke seem deliberate in never using the word 'sign' in his Gospel narrative to describe any of Jesus' miracles,[15] including his raising of the widow of Nain's son and Jairus's daughter from the dead (Lk. 7.11-17; 8.41-42, 49-56), he also does not apply it to Jesus' own resurrection.[16] In fact, at the end of Jesus' parable of the rich man and Lazarus (16.19-31), Luke has Jesus say that resurrection is not sufficient in and of itself to provoke faith and repentance (v. 31), the two ingredients most often deemed essential in the human response to Jesus' message and mission (cf. Lk. 5.20; 7.50; 8.50; 18.8, 42; and also 5.32; 13.1-5; 15.7). From Luke's perspective, then, it would have been most uncharacteristic of Jesus to have acceded to the people's wish for a 'sign from heaven' that would have authenticated beyond question his identity as one sent from God, when their response to his ministry up to that point was marked neither by belief in what his works manifested nor by a turning away from their sins.

For these reasons, then, it would seem propitious to look at places in the book of Jonah other than in the second chapter for the context that Luke may have had in mind when he described Jonah as 'a sign to the Ninevites'. There are two possibilities: Jonah 3 and Jonah 4. Since almost no one thinks Jonah 4 a suitable biblical source underlying Lk. 11.30a, I will not devote any consideration to it here, even though one can discern in certain features of this chapter content that might have been understood as defining a 'sign'. However, that neither Luke nor any of his subsequent interpreters ever betray a hint of such an understanding suggests that it is more appropriate to seek another setting in Jonah for the story element that inspired what Luke may have meant by Jonah as 'a sign to the Ninevites' in 11.30a.

15. The reason for this is not clear. In Acts Luke uses σημεῖον some 13 times, either by itself or in combination with τέρας and/or δύναμις to indicate miraculous acts very much like those performed by Jesus during his ministry. From this it would seem a proper inference that Luke could have employed σημεῖον to describe Jesus' miracles in his Gospel, but he does not. See K.H. Rengstorf, 'σημεῖον', *TDNT*, VII, p. 239.

16. It is doubtful that the Q community would have either, since Q contains no sayings of Jesus relating either to his passion or resurrection. For a synoptic presentation of Q, see J.S. Kloppenberg, *Q Parallels: Synopsis, Critical Notes, and Concordance* (Sonoma, CA: Polebridge Press, 1988). See also J. Bowman, 'Jonah and Jesus', *AbrN* 25 (1987), pp. 1-12, esp. 6-7.

III

But if this setting must be within Jonah 3, what in this chapter would move Luke to say that 'Jonah became a sign to the people of Nineveh', since none of this wording appears anywhere here? Let us begin by suggesting that what seems to have caught Luke's attention was the content of 3.4-8. There Jonah proclaims, 'Yet forty days and Nineveh shall be overthrown', followed by the people's belief in God and the king's edict implementing their response in acts of contrition and repentance. The perception would thus be that Jonah became a sign to the Ninevites, not through anything that he had previously experienced, however prodigious and impressive that was, but through what he said to them, through his proclamation of an imminent judgment, communicated with divine authority.[17] It is clearly to that proclamation and what they inferred from it that the Ninevites respond. This would seem to mean, then, as I have already had occasion to mention, that for Luke the 'sign of Jonah' was not some kind of miraculous prodigy, a 'sign from heaven', which Luke says some of the people (11.16) had sought from Jesus. To the demand for this kind of sign, Jesus' response was an unqualified rejection, as Mark (8.12) has most trenchantly expressed it. By retaining the words καὶ σημεῖον οὐ δοθήσεται αὐτῇ, both Matthew and Luke show essential agreement with Mark, even though they add the apparent exception, εἰ μὴ τὸ σημεῖον Ἰωνᾶ [τοῦ προφήτου], which is not really an exception at all, since what Jesus offers is not a sign in the way that the people wanted. For Luke the only sign Jesus will give to the 'sign-seekers' is one precisely not 'from heaven' (in the sense of some kind of supernatural phenomenon or event), but from earth, indeed from earthly history,[18] from ancient Nineveh. At the same time, this does not imply that God has no involvement in it, since,

17. While Jonah does not preface his brief message with the familiar oracular formula, 'Thus says Yahweh', readers would infer from Jon. 3.2 (וקרא אליה את־הקריאה אשר אנכי דבר אליך) that Jonah's words had their origin in God. Moreover, Jonah's use of the passive voice in the last word of his oracle (נהפכת) hints at the divine agency to be involved in the destruction of Nineveh.

18. So T.W. Manson, *The Sayings of Jesus as Recorded in the Gospels according to St. Matthew and St. Luke Arranged with Introduction and Commentary* (London: SCM Press Ltd, 1949), p. 89, followed by Fitzmyer, *The Gospel according to Luke X–XXIV*, p. 935.

as we have seen, Jonah's prophecy to the Ninevites was obviously thought to be God-inspired.

But now we must ask, if Luke does have Jon. 3.4-8 in mind when he records Jesus as saying, 'For just as Jonah became a sign to the people of Nineveh...', how from this scriptural locus did he understand Jonah to have been a sign to the Ninevites? A careful study of the text of Jonah 3 gives no clear indication that the narrator was intentionally portraying Jonah as such. Hence, what we appear to be dealing with here is Q and Luke's own unique interpretive approach to Jon. 3.4-8. Taking the text of Lk. 11.30a at its face value, it would seem to convey that Jonah himself, in his own person and presence, was a sign to the Ninevites, much as earlier Isaiah (together with his sons) and Ezekiel were said to be signs to the Israelites (cf. Isa. 8.18; 20.3; Ezek. 12.6, 11; 24.24, 27).[19] But the parallelism with Isaiah and Ezekiel is only partial at best. While in Isa. 8.18 one can see how the witness of Isaiah and his sons represented God's word among the people,[20] their sign-character would also be defined by their actions, and possibly even their names, which testified to God's power in history.[21] In 20.3 it is substantially the symbolic action of Isaiah, walking 'naked and barefoot', that makes him 'a sign and a portent against Egypt and Ethiopia'. Similarly Ezekiel, in digging through the wall and taking his baggage through it (12.3-6, 11), and in acquiescing to the divine command not to engage in mourning rites for his deceased wife (24.16-27), manifests himself as a sign for the house of Israel. But when Q and Luke (or even Jesus, for that matter) read about Jonah's confrontation with the Ninevites, it is not likely that they thought it was his name or any kind of unusual action, other than the delivery of his laconic message, that qualified him for the designation 'a sign to the Ninevites'. Jonah was a sign, not because of anything about his person, demeanor, or appearance, or because of some type of symbolic deed that he performed, or even because, as we noted earlier, he

19. See the discussion of R.B.Y. Scott, 'The Sign of Jonah', *Int* 19 (1965), pp. 18-19. The Hebrew text of the Isaiah passages employs the compound expression אות ומופת (in the plural in 8.18), whereas it is only מופת that is used in the Ezekiel texts (the plural form in 12.11). The LXX is virtually consistent in rendering Hebrew אות by σημεῖον, מופת by τέρας, though in these texts their meaning is practically synonymous (so in the Ezekiel passages the NRSV regularly renders מופת by 'sign[s]').

20. So Scott, 'The Sign of Jonah', p. 18.

21. O. Kaiser, *Isaiah 1–12: A Commentary* (OTL; Philadelphia: Westminster Press, 2nd edn, 1983), pp. 197-98.

had experienced an extraordinary divine deliverance, but simply because of what he said (and possibly the conviction with which he said it).

According to this interpretation, then, the 'sign' which Jonah became to the Ninevites was that of a prophet proclaiming a threatened judgment of destruction, together with a subtle hint that it could be allayed only if the people of Nineveh repented of their 'evil ways' (cf. Jon. 3.10). The hint is suggested in two usages: first, through the temporal phrase 'yet forty days', the number 40 often being employed in the Hebrew Bible to indicate a time of trial and testing, but perhaps more particularly here in Jonah to specify the interval which the Ninevites were being granted, not simply to agonize over their impending doom, but to decide whether or not they wanted to do something that might prevent it; and secondly, through the use of the double-sided verb, נהפכת, which from Jonah's perspective doubtless refers only to the 'transformation' of Nineveh into a ruin,[22] but from the divine perspective may suggest the possibility of the Ninevites' own 'transformation', should they decide to turn away from their sinful deeds.[23] Thus, the import of Jon. 3.4, which I would suggest was most likely perceived by Luke, was twofold: on the one hand, the surface meaning of a prophetic judgment oracle, involving Nineveh's threatened destruction, but on the other, the deeper meaning suggesting to the hearers of the oracle that their repentant response might halt the execution of that judgment. If this understanding is in the right direction, then what Luke has Jesus telling the 'sign-seekers' is that the only sign they will be given is one like the prophet Jonah once manifested to the ancient Ninevites through his proclamation of a sure promise of judgment unless they rather quickly and radically changed their lifestyle.

There is, of course, nothing new about this interpretation that for Luke the 'sign of Jonah' consisted of the content of Jonah's preaching

22. As often noted, it is the root הפך which is regularly used when allusion is being made to the classic destruction of Sodom and Gomorrah (cf. Gen. 19.25, 29; Deut. 29.23; Isa. 13.19; Jer. 20.16; 49.18, 50.40; Amos 4.11; Lam. 4.6), and this may have been what the Jonah narrator wanted the readers to impute to Jonah's mind when he delivered his prophecy against Nineveh.

23. Cf. E.M. Good, *Irony in the Old Testament* (Philadelphia: Westminster Press, 1965), pp. 48-49. While in his commentary on the book of Jonah, Leslie Allen thinks reading a *double entendre* in נהפכת is 'oversubtle' (see *The Books of Joel, Obadiah, Jonah and Micah* [NICOT; Grand Rapids: Eerdmans, 1976], p. 222 n. 14), this opinion may be unjustified given the way God responds to the Ninevites' contrition (Jon. 3.10).

to the Ninevites and its implications. Many scholars support this understanding, in one form or another.[24] But because a significant number have also rejected it, we need to pause and examine how valid their chief reasons are for this rejection.

The first has to do with the definition of the word 'sign', and with what it conveys, especially in the context of Lk. 11.30. It is argued that here it must refer to some kind of miraculous deed, which for Jonah must be his extraordinary deliverance from the fish and/or the sea.[25] Nothing else, it is thought, would authenticate Jonah as a genuine prophet in whom the power of God was at work. Jonah's preaching alone was not self-authenticating. Moreover, the Ninevites would not respond to a mere sign of warning, but only to a sign of verification that would serve to convince them that Jonah was indeed a divine messenger. For this, only his rescue from the fish and the sea qualified.[26]

But as we have already observed above, there are good reasons for concluding that Luke did not necessarily find in Jonah 2 the biblical grounding for 'the sign of Jonah'. Moreover, nowhere in Jonah 3 are the Ninevites portrayed as either needing or receiving a particular kind of divine authentication for Jonah—other than his proclaimed prophetic message—in order for them to initiate their rituals of contrition and change of conduct. Since the text makes good sense without such an imposition from Jonah 2, it is not requisite to think that Luke presupposed

24. For a representative sampling of scholars who favor it, see Manson, *The Sayings of Jesus*, p. 89; W.G. Kümmel, *Promise and Fulfilment: The Eschatological Message of Jesus* (trans. D. Barton; Naperville, IL: Alec R. Allenson, 1957), p. 68; O. Glombitza, 'Das Zeichen des Jona (Zum Verständnis von Matth. XII.38-42)', *NTS* 8 (1961–62), p. 365; H.E. Tödt, *The Son of Man in the Synoptic Tradition* (London: SCM Press, 1965), p. 53; Edwards, *The Sign of Jonah*, p. 95; C.H. Talbert, *Reading Luke: A Literary and Theological Commentary on the Third Gospel* (New York: Crossroad, 1982), p. 138; Fitzmyer, *The Gospel according to Luke X–XXIV*, p. 933; M.D. Goulder, *Luke: A New Paradigm* (JSNTSup, 20; Sheffield: JSOT Press, 1989), II, p. 512.

25. Actually, the real miraculous event in Jon. 3 is not what Jonah experienced, but what the Ninevites did in response to Jonah's prophecy: their universal conversion. To the Israelite hearers/readers of Jonah's story, such an event was totally unparalleled in the history of Israel's response to the warnings of its prophets, to say nothing of foreign nations. The comprehensiveness of the Ninevites' actions was not simply unexpected, it was an unprecedented miracle!

26. For the points in this line of reasoning, see Vögtle, 'Der Spruch vom Jonaszeichen', p. 264; Jeremias, *TDNT*, III, p. 409; Marshall, *The Gospel of Luke*, p. 485; Swetnam, 'No Sign of Jonah', pp. 126-27.

it. Further, while the Greek word σημεῖον, like its Hebrew analogue אות, often does refer to divine marvels, it is not restricted to such a definition. According to the Arndt–Gingrich Greek lexicon, the first meaning given to σημεῖον is 'the sign or distinguishing mark by which something is known, token, indication' (cf. Lk. 2.12), under which is included 'a sign of things to come' (cf. Lk. 21.7), and 'a sign of warning' (cf. Lk. 2.34).[27] As 'a sign of warning', Arndt and Gingrich cite the meaning of σημεῖον in Lk. 11.29-30. Since it is a well recognized feature of prophetic oracles of judgment to function as signs of warning to the people, it is not surprising that Luke could understand Jonah's judgment oracle (Jon. 3.4) as a warning-σημεῖον, one which not only apprised the Ninevites of the seriousness of this prophet's announcement of judgment, but also motivated them to believe in God (Jon. 3.5). So while it is true that nowhere outside of Lk. 11.30 and 32 are σημεῖον and κήρυγμα ever correlated,[28] when prophets function as signs, the latter may be defined not simply by what the prophets do but also by what they say.[29] To argue that Lk. 11.30a, then, could not have understood Jon. 3.4 as depicting the prophet as a sign to the Ninevites epitomized in his proclamation of judgment seems unjustified.

A second—and possibly more serious—objection to the identification of the 'sign of Jonah' with his preaching arises because of the comparison drawn with the Son of Man in Lk. 11.30b. If the unspoken *tertium comparationis* is the message of Jonah/the Son of Man (= Jesus), then the verb one expects in Lk. 11.30b should be a *present* tense form (ἔστιν), not a future (ἔσται), since Jesus as the Son of Man was *already* a sign of judgment and repentance through what he proclaimed to 'this generation' (i.e., those unwilling to change and accept Jesus' 'good news').[30]

There are several matters to consider here. First, in 11.30b is Luke employing ἔσται rather than ἔστιν to convey that 'this generation' will not acknowledge or respond to Jesus' proclamation of judgment-repentance until sometime in the future, even though this proclamation is given

27. BAGD, p. 755a.

28. Aside from their parallels in Mt. 12.40, 41. There is not, of course, unanimous agreement among scholars that they actually *are* in correlation here, and I shall look at this more closely in the discussion below.

29. Cf. my comments above on Isaiah and Ezekiel.

30. See Vögtle, 'Der Spruch vom Jonaszeichen', p. 264, and Swetnam, 'No Sign of Jonah', p. 127.

in and is relevant to the present? But in Luke's perspective (or that of any of the Gospel writers, for that matter), it would appear that a time never came, whether in Jesus' lifetime or after his death and resurrection, when 'this generation' acknowledged Jesus' message as a 'sign' that they must repent to escape judgment. Moreover, the understanding of the meaning or significance of a 'sign' is not dependent upon its being acknowledged or accepted. Thus Lk. 11.30b does not appear to be implying that although Jesus is not now recognized as the 'sign' (through his preaching) that 'this generation' is in danger of judgment if it does not repent, this *will* happen in the future.

Secondly, there is the grammatical issue of *the kind of* future meaning to which ἔσται points. There are two possibilities. The first is that ἔσται may be construed simply as a logical future on the same level as δοθήσεται in 11.29.[31] This happens when two logically connected events or actions are mentioned, the second occurring subsequent to the first, so that it is marked by a future tense verb. Jesus says that when 'this generation' asks (in the present) for a sign, no sign *will be given* it, that is, following the request, though not necessarily at some distant point in the future. Similarly, in 11.30 we have reference to two analogous events, the first earlier than the second, making the latter in the future of the former. But while the distance between Jonah becoming a sign to the people of Nineveh and the Son of Man becoming a sign to 'this generation' is much greater than that between the demand for a sign and Jesus' response to it (v. 29), in both cases the second event need not be placed at some remote time-point in relation to the one who speaks about it. If one agrees with this interpretation, then the meaning would be that Jesus as the Son of Man will be a sign to 'this generation' as Jonah once was to the people of Nineveh, that is, a preacher for repentance and faith. What he has been, he will continue to be throughout the remainder of his ministry. No sign such as the people want will be granted; the sign that Jesus was is in continuity with the sign that he will keep on manifesting. The difficulty with this interpretation is that it

31. Marshall, *The Gospel of Luke*, p. 485. Note also the comments of Fitzmyer, *The Gospel according to Luke X–XXIV*, pp. 933, 936 (in relation to Lk. 11.30). What he says here, however, seems to be in tension with his classifying 11.30b as a Son of Man saying having only a future sense of Jesus' coming in glory and judgment. See the first volume of Fitzmyer's commentary on Luke, *The Gospel according to Luke I–IX: A New Translation with Introduction and Commentary* (AB, 28; Garden City, NY: Doubleday, 1981), p. 211. On this issue, see further below.

radically distinguishes Lk. 11.30 from the three other Son of Man sayings that are very clearly 'eschatological correlatives' (all of them in Lk. 17, vv. 24, 26, 28-30, and all featuring ἔσται) referring to the revelation of the Son of Man at some future time. While it is possible that 11.30 *could* have a different nuance from the similarly formed sayings in Luke 17—certainly 11.30 has a somewhat different context from the sayings in ch. 17—its distinctiveness from the other Son of Man sayings which do relate to Jesus' earthly ministry suggests caution in assigning primarily a logical future meaning to ἔσται here.

This brings us to the second possibility with regard to the type of future meaning ἔσται might have, that is, referring to a so-called real future, one pointing to an event occurring after Jesus' death, possibly his parousia, or even God's final judgment. This is the usual scholarly understanding of ἔσται in 11.30,[32] and it fits well with the future direction indicated in the following verses, 31-32 (and their parallel in Mt. 12.41-42).[33] In these verses the future context would seem to be that of the final judgment, so that if this same setting was thought to prevail in 11.30b, it would suggest the meaning that the Son of Man will be a sign to 'this generation' at the time of the final judgment.

But if this interpretation is adopted, it is not without certain difficulties. First, the comparison with Jonah is less exact than would be the case with Mt. 12.40, for clearly in Jonah 3 the prophet's preaching was not a future sign in any eschatological sense, but a present indication that an imminent judgment is being threatened. Jonah, through his word of judgment, was a sign to the Ninevites *at that very moment*. In the analogical Son of Man logion, however, the more distant future of the sign seems intimated. The Son of Man is apparently not now a sign to the present generation, but will be in the future, at the time of the eschaton. Yet at the final judgment, will the Son of Man do more than proclaim judgment on the present generation? Will there also be a respite for repentance? Apparently not, in light of Lk. 11.31-32 (//Mt. 12.41-42; cf. also Mt. 25.31-46), where only condemnation is mentioned. Thus, we would appear to have here a second difference within the analogy between Jonah as 'a sign to the people of Nineveh' and the Son of Man as a future sign 'to this generation'. Whereas Jonah's proclama-

32. Marshall, *The Gospel of Luke*, p. 484.

33. Assuming, of course, that these verses were intended to be read in conjunction with 11.30 (Mt. 12.40 respectively), if not at an early stage of the tradition, then clearly in its final form. I shall return to this matter below.

tion to the Ninevites clearly did allow time for repentance, the Son of Man's pronouncement to 'this generation' at the final judgment will not.

Nonetheless, it would seem that the reason Luke has Jesus announce the meaning of the 'sign of Jonah' now is precisely to indicate that the time for repentance is at hand: 'this generation' can repent immediately and receive salvation (as once the ancient Ninevites did). On the other hand, at the final judgment, when they will again be confronted by the Son of Man, the time for repentance will have passed—forever. Hence the function of the 'sign of Jonah' sayings in Luke would seem to be the same as in Matthew: to warn the contemporaries of Jesus who have rejected his message of the decisiveness of their *present* response to the Son of Man's proclamation of judgment and call for repentance. If they fail to respond but wait until they see and hear the sign again at the final judgment, it will be too late.

A third objection to correlating the 'sign of Jonah' with Jonah's preaching is predicated on how the verses immediately following Lk. 11.30 are to be understood. That is, if, as a number of scholars contend, the original function of the content of vv. 31-32 was for a different setting, where illuminating the meaning of the phrase 'the sign of Jonah' was not at issue, does the present collocation of these verses after v. 30 suggest that for Luke they cannot function to help interpret v. 30? Of course, the way vv. 31-32 became linked to vv. 29-30 (or to 27-30, if Catchpole is correct in seeing a close connection between vv. 27-28 and 29-32[34]) is a vexed traditio-historical question, though in general there seems to be a scholarly consensus that vv. 31-32 did not originally function in Q as sayings illustrating the meaning of the 'sign of Jonah' in vv. 29-30, but rather served a polemical function to shame the Jews for their refusal to believe in Jesus' message or his powerful deeds (thus belonging to the same category as Lk. 10.13-15).[35] However, because the 'sign-seekers' were associated with those lacking faith in Jesus' words and acts, it is easy to see how traditions about the demand for a sign, and the introduction and explanation of 'the sign of Jonah' (Lk. 11.29-30), could become linked with minatory sayings (11.31-32) condemning unrepentant Israel by contrasting the latter with more appro-

34. See D.R. Catchpole, 'The Law and the Prophets in Q', in G.F. Hawthorne and O. Betz (eds.), *Tradition and Interpretation in the New Testament: Festschrift for Earle E. Ellis* (Grand Rapids: Eerdmans, 1987), p. 100.

35. Cf. R. Bultmann, *The History of the Synoptic Tradition* (trans. J. Marsh; Oxford: Basil Blackwell, 1968), pp. 112-13.

priately responsive Gentiles.[36] In any case, at least in Luke's final redaction, if not earlier, a perceived meaningful point of contact could be thought to exist between v. 30 and vv. 31-32, which, given the biblical background I think most likely for v. 30a, seems best provided by what Jonah has to say, his proclamation of judgment to the Gentile Ninevites, and their positive response to it. Hence, an alternative Q understanding of the substance of vv. 31-32 in a different context does not necessarily preclude Luke from adapting this material in his own context to support an understanding of the 'sign of Jonah' as alluding to the prophet's preaching.

But even at the level of Luke's final redaction, questions have been raised as to whether vv. 31-32 served to reinforce the identification of 'the sign of Jonah' with Jonah's preaching. The problem is not just with v. 31, which seemingly has nothing to do with Jonah at all, but also with v. 32: although it highlights the repentant response of the Ninevites to 'the proclamation of Jonah', this κήρυγμα 'Ιωνᾶ is said to be in parallelism with τὴν σοφίαν Σολομῶνος in v. 31, not with σημεῖον 'Ιωνᾶ or simply σημεῖον in vv. 29 and 30, respectively.[37] But are we limited to only one parallelism here, or are there not two? Certainly Luke, by reversing the Matthean order of vv. 31-32, highlights a wisdom component in Jonah's/Jesus' preaching,[38] and indeed it would appear that that preaching, characterized by wisdom, is what constitutes the 'something' greater than Solomon and Jonah, not simply Jesus himself.[39] But in each

36. Edwards (*The Sign of Jonah*, pp. 83-87) has argued for a different and somewhat more complex scenario, according to which Q combined two units of tradition: Jesus' refusal to grant a 'sign' (as represented in Markan tradition, i.e., without the phrase 'except the sign of Jonah') and the double saying about the queen of the south and the judgment and repentance of the people of Nineveh. On the basis of the latter, Q invented the phrase 'the sign of Jonah' (as in Lk. 11.29), and then proceeded to add an explanation for it (as in Lk. 11.30). In reaction to this, I am inclined to agree with Marshall's criticism that 'Edwards fails to justify his assumptions…' (Marshall, *The Gospel of Luke*, p. 483). Moreover, if Q was Luke's source for the content of vv. 29-32, as is generally agreed, it is possible that their alignment in Q was much as we now find them in Luke (but see section IV below for another argument).

37. Cf. Vögtle, 'Der Spruch vom Jonaszeichen', p. 235; V. Mora, *Le signe de Jonas* (Paris: Cerf, 1983), pp. 64, 68-69.

38. Fitzmyer, *The Gospel according to Luke X–XXIV*, p. 933.

39. Taking seriously the neuter gender of πλεῖον in vv. 31-32, referring to a thing rather than a person. A surprising number of scholars either discount or ignore this (cf. Bultmann, *The History of the Synoptic Tradition*, p. 129; Glombitza, 'Das

of the verses, 29-32, there is reference to a spoken communication, three times in the form of a genitive phrase composed of a noun followed by a personal name: 'the sign of Jonah' (v. 29); 'the wisdom of Solomon' (v. 31); and 'the proclamation of Jonah' (v. 32). The parallelism of the latter two is obvious, based on their shared formal structural features, but a linkage of these with 'the sign of Jonah' in v. 29 (and 'the sign' in v. 30, which purports to allude to what 'the sign of Jonah' is) should not easily be dismissed, even though the overall structural shaping of vv. 31-32 is not matched in vv. 29-30. What is matched is a common grammatical phrase that refers to something being spoken, whether by Jonah (vv. 30, 32) or Solomon (v. 31).[40] Moreover, *what* Jonah says is labeled in v. 32 as κήρυγμα, the same word employed in the LXX of Jon. 3.2 (translating the Hebrew קריאה) to refer to what God is going to tell Jonah to proclaim to the Ninevites, which he carries out in 3.4, the verse I believe underlies Lk. 11.30a. Finally, v. 32 has three catchwords in common with v. 30: the Ninevites, 'this generation', and Jonah.[41] So whether on the basis of similar grammatical expressions indicating the same kind of meaning, or shared vocabulary, vv. 31-32 manifest clear ties with vv. 29-30, leading to the conclusion that they were placed in this context further to explicate the meaning of 'the sign of Jonah' in these verses.[42]

But if the structure, vocabulary and meaning of vv. 31-32 do not necessarily preclude them from reflecting an understanding of 'the sign of Jonah' as referring to Jonah's preaching to the Ninevites, what about their order? I have mentioned above that the Matthean order of the

Zeichen des Jona', pp. 363, 365; Mora, *Le signe de Jonas*, pp. 65, 69; Vögtle, *Der Spruch vom Jonaszeichen*, p. 234). Among scholars who acknowledge the significance of the neuter usage of πλεῖον, there is some disagreement as to what the 'something' refers to: aside from proclamation of judgment and/or wisdom (Catchpole, 'The Law and the Prophets in Q', pp. 100-101; Marshall, *The Gospel of Luke*, pp. 486-87; Tödt, *The Son of Man in the Synoptic Tradition*, p. 53), the suggestions range from 'the Kingdom of God' (Manson, *The Sayings of Jesus*, p. 92), to 'the presence of the Holy Spirit in the ministry of Jesus' (Talbert, *Reading Luke*, pp. 138-39; A.Y. Collins, 'The Son of Man Sayings in the Sayings Source', in M.P. Horgan and P.J. Kobelski [eds.], *To Touch the Text: Biblical and Related Studies in Honor of Joseph A. Fitzmyer* [New York: Crossroad, 1989], p. 378).

40. Assuming, of course, that my analysis of the meaning of 'the sign of Jonah', argued above, is in the right direction.

41. Vögtle, 'Der Spruch vom Jonaszeichen', p. 249.

42. This is also Mora's conclusion (*Le signe de Jonas*, p. 60), but with a different understanding of what 'the sign of Jonah' meant. See above, n. 37.

'people of Nineveh' saying and 'queen of the south' saying are reversed in Luke, and so some[43] suggest that for Luke, at least, vv. 31-32 do not indicate that 'the sign of Jonah' refers to Jonah's preaching. By his rearrangement, Luke breaks up the close Matthean association between the saying about the people of Nineveh repenting at the preaching of Jonah (Mt. 12.41 // Lk. 11.32) and the explanation of 'the sign of Jonah' in the preceding verse (Mt. 12.40 // Lk. 11.30). But does this mean that Luke saw no connection between v. 32 and vv. 29-30? It does not necessarily follow, as I have tried to show above in pointing out certain grammatical, linguistic and semantic commonalities between v. 32 and vv. 29-30. Hence, Luke's reordering of vv. 31-32 is not a solid clue for concluding that he discerned no connection between 'the sign of Jonah' and Jonah's preaching. But why did Luke tamper with the Matthean order here?[44] It is my contention that investigation of this casts some interesting light on Luke's redaction of the 'sign of Jonah' pericope, and to that issue I now turn.

IV

Investigators have long been concerned about how to explain the different ordering in the Matthean and Lukan renderings of the concluding verses (Mt. 12.41-42 // Lk. 11.31-32) of 'the sign of Jonah' pericope. While there are minor textual differences between these versions, most of which can be satisfactorily accounted for by traditio-historical and stylistic considerations,[45] when one compares the two Gospels at this point it is the inversion of these verses that has attracted most attention.

Probably the majority of scholars would now designate the Lukan ordering as the most primitive and closest to Q, assigning the reversal to Matthew. Matthew's arrangement, however, appears to be the most natural one for explaining 'the sign of Jonah', because it brings into juxtaposition all the material drawn from the book of Jonah (Mt. 12.40-

43. For instance Vögtle, 'Der Spruch vom Jonaszeichen', p. 235.

44. Of course the 'tampering', if such it was, may have been Matthew's work, not Luke's, though the matter is not easily resolved. After making a case for Matthew's order as being more original, Fitzmeyer judiciously concludes: 'In the final analysis, however, we cannot say for certain who inverted the order of "Q" in these sayings' (Fitzmyer, *The Gospel according to Luke X–XXIV*, p. 932).

45. See, for example, J. Jeremias, *Die Sprache des Lukasevangelium: Redaktion und Tradition im Nicht-Markusstoff des dritten Evangeliums* (Göttingen: Vandenhoeck & Ruprecht, 1980), p. 204.

41).[46] Though assurance is not possible, I think it is more likely Luke than Matthew who has manipulated the reordering of the traditions here. His reasons for doing so can only be conjectured, but there are several plausible possibilities. First, the Lukan arrangement preserves an ordering that is both biblically (and historically) correct. In the Hebrew canon the Queen of Sheba's visit to Solomon is recounted in 1 Kings 10, prior to the rendition of Jonah's story in the prophetic corpus. If that visit does have a historical nucleus to it, as is widely accepted, it would have taken place several centuries before the historical Jonah lived. But did Luke favor this ordering principally on the basis of a scriptural or historical understanding? He may have decided that to end the pericope with the 'queen of the south' logion (as does Matthew) was not as strong or as effective a way to conclude the unit as with the saying about 'the people of Nineveh'. Luke may also have observed that since the unit began with an allusion to Jonah (v. 29), it was only appropriate that it climax with 'something greater than Jonah', the preaching of Jesus as the Son of Man (v. 32). While none of these suggestive explanations can be eliminated, I would like to add yet another one to the mix.

In his provocative 1957 study,[47] C.F. Evans presented the intriguing hypothesis that in shaping the Central Section of his Gospel (9.51–18.14, according to Evans), Luke was guided by the book of Deuteronomy for

46. Cf. Fitzmyer, *The Gospel according to Luke X–XXIV*, p. 932; Catchpole, 'The Law and the Prophets in Q', p. 99; Marshall, *The Gospel of Luke*, p. 482. D. Correns ('Jona und Solomon', in W. Haubeck and M. Bachman [eds.], *Wort in der Zeit. Festschrift für K.H. Rengstorf* [Leiden: Brill, 1980], pp. 68-94) points out that in connection with the fast liturgy referred to in the Mishnah (*m. Ta'an*. 2.4), we have another textual instance (outside of Mt. 12.41) where the immediate juxtaposition of Jonah, then Solomon, occurs (actually it is not simply Solomon who is mentioned, but David and his son Solomon), and because this liturgy is based on very old tradition, it may go back even as far as Jesus' time. But there is no certainty about this, and that the ordering of the sayings in Mt. 12.41-42 was somehow dependent upon this tradition seems rather unlikely. In supporting the Matthean order, Goulder (*Luke: A New Paradigm*, II, p. 512) gives an interpretation of Luke's modus operandi in vv. 31-32 that in my view is inappropriately subjective. I would also deem somewhat frivolous a couple of the scholarly conjectures H. Green mentions in his study, 'Matthew 12.22-50 and Parallels: An Alternative to Matthean Conflation', in C.M. Tuckett (ed.), *Synoptic Studies* (JSNTSup, 7; Sheffield: JSOT Press, 1984), pp. 157-76, esp. p. 166: that Luke inverted the Matthean order simply to create a variation for its own sake, or to avoid the offense of plagiarism (surely a more modern than ancient concern).

47. 'The Central Section of St. Luke's Gospel'.

both his choice and arrangement of tradition content. While Evans's theory is not without its flaws,[48] there seems to be enough validity to his basic thesis to accord it at least a tentative acceptance.[49] If we do, it is

48. The most thoroughgoing critique of it that has come to my attention is the study by C.L. Blomberg, 'Midrash, Chiasmus, and the Outline of Luke's Central Section', in R.T. France and D. Wenham (eds.), *Gospel Perspectives: Studies in Midrash and Historiography* (Sheffield: JSOT Press, 1983), pp. 217-61. His basic criticism is that most of the verbal parallels Evans offers are too vague to establish a convincing demonstration that Luke did use Deut. 1–26 as the model for 9.51–18.14. He concedes only that the Lukan parables in 14.15–16.13 may have been dependent on Deuteronomy for their themes (p. 228). So while the general absence of genuine parallels to Deuteronomy does not necessarily discredit Evans's theory per se (p. 225), Blomberg does not think Evans has solved the problem of the outline of Luke's Central Section (p. 233). In his commentary on Luke (*The Gospel according to Luke I–IX*, p. 826), though listing Evans's study in his bibliography, Fitzmyer does not offer any direct critique of it, except the comment that he does not agree with Evans when he interprets Luke as depicting Jesus as 'the new Moses' (an important component in Evans's thesis). However, the way he describes Luke's organization of the material in his so-called 'travel account' shows that Fitzmyer would not agree with Evans's general proposal. For other criticisms of Evans's article, see E.E. Ellis, *The Gospel of Luke* (Century Bible; Grand Rapids: Eerdmans, 1974), p. 147; J.W. Wenham, 'Synoptic Independence and the Origin of Luke's Travel Narrative', *NTS* 27 (1980–81), pp. 509-10; and the studies surveyed recently in C.A. Evans, 'Luke 16:1-18 and the Deuteronomy Hypothesis', in *idem* and Sanders (eds.), *Luke and Scripture*, pp. 121-39, esp. pp. 122-26.

49. Since the publication of the monographs by J. Drury (*Tradition and Design in Luke's Gospel* [London: Darton, Longman & Todd, 1976]) and M.D. Goulder (*The Evangelists' Calendar* [London: SPCK, 1978]), both of which not only warmly embraced Evans's proposal, but also developed it in more detail (in ways that are roundly criticized by Blomberg; see 'Midrash, Chiasmus, and the Outline of Luke's Central Section', pp. 228-33), I know of only one major recent study which has treated Evans's article in a very positive way: D.P. Moessner's *Lord of the Banquet: The Literary and Theological Significance of the Lukan Travel Narrative* (Minneapolis: Fortress Press, 1989). While Moessner admits that some of the parallels that have been suggested between Luke's Central Section and Deut. 1–26 'are tenuous at best', he thinks a number of others 'are indeed startlingly close' (p. 32), and he goes on to develop the most plausible demonstration so far published of the connection between Lk. 9.51–19.44 (he argues for the extension of Luke's travel account well into Lk. 19) and the book of Deuteronomy. However, he seems less interested in a detailed textual comparison between Luke and Deuteronomy than in themes and motifs that they share in common. Perhaps the most recent (nuanced) general support for C.F. Evans's thesis is in C.A. Evans's study, 'Luke 16:1-18 and the Deuteronomy Hypothesis', esp. pp. 126-30.

instructive to study carefully Deut. 10.12–11.32 (LXX), the portion of Deuteronomy that Evans posits as guiding Luke as he put together the material now included in Lk. 11.27-36, in which the 'sign of Jonah' pericope is centered.[50] There are several things of interest about this portion of Deuteronomy that may have influenced Luke to place 11.27-36 precisely where he does.

First, Deuteronomy 10 and 11 repeatedly stress 'hearing' and 'keeping' the divine commandments. Compare the following excerpts from Deuteronomy 10 and 11 (LXX) with Lk. 11.28:

Deut. 10.13	Lk. 11.28
φυλάσσεσθαι τὰς ἐντολὰς κυρίου τοῦ θεοῦ σου...	αὐτὸς δὲ εἶπεν· μενοῦν μακάριοι οἱ **ἀκούοντες** τὸν λόγον τοῦ θεοῦ καὶ **φυλάσσοντες**.
Deut. 11.1	
...καὶ **φυλάξῃ** τὰ φυλάγματα αὐτοῦ...	
Deut 11.8	
κὰι **φυλάξεσθε πάσας** τὰς ἐντολὰς αὐτοῦ...	
Deut. 11.13	
ἐὰν δὲ ἀκοῇ **ἀκούσητε** πάσας τὰς ἐντολὰς ταύτας...	
Deut. 11.22	
καὶ ἔσται ἐὰν ἀκοῇ **ἀκούσητε** πάσας τὰς ἐντολὰς ταύτας...	

The strong Deuteronomic emphasis on a faithful and wholehearted response expressed in the 'keeping' and 'hearing' of the divine commandments is virtually the same point with which Luke introduces the section on 'sign-seeking' in 11.28: 'But he [Jesus] said, "Blessed rather are those who *hear* the word of God and *keep* it".' Admittedly, the key verbs 'to keep' and 'to hear' are never used in the same verse in Deuteronomy 10–11, as they are in Lk. 11.28, and the Deuteronomy texts introduce 'to keep' before using 'to hear', reversing the Lukan order. But the more important point is that the same two key Greek verbs—φυλάσσω and ἀκούω—are both used in Deuteronomy 10–11 and in Lk. 11.28, and with the same essential meaning. Moreover, an

50. Evans, 'The Central Section of St. Luke's Gospel', p. 44.

important thrust of Deuteronomy 11, explicitly as well as implicitly, is that those who heed the divine commandments will receive a blessing. Note Deut. 11.26-27 (LXX): Ἰδοὺ ἐγὼ δίδωμι ἐνώπιον ὑμῶν σήμερον **εὐλογίαν** καὶ κατάραν, τὴν **εὐλογίαν**, ἐὰν **ἀκούσητε** τὰς ἐντολὰς κυρίου τοῦ θεοῦ ὑμῶν..., and the clear implications of Deut. 11.13-15 and v. 21. In Lk. 11.28, the third Evangelist has Jesus pronounce those 'blessed' (μακάριοι) who 'hear' (ἀκούοντες) the word of God and obey it. While Jesus uses the adjective μακάριοι over against Deuteronomy's synonymous but differently rooted noun εὐλογίαν, the meaning in both texts is quite similar.

Secondly, in Deut. 10.14-16, the Deuteronomist has Moses remind Israel that though God is the creator of all, the Deity has especially set the divine love upon the people of Israel that they might serve God faithfully in the land given them. But this implies a life of obedience, which will inevitably be characterized by repentance. This is expressed in Deut. 10.16 through the metaphor of circumcision: 'Circumcise, then, the foreskin of your heart, and do not be stubborn any longer' (NRSV). When in Lk. 11.29 Jesus calls this generation 'evil', seeking after a sign, it presupposes their stubborn impenitence. The point behind all of Lk. 11.29-32 is to get the people to do precisely what Moses commands Israel to do in Deut. 10.16, though in this instance Luke's language does not pick up on the metaphor in Deuteronomy.[51]

Thirdly, both Deuteronomy 11 and Lk. 11.29-30 employ the same word for 'sign' (σημεῖον), and both use it in the same two different senses. Note the following texts:

Deut. 11.3	Lk. 11.29
...καὶ τὰ **σημεῖα** αὐτοῦ καὶ τὰ τέρατα αὐτοῦ, ὅσα ἐποίησεν ἐν μέσῳ Αἰγύπτου Φαραὼ βασιλεῖ Αἰγύπτου...	...ἡ γενεὰ αὕτη γενεὰ πονηρά ἐστιν· **σημεῖον** ζητεῖ, καὶ **σημεῖον** οὐ δοθήσεται αὐτῇ...

51. It should perhaps be added here that for Luke, as well as probably for Jesus, the 'crowds' who gather to hear Jesus and whom he calls 'this generation' are also representatives of the people of Israel whom God loves. While Jesus' words to them are harsh, it is not because he rejects and hates them, but because he wants them to repent and love God. He seeks to win 'this generation' to God's will, much as Moses pursued the Israelites in the wilderness to get them to listen and respond to God's commandments.

Deut. 11.18	Lk. 11.29-30
καὶ ἐμβαλεῖτε τὰ ῥήματα ταῦτα εἰς τὴν καρδίαν ὑμῶν καὶ εἰς τὴν ψυχὴν ὑμῶν· καὶ ἀφάψετε αὐτὰ εις **σημεῖον** ἐπὶ τῆς χειρὸς ὑμῶν...	...εἰ μὴ τὸ **σημεῖον** Ἰωνᾶ· καθὼς γὰρ ἐγένετο Ἰωνᾶς τοῖς Νινευίταις **σημεῖον**...

Through what God did for Israel in the exodus, the Israelites witnessed and experienced God's 'signs' (σημεῖα), that is, the Deity's miraculous delivering acts (τὰ τέρατα αὐτοῦ). In Jesus' day, many of the people were demanding of him the same type of 'sign', that is, some kind of prodigious wonder that would authenticate his mission beyond question, or firmly establish his credentials as one sent from God. This is the sense of the first two instances of σημεῖον in Lk. 11.29. Jesus refuses categorically to grant such a 'sign' to 'this generation', most probably because, like the Israelites coming out of Egypt, they have already seen such 'wonders', most recently in the saving deeds that Jesus has performed through his exorcisms, yet they have not believed him. Jesus will not grant additional 'signs' of this type when those previously given have only been discounted or ignored.

But to the wilderness generation, Moses spoke of another kind of 'sign', one that consisted of God's words which the people were not only to take to heart, but also to bind as a σημεῖον on their hands as an external reminder of the divine will (Deut. 11.18, LXX). Similarly, Jesus had another 'sign' for his generation, τὸ σημεῖον Ἰωνᾶ, a 'sign' which Jonah became to the Ninevites, thus an external 'sign' to them of God's word of threatening judgment for their evil deeds. In Deut. 11.3 and 18 (LXX), and in Lk. 11.29-30, we therefore have two different usages of the word σημεῖον, which may have impressed Luke as he arranged his 'demand for a sign' and 'sign of Jonah' materials precisely at this juncture.

Fourthly, and most intriguingly from my perspective, careful scrutiny of Deuteronomy 11 suggests perhaps another reason (in addition to the ones already proposed by scholars) why Luke may have ordered the content of 11.31-32 in the manner he has. I call attention to Deut. 11.2-3, 5, and 8 (LXX) over against Lk. 11.31, and Deut. 11.25 (LXX) over against Lk. 11.32a:

Deut. 11.2-3, 5, 8	Lk. 11.31
[2]καὶ γνώσεσθε σήμερον ὅτι οὐχὶ τὰ παιδία ὑμῶν, ὅσαι οὐκ οἴδασιν οὐδὲ εἴδοσαν τὴν παιδείαν κυρίου τοῦ θεοῦ σου καὶ τὰ μεγαλεῖα αὐτοῦ καὶ τὴν χεῖρα τὴν κραταιὰν καὶ τὸν βραχίονα τὸν ὑψηλὸν [3]καὶ τὰ σημεῖα αὐτοῦ καὶ τὰ τέρατα αὐτοῦ, ὅσα ἐποίησεν ἐν μέσῳ Αἰγύπτου Φαραὼ βασιλεῖ Αἰγύπτου καὶ πάσῃ τῇ γῇ αὐτοῦ...[5]καὶ ὅσα ἐποίησεν ὑμῖν ἐν τῇ ἐρήμῳ, ἕως ἤλθετε εἰς τὸν τόπον...[8]καὶ φυλάξεσθε πάσας τὰς ἐντολὰς αὐτοῦ, ὅσας ἐγὼ ἐντέλλομαί σοι σήμερον, ἵνα ζῆτε καὶ πολυπλασιασθῆτε καὶ εἰσέλθητε καὶ κληρονομήσητε τὴν γῆν, εἰς ἣν ὑμεῖς διαβαίνετε τὸν Ἰορδάνην ἐκεῖ κληρονομῆσαι αὐτὴν...	βασίλισσα νότου... ἦλθεν ἐκ τῶν περάτων τῆς γῆς ἀκοῦσαι τὴν σοφίαν Σολομῶνος...

Deut. 11.25	Lk. 11.32
οὐκ **ἀντιστήσεται** οὐδεὶς κατὰ πρόσωπον ὑμῶν· τὸν τρόμον ὑμῶν καὶ τὸν φόβονυμῶν ἐπιθήσει κύριος ὁ θεὸς ὑμῶν ἐπὶ πρόσωπον πάσῆς τῆς γῆς, ἐφ᾽ ἧς ἄν ἐπιβῆτε ἐπ᾽ αὐτῆς, ὅν τρόπον ἐλάλησες κύριος πρὸς ὑμᾶς.	ἄνδρες Νινευῖται **ἀναστήσονται** ἐν τῇ κρίσει μετὰ τῆς γενεᾶς ταύτης καὶ κατακρινοῦσιν αὐτήν·

Though aside from Deut. 11.25 and Lk. 11.32 there are no catchword connections between Deut. 11.2-3, 5, 8 and Lk. 11.31, it is not difficult to see how Luke may have been struck by a thematic analogy between the Israelites coming from Egypt to the Promised Land, and the queen of the south coming from afar ('from the ends of the earth') to hear the wisdom of Solomon (which surely would have been thought to embody the divine wisdom). The point of comparison would be between two persons/peoples coming from outside Palestine to the Promised Land to hear and obey God's teaching, which if not done would surely bring judgment. This is the main burden of Deuteronomy 11 as a whole. However, in v. 25 the words, 'No one will *stand* against you...' (LXX οὐκ ἀντιστήσονται οὐδεὶς κατὰ πρόσωπον ὑμῶν) may have had special significance to Luke in light of the 'people of Nineveh' saying which begins with the Ninevites '*standing up* in the judgment with this generation' (ἀναστήσονται ἐν τῇ κρίσει μετὰ τῆς γενεᾶς ταύτας). In other words, Luke may have been conscious of a contrasting relationship between his Deuteronomic material (Deut. 11.25) and the Ninevite saying at this point. Whereas the Israelites will have no one to stand against them in battle to prevent them from taking possession of the Promised Land if they are fully obedient to God's will, the present generation of Israel in Jesus' day *will* have Gentiles standing up against them in judgment, because they have not been responsive to the proclamation of the divine will through Jesus. Because the motif of coming from afar to Palestine to respond to the divine instruction occurs first, at the beginning of Deuteronomy 11 (esp. vv. 1-8), whereas the motif of 'standing against' those who have come does not occur until later (v. 25), this may have been sufficient cause for Luke to order vv. 31-32 as he has, thereby inverting the Matthean order. This would suggest that the inversion was indeed Luke's doing, and not necessarily something already present in Q.

One further observation with regard to Deuteronomy 11 and Lk. 11.31-32: whenever the Israelites refused to repent and respond in obedience to what God has said and done, divine judgment was almost an inevitable consequence. In Deuteronomy 11 it is expressed through the denial of blessing (vv. 16-17) and the onset of curse (vv. 26-28). In Lk. 11.31-32, the background is the scene of the final judgment, with the Son of Man presiding, and the queen of the south and people of Nineveh acting as accusers against those who did not heed the divine wisdom or who, having heard a message of judgment, could not bring themselves to repent.

I would be the first to acknowledge that these proposed points of contact between Deuteronomy 10–11 and Lk. 11.27-32 are principally my own (Evans does not mention any of these suggestions, nor have I seen them in any other work that gives his hypothesis credence), and I obviously cannot demonstrate that Luke was aware of them. But I think that the indicators discussed above, particularly the first, third and fourth, suggest that Luke may have been aware of these connections.

V

In his 1962 article on 'The Sign of Jonah', Dom John Howton quotes E. von Dobschütz as saying: 'Nobody until this day has succeeded in giving a fair explanation of what the sign of Jonah might mean'.[52] That honest assessment of previous scholarship on this intriguing expression could just as accurately be affirmed today, despite a great deal of further work on it, including my own. I would not claim that either the present study of the Lukan 'sign of Jonah' pericope or my earlier one on the Matthean passage have definitively cracked the enigma of how this elusive saying should be interpreted. Such an effort is severely handicapped by the lack both of sufficient external and internal evidence to support an unambiguous univocal meaning with utmost confidence. For that reason, this study has not ventured to offer any new interpretation 'of what the sign of Jonah might mean', but rather, on the basis of a fresh examination of its biblical base in the book of Jonah (probably the most important external source we have for explaining it), an analysis of how the semantics of σημεῖον would affect Luke's use of it, and an assessment of the whole Lukan context, it seeks to decide which interpretation, among the more plausible ones that have been proposed, better fits the data. I have concluded that this is the one which sees Jonah's judgment proclamation to the Ninevites (in Jon. 3.4) providing a more likely definition of the 'sign of Jonah' in Luke[53] than any miraculous deed of deliverance of the prophet, based upon his fish and sea experience (in Jon. 2). The comparison that Luke makes in 11.30 between Jonah as a 'sign' to the Ninevites and the Son of Man as a 'sign' to 'this generation' also makes good sense when the *tertium comparationis* is simply an announcement of judgment (rather than more specifically an announcement of judgment involving the threatened destruction of Nineveh).[54]

52. E. von Dobschütz, 'Eschatology of the Gospels', *JTS* (1920), pp. 111-12, *pace* J. Howton, 'The Sign of Jonah', *SJT* 15 (1962), p. 298.

53. I argue in my study of Mt. 12.40 ('Matthew 12.40 as an Interpretation of "The Sign of Jonah" Against its Biblical Background') that Matthew also had a similar understanding, though he employs some different wording and imagery, as well as another textual basis in the book of Jonah, viz. Jon. 2.

54. Then the implied comparison in Lk. 11.30 would be something like the following: 'Just as Jonah became a sign to the Ninevites (that Nineveh would be destroyed), so the Son of Man will be a sign to this generation (that Jerusalem will

Before bringing this essay to a close, I want briefly to address an issue of no small importance to Professor Sanders's interests: the application of canonical criticism (which Professor Sanders has played a highly significant role in developing[55]) to the interpretation of a biblical text, in the present instance Lk. 11.29-32.

For this text, the exercise is more difficult than it was for Sanders when he did his studies of 'From Isaiah 61 to Luke 4',[56] and 'Isaiah in Luke'.[57] This is because, unlike for Isaiah, we have no sure knowledge about the original audience of the book of Jonah, or its historical setting and date. The way Jonah 3, or more specifically 3.4, addressed subsequent communities of faith prior to the New Testament is almost totally unknown. Except in two manuscripts of the Book of the Twelve associated with the Qumran discoveries,[58] Jon. 3.4 does not appear to be either quoted or alluded to in any literary sources before or near the time of the Gospel of Luke, though of course it was translated into Greek in the LXX. Interestingly, this translation does contain a variant from the MT Hebrew of 3.4, but because it is probably best explained as arising from a scribal copying error,[59] its legitimacy as a better reading

be destroyed)'. G. Schmitt moves in this direction in his article, 'Das Zeichen des Jona', *ZNW* 69 (1978), pp. 123-29 (esp. pp. 128-29), based on his interpretation of an apocryphal prophecy attributed to Jonah in the pseudepigraphical work *The Lives of the Prophets* (first century CE), according to which whenever all the Gentiles would be seen in Jerusalem, 'the entire city would be razed to the ground' (*Liv. Proph.* 10.11). But the immediate Lukan context of 11.30 lends no support for interpreting this verse in terms of a destruction, and Luke elsewhere seems to make no connection between the Son of Man and the fall of Jerusalem.

55. For a good explication of what is involved in canonical criticism, see Sanders's monograph, *Canon and Community*.

56. In J. Neusner (ed.), *Christianity, Judaism and Other Greco-Roman Cults: Studies for Morton Smith at Sixty* (Leiden: Brill, 1975), Part I, pp. 75-106; republished in revised form in Evans and Sanders (eds.), *Luke and Scripture*, pp. 46-69.

57. *Int* 36 (1982), pp. 144-55; republished in revised form in Evans and Sanders (eds.), *Luke and Scripture*, pp. 14-25. In the task of canonical criticism, Sanders acknowledges that sometimes its results may be severely limited for lack of certain kinds of information. See his comment in *Canon and Community*, p. 77.

58. A very fragmentary Greek scroll of the Minor Prophets, and a more complete Hebrew scroll of the Minor Prophets. For the former, see now E. Tov, *et al.*, *The Greek Minor Prophets Scroll from Naḥal Ḥever (8ḤevXIIgr)* (DJD, 8; Oxford: Clarendon Press, 1990), esp. pp. 30-31; for the latter, P. Benoit, *Les Grottes de Murabbaʿat: Texte* (DJD, 2; Oxford: Clarendon Press, 1961), esp. p. 91.

59. This error would have been precipitated by MT שלשת ימים (= LXX ἡμερῶν

of the text is questionable.[60] In any event, it does not seem to have any bearing on the way Luke interpreted this verse. Thus, we have so far discovered no literary evidence from before the time of Jesus attesting the existence of an expression like 'the sign of Jonah', even though in the Hebrew Bible, as we noted earlier in the case of Isaiah and Ezekiel, we have the word 'sign' occasionally associated with these prophets' words or deeds. Yet the label 'sign of Isaiah' or 'sign of Ezekiel' never seems to have developed.

The earliest extant written evidence for the phrase 'the sign of Jonah' comes from the Gospel traditions of Matthew and Luke, who assign the words to Jesus. But if Matthew and Luke were dependent upon a putative 'sayings-source', traditionally called 'Q', for what information they have about 'the sign of Jonah', should we conclude from this that it was the Q-community which originated the saying, though attributing it to Jesus? While this is not susceptible to proof, I see no reason why it could not have been Jesus himself who first made the genitive combination of the word 'sign' and the name of a prophet, in this case, Jonah.[61] He would have done this on the basis of a fresh interpretation of the book

τριῶν) at the end of v. 3, which the Greek translator carried over to the beginning of v. 4 (as τρεῖς ἡμέραι), either due to vertical dittography or a desire to harmonize with the same number in v. 3 (with a further reminiscence of the 'three-day' motif in 2.1). The first-century CE fragmentary Greek scroll of the Minor Prophets (8ḤevXIIgr), found in the Naḥal Ḥever, the later Greek recensions of Aquila, Symmachus and Theodotion, as well as the Targum, all support the MT reading here, probably in recognition of its superiority. For a recent discussion of the textual evidence and its implications for interpretation, see now J.M. Sasson, *Jonah: A New Translation with Introduction, Commentary, and Interpretations* (AB, 24B; Garden City, NY: Doubleday, 1990), pp. 233-34.

60. Nonetheless, the Greek reading does have its modern scholarly defenders (see H.W. Wolff, *Obadiah and Jonah—A Commentary* [trans. M. Kohl; Minneapolis: Augsburg, 1986], p. 144, textual note 4b), principally on the grounds of the rapid dissemination of Jonah's prophecy among the Ninevites, and their equally quick response to it, and this could well be the interpretation that the Greek-speaking Jews in Alexandria found most meaningful and worthy of perpetuation as they read Jon. 3. One might also observe here that had Jonah predicted the fall of Nineveh before the end of only three days, and the Ninevites had not repented and moved God to revoke the threatened destruction, his own life would have been endangered, since it took him three days to traverse the city and emerge on its eastern side (cf. 3.3 with 4.5). Moreover, he presumably would have had no time at all to build his סכה and wait in its shade to see what would happen to the city!

61. On this see now Catchpole, 'The Law and the Prophets in Q', pp. 100-101.

of Jonah, introducing the word 'sign' (which occurs nowhere in Jonah) to describe (as we have it in Luke's rendition) the oracle of judgment Jonah delivers to the Ninevites. He thereby adapts the text of Jonah to meet a present need in his ministry: that is, to respond to those demanding of him a 'sign' to verify his messiahship beyond dispute. In so doing, he shifts the focus away from his personal identity to the content of his message, in which he hopes the people will discern the voice of God warning them of the consequences if they do not repent and amend their lives, so that they can receive the gift of the Kingdom. With this contemporizing hermeneutic, Jesus as Son of Man compares himself to the prophet Jonah, making them both signs of warning to a people who must change if they are not to receive an irrevocable judgment.

Another, later stage in the canonical interpretation of Lk. 11.29-32 would be in the time of the church (after Luke's Gospel), when in the face of persecution, defection, increasing despair, and the realization that the split between the synagogue and the church was most likely going to be permanent, Christians felt the need for a bolstering of their faith that in Jesus a victory over sin and death had indeed been won, and that in his resurrection he was vindicated as God's true messiah. In light of this need, it could be seen why subsequent readers of Lk. 11.29-32 (as well as of Mt. 12.38-42) would resignify these somewhat elusive words as referring to the 'sign' of Jesus' deliverance from death. As the above study has endeavored to show, I do not think the earlier stages of this tradition had such a meaning in mind, but because a new situation motivated a fresh interpretation, and the wording of the text allowed it, 'the sign of Jonah' was recontextualized to address a pressing need in a post-Lukan community of faith.

Obviously, for the concern of the present study, the central interest has been focused on how Luke himself dealt with the 'sign of Jonah' tradition. If my analysis is acceptable, Luke's treatment of this tradition has involved two major items of significance for canonical-critical assessment. The first was his move (probably following Q, except perhaps for the ordering of the verses) to conjoin vv. 31-32 to the 'sign of Jonah' sayings in vv. 29-30. As we saw earlier, the former probably derive originally from a somewhat different context, wherein Jesus' Jewish hearers are compared unfavorably with others (including certain Gentiles) because, unlike the former, the latter make a positive response to Jesus' message and mission.[62] By attaching these verses to the 'sign

62. For texts in Luke which share this theme, note 10.13-15, 30-39; 13.10-17,

of Jonah' sayings, Luke adapts them to function as elucidations of what 'the sign of Jonah' might mean. With this move, not only do they both signify that the 'sign' resides in what Jonah and the Son of Man say, but v. 31 adds the thought that what is said is tantamount to the divine wisdom, which should inspire an unusual effort to be heard. Yet even though these verses are made to serve a new function, their original one is left intact, and unobscured. At the same time, they serve to underline the seriousness of the people's persistent refusal to hear and respond to God's word, because it could result in a moment when only judgment—not repentance—is any longer possible. Hermeneutically, then, the way vv. 31-32 are to be interpreted in their present context would seem to meet a need, not only for the hearers of Jesus' teaching during the days of his earthly ministry, but also for the largely Gentile Christian audience of Luke's Gospel,[63] to bring them to a more immediate acceptance of what Jesus has said, before it is too late.

A second facet in Luke's handling of the 'sign of Jonah' tradition important for the canonical-critical analysis of Lk. 11.29-32 resides in the possibility that Luke may have used Deuteronomy 1–26 as a template guiding his organization of the traditions he included in the Central Section of his Gospel. But by placing the content of 11.27-32 over against the traditions in Deuteronomy 10 and 11, Luke has not produced a marked hermeneutical shift. Indeed, if it was Luke's intention to portray Jesus as the new Moses (as Moessner, following C.F. Evans, has forcefully argued[64]), then, like the old Moses, Jesus finds himself confronted by a people largely recalcitrant and unbelieving, who need to be reminded of the importance of hearing and keeping the divine commandments, since their failure to do so can only result in their judgment. This was the major burden of Deuteronomy 10–11, as it is of Lk. 11.27-32.

However, at two points Luke seems to have adapted his Deuteronomic base to serve more his own than the Deuteronomist's purposes. First,

22-30; 14.15-24; 15.1-10; 17.11-19; 19.1-10. Interestingly, Luke has placed most of these texts, just as 'the sign of Jonah' pericope, in his Central Section, where special prominence is given to the motif of judgment for those who are unwilling to repent.

63. Fitzmyer (*The Gospel according to Luke I–IX*, p. 59) acknowledges that in this audience were doubtless some Jews and Jewish Christians, but that predominantly Luke wrote for Gentile Christians in a Gentile setting. See also the comments of R. Maddox, *The Purpose of Luke–Acts* (Göttingen: Vandenhoeck & Ruprecht, 1982), pp. 186-87.

64. See Moessner, *Lord of the Banquet*, especially ch. IV.

with regard to the two types of sign mentioned in Deut. 11.3-7 and 18, respectively, by comparing these to the sign the people demand of Jesus and the sign Jesus wants to emphasize, that is, 'the sign of Jonah', Luke has Jesus attribute more significance to the latter than to the former, something which does not derive from the Deuteronomic context. Secondly, by placing the 'queen of the south' saying before the 'people of Nineveh' saying, if this was motivated by the order of certain motifs in Deuteronomy 11, as I have argued above, Luke has used his Deuteronomic model primarily to serve his interest (if not the interest of earlier Jesus tradition) of giving further definition to the meaning of 'the sign of Jonah', by assigning precedence to the wisdom character of the divine word before stressing its important function of calling for—and eliciting—repentance. In so doing, Luke has expanded the function of his Deuteronomic material in a way the Deuteronomist could never have envisaged, but quite in keeping with the way canon often works.

What I have tried to do, then, is to add a chapter in the story of the use of the 'sign of Jonah' tradition in the faith communities of the Gospel writers Matthew and Luke (but especially Luke), and of the early church. Whereas many have assimilated Luke's usage to Matthew and/or the early church's understanding, the force of this essay has been to marshal the data for Luke's understanding as a distinctively different one from that of the traditions which followed him. While in my view he is in agreement with the basic thrust of the Matthean interpretation, he utilizes different material to support it, which at the same time produces some unique nuances.

Though it may still be true that we do not have 'a fair explanation of what the sign of Jonah may mean', Lk. 11.29-32 continues to evoke efforts to interpret and illuminate it, with varying degrees of plausibility. At the same time, there remain available some of the past meanings that have been suggested, waiting to be appropriated or reappropriated, as new contexts invite them.

Part II
Ancient and Modern Transmission, Translation and Appropriation of the Canon

Adaptable for Translation: Deuteronomy 6.5 in the Synoptic Gospels and Beyond

Robert A. Bascom

1. *Introduction*

James Sanders, at the beginning of an essay key to understanding much of his approach to biblical interpretation, has written: '*hermeneutics must be viewed as the midterm of the axis which lies between stability and adaptability*'.[1] The same thing could be said of biblical translation. Those who have either studied bible translation or tried their hand at it realize sooner or later that no matter what kind of translation technique is being employed, the translator must first interpret the text before translating it. One of the more interesting places to view this double phenomenon of interpretation and adaptive translation is in the New Testament treatment of the Old Testament[2] via its various forms—Hebrew Bible, LXX, Targums and Midrash. Sanders has made this subject a matter of frequent research, and his fundamental approach to the matter informs what follows.[3] The other methodological system being employed is modern translation theory, as developed by E.A. Nida and others over the last fifty years or so.[4] The results are not so much surprising as is the fact

1. 'Adaptable for Life', in F.M. Cross, W.E. Lemke and P.D. Miller (eds.), *Magnalia Dei: The Mighty Acts of God. Essays on the Bible and Archeology in Memory of G. Ernest Wright* (Garden City, NY: Doubleday, 1976), pp. 531-60.

2. 'Old Testament' instead of 'Hebrew Bible' will be used throughout this paper, to avoid having to distinguish between Hebrew and Greek forms of the text where it is not significant to do so.

3. See for example *Torah and Canon* (Philadelphia: Fortress Press, 1972); 'Hermeneutics of True and False Prophecy', in G. Coats and B.O. Long (eds.), *Canon and Authority* (Philadelphia: Fortress Press, 1977), pp. 21-41; 'Torah and Paul' in W. Meeks (ed.), *God's Christ and His People* (Oslo: Universitets forlaget, 1977), pp. 132-40; *Canon and Community: A Guide to Canonical Criticism* (Philadelphia: Fortress Press, 1984).

4. See for example E.A. Nida, *Toward a Science of Translating, with Special*

that despite a general agreement among both biblical and translation scholars for some time about the matters involved, their insights have yet to be applied in key cases in modern translations of the Bible into English. One such case is Deut. 6.5 and its citation in the New Testament.

The well-known verse Deut. 6.5 is quoted in all three Synoptic Gospels, with some slight variations. These variations, I shall argue, show that the New Testament authors not only were aware of the Old Testament meaning of the quotation, but also were aware of subtle shifts in the semantic domains between key words of this text in biblical Hebrew and koine Greek. The variations indicate the attempt, not altogether successful, to make the necessary adjustments in the translations from Hebrew to Greek. In understanding what the Gospel writers were trying to do, we not only recover the meaning of the Old Testament and New Testament versions of the text, but also gain an appreciation of the antiquity of at least some principles of functional equivalence translation.[5] Unfortunately, modern translators into English (as well as more than a few commentators) have not followed the logical consequences of what the New Testament authors did, but instead render all the texts in question rather formally (word for word). This has led to a history of misinterpretation of this Old Testament text and its translation in the New Testament. The result has been a sentimental or emotional understanding of Deut. 6.5 and its New Testament citations in modern translations, rather than one that focuses on loyalty and obedience. The latter, I will argue, is the true force of the words in Deuteronomy. I will also argue that this focus was what the New Testament writers, given their own limitations in translation, were trying to preserve. The basic outlines of the problem and its resolution are not a matter of much discussion or debate in either biblical studies or translation theory. Readers of modern English translations at

Reference to Principles and Procedures Involved in Bible Translating (Leiden: Brill, 1964); E.A. Nida and C.R. Taber, *The Theory and Practice of Translation* (Leiden: Brill, 1982 [1969]); E.A. Nida, *Componential Analysis of Meaning: An Introduction of Semantic Structures* (The Hague: Mouton, 1975); E.A. Nida and W.D. Reyburn, *Meaning Across Cultures: A Study on Bible Translating* (Maryknoll, NY: Orbis Books, 1981).

5. Cf. a similar observation about the translational strategies of the writers of the Synoptic Gospels made by P. Ellingworth in 'Parallel Passages in the Gospels', *TBT* 34.4 (1983), pp. 401-407. Unfortunately, the suggestions for translation made in the present paper will most likely only be accepted in areas where there is no existing translation as yet, since the texts in question are otherwise so well known, and thus difficult to change, at least for now.

least are left with the impression that loving God with all one's heart is something more akin to romantic involvement than to loyal commitment.

2. *Deuteronomy 6.5 in the Hebrew Bible*

Analysis

> וְאָהַבְתָּ אֵת יְהוָה אֱלֹהֶיךָ בְּכָל־לְבָבְךָ וּבְכָל־נַפְשְׁךָ וּבְכָל־מְאֹדֶךָ׃
>
> ...and you shall love the LORD your God with all your heart, and with all your soul, and with all your might. (Deut. 6.5)[6]

This verse is interesting for interpreters in that it forms the last part of the Shema (Deut. 6.4-5), and the first part of the recital of the (two) greatest commandment(s) of New Testament-era Judaism according to the Synoptic tradition. Thus it never really stands on its own, but must be understood against the background of the affirmation of the uniqueness of Yahweh (in Deuteronomy) on the one hand and the command to love one's neighbor (illustrated by the parable of the Good Samaritan in Luke) on the other. Most commentators correctly note that both in the Hebrew Bible and the New Testament the point of this text is holistic, not atomistic. Thus while analyzing the internal structure of the text (as I shall do later on) may teach us something about the translation principles of the New Testament authors and redactors, we should never lose sight of the meaning of the text as a whole.[7]

The concept of 'loving' God with all one's לב (and sometimes נפש as well) is common enough, though this wording is restricted to Deuteronomy.[8] A Deuteronomistic note about King Josiah in 2 Kgs

6. Unless otherwise noted, the RSV will be used throughout this paper.

7. B.M. Newman and P.C. Stine (*A Handbook on the Gospel of Matthew* [New York: United Bible Societies, 1988], p. 716) give a succinct version of this argument. They go too far, however, in saying that 'no distinction can be drawn between the meaning of the individual terms'. The holistic thrust in both Old Testament and New Testament is achieved by the bringing together of such an all-encompassing list. The terms are not synonyms elsewhere, and while it may be true that 'Any one of them would have been sufficient', that is due to the discourse ('You shall love God with all your...') and not to the general nature of these terms. Their suggestion for translation, however, is absolutely on the mark, except that they still use 'love' instead of 'commit' or 'be loyal'. Cf. also among others J.A. Fitzmyer, *The Gospel according to Luke X–XXIV* (Garden City, NY: Doubleday, 1981), pp. 878-79.

8. Cf. the NJB note on this verse (p. 233).

23.25 almost quotes our text verbatim, but with an important change: אהב ('love') becomes שוב ל' ('turn to'). Yet what is an apparent shift in meaning is entirely in accord with Deuteronomy itself, since in 30.10 שוב ל' is used in connection לב and נפש. Thus אהב and שוב ל' seem to be nearly identical terms in these contexts, and it would appear further that Deuteronomy, while unique in using אהב here, uses it to mean 'demonstrate love/commitment', that is, loyalty or obedience.

This usage for אהב is backed up by ancient Near Eastern texts. Even in the rest of the Hebrew Bible, אהב is not uniquely an emotional word, but is used of preference ('Jacob have I loved...'), especially in cases of treaties.[9] Thus the meaning in 1 Kgs 5.15 (5.1 in English), when the text says that Hiram 'loved' David, is likely *loyalty*, and not (at least primarily) love as an emotion or sentiment. This is substantiated by the language of treaties from the ancient Near East, where the vassal is to proclaim his love for his lord in no uncertain terms, even when there can be no doubt that there is no love lost between the parties in question.[10]

William Moran and others have written a series of closely related articles, starting from the idea that in Deuteronomy אהב refers to loyalty, as noted above. These articles make the point that the popular idea that Deuteronomy was influenced by Hosea's concept of filial love between God and humankind not only starts with God's love for humans and incorrectly extrapolates to humans' love for God, but in fact has the matter somewhat backwards from the start. It is Hosea who is influenced by the covenantal understanding of the relationship so apparent in Deuteronomy, though of course he makes it his own. The point is, for those who take this view, that this human love for God in Deuteronomy can be *commanded*, and thus cannot easily be understood as primarily emotional at all. For how does one command a feeling?[11]

J. Gerald Janzen has gone further, seeing אחד ('one') in the opening

9. *The NIV Study Bible* (Grand Rapids: Zondervan, 1985), p. 320, note on Josh. 22.5: 'In the ancient Near East, love was also a political term, indicating true-hearted loyalty to one's king'.

10. W.L. Moran, 'The Ancient Near Eastern Background of the Love of God in Deuteronomy', *CBQ* 25 (1963), pp. 78-82.

11. Moran, 'The Love of God in Deuteronomy', pp. 77-87; N. Lohfink, 'Hate and Love in Osee 9.15', *CBQ* 25 (1963), p. 417; D.J. McCarthy, 'Notes on the Love of God in Deuteronomy and the Father–Son Relationship between Yahweh and Israel', *CBQ* 27 (1963), pp. 144-47; S.D. McBride, 'The Yoke of the Kingdom', *Int* 27 (1973), pp. 273-306; P.D. Miller, 'The Way of Torah', *The Princeton Seminary Bulletin* 8.3 (1987), pp. 17-27.

verse of the Shema (Deut. 6.4) as referring to the moral integrity of God, and thus his faithfulness, rather than the more common interpretations of this word as radically monotheistic or specifying Yahweh's unique character. Janzen supports this by means of a chiastic comparison of Deut. 6.4-5 with Jer. 32.38-41, in which the people will be given *one* heart (the ability to be faithful), and it is Yahweh who will do them good (that is, love them) with all his heart and all his soul. In Janzen's explication of these texts there is thus a correspondence established in the mutual love (with heart and soul) between God and humans which has at its core the meaning 'to be faithful' or 'loyal' above all else.[12]

The argument is not that אהב does not have an emotional component in many of its uses in the Hebrew Bible, or even in Deuteronomy, but rather that when אהב is used in speaking of humans' relation to *God*, and especially with reference to their hearts, it denotes something more like loyalty. Recognizing that the meaning of words cannot be determined in isolation, we turn to the rest of the text to see if this understanding of אהב can be justified.

It is not אהב alone which creates the problem for modern interpreters, but its combination with לב. For a modern English speaker, to love with all one's heart is usually nothing other than romantic love. It is hard to imagine saying to anyone 'I love you with all my heart', and meaning anything other than romantic love. In fact, this usually indicates a situation between lovers.[13] While 'God' as a object necessarily changes the focus of the meaning away from romantic love, 'loving God with all your heart' in English (or in a great number of other modern languages) still falls well within the domain of sentiment and feeling more than that of loyalty or commitment.

Hans Walter Wolff has documented the fact that לב is not the primary seat of emotion in Hebrew as it is in English, but of intentionality. It

12. J.G. Janzen, 'On the Most Important Word in the Shema (Deuteronomy VI 4-5)', *VT* 37 (1987), pp. 280-300.

13. Of course this is a generalization regarding the use of 'heart' in English, and counter-examples can be given, but only if we change the environment and thus the idiom (e.g. lack of enthusiasm: 'his heart was not in it', loyalty: 'true-hearted' [used in NIV note to Josh. 22.5], etc.). Cf. A. Nygren, *Agape and Eros* (London: SPCK, 1953), who among others has studied the issue from a more philosophical/historical perspective. His study in general supports the thesis of this paper, though more from the point of view of explaining how it is we have derived our own modern views of love. Furthermore, he stops at the Reformation, which he considers to have solved the problem as it had existed up to that time.

reflects human thoughts directed towards the future, in planning, willing or wishing.[14] What Wolff does not go on to say, but is surely an important expansion of his explication, is that לב may well never be literal (meaning the organ of the body) in the Hebrew Bible. The one possible exception is the case of Nabal in 1 Sam. 25.37, where his heart is said to have died within him, referring perhaps to a stroke or a heart attack. Yet even here there is doubt, since the next verse says that ten days later Yahweh smote Nabal, and he died. Thus the first instance could just as easily be describing deep discouragement or depression. Interestingly, the New Testament does not use καρδία in a literal sense either, as we shall see below.[15]

Furthermore, אהב and לב are never used together in Hebrew outside of the usages in Deuteronomy referring to loving God. More importantly, only rarely can one find any connection between even the *concept* of love and the heart in the Hebrew Bible (cf. Song 4.9, 'you have ravished my heart...'). In Deuteronomy, while the human לב can stand for emotions, unless we count the text under discussion (and related ones) those emotions are never love or compassion, but discouragement (1.28 'melt'), pride (8.12; 17.20 'lifted up'), stubbornness (15.7 'hardened'), sadness (15.10 'grieved'), anger (19.6 'hot'), fear (20.8 'faint'), or shock/surprise (28.28 'astonish'). Yet even these texts are fewer and less significant than those which show the לב as the center of intentionality (planning, willing, wishing). In Deuteronomy alone, outside the text(s) under consideration people *consider* in their hearts (4.39; 8.5), *say/speak/congratulate* in their hearts (7.17; 8.17; 9.4; 29.19), are *deceived* in their hearts (11.16), *ponder/memorize* in their hearts (11.18), *think* in their hearts (15.9), and *perceive* in their hearts (29.4).[16] The richness of idioms connected with לב, including a number of examples denoting

14. H.W. Wolff, *The Anthropology of the Old Testament* (Philadelphia: Fortress Press, 1974), pp. 40-58.

15. J. Louw and E.A. Nida, *Greek–English Lexicon Based on Semantic Domains* (New York: United Bible Societies, 1989), I, p. 321.

16. One never finds, for example, as in Mayan languages, that the heart 'hurts' (= love), or is 'delicious' (= happiness). If Janzen (above) is correct, that 'one' means moral integrity or faithfulness within a relationship, it is like the Mayan 'one-hearted' (= solidarity, used for trust and faith as well). After such a list, the very idea of semantic domains being applicable to productive metaphors is called into question. Nevertheless 'superdomains' or ranges of meaning can still be mapped, and in the end, it is the fact that 'love' and 'heart' never combine in any text (unless the premise of this paper is in error) to mean emotional attachment that is significant.

emotions, coupled with the lack of any idioms with לב denoting love (no 'tender' or 'delicate' or 'soft' לב, for example) seem to point to a lack of connection between לב and the concept of love in general.[17]

One could almost say that, given the semantic domain of לב, for this discussion we need to understand what אהב means to define לב, and that, given the semantic domain of אהב, we need to understand what לב means to define אהב. It is helpful, therefore, that the context for 'loving' God (usually with 'heart/soul') in Deuteronomy invariably points to commitment ('obey, serve, walk in the ways of, turn to') rather than emotion.

Samuel Terrien has translated the text accurately if not elegantly:

> ...And thou shalt love Yahweh, thy Elohim, with thy whole mind, and with thy whole drive for self-preservation, and with the 'muchness' of thy whole being.[18]

Terrien goes on to say (in a footnote) that the words which are usually translated 'heart' (לבב) 'soul' (נפש) and 'might' (מאד) 'designate aspects of the human person which do not correspond exactly to English notions'.[19] His translation reflects that belief, and thus it sounds strange. Translators of modern versions intended for audiences with a knowledge of Scripture usually do not have the luxury of making strange-sounding

17. Recently Rolf Knierim has taken Wolff's analysis considerably further with regard to the key terms for my own discussion, לב and נפש. Knierim's argument, which is really about spirituality in the Old Testament, seems at first like the traditional one, in that he does not stake out a semantic space for 'heart' as volitional-intellectual as opposed to emotive. He goes on to describe the role of the heart as fundamentally different than heretofore understood, as he locates the central animating force within the individual as רוח, or spirit, which is given to humans (and all creation) from God, and has a specific content (such as 'wisdom'), which acts upon or in the heart in a number of different ways. This discussion is of great value and will provide a new starting point for any discussions involving these terms. Even so, the terms of this particular discussion are specific enough (especially with regard to translation) to remain valid even in light of Knierim's thesis (see R. Knierim, 'The Spirituality of the Old Testament', in *The Task of Old Testament Theology* [Grand Rapids: Eerdmans, 1995], pp. 269-97). More relevant to the discussion here are Knierim's observations (in oral discussion) that the idea in Deuteronomy is that the heart is capable of love for God ('the word is near to you'), while Jeremiah, on the one hand, and the New Testament, on the other, are much more critical of this capacity, and must solve the problem in more radical ways ('I will give you a new heart', and 'After that you will receive the Holy Spirit'). Still, 'love' in these contexts may well be better understood as *loyalty* than sentimental love.

18. S. Terrien, *The Elusive Presence* (New York: Harper & Row, 1978), p. 201.

19. Terrien, *Presence*, p. 223.

translations and then explaining them in a commentary, as much as they would like to at times. Yet Terrien makes an important point. Accuracy at times will be at odds with 'naturalness', or put another way, the harder reading is to be preferred at the beginning of the translation process, though the eventual goal should of course be a readable text in the target language. Fortunately, in this case the translator of the Hebrew text has some good natural-sounding equivalents in English. It is a matter of finishing what Terrien began.

Though נפשׁ (usually inaccurately translated 'soul' in English) is not directly a part of the problem being discussed at this point, it can serve as part of the solution.[20] As is well known, it can often be best translated as 'person', or 'self', depending on the context. In some contexts, including Deut. 6.5, it should probably be taken as the vital force, or the center of emotional intensity or desire. Thus it would most naturally be rendered in these cases as 'heart' (or 'self') in English.[21] That leaves לב free to be translated as it should be, 'mind'. Interestingly, the translators of the TEV followed this course in 2 Kgs 23.25 but not in Deut. 6.5 and related cases.[22] The problem for the TEV translators was the word 'love', which they were unwilling to change to 'show loyalty to' (or some such), and thus could not bring themselves to say 'love God with all your mind...' Interestingly, this is precisely what the Gospel writers did when they quoted the verse in the New Testament.

Therefore a possible translation would be 'Be loyal to God with all your mind, heart (or self) and strength.' The last of the terms in this list, מאד, is rarely translated as a noun, as it is traditionally in Deut. 6.5 (with the bound possessive pronoun), but is usually adverbial. However, in this case it should be translated semantically as adverbial with a superlative force, and not *grammatically* as a noun. Thus for the last part 'and do it

20. Of course it will enter into the discussion of the New Testament use of this text. It may be the least well translated of all the terms, given the history of 'soul' in subsequent interpretation. It is of course a bit untidy for modern translators that 'soul' is the center of desire both in Hebrew and Greek, and even of affection in Greek, but has not yet in either language become what 'heart' is for English speakers—the center of romantic love.

21. Even so 'heart' should not have a primarily sentimental force here. It works well only if we take 'heart' in the sense in which it is used in the idiom 'his/her heart was/was not in it'. This shows how close this meaning of 'heart' is to 'self', and the argument can be made that 'self' may actually be best in some of these contexts in English as well.

22. *Good News Bible* (New York: American Bible Society, 1976), pp. 425, 198.

as strongly/completely as you can' may be closer to the force intended.[23] As we shall see below, at least one of the New Testament writers was apparently aware of this possibility as well.

Modern Interpreters

Many modern commentators, and especially translators of modern versions, have been slow to make what should be by now the obvious equivalent translations of אהב as 'commitment', לב as 'mind', and נפש as 'heart' (or 'self') in texts such as these, much less recognizing the very possible adverbial/superlative force of מאד as 'strongly/completely'. This is in spite of the fact that the covenantal (i.e. juridical/treaty) background for humankind's love of God is nearly universally recognized. A few examples will suffice.

The *Jerome Biblical Commentary* explicitly attributes to Deuteronomy the addition of emotional depth to 'a basically juridical expression'.[24] While this might well be so, *JBC* allows modern readers to think (as they most certainly would) that this emotional depth comes from loving God with the *heart* (לב), while in fact that is the juridical part, and any emotional content comes with loving God with the *soul* or *self* (נפש).

Both Peake's Commentary and the Oxford Annotated Bible on the RSV (cf. NRSV also) explain in their notes what the terms in Deut. 6.5 mean, but in fact comment on translations which contradict their notes.[25]

23. BDB, p. 547, and M. McNamara, *Targum and Testament* (Grand Rapids: Eerdmans, 1972), p. 125: '*Me'od*, in the sense found in the Shema' is used only in Deut. 6.5 and 2 Kgs 23.25. Elsewhere the word occurs only in adverbial phrases, with the meaning of "greatly".' Cf. also G.H. Davies, 'Deuteronomy', in M. Black and H.H. Rowley (eds.), *Peake's Commentary on the Bible* (Hong Kong: Nelson, 1962), p. 273: '*might* is a metaphor of the superlative, completely'. This would make an even more natural translation as follows: 'Be completely loyal to God, with all your mind and heart'. Of course לב could be rendered as 'be committed to', and נפש could be rendered 'directing your self toward', for the following: 'Be completely loyal and committed to God, directing your whole self toward him'. This last is the most clear, but loses all the imagery.

24. J. Blenkinsopp, 'Deuteronomy', in R. Brown, J.A. Fitzmyer and R. Murphy (eds.), *The Jerome Biblical Commentary* (Englewood Cliffs, NJ: Prentice-Hall, 1968), p. 107.

25. Davies, 'Deuteronomy', p. 273. B.W. Anderson, in *The New Oxford Annotated Bible: RSV Edition* (ed. H.G. May and B. Metzger; New York: Oxford University Press, 1973), p. 223. B.W. Anderson in *The New Oxford Annotated Bible: NRSV Edition* (ed. B. Metzger and R. Murphy; New York: Oxford University Press, 1991), pp. 226-27.

If לב is mind and נפש is heart or self (emotional center) and strength is adverbial/superlative ('strongly/completely') in English, as many commentators have recognized, the terms should be rendered thus in at least some English translations.

Gerhard von Rad compares the love required in Deut. 6.5 to that between a son and his father, and cites Deut. 8.5 and 14.1 in support. He thus also reads the text sentimentally, though more biblically than many other commentators. It should be noted, however, that the basis of the comparison in 8.5 is *discipline*, not love as von Rad would have it, and in 14.1 'sons' should not be understood (even metaphorically) as biological, but rather as is often the case in the Hebrew Bible, as 'servants, followers, disciples'.[26]

The NIV Study Bible, in its note on Deut. 6.5, indicates that the love spoken of in this verse must be total, and in so doing follows most commentators. It does even better in its note on Josh. 22.5, where it states that אהב can be a political term (as we saw above). The same note, however, speaks of loving God from the heart in a way which would most naturally be understood as sentimental or emotional.[27]

Of course there are a number who have seen it otherwise. It is only fair to recognize that at least two major commentators on Deuteronomy fundamentally agree with the interpretation put forward here, and cite it in their commentaries. A.D.H. Mayes states not only that אהב in this context means obedience, but that לב means mind and נפש represents emotions or desire (see my discussion below, which supports this as well). More recently Moshe Weinfeld equates אהב with loyalty and allegiance, לב with mind, and נפש with a willingness to die for the sake of the covenantal relationship.[28] These are important contrary voices in what has otherwise been a reinforcement in English translation tradition of the force of the text as emotional, rather than as signifying loyalty and commitment.

26. G. von Rad, *Deuteronomy* (Philadelphia: Westminster Press, 1966), pp. 63-64. This is in no way meant to deny the importance of the imagery of the father–son (or father–daughter) relationship with reference to God and Israel elsewhere, but those cases distinctively use the direct singular metaphor, 'son' (e.g. Exod. 4.22; Hos. 11.1) or 'daughter' (Jer. 3.19) for Israel.

27. E.S. Kalland and K.L. Barker, 'Deuteronomy', p. 254, and A. Lewis, 'Joshua', p. 320, in *The NIV Study Bible*.

28. A.D.H. Mayes, *Deuteronomy* (Grand Rapids: Eerdmans, 1987), pp. 156, 176; M. Weinfeld, *Deuteronomy 1–11* (Garden City, NY: Doubleday, 1991), pp. 338, 351.

However, this understanding is not as yet reflected in any major translation in English, nor quite possibly in any other major modern translation either. All of this creates a comparative context for what happens to the text in translation in the New Testament. The argument being made here is that while the writers of the Synoptics certainly would never have discussed it in the way I have done above, they knew what the semantic ranges were for the key terms in question. But perhaps unfortunately for later translators, they had somewhat limited resources for dealing with these terms in translation. Nevertheless, as we shall see, they made adjustments within the parameters available to them. Modern translators of the Bible may follow through the logical consequences of such adjustments and do the same thing for their readers.

3. *The 'Afterlife' of Deuteronomy 6.5 in Biblical Tradition*

The LXX

Our Deuteronomy text takes a turn in subsequent biblical tradition when the Synoptic Gospels unanimously quote and adapt it in the New Testament. This adaptation turns out to be significant evidence for my present argument. Still, no discussion of the subject of Old Testament quotes in the New Testament is in order without a first look at the LXX. In looking at the LXX version of Deut. 6.5, the significant thing for our discussion is that some textual witnesses have διάνοια (mind) instead of καρδία (heart) for the first term of the list.[29] Be that as it may, the LXX is significant because it uses both καρδία (usually) and διάνοια (more rarely) to translate the Hebrew לב. Thus the New Testament authors were not operating in a vacuum, but already had the help of the LXX translators in understanding the force of לב in Hebrew.[30]

29. The Göttingen LXX prefers διάνοια to καρδία in Deut. 6.5, showing the strength of the textual tradition at that point. Weinfeld recently (*Deuteronomy*, p. 338) as well as P.M.-J. Lagrange earlier in *Evangile selon Saint Marc* (Paris: Gabalda, 1929), p. 322 have preferred the LXX text of B with διάνοια here.

30. E.C. Blackman, 'A Study of the Words "Thought", "Mind", and "Heart"', *BT* 4.1 (1953), pp. 36-40; R. Bratcher and E.A. Nida, *A Translator's Handbook on the Gospel of Mark* (New York: United Bible Societies, 1961), p. 383; V. Taylor, *The Gospel according to St. Mark* (Grand Rapids: Baker, 1966), p. 486. My colleague Harold Scanlin has pointed out to me that the actual LXX לב-translation count is 709 for καρδία to 51 for διάνοια (taken from E.C. dos Santos, *An Expanded Hebrew Index for the Hatch–Redpath Concordance to the Septuagint* [Jerusalem: Dugith, 1973]).

In fact, it has been suggested that this was the source of the subsequent Markan (and thus the other Synoptic) insertion of 'mind' into the list (see below). This explanation fails to account for too much in the New Testament tradition, such as why διάνοια was inserted where it was, or why Mk 12.33 uses σύνεσις instead, or why Mk 12.33 can leave out 'soul' and Matthew can leave out 'strength', and Luke can follow a different order than Mark, whom he is supposedly following. Newman and Stine explain Matthew's omission as 'a preference for the three-membered form of the Hebrew text'.[31] This has simplicity in its favor, but lacks explanatory power. In any case, the New Testament authors were doubtless aware of a multiplicity of text-forms.

The Greek lexicons list καρδία associated with love in Greek literature, but also list 'mind' as a secondary meaning. Thus, by means of a formal equivalence of καρδία for לב, there seems to be a move away from the semantic domain of thoughts and feelings but never love (לב) toward the semantic domain of feelings, and especially love, as well as thoughts (καρδία).[32]

New Testament Era Usage

In the New Testament the relevant citations are the Synoptic cases I shall deal with below, except for the usage 'to be/have a place in the heart' (2 Cor. 7.3; Phil. 1.7). The lexicons also list ψυχή (usually translated as 'soul' in English, as the equivalent of נפש) as occurring with various Greek terms for love to mean affection both in the New Testament (1 Thess. 2.8) and in other contemporary Greek literature.[33] Moulton and Milligan do not list any meanings for καρδία, but agree with the other lexicographers that ψυχή is the seat of feeling and desire (among other things), for the Greek speaker of the New Testament era.[34] All this indicates that a semantic shift has occurred in the text of Deut. 6.5 as it was translated from Hebrew to Greek: from intentionality (לב) plus desire (in a self-preservation sense: נפש) to feelings and thoughts (καρδία) plus desire and affection (ψυχή). This of course is what the New Testament authors were aware of, and most likely why they added 'mind' to the quotation from Deut. 6.5. In English (and other languages with similar

31. Newman and Stine, *Matthew*, p. 716.

32. LSJ, p. 877b.

33. BAGD, pp. 405a, 901b.

34. J. Moulton and G. Milligan (eds.), *The Vocabulary of the Greek Testament* (Grand Rapids: Eerdmans, 1930), pp. 321, 698-99.

domains for 'heart') the shift becomes even greater, and further corrections in translation are required.

The following table indicates the shifts in semantic domain regarding centers of thinking and feeling in particular.

	Thinking	Feeling
Old Testament Hebrew	לב	לב: feelings, but not love? נפש: desire, self
New Testament Era[35] Greek	διάνοια καρδία	ψυχή: desire, affection καρδία
English	mind: thoughts	heart: love

Table 1: *Semantic Domains*

Nida and Louw's *Greek–English Lexicon Based on Semantic Domains* attempt to go beyond the standard lexicons for the study of such matters in New Testament Greek. This resource allows one quickly to check the working hypothesis represented by Table 1. Both καρδία and ψυχή are listed on the same page, as 'inner self, desire', and so on, and for 'heart' a note is added, mentioning the Hebrew Bible influence on the use of this word in the New Testament as 'mind'.[36] Of course, if 'heart' in the New Testament really could mean 'mind', there would have been no need for the Synoptic translators to add διάνοια, listed unambiguously by the lexicon as 'mind'.

More interesting is the entry for 'love' (ἀγαπάω). Here there are two entries, the first of which is love 'based on sincere appreciation and high regard', and the second of which is 'to demonstrate or show one's love'. It is this second meaning which fits best in the Synoptic citations of Deut. 6.5, and is in general agreement with the usage outlined above for 'love' as loyalty or commitment.[37] If final support were needed, Luke's use of the parable of the Good Samaritan as the definition of the kind of love involved in both commandments (the second is 'like' the

35. Since one of the points being made in the paper is that the New Testament authors were adjusting their Old Testament citation in order accurately to render the sense, the comparison is not between New Testament Greek and Old Testament Hebrew, but between the Greek the New Testament writers were accustomed to hearing and using and Old Testament Hebrew. New Testament Greek itself, as has been amply demonstrated elsewhere, was highly Semiticized.

36. Louw and Nida, *Lexicon*, I, p. 321. Here the compilers note that καρδία never has a literal meaning in the New Testament either (see above discussion on לב in this regard).

37. Louw and Nida, *Lexicon*, I, pp. 293-94.

first) must be this kind of commitment in spite of what could only have been feelings of pity at best for a stranger and traditional enemy.[38]

The Synoptic Translations

The text on Deut. 6.5 is arguably cited four times in the Synoptic Gospels: twice in Mark, and once each in parallel passages in Luke and Matthew. To set the following discussion in perspective, all four quotations are displayed in tabular form, alongside the text of Deut 6.5:

Deut. 6.5	Mk 12.30	Mk 12.33	Lk. 10.27	Mt. 22.37
ואהבת את יהוה אלהיך	καὶ ἀγαπήσεις κύριον τὸν θεόν σου	καὶ τὸ ἀγαπᾶν αὐτὸν	ἀγαπήσεις κύριον τὸν θεόν σου	ἀγαπήσεις κύριον τὸν θεόν σου
בכל־לבבך	ἐξ ὅλης τῆς καρδίας σου	ἐξ ὅλης τῆς καρδίας	ἐξ ὅλης [τῆς] καρδίας σου	ἐν ὅλῃ τῇ καρδίᾳ σου
ובכל־נפשך	καὶ ἐξ ὅλης τῆς ψυχῆς σου		καὶ ἐν ὅλῃ τῇ ψυχῇ σου	καὶ ἐν ὅλῃ τῇ ψυχῇ σου
	καὶ ἐξ ὅλης τῆς διανοίας σου	καὶ ἐξ ὅλης τῆς συνέσεως	καὶ ἐν ὅλῃ τῇ ἰσχύϊ σου	καὶ ἐν ὅλῃ τῇ διανοίᾳ σου·
ובכל־מאדך	καὶ ἐξ ὅλης τῆς ἰσχύος σου·	καὶ ἐξ ὅλης τῆς ἰσχύος	καὶ ἐν ὅλῃ τῇ διανοίᾳ σου·	
		καὶ τὸ ἀγαπᾶν τὸν πλησίον ὡς ἑαυτὸν	καὶ τὸν πλησίον σου ὡς σεαυτόν.	

Table 2: *Texts*

Several things should be noted about the context of the Old Testament citations in the Synoptics. As was mentioned above, the context for the Deut. 6.5 text is as the second part of the Shema, yet only Mark preserves this context. Furthermore, all three Evangelists make the text a part of another complex unit comprised of Deut. 6.5 + Lev. 19.18, namely, a combination apparently known to the Synoptic writers as the (two) greatest commandment(s). Finally, the Evangelists differ somewhat on who speaks the words. Mark has what should be considered the

38. Cf. C. Spicq, *Agape in the New Testament* (St Louis: Herder, 1963); V.P. Furnish, *The Love Command in the New Testament* (Nashville: Abingdon Press, 1972), who both make the point of the unity of the two commandments in the Synoptics, and point out that 'love' in this context must be something like 'serve' or 'obey'.

original form of the citation in the Synoptics, not simply because he is generally believed to have written his Gospel first, but because the forms in Matthew and Luke can best be explained as using Mk 12.30 and 33 respectively. Dependence at this point has been notoriously difficult to show, possibly due to a complex dependence in which different aspects from the two quotations in Mark are used and combined creatively by Matthew and Luke.[39] Mark has Jesus speak the two commandments (with the first in the full Shema-form as well), and the 'scribe' paraphrastically repeats what Jesus says. Luke puts something closer to what Jesus says into the mouth of his 'lawyer', while Matthew, following Mark's 12.30 text even more closely than Luke (with the exception of the deletion of 'strength'), keeps the words on the lips of Jesus.[40]

That Luke is using Mk 12.33 as much as he is 12.30 is shown not only by the fact that he has the lawyer speak the text, but by the fact that he (with Mk 12.33 and against Mk 12.30 and Matthew) collapses the two commandments into one (see Table 2), while Mk 12.30 and Matthew explicitly name a first and a second commandment, listing them in separate sentences. Matthew also elaborates by saying that the second is like the first. Yet it is Luke who is most aware of the internal structure of the quotation, and refuses to insert 'mind' into the list, adding it instead onto the end.

The striking thing in the table is that, except for the common use of the phrase 'to love God', the only other term common to all the quotations is καρδία. Beyond this, all the Synoptic quotes/paraphrases add a

39. For example, in spite of the following analysis, there is the matter of the three versus four 'tones', which would point in the opposite direction for dependence. Cf. R.H. Gundry, *The Use of the Old Testament in St. Matthew's Gospel* (Leiden: Brill, 1975), pp. 22-24.

40. That Matthew has a 'lawyer' ask Jesus the initial question is not significant for this discussion, but is interesting in its own right for the Synoptic problem, particularly in view of the questionable nature of the term text-critically. It is likely that originally Matthew and Luke went their own ways with regard to this text even with regard to the identification of the questioner. Luke would have adjusted Mark's Jewish-sounding 'scribe' to 'lawyer', with Matthew interpretively assigning the speaker to the Pharisees by anaphora ('one of them'). The existence of 'lawyer' in Matthew's text would then be explained by secondary textual dependence on Luke (cf. B.M. Metzger, *A Textual Commentary on the Greek New Testament* [London: United Bible Societies, 1975], p. 59). That Matthew would blame the Pharisees for something the tradition he received did not, fits his redactional pattern as well, as commentators of Matthew have noted.

term equivalent to 'mind'.[41] The apparent reason is that while καρδία (heart) covered a good deal of the emotional sphere, the New Testament writers wanted to make sure that their readers understood heart (καρδία) in an Hebrew Bible sense and not 'as the seat of feeling and passion' as Liddell, Scott and Jones list it in their lexicon.[42] To be sure, in that lexicon 'love' is not explicitly listed among those feelings and passions, and the meaning 'mind' is also listed (as meaning number three, after feelings and desire), but a simple look at the lexical entries shows a dramatic shift from the meaning of לב in the Hebrew Bible, on the one hand, to the corresponding meaning of καρδία in Greek leading up to and including the New Testament era, on the other hand.

The term for mind or understanding is placed between καρδία and ἰσχύς in both Markan quotations, preserving the last position for ἰσχύς (= מאד) as in Deut. 6.5. Meanwhile Matthew omits this last element. The apparent adverbial/superlative force of מאד in the original Hebrew text, and the Evangelists' awareness of this fact, explains both of these seemingly diverse treatments of the term. Thus it belongs at the end, to modify the whole list ('and do it strongly/completely'), or it is regarded as superfluous (by Matthew) after such an all-encompassing grouping of terms.[43]

Only Luke, who, as I noted above, seems to be aware of the internal structure of the quotation, puts the terms in the order they occur in Deut. 6.5, and adds διάνοια at the end. This strategy, while divergent from that of the other Evangelists, supports the contention that resources for dealing with quotations in translation were limited in the New Testament era. What is apparent in all of the different ways of dealing with the Old Testament citation is that there was less freedom available to the ancient translator than there is today in respect of substitution of terms, and more freedom in respect of addition or deletion of terms. Thus the Evangelists all *add* some term for 'mind', rather than substituting it for καρδία.

41. Only Mark's scribe paraphrases the term, using σύνεσις instead. At the same time, he omits ψυχή altogether (the only one in the list to do so). This supports further the idea that καρδία in Greek could cover the emotional sphere, leaving ψυχή with no work to do.

42. LSJ, p. 877b.

43. The switch from the LXX's δύναμις to ἰσχύς does not seem to have any special meaning.

4. *Conclusion*

Deut. 6.5 has often been misunderstood due to the failure of any modern translation to translate the various terms of this verse precisely into English:

אהב as 'commit/be loyal to'	rather than 'love'
לב as 'mind'	rather than 'heart'
נפש as 'desire', or 'heart', or 'self'	rather than 'soul'
מאד as 'strongly/completely'	rather than 'strength'

A possible translation would be 'commit your minds and whole selves (or hearts) completely to Yahweh your God',[44] or perhaps 'commit yourselves whole-heartedly to Yahweh your God'.

The Synoptic translators tried to keep the force of the original as commitment by means of the addition of the term 'mind', or 'understanding' (διάνοια or σύνεσις), but their texts nevertheless have been interpreted sentimentally due to further semantic shifts between Greek and English. This was not so much their fault as the fault of subsequent translators who did not take sufficient notice of the differences in the meaning of 'heart' in various languages. If modern translators make the adjustments in Deut. 6.5 taking into account their own modern target language semantic domains, however, the problem of misunderstanding the New Testament citations of this text largely disappears since the quotation would now read a Deuteronomy text which speaks of whole-hearted commitment rather than deep emotion. The loss would be that the New Testament writer's adjustments may be obscured thereby. In translation, the quotation in the Synoptics might well collapse certain terms (e.g. for 'heart', 'soul' and 'mind') in the translation of the Deuteronomy text into English, as the suggested translations above indicate. There still might be some justification for stylistic variation between Mk 12.30 and 12.33, however, and Matthew would lack 'completely' or its equivalent. It should be noted again that the limitations of translation of a 'famous' text are such that not many modern translators would in fact be willing to attempt the above suggestions. In any case, it should not stand unchallenged, especially since many translations remain which reflect more formally the wording of the original languages.[45]

44. The older form of the imperative in English ('you shall/thou shalt') has been dropped in favor of the simpler modern form (bare verb first).

45. Cf. the traditional rendering of 'for length of days' as 'forever' at the end of Ps. 23.

The interesting point for modern translators of the Bible is that within the parameters of translation methods which existed at the time, the New Testament translators of this Old Testament text show an awareness of shifts in meanings of terms between biblical Hebrew and the Greek of their day, and try to make the necessary adjustments. The kinds of adjustments New Testament writers made to their religious traditions have variously been described as midrashic, allegorical, typological, rhetorical, traditio-historical and more. While these labels have been at times been and continue to be useful, it is also the case that at times the New Testament writers were simply trying to conserve the meaning of the tradition they were using or the text they were citing in the new contexts in which they were writing. While new contexts for old texts or traditions invariably involve semantic shifts, the processes which produce new meaning may be nothing other than the application of sound translation principles which attempt to conserve essential source meaning through the adaptation of form to context. It is thus that the New Testament writers, as well as their LXX predecessors,[46] have demonstrated sensitivity to some of the basic principles of functional equivalence translation. We would do well to learn from them. In the words of James Sanders, 'Adaptability and stability. That is canon.'[47] That is also translation.

46. The LXX translators or scribes responsible for the reading 'mind' (διάνοια) for 'heart' (לב) in Deut. 6.5 actually go further than Mark and his followers, replacing rather than simply adding terms which have shifted in meaning.

47. Sanders, 'Adaptable for Life', p. 561.

THE AUTHORITY AND INTELLIGIBILITY OF TORAH: REFLECTIONS ON A TALMUDIC STORY

Merrill P. Miller

I

Neither the closure nor the boundaries of the canon have been the decisive issue in James A. Sanders's seminal contributions to the field of canonical criticism. Rather, in my judgment, the decisive issue has been the hermeneutical process that Sanders regards as determinative both for the formation of the canon in the biblical communities and for the identity of the biblical communities shaped by the canon. The authority and intelligibility of Torah as well as the stability and adaptability of canon are only in subsidiary ways the expressions of canonical closure, textual standardization, and *relecture*. In Sanders's work, Torah and canon are chiefly the expressions of a theological hermeneutic that is evident in the selection and adaptation of tradition, and that operates in the subsequent shaping of the canon. Sanders has called it the monotheizing hermeneutic of the Bible, or, in a more philosophical vein, the affirmation of the integrity of reality. The community is constituted in the process of retrieving the monotheizing ethos of the Bible from earlier traditions and reworking it for ever new challenges. This hermeneutical process and ethos has also made it possible for Sanders to name what it is that links scholarly retrieval of the past to communal renewal in the present.[1]

1. Besides the volumes by Sanders, *Torah and Canon* (Philadelphia: Fortress Press, 1972) and *Canon and Community* (Philadelphia: Fortress Press, 1984), see especially the prologue and epilogue in *idem*, *From Sacred Story to Sacred Text* (Philadelphia: Fortress Press, 1987) and the essay by Sanders, 'The Integrity of Biblical Pluralism', in J.P. Rosenblatt and J.C. Sitterson, Jr (eds.), *'Not in Heaven': Coherence and Complexity in Biblical Narrative* (Bloomington and Indianapolis: Indiana University Press, 1991), pp. 154-69.

By emphasizing the centrality of a hermeneutical process in Sanders's contributions to canonical criticism, I am also taking account of recent discussion of the rabbinic canon and the criticism of an approach that restricts the adaptability of canon to the activity of reinterpretation without recognizing the redefinition of the boundaries of canon. In a recent article, David Kraemer has argued that the formation of the rabbinic canon entails as much movement toward reopening the canon as movement toward closure of the canon.[2] This double movement is also relevant to the wider issue of degrees of authority within a canon.[3] But if my judgment is correct, the more pertinent issue for Sanders would not be the changing boundaries of the rabbinic canon, but the hermeneutic that guided redefinition of the 'whole Torah' in rabbinic communities. However that hermeneutic might be precisely identified, what guided an expanded understanding of Torah among post-Mishnaic sages of Palestine and Babylonia clearly presupposed and built upon the association of wisdom and Torah.

To the question of the poet of Job 28, 'But where shall wisdom be found?' (v. 12), the sages of the Talmud had a ready and to them compelling answer. It is acquired in תַּלְמוּד תּוֹרָה, the study of Torah, in the discipline of scholastic dialogue and argument, and in the service rendered the teacher by the disciple.[4] It is acquired in the setting of the supernatural family constituted by the master–disciple circles of Palestine and Babylonia.[5] The study of Torah not only leads to a life of sagacity; it

2. D. Kraemer, 'The Formation of Rabbinic Canon: Authority and Boundaries', *JBL* 110 (1991), pp. 613-30.

3. Kraemer, 'Formation of Rabbinic Canon', esp. pp. 626-28.

4. On Job 28, see *b. Šab.* 89a and ch. 12 of *'Abot de Rabbi Nathan* in A.J. Saldarini, *The Fathers According to Rabbi Nathan Version B: A Translation and Commentary* (Leiden: Brill, 1975), pp. 94-97; cf. ch. 6 of *'Abot de Rabbi Nathan* in J. Neusner, *The Fathers According to Rabbi Nathan* (Atlanta: Scholars Press, 1986), translation based on S. Schechter, *Aboth de Rabbi Nathan* (Vienna: Ch. D. Lippe, 1887; repr., New York: Philipp Feldheim, 1945), pp. 51-52. On Torah as a symbolic abstraction, see J. Neusner, *Torah: From Scroll to Symbol in Formative Judaism* (Philadelphia: Fortress Press, 1985), esp. pp. 136-40, on Torah as an activity. For the centrality of argumentation in what constituted Torah from the middle Amoraic generations to the *gemara*'s final, anonymous editors, see D. Kraemer, *The Mind of the Talmud* (New York and Oxford: Oxford University Press, 1990).

5. Neusner, *Torah*, pp. 146-54. The study by David Goodblatt, *Rabbinic Instruction in Sasanian Babylonia* (Leiden: Brill, 1975), makes a strong case for the position that rabbinic instruction in Babylonia from the third to the fifth centuries was delivered in the setting of master–disciple circles rather than in the corporate setting

is the expression of it.[6] As in other sage traditions of late antiquity, the teacher is honored above one's natural father, for the teacher has drawn the disciple close to wisdom and thus has brought the disciple not merely into this world but into the world to come.[7]

The association of wisdom and Torah, an association that by Talmudic times was many centuries old, not only served to link the spiritual heritage of a people with primordial orders, or the typicalities of social experience with the revealed order at the foundation of the nation, it also served to account for the intense preoccupation with Torah as the object of study and meditation, of longing and desire among the pious and wise.[8] In turn, whatever the sages cultivated and transmitted in the

of an academy. The position that instruction took place in academies has been defended recently by Y. Gafni, *Yehude Bavel bi-Tequfat ha-Talmud* (Jerusalem: Merkaz Shazar, 1990), pp. 177-236, cited in R. Kalmin, 'Collegial Interaction in the Babylonian Talmud', *JQR* 82 (1992), p. 384 n. 2. Kalmin argues that encounters between masters (and not only between masters and their disciples) were quite frequent, formal and hierarchical, though it cannot be demonstrated that they took place in academies (p. 384).

6. For *'Abot* and *'Abot de Rabbi Nathan*, see A.J. Saldarini, *Scholastic Rabbinism* (Atlanta: Scholars Press, 1982) and J. Neusner, *Judaism and Story* (Chicago: University of Chicago Press, 1992), pp. 30-39. Neusner (*Torah*, pp. 54-56) sees study of Torah in *ʾAbot* as instrumental, an indicator of the status of the sage; in the Talmuds, especially the Bavli, Torah-learning brings salvation.

7. *m. B. Meṣ.* 2.11; *b. B. Meṣ.* 33a.

8. For discussions of this association and related expressions of piety in different historical periods, see J. Levenson, 'The Sources of Torah: Psalm 119 and the Modes of Revelation in Second Temple Judaism', in P.D. Miller, Jr, P. Hanson and S.D. McBride (eds.), *Ancient Israelite Wisdom: Essays in Honor of F.M. Cross* (Philadelphia: Fortress Press, 1987), pp. 559-74; B. Mack, *Wisdom and the Hebrew Epic: Ben Sira's Hymn in Praise of the Fathers* (Chicago: University of Chicago Press, 1985), esp. pp. 89-110; 112-20; on Ben Sira and Deuteronomy, see G. Sheppard, *Wisdom as a Hermeneutical Construct* (Berlin: de Gruyter, 1980); M. Fishbane, 'From Scribalism to Rabbinism: Perspectives on the Emergence of Classical Judaism', in *The Garments of Torah* (Bloomington and Indianapolis: Indiana University Press, 1989), pp. 64-78. This is not to suggest that what constitutes Torah is identical in late biblical and rabbinic literature, but only that it is the activity and piety of sages that establishes the link between wisdom and Torah; cf. expressions such as 'taking the yoke of Torah', 'drawing near to Torah', 'speaking words of Torah', and 'acquiring Torah' in *'Abot* with similar language applied to wisdom in Ben Sira and in the biblical wisdom Psalms. On the curriculum of the sage, cf. Sir. 39.1-3 and *ARN*, Version B, chs. 12; 28; *b. Suk.* 28a.

course of their study and life together eventually would come to have the status of Torah.[9]

II

For Sanders, 'monotheizing' refers to the struggle to affirm the ethical and ontological integrity of reality or oneness of God. This struggle gives the canonical process its intelligibility as a dialogue carried on across the ages in communities of faith.[10] Similarly, the intelligibility of Torah in the formative age of rabbinic Judaism is often described in terms of dialogue or conversation carried on across the generations and within each generation of the circle of sages.[11] This essay examines a familiar story in the Babylonian Talmud which shows, however, that at least on some occasions the conversation can prove to be unintelligible. And not only for outsiders (for whom it is almost always unfollowable). Indeed, as the story has it, it once happened to Moses, the one with whom the conversation began. In the course of the essay I will seek to identify the oppositions that are present in the story and suggest the sort of reflections that these oppositions invite. The goal will be to retrieve a dimension of the intellectual experience of a textual community and clarify the conditions of intelligibility of the object of its study. The story is cited in *b. Men.* 29b by R. Judah in the name of his teacher, Rav, the famous sage whose return from Palestine to his native Babylonia in the early part of the third century has conventionally marked the beginning of the Amoraic period.[12]

9. On the development of the conception of an Oral Torah, see most recently Neusner, *Torah*; P. Schaefer, 'Das Dogma von der mündlichen Torah im rabbinischen Judentum', in *Studien zur Geschichte und Theologie des rabbinischen Judentums* (Leiden: Brill, 1978), pp. 153-197; M.I. Gruber, 'The Mishnah as Oral Torah: A Reconsideration', *JSJ* 15 (1984), pp. 113-22; M.S. Jaffee, 'Oral Torah in Theory and Practice: Aspects of Mishnah-Exegesis in the Palestinian Talmud', *Rel* 15 (1985), pp. 387-410; Kraemer, 'Formation of Rabbinic Canon', pp. 616-19; *idem*, *The Mind of the Talmud*, pp. 117-18.

10. See Sanders, *From Sacred Story to Sacred Text*, esp. pp. 4-8; *idem*, 'The Integrity of Biblical Pluralism', esp. pp. 164-69.

11. For a statement of this in the context of midrash, see G.L. Bruns, 'The Hermeneutics of Midrash', in R. Schwartz (ed.), *The Book and the Text: The Bible and Literary Theory* (Oxford: Basil Blackwell, 1990), pp. 198-99.

12. J. Neusner, *A History of the Jews in Babylonia: The Early Sasanian Period*, II (Leiden: Brill, 1966), pp. 27-39; 126-34.

A. When Moses went up to the height [to receive the Torah], he found the Holy One, blessed be He, sitting and affixing crowns to the letters.
B. Moses said to him, 'Lord of the universe, who stays your hand?'
C. God said to him, 'There is a certain man who will arise at the end of some generations, and his name is Akiba b. Joseph. He is going to expound on each and every tittle heaps and heaps of laws.'
D. 'Lord of the universe, show him to me,' Moses requested.
E. 'Turn around,' God replied.
F. He turned around and went and sat at the back of eighteen rows[13] and did not know what they were saying. Moses grew weak.
G. When discussion reached a point,[14] the disciples of Akiba said to him, 'Master how do you know this?'
H. Akiba said to them, 'It is a law revealed to Moses at Sinai.' Moses was relieved.
I. He returned and came before the Holy One, blessed be He. Moses said to him, 'Lord of the universe, you have a person like this and you give Torah by my hand?'
J. God said to him, 'Be silent! That is what I have decided.'
K. 'Lord of the universe, you have shown me his Torah, show me his reward,' Moses [further] requested.
L. 'Turn around,' God replied.
M. He turned around and saw them weighing Akiba's flesh on the scales [in the market].
N. 'Lord of the universe, this is [his mastery of] Torah and this is its reward?!' cried Moses.
O. God said to him, 'Be silent! That is what I have decided.'

The striking and half-amusing scene that finds Moses in the classroom of Akiba stands in the center of the story (F-H). Taking his seat behind eighteen rows and hearing a discussion of Torah he cannot follow, Moses is at first distressed.[15] His mind is put at ease, however, when he

13. The variant reading (rather than 'eight rows') is well attested; see R. Rabbinovicz, *Diqduqei Soferim*, ad. loc. (New York: M.P. Press, 1976).

14. The printed edition has כיון שהגיע לדבר אחד. J. Fraenkel ('Hermeneutic Problems in the Study of the Aggadic Narrative', *Tarbiz* 47 [1978], pp. 168-69) argues that the reading כיון שהגיע לדבר is correct and that therefore we should understand that Akiba's disciples are asking for the source of their master's knowledge of a halaka that had been the subject of the midrashic discussion that Moses could not follow.

15. Moses sits in the back rows, which are for students who cannot follow the words of the sages and who therefore do not participate in the Torah-talk. Cf. *b. Ḥul.* 137b where R. Yohanan reports a similar experience: 'I remember when I was sitting before Rabbi, seventeen rows behind Rav, seeing sparks of fire leaping from the mouth of Rav into the mouth of Rabbi, and I did not know what they were

hears Akiba refer to him as the source of his knowledge of a law. We might conclude that the meeting between Moses and Akiba reflects contemporary debate about the authoritative sources of rabbinic behavioral norms. Are these norms generated by means of exegetical ingenuity applied to the Written Torah (F), or are they made available to the community through faithful transmission of the Oral Torah received by Moses at Sinai (G-H)?[16] The opposition that is given narrative expression in this scene seems to me to relate to a more general issue than the question of the sources of rabbinic halaka. To begin with, we must ask how this scene is related to a second one that is surely not amusing, in which Moses is shown the flesh of the martyred Akiba being weighed in the butchers' shops (M). Moreover, we will have to relate these two interior scenes (F-H; M) to the dialogue between Moses and God that frames them (B-E; I-L; N-O).

The story is cited in a discussion of the Mishnah's statements about conditions that invalidate the script of biblical texts contained in the mezuzah and the *tefillin*. A single imperfect letter invalidates the whole. The discussion includes teachings of Rav quoted by R. Judah on the conditions that must obtain in order for letters to be properly deciphered. Thus, in its literary context, the story highlights the perfection of every letter of the Torah. Moses finds God drawing תָּגִּין, the crowns consisting of three strokes that adorn seven letters of the Torah (A). In other instances in the Talmud, the binding of crowns is a gesture of

saying'; cf. Goodblatt, *Rabbinic Instruction*, pp. 252-59, on the order of seating at instructional sessions. Goodblatt believes it is Palestinian practice that is reflected in these seating arrangements.

16. One problem with this formulation of the issue is that the matter is hardly in doubt here, since Akiba himself resolves it. Akiba's midrash does not compete in the story with the view that rabbinic law (or at least some particular rabbinic laws) derives its authority from having been revealed to Moses at Sinai; see *b. Nid.* 45b where Akiba tells his disciples that the whole Torah is 'halaka revealed to Moses at Sinai'. Here, the perspective may be similar to that of *y. Pe*ʾ*ah* 2.17a and *y. Ḥag.* 1.76d where it is said that even what an accomplished disciple will teach before his master was said already to Moses at Sinai; thus, all innovations are somehow already implicit in the Torah received by Moses at Sinai. On the other hand, the tension reflected in the classroom scene in our story may be closer to the issue found in *b. 'Erub.* 13b where it is said that no one was comparable to R. Meir in his generation but that the sages did not fix the law according to him because they could not fully comprehend the subtleties of his views; see Kraemer's discussion of this text along the lines of opposition between practice and truth, *The Mind of the Talmud*, pp. 141-36.

praise.[17] Thus, we can probably assume that Moses has found God adding symbols of praise to the Torah, and since Moses is explicitly told that the crowns on the letters are affixed with a view to the future activity of Akiba b. Joseph, it would follow that Akiba's skill in drawing out a multitude of laws from each and every stroke redounds to the praise of the Torah and demonstrates its perfection.[18]

Yet this is not the aspect of the matter that evokes the response of Moses. In the first of three rhetorical responses that Moses addresses to God, the opacity of divine gestures is already to the fore. 'Who stays your hand?' (מי מעכב על ידיך) asks Moses (B). As a rhetorical question, this registers not only puzzlement about the necessity of these decorative strokes and the reason for delay in giving the Torah, but also expresses the inappropriateness and uselessness of questioning God's actions, unintelligible though they may be. Thus, in *b. B. Bat.* 16a, the sage, Raba, has Job say, 'you have created the righteous and you have created the wicked, and who stays your hand?' (i.e., who will prevent you or tell you what you may do?)[19] This response already anticipates the course of the dialogue with God, for later, Moses will return to ask in wonder, 'You have a person like this and you give Torah by my hand?' (I). Finally, he will express dismay over Akiba's fate and lament, 'This is Torah and this is its reward?!' (N). In both of these latter instances Moses will be told emphatically to cease (J; O), but not in the first instance. At first, he is met not with challenge but with irony, and is answered by God as though his question were a straightforward one.[20] There *is* someone who restrains God from giving the Torah before attaching crowns to the letters (C). The story then moves forward from Moses' desire to be shown Akiba (D). His request is granted (E), and later gives rise to a second request. Moses wishes to see not only Akiba's mastery of Torah, but also the reward it will bring: 'You have shown me his Torah, show me his reward' (K).

17. *b. Šab.* 88a; 104a; *b. Ḥag.* 13b and see Fraenkel, 'Hermeneutic Problems', p. 166.

18. In *Lev. R.* 19.1 (ed. Margaliouth, תיב־תיג), R. Joshua and R. Eliezer are also said to have interpreted the strokes (קוצים) of the letters. The statement is probably based on a midrash on the words in Song 5.11, קצוותיו תלתלים שחורות (see *Cant. R.* 5.11.1). For examples of Akiba's independent exposition of Scripture and its harmonization with halakic tradition, see *b. Sanh.* 51b and *Sifre* 75 (ed. Horovitz, p. 70); cf. *t. Zeb.* 1.8.

19. Cf. Fraenkel, 'Hermeneutic Problems', p. 166.

20. Fraenkel, 'Hermeneutic Problems', p. 166.

The fact that this second request follows the encounter with Akiba, and especially that it is made after Moses is told to be silent, suggests that in its present form the story may be composite. There is also some disparity between a story that seems to be focused on the relationship between Moses and Akiba in the context of the giving of the Torah (A-J), and a story that ends in response to the martyrdom of Akiba (K-O). Nevertheless, the second request of Moses presupposes the scene in the classroom and is explicitly linked to it. I would suggest that the story is constructed by means of a doubling in which a first climax (J) is heightened and intensified by a second (O). To achieve this effect, a second request by Moses serves to complete the original request to be shown Akiba.[21] This is followed by a second scene in the market (M), and concludes with a second silencing of Moses. The segments of the two-part narrative can be divided as follows:

[a] The puzzlement of Moses and his initial response to the crowns. (A-B)
- [b] God's description of Akiba and his activity. (C)
  - [c] Moses' request to be shown Akiba which is granted. (D-E)
    - [d] The scene in the classroom and the reactions of Moses. (F-H)
      - [e] Moses' return and the reference to Akiba and the giving of the Torah followed by the first silencing of Moses. (I-J)
  - [c′] Moses' second request which is also granted. (K-L)
    - [d′] The scene in the market. (M)
      - [e′] A second reference to Akiba (his mastery of Torah) and the second silencing of Moses. (N-O)[22]

I have briefly reviewed the major components of the story—setting, dialogue, scenes in the classroom and in the market—and have suggested the way in which the story is constructed. The problem of determining the sort of reflections invited by the story depends upon grasping its internal unity and correctly deciphering the oppositions that are present in the story.

21. Cf. Fraenkel, 'Hermeneutic Problems', pp. 170-71.

22. According to this division, the two parts of the narrative are of unequal length. It is important to see, however, that segment e not only points ahead to Moses' response to the martyrdom of Akiba and the silencing of Moses that concludes the narrative but also points back to segments a and b and God's initial description of Akiba and his activity. Cf. 'a certain man' (C) and 'a man like this' (I); 'your hand' (B) and 'my hand' (I).

III

Our story can be usefully compared in its narrative features to five other stories. Four of these are also found in the Babylonian Talmud. Three are attributed to the first-generation Palestinian Amora, R. Joshua b. Levi, at *b. Šab.* 88b-89a, while one is introduced as a *baraita* (a Tannaitic tradition not found in the Mishnah) at *b. Sanh.* 111a-b. The first story appears in *Pesiqta deRab Kahana* and is attributed to R. Jose bar Ḥanina, a second-generation Palestinian Amora (at *Pisqa* 4.7 on Num. 19.2, ed. Mandelbaum, p. 73). All six stories have as their setting the giving of the Torah to Moses at Sinai and, with one exception, are introduced by the temporal clause, 'When Moses ascended to the height'. (The other begins, 'When Moses descended from before the Holy One, blessed be He'.) In each story, the occasion and circumstances provoke a question, and an implied objection or the registering of astonishment. The stories consist mainly of dialogue between God and Moses, but in two instances also include members of the heavenly world.[23] In each case, circumstances, gestures and verbal exchanges create some point of tension which is resolved. At the same time, the dialogue reveals particular characteristics of Moses and different faces of Torah while showing that God is at once like a sage and yet God.[24] Passages of Scripture figure in all of the stories except ours, either as part of the dialogue, as commentary on the dialogue, or as prooftexts. Our story is also the only one that includes scenes that involve Moses directly in a time different from his own.

The six stories can also be arranged into three pairs. The first pair of stories turns on the wisdom and humility of Moses. Because of his responses to the objections of the angels and Satan against giving God's 'hidden treasure' to humankind, Moses is honored, and the Torah is seen as a boon for humankind.[25] Moses is corrected in the second pair of stories with the result that the difference between divine and human perspectives is highlighted while the intercession of Moses on behalf of Israel is also shown to be essential to the success of the project.[26]

In the third pair of stories the requests of Moses are granted but with

23. *b. Šab.* 88b-89a.

24. Our story does not differ significantly from the others with respect to these characteristics, even though the particular issues of our story are distinctive.

25. *b. Šab.* 88b-89a.

26. *b. Šab.* 89a; *b. Sanh.* 111a-b.

radically different consequences and implications. The story found in *Pesiqta deRab Kahana* is closest to ours. It appears in the context of a discourse for Sabbath *Para* (the ashes of the red heifer) on Num. 19.2. It is said that even Solomon in all his wisdom did not understand the rational grounds for the ashes of the red heifer. In another part of the discourse, R. Azariah, a fourth-generation Amora, delivers the views of a number of earlier Palestinian Amoraim to the effect that the instruction concerning the ashes of the red heifer is a decree that must be obeyed without rational explanation, which will be given only in the time to come, although one teacher states that the explanation was already revealed to Moses and another states that it was revealed only to R. Akiba. Then R. Azariah continues:

> A. R. Aha in the name of R. Jose bar Ḥanina: When Moses ascended to the height of the heavens he heard the voice of the Holy One, blessed be He, as he sat engaged in the passage on the ashes of the red heifer and cited the law in the name of the one who stated it: 'R. Eliezer says, "A heifer whose neck is broken is to be one year old and the red heifer, two years old."'
>
> B. Said Moses to the Holy One, blessed be He, 'Lord of the universe, the upper and the lower realms are under your authority and yet you sit and recite a law in the name of flesh and blood?'
>
> C. The Holy One, blessed be He, said to him, 'Moses, a certain righteous man is destined to arise in my world and destined to open his discourse with the passage on the red heifer beginning, R. Eliezer says, "A heifer whose neck is broken is to be one year old and the red heifer, two years old."'
>
> D. Moses said to him, 'Lord of the universe, may it be your will that he be from my loins.'
>
> E. God said to him, 'By your life, he is to be from your loins.' That is what is written (in Exod. 18.4), 'The name of the one Eliezer.' And the name of that special person is Eliezer.

Just as in our story, here too Moses finds God engaged in Torah, not, however, in inscribing the written one, but in reciting the discourse of a sage of the Mishnah. Here too Moses' initial response to the situation registers puzzlement, or better, astonishment, and in both cases Moses is pointed toward a future destined to bring forward a famous sage. Furthermore, in both stories Moses makes a request with respect to the named sage and in each case the request is granted. But these similarities serve to heighten the differences. In *Pesiqta*, not only is the Torah given to Moses at Sinai, but he quite literally embodies Torah. He is the progenitor of Torah in the person of his lineal descendant, R. Eliezer. The continuity and identity of the Torah across the generations is guaranteed by the self-same spiritual concern for the purification of Israel, by the verbatim repetition (by God!) of the sage's Torah, and by lineal descent. Here, the present and future face each other in complete transparency and merge in the physical and spiritual transmission of sages.

By contrast, our story reveals the future not as a matter of foreknowledge, but as a dimension that Moses is granted to enter in order to be shown the later sage. Here, though Moses is named in order to authorize a rabbinic law, it is not because he embodies the future of Torah, but in spite of the fact that it is unintelligible to him. Here, present and future do not stand in a continuous transparent relationship, but in one that is darker and more problematic.

IV

In order to relate the narrative oppositions in our story to the broader social context of a life of Torah study in the circles of sages, we need to take note of more general oppositions reflected in rabbinic cultures and literatures. First, there is the context of relations between circles of sages and the wider Jewish society. Recent studies have made it increasingly problematic to assume that the rabbis or rabbinical interests dominated the positions of political authority or represented the conventional social ideas of the larger society. For example, the study of Martin Goodman suggests that for second-century Roman Palestine it would be more appropriate to think of rabbinic circles in Galilee after the Bar Kochba revolt as a counter-culture. This counter-culture found it necessary to accommodate itself to the social and economic interests of Galilean farmers in order subsequently to enhance its claims and exercise functions of bureaucratic and judicial leadership.[27]

Although the interaction and influence of sages and their disciples on the wider society increases in the land of Israel and in Babylonia in the third century, the case remains that rabbinic circles were occupied with a special way of life.[28] The demands of Torah study, which involved long periods of apprenticeship to a particular master, often took priority over

27. M. Goodman, *State and Society in Roman Galilee, A.D. 132–212* (Totowa, NJ: Rowman & Allanheld, 1983), pp. 175-81.

28. See W.S. Green, 'Storytelling and Holy Man: The Case of Ancient Judaism', in J. Neusner (ed.), *Take Judaism, For Example* (Chicago: University of Chicago Press, 1983), pp. 39-42.

and created tensions with the requirements of earning a living and ordinary familial responsibilities, and even with the customary religious duties associated with the synagogue.[29] The supernatural power that accrued to the study of Torah formed the circles of disciples and their teachers into a supernatural family. Debates over the relative priority of deeds to learning, study of Torah to communal service, and the constant need to encourage local support for Torah scholars give evidence of a permanent tension between exalting Torah study to a supreme value and seeking to influence the patterns of social behavior and the institutions of the wider society.[30]

A second context concerns dynamics that are internal to the culture of master–disciple circles viewed as a textual community. Here, we need to take account of recent work of literary analysis of rabbinic texts and the program of documentary analysis of the rabbinic corpus in the work of Jacob Neusner. This work, which views the Judaisms of late antiquity as cultural systems, has helped to differentiate periods and styles within the rabbinic forms of the first six centuries and to distinguish stages in the formation of the rabbinic corpus. As a consequence, our view of intergenerational conflicts and tensions in rabbinic circles is also sharpened. From this perspective, later sages did not merely transmit and develop the programs of earlier generations, but, on the contrary, honored and gave recognition to their predecessors in the measure that they broke with their programs, aims and outlooks and appropriated what they received for their own purposes. One sees the process in the relationship of the two Talmuds to Scripture and Mishnah. Just as the midrash of the Talmudic era cites the Written Torah in an atomistic fashion and sets diverse comments side by side, so the *gemara* cites the Mishnah as Oral Torah, atomizing and deconstructing its formal and conceptual framework in the process and appropriating the words for its own extended discussions.[31]

29. For example, *b. Šab.* 10a; *b. Ber.* 8a, and see J. Neusner, 'Transcendence and Worship Through Learning: The Religious World-View of Mishnah', *Journal of Reform Judaism* 25 (Spring, 1978), pp. 15-29, esp. pp. 15-16; *idem*, *Judaism and Story*, pp. 30-39.

30. For example, *b. Meg.* 16b; *b. ʿErub.* 63b; cf. *b. Pes.* 50a on the altogether different relationship of the sages to the world to come from that of the wider society. See the discussion in E.E. Urbach, *The Sages: Their Concepts and Beliefs* (trans. I. Abrahams; 2 vols.; Jerusalem: Magnes, 1976), I, pp. 603-19, 626-28.

31. See the discussion of J.N. Lightstone from the perspective of the sociology of knowledge, *Society, the Sacred, and Scripture in Ancient Judaism* (Waterloo,

If rabbinic culture is not simply a reflection of the commonplaces and ideals of the wider society, and if rabbinic literature does not represent merely the continuous unfolding of what is already implicit in earlier sources, we have reason to question whether the largely collective voice of the sages in the redacted rabbinic texts is a simple reflection of the social experience of rabbinic circles. Such features of the texts as the ubiquitous citing of earlier authorities, the oppositional structure of many preserved traditions, the presentation of diverse views and different sources of authority side by side, and the abundance of stories about sages scattered throughout the literature which are never compiled to form a single biography[32]—all of these features create an impression of a society in which diversity and individuality certainly exist, but are modulated in a harmonious collective experience involving mutual recognition and common participation in an enterprise that spans the generations.[33]

But we must ask whether the impression of reciprocity, of acceptance and cultivation of opposing views, of continuity of tradition and intelligibility of discourse is not a deliberate aim of the authorships of rabbinic documents to express ideals and values that also serve to offset tendencies of excessive competition for disciples, for recognition of mastery of Torah, and for influence.[34] Rabbinic writings do speak largely in the collective voice of different authorships about a common enterprise to which all sages contribute. But they also give evidence of the warfare of Torah, the battlefield of rabbinic debate, particularly in the later strata of the Babylonian Talmud.[35]

Ontario: Wilfrid Laurier University Press, 1988), pp. 71-94. From a literary and rhetorical perspective, see Kraemer, *The Mind of the Talmud*, pp. 127-38.

32. See J. Neusner, *Why No Gospels in Talmudic Judaism* (Atlanta: Scholars Press, 1988).

33. Green, 'Storytelling', pp. 39-40; see D. Stern, 'Midrash and Indeterminacy', *Critical Inquiry* 15 (1988), pp. 153-61, and Bruns, 'Hermeneutics of Midrash', pp. 197-206 on *b. Ḥag.* 3a-b and related texts; R. Goldenberg, 'History and Ideology in Talmudic Narrative', in W.S. Green (ed.), *Approaches to Ancient Judaisms* (Chico, CA: Scholars Press, 1983), IV, pp. 159-71; Urbach, *Sages*, I, pp. 623-24, cites *b. Ket.* 75a: 'Of the stubborn and disputatious R. Jeremiah, who called Rav Sheshet, Abbaye, and even Rava "foolish Babylonians", Rava said: "When one of us goes up there (to Eretz-Israel), he is worth two of them. For R. Jeremiah, who did not know what the Rabbis were talking about, when he went up there called us foolish Babylonians".'

34. See the literature in the preceding note, esp. Stern, 'Midrash and Indeterminacy', pp. 155-56.

35. See *b. Ḥag.* 14a; *b. Sanh.* 111b.

The war was conducted at close quarters, and therefore among the casualties of the battlefield would certainly be overweening pride, pretensions to special powers, and fantasies of total victory.[36] But the battlefield would also produce brilliant strategists and attempts to outwit and outmaneuver opponents, and therefore in certain instances one might find that one did not know what the other was doing or saying.[37]

It is in thinking about Torah metaphorically as conversation and as warfare that we see the pertinence of the oppositions in our story. In other words, I am suggesting that the conceptual background of our story presupposes that Torah study is the ground of a common life and collective identity, but that the intelligibility of Torah also depends on the continuing acts of thought and imagination of singular human agents.[38]

V

To focus on the insular life and imaginative world of the sages may appear to ignore the climax of the story which relates to the martyrdom of Akiba by the Romans.[39] Moreover, if the story actually comes from the first generation of Amoraim, we might suppose that the memory of Akiba's fate was pertinent to Rav, who had studied among disciples of Akiba (and their disciples), and to other early third-century Babylonian Amoraim in view of the new Persian dynasty that had conquered, and that threatened the security and religious autonomy of Babylonian Jewry.[40] In any case, the closing scene in the story raises the question of theodicy.

36. Green, 'Storytelling', pp. 40-41.

37. References in the Bavli to not knowing what a sage (or sages) is saying usually signify recognition or a claim of superior Torah. But some of the contexts also show that this situation is problematic, especially with respect to claims of authority; see above, the references to *b. Ḥul.* 137b, *b. ʿErub.* 13b, and *b. Ket.* 75a in nn. 15, 16 and 33 respectively. To imagine Moses, the sage of sages, in that situation would tend to make the situation paradigmatic and suggest that it reflects a problematic or concern that is in some way definitive for the ethos of the community.

38. The idea that the locus of authority is to be found in a social process that shapes a collective enterprise seems to me to stand in the foreground of the articles by Stern and Bruns (above, n. 33) in dealing with the phenomena of polysemy in midrash. At the same time, it is clear from what they have written that they are aware that this expresses an ideal that was often far from the social experience of the rabbis.

39. On the imaginative world of the sages, cf. W.S. Green, 'Reading the Writing of Rabbinism: Toward an Interpretation of Rabbinic Literature', *JAAR* 51 (1983), pp. 203-204.

40. See Neusner, *A History of the Jews in Babylonia*, II, pp. 230-36.

The lament which Moses addresses to God, 'This is Torah and this is its reward?!', is found in other contexts as a form of questioning divine justice. This particular form is also related to others. In one of a number of studies designed to demonstrate the presence of Greco-Roman rhetorical forms in rabbinic literature, Henry Fischel compared several Aramaic and Hebrew *sententia* denying Providence with similar Greek and Latin coinages, and attributed the similar formal patterns to the widespread influence of Epicurean ideas and polemics against Epicureanism among similarly structured scholar-bureaucracies, namely, Greco-Roman rhetoricians and rabbinic sages of the first and second centuries.[41] The formal patterns discussed by Fischel entailed word repetition at the beginning of stichoi as well as types of alliteration, approximation of rhyme and additional repetitions at the end of stichoi. Examples of the pattern are, 'There is no justice and there is no judgment' (לית דין ולית דיין), 'Where is the goodness promised this one? Where is the length of days promised this one?' (איכן היא אריכות ימין של זה איכן היא טובתו של זה), 'There is no reward and there is no resurrection of the dead' (אין שכר ואין תחיית המתים), and also the one that appears in our story, 'This is Torah and this is its reward?!' (זו תורה וזו שכרה). Such sentences are attributed to biblical arch-heretics such as Cain and Esau as well as to the second-century heretic-sage Elisha ben Abuyah. They are also the sentiments of a whole biblical generation, the generation of the flood, and they are the conclusions that could be drawn from sayings of Solomon in Ecclesiastes, for which reason some sages sought to 'hide away' the biblical book.[42]

The instances of *sententia* of this kind that Fischel surveyed in rabbinic literature are clearly polemical. They are either placed in the mouths of the wicked, the unrepentant, so that they constitute speeches in character, or they are expressed and explicitly refuted. Nevertheless, as Fischel points out,

> in most of the Hebrew sources the 'Epicurean' speaker, likewise, speaks with great conviction but he speaks apparently in shock and despair, after a decisive event that seems to prove the non-existence of justice. This is true for Cain, Esau, Acher [Elisha ben Abuyah] and even the Sages who question Solomon.[43]

41. H. Fischel, 'An Epicurean Sententia on Providence and Divine Justice', in *Rabbinic Literature and Greco-Roman Philosophy* (Leiden: Brill, 1973), pp. 35-50.

42. Fischel, 'An Epicurean Sententia', pp. 35-40.

43. Fischel, 'An Epicurean Sententia', p. 48.

This is also true in one of the accounts of the martyrdom of Akiba. Even the ministering angels express shock and dismay over the disparity between Akiba's great learning, his Torah, and his fate. 'This is Torah and this is its reward?!' they cry, whereupon a heavenly voice goes forth and proclaims, 'Happy art thou, R. Akiba, that thou art destined for the life of the world to come.'[44]

In our story there is no heavenly voice that goes forth assuring Akiba's place in the world to come, but a rebuke that brings Moses to silence before what appears to be an absolutely closed case. Clearly, this is an instance of questioning divine justice that does not conform to the usual intent to characterize apostasy or to present a satisfactory theodicy.[45] Here there is a subversive posture that seems to counter the conventional wisdom, 'The more Torah the more life' (*m. ʾAb.* 2.7). The reason for this is that our story is not focused on the specific issue of divine justice but on the enduring tension and reciprocity between the authority and the intelligibility of Torah.

VI

A review of two recent discussions of our story will bring the issues of interpretation into sharper focus. Jonah Fraenkel has applied to the story the methods of structural analysis of folktales in an effort to show how artistic and didactic features are joined in tales found in the two Talmuds.[46] According to Fraenkel (and many others), rabbinic tales reflect the worldview of the story-teller and not the historical personality of the hero. Whether the tales have as their background and setting historical events or a supernatural world, they take no account of historical process or broader historical factors. The stories are carefully

44. *b. Ber.* 61b.

45. For the idea of erotic, mystic death and the ideology of martyrdom, and its connection with a midrash attributed to R. Akiba, see D. Boyarin, *Intertextuality and the Reading of Midrash* (Bloomington and Indianapolis: Indiana University Press, 1990), pp. 117-29. Neither theodicy nor martyrdom and mystic vision appear to be in view in our story.

46. Fraenkel, 'Hermeneutic Problems'; *idem*, '*Ma'aseh be-R. Shila*', *Tarbiz* 40 (1970), pp. 33-40; *idem*, 'Paranomasia in Aggadic Narratives', *Scripta Hierosolymitana* 27 (1978), pp. 27-51; *idem*, 'The Portrait of R. Joshua b. Levi in the Stories of the Babylonian Talmud', *Proceedings of the World Congress of Jewish Studies* 6 (1973), pp. 403-17; cf. N.J. Cohen, 'Structural Analysis of a Talmudic Story: Joseph-Who-Honors-The-Sabbaths', *JQR* 72 (1982), pp. 161-77.

plotted, each part being planned with a view to the whole, and the details and concerns of the stories make sense only internally.[47]

In Fraenkel's reading of our story, Moses is no straight man. The movement of the plot depends on his questions and requests, and interest is in fact focused on his responses; in particular, his response to the meeting of Akiba.[48] Fraenkel argues that Moses is 'set up' by God's curious delay in giving the Torah in order to test his response to those who will engage in its study in the future.[49] At the outset, Moses is ready to receive the Torah and is puzzled by the delay. But when he returns to his own time he is astonished that God, who has someone like Akiba, gives the Torah through him. According to Fraenkel, the astonishment of Moses demonstrates that he is not jealous of Akiba and therefore is worthy to receive the Torah.[50] In a similar manner, Moses knows that he will be honored throughout the generations, which dramatizes the absence of reward for Akiba. Moses' dismay over Akiba's fate is a further expression of the hero's concern for his fellow mortal.[51] Fraenkel goes on to argue that although the story takes place in a supernatural setting, it reveals an opposition in the history of Torah. Moses knows about the crowns but will never understand what 'they are saying' in the schools. Akiba knows how to do midrash but will never know about the crowns. Moses will be given the Torah and will always be honored for his role. Akiba will engage in midrash through his own ingenuity, but will depend on Moses' authority and never know that there is a reward for this.[52]

Fraenkel's reading stresses the humility and humanity of Moses as revealed by his responses to Akiba. But this reading depends on setting aside the responses of God. For Fraenkel, God's responses point to matters already decided and interest is focused on what is to be decided in the course of the story, namely, the worthiness of Moses to receive the Torah.[53] I agree that the internal coherence of the story depends on

47. Fraenkel, 'Hermeneutic Problems', pp. 139-45.

48. Fraenkel, 'Hermeneutic Problems', p. 165.

49. Fraenkel, 'Hermeneutic Problems', pp. 166-69.

50. Fraenkel, 'Hermeneutic Problems', p. 169.

51. Fraenkel, 'Hermeneutic Problems', p. 172.

52. Fraenkel, 'Hermeneutic Problems', p. 172.

53. Fraenkel ('Hermeneutic Problems', pp. 169, 171) takes God's final statements as declarations that the history of the unfolding of Torah and the roles of those who engage in Torah have already been appropriately determined by divine decree. Within these established boundaries, the humility and humanity of Moses are revealed in his responses.

following the experience of Moses and that Moses' initial response to the crowns implies a suspicion that delay involves the choice of someone else to receive the Torah. But before Moses has returned to God he already knows that he will receive the Torah because of Akiba's response to the disciple's question and now, knowing what he knows as one who cannot follow or participate in the Torah-talk of the classroom, he returns with a question of astonishment. God's response to Moses is a rebuke and is surely not meant in praise of his humility. Rather, Moses' astonishment unfolds the second stage of a sequence that moves from puzzlement about decorative flourishes (B) to astonishment about divine choices (I) to dismay about human consequences (N).

However, the oppositions that Fraenkel discerns in the story are instructive. In particular, the oppositional relationship of Mosaic authority and Akiban ingenuity is clearly present in the classroom scene. But there seems to be little connection between the oppositions enumerated by Fraenkel and the claim that the story highlights the humility of Moses. Moreover, the contrasting situations of Moses and Akiba in the story are hardly to be accounted for by their different historical locations, as I think Fraenkel implies.[54] The details of the story, as well as the rabbinic worldview, would seem to defy that particular kind of historical realism. It is more likely that the contrasting situations reflect oppositions that are felt to be inherent in the life of a community engaged in the study of Torah.

Despite the tradition of Akiban exegesis with its attention to extraneous words as pegs for legal deductions, there is no report of his deducing laws from the decorative strokes of certain Hebrew consonants.[55] To do so means deriving rules of behavior from mute features of a sacred artifact.[56] What is suggested is that the perfection of the Written Torah depends on the ingenuity of Akiba; the adorning is done for the sake of his unrepeatable feats of genius. Akiba does not merely take his place in a line of tradents. He makes his own discoveries, and his singular mode

54. In Fraenkel's view ('Hermeneutic Problems', p. 168), Moses does not know what they are saying in the classroom because midrash as a historical phenomenon belongs to the future. But the contrast between Moses' authority and Akiba's ingenuity is surely more than a matter of their different historical locations for those who have imagined such a scene.

55. See B. Visotzky, 'Jots and Tittles: On Scriptural Interpretation in Rabbinic and Patristic Literatures', *Prooftexts* 8 (1988), p. 258.

56. See W.S. Green, 'Romancing the Tome: Rabbinic Hermeneutics and the Theory of Literature', *Semeia* 40 (1989), p. 158.

of engagement with the Mosaic legacy abounds to the praise of Torah, though this achievement earns him neither authority nor reward. Moses, on the other hand, does not share in Akiba's mastery of Torah, yet his authority as the source is honored. The opposition of Moses and Akiba is between the authority of a collective voice that is faithfully transmitted from generation to generation and the idiosyncratic achievements of individual sages.

The daring of the story may be felt to lie in its capacity to question whether the Torah received by Moses is the same Torah that Akiba (or third-century masters) studies and teaches.[57] But the issue appears to be dodged by Akiba's appeal to the authority of Moses. The identity and authority of Torah is not what is in question here. The issue is making sense of how Torah matters for life.[58] What are the conditions of its intelligibility from generation to generation? If authority rests in what is already given, one's own particular contribution to the ongoing conversation can only arise as a consequence of the loss of intelligibility of earlier voices. Akiba has made Torah make sense in his own inimitable way and with respect to that achievement every preceding generation beginning with Moses will take a back seat. It is not just that future expressions of Torah are not exhausted in the revelation of Sinai, but that the future direction of the conversation is unpredictable. However, the achievement of intelligibility cannot be at the expense of the authority and identity of Torah. Citing earlier authorities is a condition of carrying authority in the conversation, even as cutting earlier authorities out of the conversation is a condition of its ongoing intelligibility. The generations are linked by a trade-off—authority for intelligibility.

VII

Jacob Neusner cites our story at the end of his study of the way in which the incarnation of God comes to expression in the later documents of the rabbinic canon.[59] Neusner has developed a taxonomy of rabbinic narrative that distinguishes between the traits of stories told

57. Cf. Visotzky, 'Jots and Tittles', pp. 266-67.

58. I am referring especially to how Torah matters for sages, that is, for a life of study and teaching of Torah in the context of master–disciple circles, and not principally to how it matters in practical application—הלכה למעשה.

59. J. Neusner, *The Incarnation of God: The Character of Divinity in Formative Judaism* (Philadelphia: Fortress Press, 1988), pp. 201-30.

about contemporary sages (sage-stories), stories told about a scriptural hero (Scripture-stories), and stories that represent God as being like a human being, especially like a sage engaging in argument and transacting exchanges (God-incarnate-stories). The sage-story has a beginning, middle and end and develops from a point of tension and conflict to a clear resolution. It does not usually cite Scripture or illustrate the meaning of a verse of Scripture. The Scripture-story, on the other hand, has little movement, tends to form a stationary tableau and has the exegesis of Scripture as its central interest. God-incarnate-stories present a more mixed picture, according to Neusner. In some, the narrative role of God is closer to that of the scriptural hero, while in others, it is closer to the characteristics of the sage. Even instances of the latter, however, exhibit the difference that they climax in the citation of Scripture.[60] In only one story, the one under discussion, is the feature of scriptural citation lacking, so that it conforms most closely to the traits of the sage-story.[61] Nonetheless, in a crucial detail it too breaks decisively with the sage-story. There is no resolution of the conflict. Neusner concludes his study in these words:

> So the one truly striking story about God in the form of not a human being in general but a sage in particular, a sage engaged in debate and argument, turns out to make precisely the opposite of the point of every other sage-story. All other such stories tell us how sages resolve points of tension and sort out conflict...But this story tells us the precise opposite, which is that God decrees and even the sage—even our rabbi, Moses, the sage of all sages—must maintain humble silence and accept the divine decree... the sage is like God, but, like all other human beings, subject to God's ultimately autocephalic decree...This I take to be the final statement of the incarnation of God of the Judaism of the dual Torah.[62]

The special place that this story occupies in Neusner's taxonomy is significant. The story does give the impression of making some final, definitive statement, as Neusner has concluded, and the absence of scriptural citation is a characteristic only of the sage-story. But the characterization of God as a sage engaged in debate and argument seems to be exactly what Neusner is showing to be missing here. To be exact, in our story God makes what first appear to Moses to be superfluous gestures,

60. Neusner, *Incarnation*, pp. 220-28. For a fuller treatment of the place of narrative in the rabbinic canon, see *idem*, *Judaism and Story*.

61. Neusner, *Incarnation*, pp. 228-29.

62. Neusner, *Incarnation*, pp. 229-30.

but who can question what God does! God grants requests which bring about responses of astonishment and protest, both of which are silenced as soon as they are uttered. Neusner has not shown in what way God is depicted as a sage in this story, since apparently the dialogue is not an engagement in debate and argument. Neusner arrives at his conclusions, in part, because Moses seems only to be a straight man who provides occasion for God's stunning replies.[63] But Moses is more than a straight man in the story, and the terms of opposition between Moses and God may not be simply those of mortal to deity.

It is the desire to make sense of things that gives the story its coherence by supplying a consistent characterization of Moses and by providing the narrative connections that link the scenes of the future to the dialogue with God. We see Moses puzzled, astonished and finally dismayed. His desire to meet Akiba is the desire of the sage to see for himself how the Torah he is to receive will matter for the future. The future affords him recognition of the honor and authority that will accompany his name through the generations ('It is a law received by Moses at Sinai') but entails a defeat of his quest for intelligibility. ('Silence! That is what I have decided.')

Since Moses cannot follow the conversation of Akiba and his disciples, he is of course unable to fathom the mind of the Holy One, blessed be He. On beginnings and endings, the case is closed; matters have already been decided. This posture would seem to assert the rules of a system that appeals to the authority of tradition and operates within the limits of intelligibility decreed by God. Akiba must appeal to Moses for the source of his knowledge and not to the ingenuity of his own discoveries. Moses must be silent before God's decrees. The pattern is certainly familiar from Israelite and ancient Near Eastern wisdom: fear of God is the beginning of wisdom and the wise make their own an age-old tradition which they have sought out and faithfully transmitted to the next generation. However, it is not difficult to see the problem of reflecting on the story only in terms of this familiar pattern. Yes, Akiba must appeal to the authority of tradition. But it is God's own scribal gesture that underwrites his ingenuity and thereby endorses the singular human agent, the unrepeatable sage and his idiosyncratic wisdom of personal discovery.[64]

63. *Incarnation*, p. 229.

64. Cf. M.V. Fox, *Qohelet and his Contradictions* (Sheffield: Almond Press, 1989), pp. 94-100.

From this perspective, we should consider whether God's decrees may not be more covertly sage-like than patently God-like. True, each entry into the future leads Moses to confront God's own statement of closure. But it is not as much a matter of silent submission to the will of God as a question of being faced with the idiosyncratic mind of God. Moses is brought to silence before a decision that arises in thought (לפני כך עלתה במחשבה)[65] A more literal translation would be, 'That is what has come to mind,' or even, 'That is what I have thought up.' What is demanded of Moses here is to risk the loss of intelligibility by letting it depend on the contingencies of personal discovery and idiosyncratic response rather than to abandon the quest for intelligibility by turning it over to the absolute authority of God. In theological terms, one might surely take the commands to silence as expressions of a monotheizing hermeneutic. But as a reflection on Torah as conversation and warfare, the matter at hand is only the ordinary puzzle of how to grasp individual human agency together with social process and collective identity.

In this story a space is provided for what cannot be simply an expression of a collective voice. Torah also increases in what is undeniably individual, in what does not come to rest completely in the authority of tradition and in what cannot always be tested by the canons of an age-old wisdom. It arises as a candid reflection about the intelligibility of Torah and how that depends on the real agents of Torah who are not only a collective voice but singular human beings.[66]

65. See *b. Pes.* 54b; *b. Ber.* 61a; *Lev. R.* 29.

66. I wish to thank the Office of Academic Affairs of Pembroke State University and the Faculty Research and Development Committee for a grant in support of research which helped defray part of the costs incurred in the writing of this essay.

L'APPROPRIATION JUIVE ET CHRÉTIENNE DU PSAUTIER

Dominique Barthélemy

Mon cher Jim, le Psautier de la grotte 11 de Qumrân que tu as édité t'a entraîné vers des analyses de la valeur canonique de ce livre ainsi que des autres qui constituent la Bible. Tu nous a aidés à nous convaincre que ces vieux livres ne trouvent leur contexte authentique qu'au sein d'un peuple qui les médite et les prie. C'est dans cette perspective que je voudrais me situer en cet hommage qui essaie de poursuivre certaines promenades que nous fîmes ensemble sur des sentiers de la Forêt Noire.

La réforme liturgique qui, dans l'Eglise catholique, a fait suite au concile Vatican II nous a permis de constater la perpétuelle jeunesse du Psautier et sa prestance supra-testamentaire. Pour une Eglise en veine d'aggiornamento, le Psautier s'impose comme la seule prière indiscutée et capable de ressusciter dans les sensibilités de chaque nouvelle génération. C'est par une concession pastorale—que j'espère provisoire—à la faible formation catéchétique de beaucoup de ceux qui ont à le réciter, que le pape Paul VI a autorisé ceux-ci à omettre dans la psalmodie de l'Office divin des versets et même certains psaumes d'imprécation. Cela n'empêche pas la plupart des communautés monastiques occidentales et, en tout cas, toutes celles des Eglises d'Orient de réciter le livre des Psaumes dans son intégralité. Il ne faudrait pas s'imaginer, en effet, que le Psautier, en tant que forme canonique de la prière du Peuple de Dieu, ait à se soumettre à la sentimalité plus ou moins fragile de ceux qui croient devoir se l'approprier.

Pour déterminer qui a le droit de s'approprier le Psautier, il faut répondre à une question primordiale qui s'est posée aux rabbins d'Israël comme aux premiers docteurs de l'Eglise: qui dit le Psautier? Je voudrai relever certaines réponses à cette question, selon le Midrash et selon S. Augustin. Je considère en effet ces réponses convergentes comme ayant une autorité traditionnelle suffisante pour qu'elles puissent être prises au sérieux en des branches diverses du Peuple de Dieu. Mon but est seulement d'ouvrir l'accès de quelques pistes sur lesquelles d'autres s'engageront.

Dans la Synagogue, qui dit le Psautier?

Sur le début du Livre des Psaumes, le *Midrash Tehillim* commence par énumérer, dans un ordre qui se veut chronologique, les dix hommes qui ont 'dit' (au sens de 'composé') les Psaumes: Adam, Melchisédec, Abraham, Moïse, David, Salomon, Asaph et les trois fils de Qorach.[1] Puis le midrash mentionne Rab Huna qui a rapporté au nom de Rab Acha:

> Quoique le livre des Psaumes ait été dit par dix personnes, il n'a été dit (au sens de 'récité') rien que par David, le Roi d'Israël. C'est comme un chœur de chanteurs qui voulait exécuter un hymne en l'honneur du roi. Celui-ci leur déclara: Quoique vous soyez tous des chanteurs aussi agréables qu'excellents et dignes d'exécuter un hymne en l'honneur du roi, ce sera seulement un tel qui l'exécutera pour vous tous. Pourquoi? Parce que sa voix est encore plus délicieuse que toutes les vôtres. C'est ce qui est écrit (2 Sam. 23.1): 'et le délicieux, quant aux hymnes d'Israël'. Qui est le délicieux, quant aux hymnes des Israélites? C'est David, le fils de Jessé.[2]

Et au nom de qui David dit-il le Psautier? C'est sur Ps. 18.1 que le même midrash nous apportera une réponse: R. Judan rapportait au nom de R. Jehudah: 'Tout ce que David a dit dans son livre, il l'a dit comme le concernant lui-même et concernant tout Israël et tous les temps'. Plusieurs exemples sont donnés de cette double interprétation. Ainsi, sur Ps. 3.6, le *Midrash Tehillim* expose:

> David a dit 'je me suis couché' par la prophétie 'et je me suis endormi' par l'Esprit saint. 'Je me suis réveillé' par Chushaï le Arkite [allusion à la fuite de David devant Absalom et à la démarche de Chushaï (2 Sam. 15.32-37 et 16.5-16) qui assurera son rétablissement sur le trône royal] 'parce que le Seigneur m'a conforté' par Nathan le prophète. Autre interprétation: c'est ce que la communauté d'Israël a dit: 'je me suis couchée' par la prophétie 'et je me suis endormie' par l'Esprit saint. 'Je me suis réveillée' par Elie, comme il est dit: voici que je vous envoie le prophète Elie (Mal 3.23) 'parce que le Seigneur m'a conforté' par le Roi messie.[3]

1. S. Buber, *Midrasch Tehillim* (3 vols.; Vilnius: ha-Almanah veha-Aḥim Rom, 1891), 1.6 (II, p. ד).
2. Buber, *Midrasch Tehillim*, 1.6 (II, p. ד).
3. Buber, *Midrasch Tehillim*, 3.7 (II, p. כ).

David et la communauté se retrouvent donc dans la récitation du Psautier. Chacun des deux le récite en son propre nom et au nom de l'autre. Mais quel est le David qui dit le Psautier? Si cette question mérite d'être posée, c'est parce que, selon le Midrash Tehillim sur Ps. 5.1,

> R. Shemuel bar Nachmani a dit: 'le pluriel הַנְּחִילוֹת signifie les deux héritages qu'a obtenus David: la royauté en ce monde et pour le monde qui vient. En effet, Il dit: 'et aussi j'en ferai un aîné' (Ps. 89.28). Mais David était-il l'aîné? N'est-il pas dit: 'et David était le plus petit' (1 Sam. 17.14). Pourquoi donc l'appelle-t-Il aîné? sinon parce que l'aîné reçoit une double part dans l'héritage. Aussi David a-t-il hérité des deux héritages de la royauté: en ce monde et pour le monde qui vient.[4]

Selon le *Midrash Tehillim* sur Ps. 57.1, R. Tachlipha de Césarée explique la déclaration faite par Saül à David:

> 'Maintenant voici que je le sais: pour régner, tu régneras!' (1 Sam. 24.21). 'Pour régner' veut dire en ce monde, 'tu régneras' dans le monde qui vient, comme il est dit: 'Et mon serviteur David sera roi sur eux' (Ezec. 37.24).[5]

Encore sur Ps. 75.11:

> 'Les cornes du juste s'élèveront.' Il s'agit de la corne du roi messie lors de son intronisation, car il est dit: 'et il élèvera la corne de son Messie' (1 Sam. 2.10). C'est la corne de David dans la lumière du monde qui vient, car il est dit: 'Alors je ferai germer une corne pour David, j'ai préparé une lampe pour mon messie' (Ps. 132.17).[6]

Le *Midrash Tehillim* n'est pas seul à offrir cette vue. En effet, déjà les *ʾAbot de Rabbi Nathan* tiennent que 'David a régné en ce monde et régnera dans le monde qui vient'.[7] Et selon un supplément à *Bereshit Rabbah* sur la bénédiction de Jacob, 'Juda, tes frères te loueront' (Gen. 49.8) porte sur ce monde et sur le monde qui vient.[8] En ce monde, David fut le premier des descendants de Juda à régner. Et il régnera de même dans le monde qui vient: 'Et David mon serviteur sera prince pour eux à jamais' (Ezec. 37.25). Ces vues sont sous-jacentes à la

4. Buber, *Midrasch Tehillim*, 5.4 (II, p. קמט).
5. Buber, *Midrasch Tehillim*, 57.3 (II, p. קל).
6. Buber, *Midrasch Tehillim*, 72.5 (II, p. ד).
7. S. Schechter, *Masekhet Avot de-Rabbi Natan* (Vienne: Ch. D. Lippe, 1887), p. 125.
8. J. Theodor et Ch. Albeck, *Bereschit rabba: mit kritischem Apparat und Kommentar* (4 vols., 2de éd.; Jérusalem: Wahrman, 1965), pp. 1207f.

déclaration du talmud *b. Roš Haš.* 25a: 'David, le Roi d'Israël, est vivant et subsiste.'

Le roi-chantre du banquet divin

A propos du pluriel 'des trônes', dans la mise en scène du jugement final en Dan 7.9, le talmud *b. Sanh.* 38b nous rapporte que R. Aqiba scandalisait ses collègues en déclarant: 'un pour Lui et un pour David'. Et R. José lui répliquait: 'Aqiba, jusqu'à quand vas-tu profaner la Shekhinah. Plutôt un pour le jugement et un pour la miséricorde.' Nous verrons que les midrashim ont développé la vue d'Aqiba. Il y eut cependant des divergences sur la position du trône de David par rapport à celui du Seigneur. Une vue classique est tenue par le *Seder Eliahu Rabbah*: 'Le Saint béni-soit-il a décidé de faire asseoir David à la droite de la Shekhinah, comme il est écrit: "Oracle du Seigneur à mon seigneur: Siège à ma droite"'.[9]

C'est le moment de citer les chapitres 4 et 5 des suppléments aux *Hékhalot Rabbati*, selon l'édition qu'en a donnée Jellinek.[10] Pour consoler R. Ishmaël ben Elisha à qui il venait d'annoncer tous les malheurs qui arriveraient à Israël du fait des Romains, l'ange Hadarniél lui fit voir de nombreux groupes d'anges de service qui préparaient de belles couronnes pour les fils d'Israël.

> Et je vis une couronne qui surclassait toutes les autres: le soleil, la lune et douze étoiles y étaient sertis. Je lui dis: 'Et cette couronne admirable, pour qui est-elle?' Il me dit: 'Pour David roi d'Israël'. Je lui dis: 'Ô transcendante splendeur, fais-moi voir la gloire de David.' Il me dit: 'Mon chéri, patiente trois heures jusqu'à ce que David arrive ici et tu verras sa majesté.' Il me saisit et me fit asseoir dans son giron. Il me dit: 'Que vois-tu?' Je lui dis: 'Je vois sept éclairs qui courent ensemble.' Il me dit: 'Ferme les yeux pour ne pas frémir. Ceux-là sortent à la rencontre de David.' Soudain furent ébranlés tous les ophanim et les seraphim et les vivants sacrés et les trésors de neige et les nuées de gloire et les constellations et les étoiles et les anges du service. Et ils disaient: 'Au Vainqueur etc. les cieux racontent etc.' Et j'entendis le bruit d'un grand ébranlement venant de l'Eden et disant: 'Le Seigneur régnera pour toujours et à jamais!' Et voici David roi d'Israël en tête et derrière lui tous

9. M. Friedmann, *Seder Eliyahu rabba ve-seder Eliyahu zuta* (Vienne: Ahi'asaf, 1902) 18.1.

10. A. Jellinek, *Bet ha-Midrash* (6 vols., 2de éd.; Jérusalem: [s.n.], 1938), V, p. 168.

> les rois de la maison de David, chacun ayant sa couronne sur la tête. Et la couronne de David était plus resplendissante et plus admirable que toutes les autres et son éclat fulgurait d'une extrémité du monde à l'autre. Puis David monta au sanctuaire qui est dans le firmament et là lui était préparé un trône de feu [...] et il s'assit sur ce trône qui faisait face à celui de son créateur et tous les rois de la maison de David étaient assis en sa présence et les rois d'Israël se tenaient debout derrière lui. Tout de suite, David se leva et dit chants et louanges comme aucune oreille ne les avait jamais entendus. Et lorsque David entonna: 'Que le Seigneur règne à jamais etc.', Métatrône, puis toute la cour céleste se mirent à entonner: 'Saint, saint, saint, le Seigneur Sabaot etc'. Et les vivants sacrés louaient en disant: 'Bénie soit la gloire du Seigneur à partir de son séjour'. Et les firmaments disaient: 'Que le Seigneur règne à jamais'. Et la terre disait: 'Le Seigneur est roi! le Seigneur est roi!' Et les rois de la maison de David disaient: 'Le Seigneur sera roi sur toute la terre. En ce jour-là le Seigneur sera unique et son nom unique.'

Rappelons ici qu'une donnée bien établie dans le *livre des Jubilés* (2.21, 31; 6.17-19; 30.18; 31.14) et dans la communauté de Qumrân (1QSb iv 23-26) est que le culte terrestre n'a de signification que par le fait qu'il s'associe à celui qui se célèbre dans le sanctuaire céleste. Si David est toujours vivant, c'est parce qu'il a été intronisé dans ledit sanctuaire comme chantre pour entonner la psalmodie universelle, alors que tous les participants de la liturgie céleste lui répondent. A ce titre, il préside à la fois la psalmodie céleste et celle de la Synagogue.

Voici maintenant une description du festin paradisiaque tirée du *Siddur de Rab Amram Gaon*:

> Le Seigneur dit aux hommes pieux: 'Allez au jardin d'Eden et célébrez le banquet qui vous a été préparé et buvez le vin qui, en ses grappes, vous a été réservé depuis les six jours de la création.' Et eux disent: 'Maître du monde! un banquet a-t-il lieu sans que le maître de maison soit présent? Si tu le veux bien, que ta Shekhinah se tienne parmi nous.' Tout de suite, David dit au Seigneur: 'Maître du monde! témoigne-nous ta bienveillance en siégeant parmi nous.' Alors le Saint béni-soit-il exauce David, comme il est dit (Isa. 58.9): 'Alors tu appelleras et le Seigneur répondra. Tu crieras et il dit: "me voici".' Tout de suite le Saint béni-soit-il fait son entrée et tous les hommes pieux se lèvent de leur trône tandis que le Saint béni-soit-il s'assied sur le trône de sa gloire. David s'assied en face de lui sur le trône qui lui a été préparé, comme il est dit (Ps. 89.37): 'et son trône est comme le soleil devant moi'. Et tous les hommes pieux s'asseyent sur leurs trônes, se réjouissent et boivent environ trois verres de vin nouveau, comme il est dit (Cant. 8.2): 'Je t'abreuve avec mon vin épicé tiré du jus de mes grenades.' Gabriel prend deux coupes, l'une pour le Saint béni-

soit-il et l'autre pour David, comme il est dit: 'et sa coupe (כֹּסוֹ au lieu de כִּסְאוֹ) est comme le soleil devant moi'. Et on leur prépare la coupe des bénédictions. Après qu'ils aient mangé et bu, Il dit: 'Qui prononce la bénédiction?' Il dit à Abraham: 'Prends-la et dis la bénédiction puisque tu es le père du monde.' Abraham répond: 'Je ne peux dire la bénédiction, car de moi est sortie une postérité qui a enflammé de colère le Saint béni-soit-il.' Il dit ensuite à Isaac: 'Prends-la et dis la bénédiction puisque tu fus couché lié sur l'autel.' Il répond: 'Je ne peux dire la bénédiction, car de moi est sortie une postérité qui a dévasté la maison du Saint béni-soit-il.' Il dit ensuite à Jacob: 'Prends-la et dis la bénédiction puisque ton camp est parfait devant Dieu.' Il répond: 'Je ne peux dire la bénédiction, car j'ai épousé deux sœurs à la fois de leur vivant, ce que la Torah interdira, comme il est dit (Lev. 18.18): "Tu ne prendras pas une femme en plus de sa sœur pour en faire une rivale".' Il dit ensuite à Moïse: 'Prends-la et dis la bénédiction puisque tu as reçu la Torah et que tu l'as observée.' Il répond: 'Je ne peux dire la bénédiction, car je n'ai pas été digne d'entrer dans le pays d'Israël.' Il dit ensuite à Josué: 'Prends-la et dis la bénédiction puisque tu as introduit les Israélites dans le pays et observé la Torah.' Il répond: 'Je ne peux dire la bénédiction, car je n'ai pas été digne d'avoir un fils.' Il dit ensuite à David: 'Prends-la et dis la bénédiction puisque tu es "le délicieux, quant aux hymnes d'Israël" (2 Sam. 23.1) et que tu es leur prince, comme il est écrit: "Et David mon serviteur sera prince pour eux à jamais" (Ezec. 37.25).' Il leur répond: 'Je dirai la bénédiction, car c'est à moi qu'il revient de prononcer la bénédiction, comme il est écrit (Ps. 116.13): "J'éléverai la coupe du salut et je prononcerai le nom du Seigneur".' Après qu'ils aient mangé, bu et prononcé la bénédiction, le Saint béni-soit-il apporte la Torah, la pose sur ses genoux et en traite à propos du pur et de l'impur, de l'interdit et du permis, des halakhot et des haggadot. David entonne un chant devant le Saint béni-soit-il et les hommes pieux lui répondent depuis le jardin d'Eden: 'Amen! que son grand nom soit loué pour les siècles et pour les siècles des siècles.' Et les Israélites infidèles répondent 'Amen!' depuis les enfers. Tout de suite, le Saint béni soit-il interroge les anges: 'Qui sont ces gens qui entonnent un "Amen" depuis les enfers?' Ils lui disent: 'Maître du monde! ce sont ceux des Israélites qui sont infidèles. Quoiqu'ils soient en grande détresse, ils font preuve de courage et disent Amen devant toi.' Tout de suite, le Saint béni-soit-il dit aux anges: 'Ouvrez-leur les portes du paradis pour qu'ils viennent chanter devant moi, comme il est écrit (Isa. 26.2): "Qu'entre le peuple juste qui a observé les Amen!"' Ne lis pas 'èmunim' mais 'aménim'.[11]

11. Jellinek, *Bet ha-Midrash*, V, pp. 45f.

Selon Louis Ginzberg, ces midrashim de rédaction assez tardive se fondent sur des sources plus anciennes.[12] Certes, les midrashim ne parlent jamais d'une seule voix. Cependant, de tous ces textes, nous pouvons tirer la conclusion que, selon la piété juive, le rôle de David à l'égard du Psautier ne se limite pas au fait que la plus grande partie de ce livre se présente comme ayant le David historique pour auteur. En effet, 'dire le Psautier' n'est pas seulement le composer, c'est le réciter en le priant. Or, l'annonce prophétique que David régnera dans l'avenir montre qu'après s'être achevé en ce monde, le règne et le trône de David ont été transférés dans l'autre monde, David y siégeant tout près du Maître des mondes et ayant pour première fonction d'entonner la récitation cultuelle du Psautier qu'exécutent les chœurs angéliques auxquels le Peuple de Dieu s'associe. C'est le second sens en lequel David 'dit' le Psautier.

Le Psautier 'dit' par le Christ

S. Augustin (*De octo Dulcitii quæstionibus* 5.3) se fonde, lui-aussi, sur Ezec. 34.23-24; 37.22-24 et Os. 3.4 pour prouver que le nom de David ne se limite pas au personnage historique qui le porta en premier.[13] C'est nécessaire pour qu'Ezéchiel (34.23) puisse dire que 'David les fera paître'. En effet,

> s'il avait dit cela au temps de Noé, ou au temps d'Abraham, ou en celui de Moïse, ou même sous le règne de Saül à qui David a succédé, nous serions en droit d'admettre que cet oracle porte sur David fils de Jessé, annonçant qu'il sera le pasteur du troupeau de Dieu qui lui fut confié durant son règne. Mais, lorsque cet oracle fut prononcé, David avait achevé de régner, quitté cette vie et avait rejoint ses pères, jouissant d'un repos mérité. De qui dit-il (Ezec. 34.23): 'Je susciterai David et je ferai de lui pour eux un unique pasteur', sinon du David qui est issu de la postérité de David?[14]

Augustin voit donc en ces oracles la preuve que le Christ peut être désigné par ce nom. Il tient donc à distinguer 'ce David de la semence duquel provient la chair du Christ' et 'notre David, Jésus en personne'.[15]

12. L. Ginzberg, *The Legends of the Jews* (7 vols.; Philadelphie: Jewish Publication Society of America, 1913–1938), VI, p. 272.
13. *PL*, 40, 168-170.
14. Augustinus, *Sermo* 47.20 (*PL*, 38, col. 308).
15. Augustinus, *Enarr. in Ps.* 77.44 (CChr, Series Latina XXXIX, p. 1095).

Il appelle ce dernier: 'notre David, le Seigneur Jésus-Christ, né de la semence de ce David-là'.[16] Il comparera le geste du jeune David déposant l'armure trop encombrante de Saül avec celui de 'notre David' déposant les observances de la Loi ancienne comme une armure pesante qui n'est d'aucun secours.[17]

D'autre part, Augustin sait bien que nous psalmodions en présence des anges: 'C'est l'assemblée des anges qui constitue le temple de Dieu. Or, Eglise d'en-haut comme Eglise d'en-bas, nous adorons au temple de Dieu: l'Eglise d'en-bas faite de tous les fidèles et l'Eglise d'en-haut de tous les anges.'[18]

Notre David, tête et corps

Citons ici un texte qui tient une place centrale dans l'herméneutique d'Augustin. Après avoir célébré la charité, il se demande qui est ce 'David' à qui le titre du Psaume 140 (141) se réfère, alors qu'en conclusion du Psaume 71 (72), il avait été dit que là s'achevaient les hymnes de David fils de Jessé.

> Qui est donc celui-ci? Je vais vous le dire tout de suite: c'est le Christ. Mais vous allez entendre des paroles qu'il serait indigne de comprendre de Notre Seigneur Jésus-Christ et celui qui manque de perspicacité me taxera de témérité pour avoir attribué ce psaume au Christ en personne. [...] Comment donc comprendre, d'une manière qui convienne à celui qui les prononce, les paroles: 'place, Seigneur, une garde à ma bouche et une porte de discrétion autour de mes lèvres, de sorte que tu ne laisses pas mon cœur pencher vers des paroles mauvaises pour trouver des excuses aux péchés'? Leur sens ne fait aucun doute: Garde, Seigneur, ma bouche par une sorte de portail et par la porte de ton précepte, pour que mon cœur ne dévie pas vers des paroles méchantes. Quelles paroles méchantes? celles qui servent d'excuse aux péchés. Que je ne préfère pas, dit-il, m'excuser plutôt que m'accuser. Ces paroles ne conviennent pas à la personne de Notre Seigneur Jésus-Christ. Quels péchés aurait-il donc commis qu'il aurait à avouer plutôt qu'à tenter de se disculper? Ces paroles sont bien les nôtres. Mais il est certain que c'est le Christ qui parle. Et si les paroles sont nôtres, comment se fait-il que ce soit le Christ qui les dise? Mais où est donc passée la charité dont je parlais tout-à-l'heure? Ignorez-vous que c'est elle qui fait de nous un seul être dans le Christ? C'est la charité qui, en notre nom, supplie le Christ; la charité qui,

16. Augustinus, *Enarr. in Ps.* 55.3 (CChr, Series Latina XXXIX, p. 679).
17. Augustinus, *Enarr. in Ps.* 143.2 (CChr, Series Latina XL, pp. 2073-74).
18. Augustinus, *Enarr. in Ps.* 137.4 (CChr, Series Latina XL, p. 1981).

au nom du Christ, supplie pour nous. [...] S'il est donc la tête et nous le corps, c'est un seul homme qui parle; que ce soit la tête qui parle, que ce soient les membres, le Christ est seul à parler. Et c'est le propre de la tête de parler aussi au nom des membres. [...] C'est à cette langue qui est dans ta tête de prendre la défense de tous tes membres, c'est elle qui est le porte-parole de tous. C'est ainsi que nous devons écouter parler le Christ. Que chacun de ceux qui font partie du corps du Christ y reconnaisse donc sa voix. Mais il lui arrivera, certes, de dire aussi des paroles en lesquelles aucun d'entre nous ne se reconnaîtra, car elles ne concernent rien que la tête. Il ne se sépare pas pour autant de nos paroles lorsqu'il use des siennes à lui, ni ne s'abstient de revenir des siennes aux nôtres. Car c'est de Lui et de l'Eglise qu'il est dit: 'Ils seront deux en une seule chair'. [...] Cela n'a rien de nouveau. Vous l'avez entendu bien des fois. Mais il ne faut pas négliger les occasions de le rappeler. [...] Si Notre Seigneur Jésus-Christ, nous représentant par la charité de son corps, quoiqu'il fut sans péché a dit: 'les paroles de mes fautes', il a dit cela au nom de son corps. Qui donc, parmi ses membres, osera dire qu'il est sans péchés? Celui là, oserait-il, en se drapant dans une fausse justice, accuser le Christ de mensonge? Confesse donc, ô membre, ce que ta tête a déclaré en ton nom![19]

Voici encore un grand texte d'Augustin prêchant sur les Psaumes:

Dieu ne pouvait gratifier les hommes d'un plus grand don que de leur donner pour tête son Verbe par lequel il a tout créé et de les lui assujettir comme membres, de sorte qu'il soit fils de Dieu et fils d'homme, Dieu unique avec le Père, homme unique avec les hommes; de sorte que, lorsque nous parlons à Dieu en le priant, nous n'en séparions pas le fils, et que, lorsque le corps du Fils prie, il ne laisse pas de côté sa tête; mais que ce soit l'unique Sauveur de son corps, Notre Seigneur Jésus-Christ Fils de Dieu, qui, tout à la fois, prie pour nous et prie en nous et est prié par nous. Il prie pour nous comme notre prêtre, il prie en nous comme notre tête et il est prié par nous comme notre Dieu. Découvrons donc nos paroles en lui aussi bien que ses paroles en nous. Et lorsque quelque chose est dit du Seigneur Jésus-Christ, surtout par mode de prophétie, qui semble relever d'un abaissement indigne de Dieu, ne répugnons pas à le lui attribuer à lui qui n'a pas hésité à se joindre à nous. [...] Contemplant donc cette suréminente divinité du Fils de Dieu qui transcende ce qu'il y a de plus sublime dans les créatures, nous l'entendons aussi en certaines parties des Ecritures qui semble gémir en priant et en s'accusant; et nous hésitons à lui attribuer ces paroles parce que notre pensée, occupée à la toute récente contemplation de sa divinité, répugne à descendre jusqu'à son abaissement et prétexte qu'on lui ferait injure si l'on situait dans

19. Augustinus, *Enarr. in Ps.* 140.2-3 et 6 (CChr, Series Latina XL, pp. 2027-29).

> l'homme les paroles de celui à qui elle s'adressait lorsqu'elle le priait en tant que Dieu. Elle se trouve souvent interloquée et s'efforce de modifier son interprétation. Mais tout ce qu'elle rencontre dans l'Ecriture ne peut que la référer à lui et ne tolère pas qu'elle le quitte. Qu'elle se ressaisisse donc et réveille sa foi; qu'elle réalise une bonne fois que celui qu'elle venait de contempler en forme de Dieu a pris la forme d'esclave, s'étant fait semblable aux hommes, et que, étant reconnu à son allure pour un homme, il s'est abaissé en se faisant obéissant jusqu'à la mort, si bien qu'il a voulu s'attribuer les paroles du psalmiste lorsque, suspendu à la croix, il disait: 'Mon Dieu, mon Dieu, pourquoi m'as-tu abandonné?' On le prie donc en forme de Dieu, tandis que lui, il prie en forme d'esclave: là créateur, ici créé, endossant, sans en être déformé, la créature qu'il s'agit de transformer, et faisant de nous avec lui un seul homme, tête et corps. Nous adressons donc notre prière à lui, par lui, en lui; et nous récitons avec lui, tandis qu'il récite avec nous; nous récitons en lui et lui récite en nous la prière de ce psaume intitulé 'prière de David' puisque Notre Seigneur est selon la chair fils de David, alors que, selon la divinité, il est Seigneur de David et créateur de David, mais aussi avant Abraham de qui vient David, et avant Adam de qui viennent tous les hommes, et même avant le ciel et la terre où toute créature se situe. Que donc personne ne dise, en entendant ces paroles: ce n'est pas le Christ qui parle, ni n'en vienne à dire: ce n'est pas moi qui parle. Bien plutôt, s'il se sait dans le corps du Christ, qu'il dise à la fois: c'est le Christ qui parle, et: c'est moi qui parle. Refuse-toi à rien dire sans lui. Lui ne dit rien sans toi.[20]

Plutôt que de dire de David qu'il est l'auteur du Psautier, Augustin préfère dire que c'est par lui que l'Esprit Saint nous a procuré ce Psautier.[21] En effet, celui qui récite le Psautier n'est pas le David historique, mais notre David, 'c'est-à-dire le Christ tête et corps'. Et l'usage que le Christ a fait durant sa passion de certains psaumes avait pour but de nous révéler qu'il en était le véritable auteur:

> Ecoutons ces mots que le Seigneur a prononcés sur la croix: 'En tes mains je remets mon esprit'. Quand nous acquérons de l'Evangile la certitude qu'il a cité ce psaume, nous ne doutons plus qu'ici c'était lui qui avait parlé. Tu trouves en effet dans l'Evangile: Il déclara: 'en tes mains je remets mon esprit, et, ayant penché la tête, il livra l'esprit'. S'il a voulu que les paroles de ce psaume fussent siennes, c'était pour t'informer qu'en ce psaume c'était lui qui avait parlé. Cherche-le donc ici. Et à propos du psaume 'pour la relève du matin', réfléchis à la manière dont il a ordonné qu'on le cherche dans 'ils ont creusé mes mains et mes pieds, ils ont compté tous mes os; eux ils m'ont contemplé et dévisagé, ils se

20. Augustinus, *Enarr. in Ps.* 85.1 (CChr, Series Latina XXXIX, pp. 1176-77).
21. Augustinus, *Sermo* 32.3 (*PL*, 38, col. 197).

sont partagé mes habits et ils ont tiré au sort mon vêtement'. Pour t'informer que c'était en lui que ces paroles s'étaient accomplies, il a donné lui-même la parole au début de ce psaume: 'Dieu, mon Dieu, pourquoi m'as-tu abandonné?' C'était la voix du corps qu'il transfigurait en lui, car jamais le Père n'a abandonné son Fils unique.[22]

Les concepts de base de l'herméneutique psalmique d'Augustin sont ceux de 'figuration' et de 'transfiguration': David 'figurait' le Christ et le Christ 'transfigure' en soi-même les sentiments des membres de son corps. Il arrive à Augustin de télescoper ces données et de dire en une formule ramassée: 'ainsi gémissent les membres de David'.[23]

Voici quelques exemples caractéristiques de ces 'transfigurations'. D'abord à propos du Ps. 140.10: 'Je demeure solitaire jusqu'à ce que j'aie disparu':

> Puisque la manière qu'avait ce grain d'être solitaire, c'était de porter en soi la grande fécondité d'une multitude, réjouissons-nous pour tant de grains qui imitent sa passion, lorsque nous célébrons les natalitia des martyrs. Donc ses nombreux membres assemblés par le lien de la charité et de la paix sous une tête unique qui n'est autre que notre Sauveur—ainsi que vous devriez le savoir, car vous l'avez entendu si souvent—ne constituent qu'un seul homme, et c'est leur voix qui se fait entendre le plus souvent dans les psaumes comme celle d'un seul homme. Ainsi un seul crie comme tous, car en un seul tous sont un.[24]

Ou encore:

> L'Eglise a faim, le corps du Christ a faim; il a faim, cet homme partout dispersé dont la tête est là-haut et les membres ici-bas. Elle vous est bien connue et très familière, sa voix dans tous les psaumes, tantôt célébrant, tantôt gémissant; tantôt heureuse d'espérer, tantôt déplorant ce qui est. Vous devez la considérer comme nôtre.[25]

Nous disposons maintenant des données qui nous permettront d'identifier celui qui psalmodie en nous:

> 'Et au milieu d'un grand nombre je le louerai.' En un autre psaume il dit: 'au milieu de l'Eglise je te chanterai'. Mais puisque celle qui chante c'est l'Eglise qui est le corps du Christ, comment l'Eglise chante-t-elle au milieu de l'Eglise? De même ici, puisque les membres du Christ sont en

22. Augustinus, *Enarr. in Ps.* 30, sermo I.11 (CChr, Series Latina XXXVIII, p. 199).

23. Augustinus, *Enarr. in Ps.* 54.3 (CChr, Series Latina XXXIX, pp. 656-57).

24. Augustinus, *Enarr. in Ps.* 69.1 (CChr, Series Latina XXXIX, p. 930).

25. Augustinus, *Enarr. in Ps.* 42.1 (CChr, Series Latina XXXVIII, p. 474).

> grand nombre, si c'est lui qu'ils louent, c'est aussi lui qui loue, puisqu'ils sont ses membres. Et c'est de la sorte qu'il loue au milieu d'un grand nombre, lorsqu'on précise que c'est lui qui loue quand eux louent en grand nombre. Ou bien cette affirmation qu'il loue au milieu d'un grand nombre signifierait-elle qu'il demeure avec son Eglise jusqu'à l'accomplissement du temps, de sorte que nous devrions comprendre 'au milieu d'un grand nombre' en ce sens qu'il est loué par eux qui sont en grand nombre? On situe en effet 'au milieu' celui qui est entouré de plus d'honneurs. Mais si le cœur est comme le milieu de l'homme, la meilleure interprétation de cette parole est que c'est dans les cœurs d'un grand nombre que je le louerai. Le Christ habite en effet par la foi en nos cœurs. C'est pourquoi il dit 'en ma bouche', c'est-à-dire dans la bouche de mon corps qui est l'Eglise. C'est en effet avec le cœur que l'on croit pour être justifié et par la bouche que l'on confesse pour être sauvé.[26]

Achevons ces citations d'Augustin par deux petites synthèses où, pour entrer en matière, il rappelle à ses auditeurs un point de vue qui doit leur être familier. D'abord:

> Nous nous rappelons avec certitude que vous avez entendu bien des fois ce que nous disons: tu n'as guère à découvrir dans les psaumes d'autres voix que celles du Christ et de l'Eglise, ou du Christ seul ou de l'Eglise seule que, certes, pour notre part, nous sommes. Et lorsque, de la sorte, nous reconnaissons notre voix, nous ne pouvons la reconnaître sans émotion, et nous sommes d'autant plus réjouis que nous nous y sentons intégrés. Le roi David ne fut qu'un homme isolé, mais ce ne fut pas un homme isolé qu'il figura, lorsqu'il figura l'Eglise constituée d'un grand nombre et dispersée jusqu'aux extrémités de la terre. Et lorsqu'il figura un seul homme, il figura celui qui est le médiateur de Dieu et des hommes, l'homme Jésus-Christ.[27]

Et enfin:

> Le titre de ce psaume est court et simple. Il ne nous retiendra pas, nous qui savons de qui David portait la figure et qui nous découvrons en celui-ci, puisque nous aussi sommes membres de son corps. Reconnaissons donc ici la voix de l'Eglise et réjouissons-nous d'avoir eu la chance de nous trouver en celle dont nous entendons chanter la voix. 'A David lui-même' suffit à constituer le titre.[28]

26. Augustinus, *Enarr. in Ps.* 108.32 (CChr, Series Latina XL, p. 1600).
27. Augustinus, *Enarr. in Ps.* 59.1 (CChr, Series Latina XXXIX, pp. 753-54).
28. Augustinus, *Enarr. in Ps.* 137.1 (CChr, Series Latina XL, p. 1979).

Deux vues convergentes

A la question 'Qui récite le Psautier?', la Synagogue répond donc par la voix de ses midrashistes et l'Eglise par celui de ses Pères qui s'est le plus attaché à prêcher les Psaumes et les deux réponses sont essentiellement convergentes.

Dans le peuple de Dieu un fidèle qui récite les Psaumes n'est jamais isolé. L'affirmation traditionnelle que le Psautier est 'de David' vise moins à situer le David historique comme en étant l'auteur humain qu'à attester que c'est 'notre David' qui le récite, c'est-à dire ce David intronisé par le Maître du monde comme présidant la psalmodie des anges et des hommes. C'est lui qui s'exprime tantôt en son nom, tantôt au nom du peuple sur lequel il est voué à régner.

Pour les chrétiens, ce David a déjà été manifesté. Pour les juifs, sa manifestation est à venir. Mais les deux peuples savent que leur prière est portée par le même intercesseur. Faut-il voir dans l'accord fondamental de ces deux herméneutiques un simple hasard? Franz Rosenzweig ne l'aurait sûrement pas cru, lui pour qui 'devant Dieu, le juif et le chrétien sont des travailleurs oeuvrant à la même oeuvre'.[29]

29. F. Rosenzweig, *Der Stern der Erlösung* (Francfort-sur-le-Main: J. Kauffmann, 1921), p. 520.

EXEGESIS AS BANQUET: READING JEREMIAH WITH THE RABBIS

Mary Chilton Callaway

> When Israel does the will of their Father in heaven, how are they spoken of? As 'a leafy olive tree, fair with goodly fruit' (Jer. 11.16), of which it is further said, 'It shall not see when heat cometh, but its foliage shall be luxuriant; and shall not be anxious in the year of drought, neither shall cease from yielding fruit' (Jer. 17.8). By what parable may the verse be understood? By the parable of ten men who assembled for a banquet. One brought large fish, another brought small fish; one brought fish salted and unsalted; one brought boiled cabbage and beets; another brought eggs; another brought cheese; another brought meat of an ox, another brought meat of a ram, and another brought meat of a fowl. All these dishes were brought at the same time to the men's table, and each took his share of all the ten kinds of food and went back to his house.
>
> So, too, when a man goes to a synagogue or a house of study, he may learn from each of the nine men already there a single verse of Torah, a single interpretation, a single Halakah. Thus each of the ten men takes away with him ten Halakot, ten verses of Torah, ten interpretations, and goes back to his house.[1]

I

While the historical-critical view envisions a multiplicity of readers slowly beginning to converge on a single truth, the rabbinic view seems to suggest a single text generating an infinite progression of interpretations. In the parable above, Torah is not a puzzle to be solved, but instead is a catalyst creating meanings. It is the occasion for a banquet after which the diners return home well-fed and the Torah remains unconsumed, ready for the next party who will feast on it.

But the Torah is not entirely unaffected by its readers either, because no generation can read it absolutely, as though it had never been read

1. *Tanna debe Eliyyahu: The Lore of the School of Elijah* (trans. W.G. Braude and I.J. Epstein; Philadelphia: Jewish Publication Society of America, 1981), p. 249.

before. Christians instinctively read Genesis 3 as the first chapter in the history of salvation. Their reading is not 'in the text' or in the intention of the ancient authors. Instead it has been transmitted along with the text by earlier readers.[2]

Even the clarifying work of historical-critical exegesis is sometimes powerless against centuries of reading: Joseph will persist in having a coat of many colors, the valley through which the Psalmist walks will most likely remain the valley of the shadow of death, and ים סוף will doubtless remain red. If translation is a form of interpretation, then these Septuagint translations have attached themselves tenaciously to their texts so as to become almost a part of them. What is authoritative in the believing communities is often not the words of the best Hebrew manuscripts but the traditions that have become attached to (or even replaced) their words.[3]

Reading the Bible is not an unmediated meeting of reader with biblical author(s), but is rather like pulling up a chair at a feast that has been under way for some time. However, this image carries another, sobering implication, for not all diners bring nourishing food to the feast. To read the Bible is also to sit at table in the company of all manner of sinners, some of whom brought bitter offerings to the feast. It is difficult to read the Gospel of John without feeling shame at later Christian anti-Semitism. Reading Noah's curse of Canaan and Ham with African American students or Genesis 3 with women reveals how deeply etched certain traditions are in Western consciousness. The scholarly plea that the biblical authors did not intend the sense that later generations attributed to these texts only partially assuages the pain; history lies heavily over the words on the page. Even knowing the original context is not enough; the words themselves have been permanently interwoven with connotations that continue to shape people's thinking.[4]

2. For a review of the differences between Jewish and Christian interpretations of Gen. 3 see G. Anderson, 'Celibacy or Consummation in the Garden? Reflections on Early Jewish and Christian Interpretations of the Garden of Eden', *HTR* 82 (1989), pp. 121-48.

3. J.A. Sanders provides valuable insight into the role of text criticism in discussion of biblical hermeneutics in 'Hebrew Bible *and* Old Testament: Textual Criticism in Service of Biblical Studies', in R. Brooks and J.J. Collins (eds.), *Hebrew Bible or Old Testament: Studying the Bible in Judaism and Christianity* (Notre Dame: University of Notre Dame Press, 1990), pp. 41-68.

4. The anti-Jewish polemic in the Gospels is especially problematic here. The process of re-contextualizing is already at work in the Gospels, where Jesus' prophetic

What do we mean when we speak of the Bible? Does it include the reality of those readers who have wedged themselves, for good or ill, between the ancient authors and us? Even someone reading for the first time is not encountering the prophet's words directly, but through the veil of redactors, cultural distance, perhaps translators, and even the nimbus that surrounds the words 'Holy Bible'. We as readers also create a historical context as we read, based on the current construction of the ancient world.[5] Such constructions of other cultures are notoriously vulnerable to the unexpressed presuppositions of the constructing scholars. Just when we think we are reading the prophet 'in his own historical context' we may in fact be reading him in a tendentious theological context.[6] Multiple layers of constructs and assumptions, hidden and overt, fill up the space between the Bible and the reader. No reader has unmediated access to an ancient text. Each reader creates the text out of shards of previous readings and layers of his or her own experience.

The problem of the nature of Scripture has preoccupied readers from the beginning—even before the canon was closed and the limits of Scripture were defined. Some of the earliest interpretations were rewritten versions in which the biblical text almost disappeared beneath the elaboration. Other interpretations, such as the Habakkuk pesher at Qumran, rejected the contextual interpretation in favor of actualization. The 'true meaning' of the prophet's words was thought to be hidden from those whom the prophet addressed (and even from the prophet himself) but revealed to the interpreter at Qumran. Likewise for the early Christians the 'true meaning' of the Scriptures had been hidden until the proper time of their fulfillment. For those Second Temple readers the point was not that the Scriptures had gained new significance

critique is heard in the early church as anti-Jewish polemic. More difficult to deal with are the frequent references to 'the Jews' in the Fourth Gospel. Here the polemic is not an overlay of later readers but seems to be part of the reality of the Evangelist's community. Sometimes the contemporary desire to distance oneself from the vitriolic words in the Gospels can lead to a denial that such sentiments motivated the Evangelists.

5. For the ways in which such constructions reflect the views of the interpreting scholars see E.W. Said, *Orientalism* (New York: Pantheon, 1978).

6. For a trenchant analysis of the 'contamination' of presuppositions in the historical-critical exegesis of the last century see J. Levenson, 'The Hebrew Bible, the Old Testament, and Historical Criticism', in *The Hebrew Bible, the Old Testament, and Historical Criticism: Jews and Christians in Biblical Studies* (Louisville, KY: John Knox/Westminster Press, 1993), pp. 1-32.

in their day, but rather that their true significance had emerged only in their day.

For most of the last two millennia both synagogue and church have assumed that Scripture is complex and multivalent. This is apparent in the rabbinic exegetical principle of *peshat* and *derash* by which a biblical text could be read for the *peshat* or 'plain sense' (the literal, philological sense of the passage when read within its own context) and then for the *derash* or the meaning found when one broadened the context to include all of Scripture and even the reader's own situation. There was never one authoritative interpretation; rabbinic commentaries are collections of rabbinic discussions and different readings of biblical passages. Similarly, in the fifth century the Christian monk John Cassian formalized the traditional exegetical practices of the church with a treatise on the fourfold senses of Scripture. Like the rabbinic principle, they moved from the 'plain' or contextual sense to readings which used specific hermeneutics, usually a form of allegory. The four senses of Scripture, the plain, the christological, the analogical and the tropological, were assumed to be inherent in Scripture, deposited by the Author; yet the same text could yield different allegorical meanings to different readers. The ancient exegetes juggled their belief in the text as a repository of divinely intended meaning with a practice of welcoming multiple readings.

Since the nineteenth century the historical-critical method at its best has had the modest goal of clarifying what traditionally had been called the plain sense of Scripture. In fact, some of the questions and observations of critical scholars are strikingly similar to those of rabbinic and patristic exegetes. One of the chief differences between critical and traditional exegesis is the modern privileging of historical context as the key to interpretation, accompanied by the positivist assumption that recovery of the historical context will yield the true sense of the text. Two developments have disturbed the hegemony of this approach. First is the increased awareness that scholars cannot be completely objective. Instead they work within sociological and theological contexts that inevitably influence the questions they pose and the way they interpret the data they find. Secondly, historians are considerably less sanguine now than they were earlier in the twentieth century about the accessibility of the past and the ability of scholars to reach consensus on the interpretation of historical data and the dating of texts. Nevertheless, chastened by its critics and aware of its own limitations, historical-critical exegesis has important contributions to make. By illuminating the otherness of the biblical world and the distance between the world of the reader and the world of the biblical authors, it helps make readers more attentive to nuances in the biblical texts, particularly when the interests of those authors do not coincide with the interests of the reader.

II

The narratives about Jeremiah and Zedekiah during the last days of Jerusalem (Jer. 37–39) provide a fruitful place to reflect on current problems of methodology in biblical studies, because they have resisted many excellent attempts to explicate the plain sense. Some exegetes, pointing to the number and quality of details in the narratives, see them as relatively unadorned historical recounting of events in the last days of Jerusalem. Others see them as multiple accounts of a single event and read them as story-telling with little historical value.[7]

Uncertainty about whether the stories represent an eye-witness account of the last days of Jerusalem or a series of elaborated fictional episodes results in radical disagreement about the purpose of the narratives and even about the political agenda of the redactors. A wide range of possibilities has been offered. The stories can be read as a theodicy, demonstrating YHWH's justification in destroying Jerusalem only after repeated pleas from the prophet to surrender the city were unheeded by king and princes. Or they can be read as a passion narrative graphically revealing how Jeremiah suffered at the hands of ruthless nobles protecting their own position.[8] This reading construes Jeremiah 37–38 as an early part of a hagiography of the prophets as martyrs which developed in both Jewish and Christian traditions. Yet one can also read these stories as a sympathetic portrait of Zedekiah, trying to hear the word of the Lord but trapped in the circumstances of his power. Such a reading sets these narratives over against the portrait of Zedekiah in the rest of the book of Jeremiah, in which he is the caricature of the wicked king. A

7. Contrast the views of J. Bright (*Jeremiah* [Garden City, NY: Doubleday, 1965], pp. 232-34) and R. Carroll (*Jeremiah: A Commentary* [Philadelphia: Westminster Press, 1986], pp. 672-73) who describe the narratives as multiple accounts of a single event, with that of W. Holladay (*Jeremiah 2* [Minneapolis: Fortress Press, 1989], p. 286), who points to the detail in the narratives as evidence of an eyewitness account.

8. H. Kremers, 'Leidensgemeinschaft mit Gott im Alten Testament: Eine Untersuchung der "biographischen" Berichte Jeremiabuch', *EvT* 13 (1953), pp. 405-16.

fourth proposal reads the narratives as an exilic redaction of an earlier chronicle of uncertain origin; the redaction intended to demonstrate that the hope for Judah's future lay only with the exiles in Babylon.[9] We are at a loss to explain even at the most basic level how the stories were intended to function in the communities where they first circulated. Even the 'plain meaning' seems inaccessible, in spite of our best tools.

One reason for the difficulty in determining the original function of the stories about Jeremiah and Zedekiah is that their construction represents the work of several hands over a period of time. The final redaction poses more than the usual number of problems for the reader, and the redactional seams are everywhere visible. Chapters 37–38 are made up of seven scenes which do not at all follow smoothly upon each other, but are both temporally and spatially disorienting. The narrative jumps backwards and forwards in time, and moves in and out of a variety of prisons. At several points parenthetical statements have been added relating the stories to the scheme of Jeremiah's life presented in chs. 26–36; they look like attempts to clarify the troubled chronology of the narratives.

If the most recent redaction criticism is right, the narratives preserve two distinct sources. The older is an account of the last days of Jerusalem and the life of the Judahites, composed by scribes who remained in the land under Gedaliah. Throughout this narrative Jeremiah counseled surrender and saw continued life in Judah under Babylonian rule as the best option for the Judahites. After the murder of Gedaliah this narrative was taken to Babylon, where it was edited by exiles who saw themselves as the true remnant of Israel. They overlaid the earlier narratives with their own perspective, largely by grafting on oracles of the prophet which had underscored the inevitability of Jerusalem's fall and the exile of the inhabitants. In this way the exilic redactors bolstered their own understanding of themselves as the true Israel with words of Jeremiah—words which had not originally intended any such meaning. Hence the words of the prophet have been reinterpreted by the very redactors who preserved them, and we can perceive the discrepancy between the 'intention' of Jeremiah and the 'intention' of his redactors. One might even argue that Jeremiah's redactors turned his words inside out. In such a case how is the reader to understand the words on the page? Even if we want our reading to follow the intention of the original author we have difficulty, for which original author should be our guide? Even the 'plain sense' seems to be multivalent.

9. C. Seitz, *Theology in Conflict* (BZAW, 179; Berlin: de Gruyter, 1989).

Further, the juxtaposition of the two sources in Jeremiah 37–38 is evidence of the process of de-historicizing that characterizes many biblical texts. Jeremiah 37–38 represents part of a trajectory of traditions about the prophet that appears to reach back to the prophet's lifetime and arches forward through the work of exilic redactors. Jeremiah's pronouncement that all who surrendered to the Babylonians would live but those who resisted would perish at the hands of their enemies meant something quite different to the Jerusalemites who heard them in 588 than to the exiles who heard them embedded in the stories of the last days of Jerusalem. The prophet's words confronted the original audience with an existential choice between two impossible political realities: surrender the holy city or hold out against the most powerful military machine in their world. However, our understanding of Jeremiah's words is limited because nowhere are those words preserved in their original context; in every case they have been set into a literary context created by redactors; that is, they have already been interpreted.

The reader of Jeremiah 37–38, even the earliest readers in the exile, cannot understand Jeremiah's words in the way that Jeremiah's audience did. The prophet does not speak directly to the reader, but is a character drawn by the author, who interposes himself between reader and prophet. In the logic of the story the prophetic warning is spoken so that the princes can arrest Jeremiah for treason and weakening the hands of the soldiers. To the reader, who knows the outcome of the story, Jeremiah's words illustrate that the intractable leadership in Jerusalem brought the destruction of the city on themselves. The prophetic warning also functions to validate Jeremiah as a 'true' prophet for the reader; events happen as he had foretold. Hence within the biblical text the words of the prophet carry at least two levels of meaning: the meaning to the characters within the framework of the story and the meaning to the readers/listeners in the exilic and post-exilic period. This distinction is worth noting because it reminds us that the process of interpretation is not only a superstructure built on top of the biblical text, but is also a part of the fabric of the story. The narrative creates a new context for the prophetic words and gives them an entirely new significance.

A similar problem is apparent in the discrepancy between the frame by which the redactors enclosed the narratives and the content of the stories themselves. The introduction (37.1-2) clearly instructs the reader with a guideline for understanding the stories that follow: Zedekiah, his princes and the people of the land did not listen to the word of the Lord which he spoke through Jeremiah. The stories, however, repeatedly portray a king eager to hear the word of the Lord, and apparently pained by his own inability to obey it. In fact, the redactor's evaluation of Zedekiah is consistent with the descriptions of him elsewhere in Jeremiah, but the characterization of the king in the stories within chs. 37–38 is unique in the book. The reader is faced with a problem. Are the stories to be read according to the rubric of the frame or the details of the narrative? In whose voice should the reader hear authority?

The history of interpretation of Jeremiah 37–38 suggests that the problem is not new. In telling the story of ch. 38, Josephus recorded a tradition that highlighted Zedekiah's good will: 'Now the king himself, because of his goodness and sense of justice, was in no way personally resentful but, in order not to incur the hostility of the leaders by opposing their wishes at such a time, he gave them leave to do as they liked with the prophet' (*Ant*. 10.121). Was Josephus 'reading against the grain' by setting aside the evaluation of Zedekiah provided at the beginning of he story? By responding to the other voice, which he heard in the narratives, he was implicitly rejecting the interpretation provided by the redactor in 37.2. The tradition that Zedekiah was a good king compelled to evil deeds by the people of Judah also appears in another first-century CE work, *2 Bar*. (the *Syriac Apocalypse of Baruch*) 1.1-3.

The shifting contexts in which the ancient redactors placed prophetic words and activities seem to discourage the possibility of a definitive reading because nowhere are the 'pure' uninterpreted words of the prophet preserved; they are always preserved in an interpretive literary context. Reading the book of Jeremiah means encountering the various readings which his words were given in the complex development from prophetic speech to canonical book. The very construction of the book invites conversation rather than closure, and the history of interpretation continues the conversation.

III

One reading of the Jeremiah tradition that seems far from the Bible at first, but on closer study promises to shed light on the problem, occurs in the midrashic homily *Pesiqta Rabbati* 26. The homily, presumably preparing the congregation for the Ninth of Ab (the commemoration of the destruction of the Temple), begins at Jeremiah's birth and ends after the destruction of Jerusalem. One part is an expansion of the story about

Jeremiah negotiating to buy his uncle's field in Anathoth. This story has two different contexts in the canonical Jeremiah. In ch. 32 Jeremiah negotiates the purchase while in captivity in Zedekiah's court of the guard. This story sets the context for the lengthy oracle promising the restoration of Judah after Babylonian domination. As the story is told, Jeremiah does not seem to understand the purpose of the divine command to buy the property; the text leaves a gap between the prophet's obedience and his understanding of the divine purpose. In ch. 37, on the other hand, Jeremiah tries to leave the city 'to claim his portion among the people' and is arrested and imprisoned. The midrash conflates the two episodes to create its climactic scene toward the end of the homily, a scene which is not biblical but which resonates with themes embedded in the canonical Jeremiah.

> In that time the Lord said to Jeremiah: 'Rise, go to Anathoth and buy the field from thine uncle Hanamel.' Thereupon Jeremiah thought in his heart: Maybe God means to turn Jerusalem over to its inhabitants and allow them to carry on their living as usual within it. Hence, [to assure them of His intention] the Lord says to me: Go, buy the field for thyself. As soon as Jeremiah left Jerusalem, the angel of the Lord came down from heaven, set his feet against the walls of Jerusalem, and breached them. Then the angel cried out, saying: Let the enemies come and enter the House, for the Master of the House is no longer within.

After a description of the burning of the Temple and the Babylonian treatment of Zedekiah and his sons, the *Pesiqta Rabbati* returns to Jeremiah:

> In the meantime, the prophet Jeremiah left Anathoth to come back to Jerusalem. He lifted his eyes and saw the smoke of the Temple rising up. So he said in his heart: Maybe Israel has returned in penitence to bring offerings, and now the smoke of incense is rising up. But when he climbed closer and stood upon the wall, he saw the Temple overturned into heap upon heap of stones and the wall of Jerusalem broken down. Thereupon he cried out to God, saying: 'Thou hast enticed me, and I was enticed; Thou hast overcome me, and hast prevailed' (Jer 20.7).[10]

The midrash reads against the plain sense of Jeremiah 37–38 when it shows Jeremiah leaving Jerusalem before the Babylonians breached the walls; the biblical version clearly shows Jeremiah in the court of the guard under Zedekiah's protection when the city falls. According to the

10. *Pesikta Rabbati: Discourses for Feasts, Fasts, and Special Sabbaths* (trans. W.G. Braude; New Haven: Yale University Press, 1968), pp. 534-36 (26.6).

Pesiqta, the date set for the destruction of the Temple, the Ninth of Ab, was approaching and Jeremiah was in the court of the guard (Jer. 38.28); the author assumes that the city could not be destroyed with Jeremiah in its midst. Whether because Jeremiah's presence signified the possibility of Zedekiah's last-minute change of heart and obedience to the divine word, or because the presence of the prophet represented the presence of the deity in the midst of the city is not stated in the *Pesiqta*. The first-century CE *Syriac Apocalypse of Baruch*, in a version of this tradition, finds explanation in Jer. 1.18: Jeremiah's works are a firm pillar to the city and his prayers are a strong wall, preventing God from accomplishing the destruction of the city.

For the midrashist the fulfillment of the divine purpose was dependent on Jeremiah's misunderstanding the purpose of the command: God had to deceive the prophet to get him out of the city. The importance of deception is subtly signaled in the way the midrash frames the episode, for it opens and closes with citations alluding to divine deception of a prophet. The opening words, 'Rise, go to Anathoth and buy the field there...' echo the divine command at the beginning of the book of Jonah, 'Rise, go to Nineveh...'. Like Jonah, Jeremiah had to be tricked into his work. When Jonah settled down to watch the destruction of Nineveh, he realized that God had deceived him into thinking he was delivering a routine proclamation before destruction whereas in fact he had brought about the salvation of Israel's enemy. The closing words of the midrash more explicitly underscore the theme of deception by having Jeremiah cry, 'Thou hast enticed me, and I was enticed' (Jer. 20.7).[11]

This midrashic departure from the plain sense of Jeremiah brings to light a shadowy aspect of the canonical book, namely the significant role of divine deception and prophetic misunderstanding. From the exilic perspective of the redactors, God had known that Jerusalem must be destroyed so that a remnant might return, but justice demanded that a prophet be sent to warn the inhabitants. The structure of the oracles in chs. 1–25, which moved from the early prophetic pleas for Judah to return to YHWH to the later oracles of doom, suggest the hopelessness of Jeremiah's task. This structure is sometimes read as genuine prophetic

11. Jeremiah's anguish at the unexpected outcome of his obedience to the divine command is also highlighted earlier in the midrash, when he says 'Woe unto me because of thee, Mother Zion! I thought I was to prophesy good things and consolations, and lo, I prophesy for thee infliction of punishment!' (*Pesikta Rabbati*, p. 528 [26.1/2]).

biography, showing that Jeremiah moved from optimism about the possibility of Judah's repentance to a sense of inevitability concerning its destruction. From another perspective the same data might suggest, in line with the confessions, that YHWH had called Jeremiah to a hopeless task and destined him for failure. The fulfillment of the divine purpose depended in part on the prophet's deception about his chances for success. The midrash in *Pesiqta Rabbati* 26 presupposes that Jeremiah was unaware of the true nature of his work more than once in his prophetic ministry.

To instruct his congregation the author of *Pesiqta Rabbati* 26 made Jeremiah a literary character whose world was not the historical Judah of the sixth century BCE, but the story-world of Scripture. But this is not so different from the canonical Jeremiah, who is not presented primarily in his own historical context but rather as a richly drawn character in a literary context. This Jeremiah always speaks on two levels, to the characters in the story and to the reader of the story. Where the reader places himself or herself in that world determines the theological messages heard. The redactors present Jeremiah's point of view, so that the readers are not encouraged to identify with themselves (Judah) in the story, but rather with the prophetic portrait of themselves. The historical reality seems to have been that few people listened to Jeremiah; the literary form of the book turns this situation around so that the prophet becomes a figure of the people, struggling with YHWH as well as with their own history.

Perhaps it is part of the divine sense of humor to keep us humble. On the one hand, Scripture suggests that the divine will unfolds in the corporate life of Israel and particularly in its political history. On the other hand, the record of that history, the locus of divine revelation, is preserved in a book that nowhere provides 'just the facts', or even the core events, in a straightforward way. Indeed, as I have suggested above, the book by its very construction interposes several interpretations between reader and event. My small example from Jeremiah is characteristic in that it does not preserve a core event with its interpretation but only stages of reflection on events beyond our reach. The reflection that began with the redactors of the canonical book continued in the commentaries and homilies of the church and synagogue in the succeeding centuries. The continuity between the redactors of Jeremiah 37–38 and the author of the midrash in *Pesiqta Rabbati* 26 lies partly in their goal, to re-interpret the Jeremiah tradition for their own day, and partly in their method, which allowed various traditions to illuminate each other.

Perhaps the rabbinic model of the banquet is after all profoundly appropriate for us. It is not possible to begin at the beginning. To read Jeremiah means to pull up a chair in the middle of a conversation that is already well under way. The history of interpretation, including critical exegesis, continues the conversation begun in the biblical text. The mix of languages, methodologies and historical contexts encourages reading from a different angle, seeing the story someone else's way. That is what makes reading a feast. The metaphor of the banquet as the model for exegesis is instructive in another way too, because it bears an ancient and indelible signification: in both rabbinic and patristic tradition the banquet is the very picture of heaven.

CANONICITY AND BIBLES TODAY

Eugene A. Nida

Torah and Canon by James Sanders has made a particularly insightful contribution to the broader and more realistic understanding of those factors which give rise to canonicity: the recognition by a believing community that a particular text is authoritative. A number of these same factors are present today in the processes of acceptance or rejection of Bible publications by various constituencies in widely differing languages. In fact, it is amazing how rapidly a particular translation of the Scriptures may be regarded as canonical. After completion of the Bible in one of the major languages of Africa, the principal translator returned to England on furlough and decided to take some courses in linguistics at the School of Oriental and African Languages. He immediately realized how many mistakes he had made in his translation of the Bible, and so upon returning to Africa he recommended to the mission that he revise the text on which he had worked for a number of years. But the mission authorities rejected his request, and although they responded politely to him, the substance of their reply was essentially equivalent to 'How can you change the word of the Lord?'

For some Bible translators even the acceptance or rejection of a particular Greek text depends not on its closeness to the original autographs, but on its agreement with certain translations which have become more or less sacrosanct. For example, some translators insist on following the Textus Receptus Greek text because they regard this 'Majority Text' as being closest to the King James Version and accordingly more authoritative. In fact, some have argued that God would not have permitted the majority of manuscripts to be other than the truest. But even the fact that the evidence for the Byzantine or Majority text is significantly divided has not seemed to diminish in the minds of many people their enthusiasm for what they regard as the canonical Greek text edited by Erasmus.

Other translators, however, turn textual scholarship on its head by insisting that the Greek text must be selected on the basis of its support for certain cherished doctrines, such as the trinity, virgin birth, deity of Jesus Christ, and inerrancy of the Scriptures. In other words, validity of a text is determined by its doctrinal content rather than doctrines being derived from the text of Scriptures. It is still incredible how many persons insist on retaining the words in 1 Jn 5.7 about 'the Father, the Word, and the Holy Spirit, and these three are one' because this statement seems to them so integral to the doctrine of the trinity.

Granting authoritative status to particular translations is not, however, a recent development. To a considerable extent this was true of the status attributed to the Vulgate Latin text by the Roman Catholic Church. For years the King James Version and the Rheims Douay Version in English, the Reina Valera in Spanish, and the Luther Bible in German became essentially canonical in the minds of many people. Even today the Bible Societies are frequently asked whether translations into such languages as Japanese, Chinese, or Arabic are based on the King James Version.

Despite the fact that many constituencies proclaim their belief in and loyalty to the entire Bible, there is often a subtle element of 'selectivity' which accords greater authenticity to some parts than to others. For example, some translators tend to harmonize parallel passages in the Gospels, and other translators give higher priority to the Gospel of John because they regard it as 'more spiritual' and therefore seemingly more true. Some translators insist on producing 'red-letter' texts because the words of Jesus are presumably more authoritative than the rest of the New Testament. A few translators have even sought first to translate and publish for new converts the books of Leviticus and Daniel because they view the Law and prophecy as indispensable for true faith in Jesus. Some translators, however, oppose any translation of the Old Testament, since there are so many stories of adultery, incest, polygamy, and wars of extermination. Furthermore, some of these translators often insist that giving people the Old Testament will inevitably lead to a doctrine of progressive revelation, something that seems to threaten the uniqueness of the divine authority of the Scriptures.

Certain key terms in a translation are sometimes important as symbols of acceptability. For example, some constituencies have insisted that only Bibles which use 'immersion' rather than 'baptism' are authoritative, while other people decide whether an English translation is authoritative by checking on the use of such terms as *propitiation*, *expiation*, *sanctification*, *predestination*, and *justification*. If a translation does not contain these 'key' terms at the appropriate places, then it cannot receive the stamp of approval. For many people, however, the most crucial test of acceptability of a new translation depends on the use of *virgin* in Isa. 7.14. Others object strongly to translating the Greek term *charis* as 'kindness' or 'goodness', and still others feel that their faith is endangered by rendering the Greek term *pistis* as 'trust' instead of 'faith'. Some insist that the romantic language of the Song of Songs be toned down, because, they say, people may otherwise never realize that this is a verbal picture of the relation of Christ to the church. In fact, many people are embarrassed by the erotic language of these marriage songs, and even Judaism has generally regarded this book as a symbolic revelation of God's relation to Israel.

Some people are so shocked at the plain, understandable words and grammar of certain popular-language translations that they insist that such translations cannot possibly be the Bible; they are simply too understandable. If the words are not mysterious, then what happens to the 'mystery of faith'?

But the acceptance of a translation as authoritative and canonical may depend on even more subtle factors. For example, some people object strongly to having different styles or levels of language in the text of the Bible. Why should Mark sound so simple and plain and the Epistle to the Hebrews be so complex and elaborate? They claim that if the Holy Spirit inspired the entire Bible, then all of it should impress readers as having the same author. This means that the same level of style should exist throughout the entire Bible, but at the same time the style must be 'sublime' in order to match the remarkable character of the content.

Some Bible translators have attempted to reach people who use non-standard language by producing a text in the very words and grammatical forms commonly used by such audiences. One translation into colloquial Arabic was totally rejected by Arabic speakers as being only in the language of pornographic literature and the comics, and a trial translation into the slang of New York City was rejected as being largely obsolete by the time it was published.

Even the order of books within a Bible may be a factor in the acceptance or rejection of a translation. Some people strongly object to the Hebrew division and order of books in the Old Testament. Placing the book of Daniel together with the 'Writings' in the final section rather than with the prophets seems like an insult to the authenticity of the book. Some Protestants totally reject the Roman Catholic practice of combining deuterocanonical books with protocanonical ones in the Old Testament and even refuse to buy Bibles that have cross-references to the deuterocanonical books (generally called 'apocryphal' by Protestants). These same persons also usually oppose the combining of the Hebrew and Greek texts of Esther into a single text.

In some instances the acceptance or rejection of a translation depends largely on sociological factors. Some persons reject the Gospel of John because of its seeming anti-Semitism, while others may adhere to a particular translation because it has become such an integral part of their liturgy. The preference for the King James Version among Black people in the United States is due in large measure to the pervasiveness of that text in the sermons and political speeches of Black preachers and politicians.

In some instances, however, there has been a far more subtle factor involved in the retention of a text which is somewhat out of date. Some years ago certain Protestant church leaders in Russia were asked about the possibility of a new translation which would reflect contemporary Russian usage and be exegetically more in keeping with present-day biblical scholarship. But the idea was rather strongly rejected, and when asked to explain more specifically their preferences for an antiquated text, the leaders said that the text had become an integral part of their liturgy and ways of speaking about their faith. Furthermore, new believers usually required one to two years to learn this language and become recognized members of the community of faith. As the leaders then said, 'Within that time we can determine whether or not such persons are members of the KGB.'

For many people the authenticity of authorship is a basic factor in acceptance or rejection of a translation. Unless the first five books of the Old Testament are listed as 'the Books of Moses' and unless a Study Bible accepts Moses' undisputed authorship of these books, the translation is likely to be rejected. Some people also insist that the Epistle to the Hebrews must be attributed to Paul; otherwise, they believe that it cannot be as inspired as some of the other letters. Any statement about the possibility of First and Second Timothy and Titus being written by someone other than Paul not only reduces the validity of these books but also of the entire publication of the Bible, because only 'unbelievers and liberals' could possibly be so heretical. The same attitudes prevail among a number of constituencies in the case of comments about a 'second Isaiah' (chs. 40–55) or a 'third Isaiah' (chs. 56–66).

Strangely enough, even the format and binding can be factors in the acceptance or rejection of a translation by some people. Other persons do not want certain poetic passages in Hebrew to be printed in poetic lines because this would suggest that the contents are not true. But some people actually prefer the poetic format for certain parts of the Bible because they claim that the prose paragraphs show what are the words of God and the poetic lines reveal what are only the ideas of people. When the Revised Standard Version was first published in red binding, some persons refused to buy and read it, because the red cover showed that the translation must have been made by communists.

With so many factors prejudicing the acceptance of a text as authoritative, one may seriously ask what kinds of factors are crucial in the acceptance of a translation. The most obvious factor is the endorsement of a publication by church authorities. For Roman Catholics this usually means an *imprimatur* by a bishop or a recommendation by a council of bishops. For Protestants the corresponding procedures would be endorsement by leaders of denominations, acceptance by denominational publishing houses, and incorporation of a translation into Sunday School literature or church liturgy. For the members of many independent and conservative churches the recommendation of a text by a well-known preacher or evangelist can be indispensable; for example, the recommendation of the Living Bible by Billy Graham. In many parts of the world the publication of a text by the local Bible Society or by the United Bible Societies provides a significant measure of validation. Even advertisers no doubt contribute a measure of authority to a text by some of their claims. For example, one advertisement for the King James Version announced, 'Read the Bible God reads.'

A number of these same kinds of factors were clearly relevant in the actual history of the canon during the first four centuries of the church, such as names associated with particular books, the legend of the 'Seventy', endorsement and use of certain writings by the Church Fathers, and the study of manuscript evidence by people such as Origen and Jerome. But there were probably other factors; for example, whether a document was on papyrus or vellum, whether it came from Alexandria or Ephesus, and whether the letters were majuscules (capitals) or minuscules (lower case letters). Canonicity in the broad sense of acceptance or rejection of a text by a believing community has been and will continue to be an unending issue.

From the above examples of the canonicity of translations, it should be obvious that there is no contradiction whatsoever with the important contribution of James Sanders to the concept of the canonicity of texts. This article simply points to the fact that the principle of canonicity can be extended from texts to translations. In fact, this same principle may be extended to cultural patterns in circumstances where particular types of behavior are regarded as authoritative for a society.

CANON AND THE COMMUNITY OF WOMEN: A FEMINIST RESPONSE TO CANONICAL CRITICISM

Nancy R. Bowen

One of the main principles of feminist biblical interpretation is that interpretation begins with women's experience. This principle is the basis for this essay, which explores the relationship between the interests and methodologies of feminist biblical interpretation[1] and canonical criticism. This exploration arises out of my reflections and observations on my own experience both as a student of Professor Sanders and the method of canonical criticism he has proposed, and as a feminist biblical interpreter. My interests in Professor Sanders's work and in feminist interpretation began at the same time and have developed together. In many ways, canonical criticism and feminist interpretation have been dance partners[2] in my work as a biblical interpreter. I am very grateful to be able to pay tribute to Professor Sanders as one of my dance instructors and to share some of the dance steps I have learned along the way.

The approach I shall take is to look first at those places where canonical criticism and feminist interpretation dance in step, that is, what these two approaches share in common. Next, I will look at places where the dance is not so smooth, where one partner might trip on the other or

1. 'Feminist biblical interpretation' includes a wide variety of perspectives and methodologies. The connections and criticisms developed in this essay do not reflect any one method. For various taxonomies that attempt to classify different approaches see E. Schüssler Fiorenza, *But She Said* (Boston: Beacon Press, 1992), pp. 21-48, 134-63; M.A. Tolbert, 'Defining the Problem: The Bible and Feminist Hermeneutics', *Semeia* 28 (1983), pp. 113-26; C. Osiek, 'The Feminist and the Bible: Hermeneutical Alternatives', in A. Yarbro Collins (ed.), *Feminist Perspectives on Biblical Scholarship* (Atlanta: Scholars Press, 1985), pp. 93-105; K. Doob Sakenfeld, 'Feminist Perspectives on Bible and Theology', *Int* 42 (1988), pp. 5-18.

2. In using dance as a metaphor I am thinking in particular of dance as based upon established steps and patterns that with creativity and innovation are combined to make new dances.

where it is not clear who should take the lead, that is, those places where these approaches are in conflict with each other. Finally, I will look at the possibility of some new dance steps, that is, how canonical criticism and feminist interpretation might learn from each other in the future.

1. *Dancing Together*

One of Sanders's primary contributions has been to call attention to, and to clarify, the process of canonization.[3] That process begins the first time a story or text is repeated or 'bridges the gap from one generation to the next'. It is only those stories and texts that continue to be repeated that get 'on the tenure track' towards canonization. One of the reasons a story becomes tradition and then canon is because of its ability to be adapted by later believing communities to their new situation. Thus, Sanders has concluded that a primary character of canon is its *adaptability* as well as its *stability*.[4]

Adaptation occurs at a number of levels. When the tradition was still primarily oral, adaptation occurred when an earlier authoritative tradition such as that of the exodus or creation was repeated and resignified. Adaptation at this stage also occurred as new authoritative traditions were added to earlier ones. The oldest manuscripts available, written long after the traditions had been stabilized, show a remarkable degree of fluidity, some of which is due to reinterpretation. After the stabilization of the Masoretic Text, adaptation continued to occur whenever a new generation read scripture in its own context. From Amos's resignification of the Day of YHWH, to the Septuagint's additions to Esther, to the rules of Hillel, to the use of allegorization in the early church, and on through Luther and up to historical criticism, each generation has sought its own way(s) to make the text adaptable.[5]

The importance of this process from a feminist perspective is that this ongoing task of adaptation is a movement in which feminist biblical interpreters are also engaged. What both canonical criticism and feminist interpreters are attempting is to define the ways in which the canon can be made adaptable in our own day. For feminist biblical interpreters,

3. J.A. Sanders, *Canon and Community* (Philadelphia: Fortress Press, 1984), pp. 21-45; *idem*, *From Sacred Story to Sacred Text* (Philadelphia: Fortress Press, 1987), pp. 133-35.

4. Sanders, *Sacred Story to Sacred Text*, pp. 19-23.

5. *Sacred Story to Sacred Text*, pp. 125-31.

rendering the canon adaptable means that the importance of gender as an aspect of interpretation must be recognized, and that women claim the right to be full participants in the interpretive process. The importance of Sanders's identification of the adaptability of canon is that it provides a warrant for feminist interpretation. Feminist biblical interpreters can thus claim both a biblical and a historical basis for their task. What they are doing is nothing new: looking for new ways to resignify the tradition is as old as the tradition itself. As Phyllis Trible has stated it, 'Liberating the Bible from patriarchy is the first theological consideration. It applies a time-honored principle to contemporary issues. From the ancient world to the present, lovers of scripture have released it from the prison of the past to speak to the living.'[6] Indeed, Trible's image of the Bible as a pilgrim[7] can be compared to Sanders's understanding of adaptability in the reuse of tradition and the process of canonization.

Another aspect of the canon that Sanders has highlighted is the multivalency of the text. Sanders has recognized that the same text can mean different things in different contexts. He cites as evidence the notorious ambiguity of poetry, the use of the same tradition to score different points, but also how many different meanings scholars in the past two hundred years have claimed as the original meaning of any given text.[8] The multivalency of the text is also a characteristic that feminist biblical interpreters have claimed in a number of ways.

First, many feminist interpreters agree with Sanders in insisting that we must give up the claim of an 'objective' reading of the text. For example, Elisabeth Schüssler Fiorenza, who has been a leader among feminist biblical interpreters in critiquing the notion of 'a value-free, objectivist study of historical texts' acknowledges a connection with Sanders's work in pointing to the obsolescence of that theory.[9]

6. P. Trible, 'Postscript: Jottings on the Journey', in L.M. Russell (ed.), *Feminist Interpretation of the Bible* (Philadelphia: Westminster Press, 1985), p. 147; also P.L. Day (ed.), *Gender and Difference in Ancient Israel* (Minneapolis: Fortress Press, 1989), p. 2.

7. P. Trible, *God and the Rhetoric of Sexuality* (Philadelphia: Fortress Press, 1978), p. 1.

8. Sanders, *Canon and Community*, p. 23; see also his essay 'Canonical Hermeneutics: True and False Prophecy', in *Sacred Story to Sacred Text*, pp. 89-105, which thoroughly discusses the issue of text and context.

9. E. Schüssler Fiorenza, *Bread Not Stone* (Boston: Beacon Press, 1984), p. 32 n. 18. See also her critique in *In Memory of Her* (New York: Crossroad, 1983), pp. xvi-xviii.

Secondly, in arguing that gender makes a difference in how one reads a text, feminists have enhanced Sanders's understanding of context. Feminist literary critics have pointed to how both gender per se and women's experience influence the reading of a text.[10] In effect, women in the act of reading form a new context. For feminist biblical interpreters, the recognition of the multivalency of the text and the effect of gender and women's experience as a new context for interpretation become the warrant for the reinterpretation of texts that have traditionally been interpreted negatively towards women. One example of such reinterpretation is Phyllis Trible's work in *God and the Rhetoric of Sexuality*, where she offers a re-reading of the Genesis 2–3 stories which portrays Eve in a much more positive light than has traditional interpretation.[11] One of Trible's justifications for her methodology is the issue of multivalency:

> A single text appears in different versions with different forms in different contexts. Through application it confesses, challenges, comforts and condemns. What it says on one occasion, it denies on another. Thus scripture in itself yields multiple interpretations of itself.[12]

There are two other aspects of the nature of canon that are important from a feminist perspective: (1) the pluralism of the canon and (2) the overall theocentric monotheizing perspective of the canon.

Sanders emphasizes that the canon comes to us from differing sources over a 1500-year period ranging from the Bronze Age to the Hellenistic-Roman. The canon speaks of its understanding of God through the norms and idioms of these cultures. The canon is pluralistic because it reflects the diversity of contexts from which the biblical sources have come and the diversity of experiences through which Israel and the church recognized God to be at work.[13] The diversity is represented in the canon in a number of ways, including the expression of multiple theologies and/or ideologies, the numerous literary genres, and the diversity of social contexts from which various works originated.

In the midst of all this pluralism Sanders speaks of the canon as a

10. For citations of some of this research see R.J. Weems, 'Reading *Her Way* through the Struggle: African American Women and the Bible', in C.H. Felder (ed.), *Stony the Road We Trod* (Minneapolis: Fortress Press, 1991), p. 58 nn. 1, 2.

11. Trible, *Rhetoric of Sexuality*, pp. 72-143.

12. *Rhetoric of Sexuality*, p. 4. In her own footnote at the end of this citation, Trible explicitly acknowledges a connection with Sanders.

13. J.A. Sanders, 'Canon (OT)', in *ABD*, I, pp. 843-46; *idem*, *Canon and Community*, p. 43.

monotheizing literature. That is, throughout the history of Israel and the church and through the centuries of various cultures, the Bible attests that there is One God who is at work.[14] There is not a God of the Bronze Age and a God of the Roman era. There is not a God of slavery and a God of kingdoms and a God of exile and a God of Jesus Christ. It is one and the same God. God is not limited to any one context or any one experience or expression of faith. This means that Scripture has built in a self-correcting apparatus that makes it impossible to absolutize any one cultural idiom or any one particular experience or expression of God's presence and activity.[15] Israel struggled to monotheize in the midst of the polytheism of its day, to affirm that it was the same God who was with them in Egypt and in exile, the same God who was with them in the West Semitic culture of the eighth century BCE and the Roman world of the first century CE.

Feminist biblical interpreters are engaged in a twofold struggle against the overall patriarchal bias of the Bible and against patriarchal structures of oppression in religious and cultural institutions. Pluralism and monotheizing work together to aid in that struggle. Since the Bible refuses to allow us to absolutize any one cultural norm and idiom, and since feminist criticism has demonstrated that patriarchy is also a cultural construct, then we cannot absolutize patriarchy in our religious and cultural institutions. Sanders states that 'To monotheize is, in part, to engage in a resistance movement against a dominant mode of thinking whether in biblical antiquity or in the present'.[16] Feminists are engaged in a resistance movement against today's dominant mode of thinking that still places 'man' at the center and 'woman' at the margins. Like our ancestors, we struggle to monotheize and to affirm that God is not limited to nor bound by a patriarchal worldview and its expression. From the perspective of monotheizing, to absolutize patriarchy is to begin to polytheize and to believe in a God of patriarchy and in a God of egalitarianism.

In addition to canonical process and an understanding of the character of canon (multivalent, pluralistic, monotheizing), canonical criticism and feminist biblical interpretation connect in their joint concern for how the canon is to be adapted or made relevant in our own day. One of the many principles that Sanders suggests is that of *dynamic analogy*. What

14. Sanders, 'Canon (OT)', pp. 843-44; *idem*, *Canon and Community*, pp. 44, 51-52, 57-60; *idem*, *Sacred Story to Sacred Text*, p. 187.

15. Sanders, *Sacred Story to Sacred Text*, pp. 7, 30.

16. Sanders, *Canon and Community*, p. 44.

this expression means is 're-presenting the tradition, consciously identifying with the character or characters in the tradition most *representative* of the new hearers or readers'.[17] For example, if Jesus challenged his own Jewish contemporaries who were faithful, responsible believers, then modern Christians, as faithful, responsible believers should hear that same challenge. By dynamic analogy, when we understand Jesus' challenge to the faithful, responsible believers of Nazareth that the year of the Lord's favor will fall upon those outside our community (Lk. 4.14-30), we too might want to drive Jesus out of town and hurl him over a cliff![18] One of the positive results that Sanders sees for such an approach is that it can seriously challenge Christianity's continuing anti-Semitism since it permits us in reading the Second Testament to identify with our just counterparts, the good religious folk who rejected Christ.[19]

Schüssler Fiorenza advocates a similar position when she argues for a paradigm that does not merely repeat or apply the biblical text but which demands a translation of the text's meaning and context into our own situation.[20] The reason for such a position is that other dominant models of biblical interpretation fail to meet the needs of the community of women struggling for liberation.[21] Schüssler Fiorenza develops her feminist theological reconstruction of Christian origins from this paradigm.[22] While her final result is very different from what Sanders proposes with dynamic analogy, she shares a recognition that biblical interpretation for today requires dynamic translation in order to bring about liberation, either from Christian anti-Semitism or Jewish and Christian patriarchy.

Finally, there are two presuppositions about the Bible that canonical criticism and feminist biblical interpreters hold in common. The first is that the Bible belongs to the community of faithful believers. Sanders's

17. Sanders, *Canon and Community*, pp. 70-71; *idem*, 'Hermeneutics', in *IDBSup*, p. 406.

18. J.A. Sanders, 'From Isaiah 61 to Luke 4', in J. Neusner (ed.), *Christianity, Judaism, and Other Greco-Roman Cults: Studies for Morton Smith at Sixty* (SJLA, 12; Leiden: Brill, 1975), pp. 75-106.

19. Sanders, *Canon and Community*, p. 74.

20. Schüssler Fiorenza, *Bread Not Stone*, pp. 32-36. See n. 25 where she cites Sanders's rule of 'dynamic analogy' as a way to make such a translation.

21. Schüssler Fiorenza identifies these models as 'the Doctrinal Paradigm', which conceives the Bible in ahistorical, dogmatic terms, and 'the Historical Paradigm', which tries to identify what actually took place; *Bread Not Stone*, pp. 25-32.

22. *A Feminist Theological Reconstruction of Christian Origins* is the subtitle of Schüssler Fiorenza's *In Memory of Her*.

Canon and Community underscores this presupposition. The canon was shaped by the existential needs of the communities of Israel and the church. The community gives life to the canon and, in turn, the canon gives life to the community. A corollary of this is that the proper locus for interpretation of the Bible lies within the community.[23] Many feminist biblical interpreters affirm the same point.[24] What they then insist upon is that this community includes the community of women.[25]

The second presupposition relates to the understanding of the Bible as the Word of God. Sanders is very clear that it is not the *text* that is the Word of God. 'The Word is the point that is made in the conjunction of text and context, whether in antiquity or at any subsequent time.'[26] Feminist biblical interpreters have also wrestled with how to understand the Bible as the Word of God, especially as it has so often been used against women. Many feminists agree that the locus of divine revelation is that conjunction between text and context and not the text itself.[27] But they go on to add that in today's context unless that conjunction *functions* to further the liberation of women from social and political oppression it cannot be understood as divine revelation and truth.[28]

In summary, in this section I have identified places of intersection between canonical criticism and feminist biblical interpretations. These places include the adaptability of the text, its multivalency, the importance of context in interpretation, the role of pluralism and the monotheizing tendency of the Bible, the importance of dynamic interpretation and some common presuppositions underlying the two approaches. I will now look at some places where each approach challenges the other.

2. *Dance Missteps*

There are at least three areas in which canonical criticism is problematic from a feminist perspective. Sanders asserts that one of the major func-

23. Sanders, *Canon and Community*, p. xv; *idem*, 'Canon (OT)', p. 843.

24. S.H. Ringe, 'Biblical Authority and Interpretation', in L.M. Russell (ed.), *The Liberating Word* (Philadelphia: Westminster Press, 1976), pp. 37.

25. Schüssler Fiorenza, *Bread Not Stone*, pp. 1-22.

26. Sanders, 'Hermeneutics', p. 404.

27. For example, Schüssler Fiorenza locates revelation in Christian experience and community as well as in women's oppression and power; *In Memory of Her*, pp. 34, 35.

28. Schüssler Fiorenza, *In Memory of Her*, p. 33; R.R. Ruether, *Sexism and God Talk* (Boston: Beacon Press, 1983), p. 19.

tions of canon is to answer the two questions, 'Who are we?' and 'What are we to do?' That is, canon has to do with mythos, or identity, and ethos, or how we live.[29] The first problematic issue is the answer to the question of identity.

Scripture can be seen as a collection of individual and community witnesses, from several millennia in the past, who chronicle their experiences of God. However, the inherent power of Scripture hinges upon our ability to find our experiences addressed in this past witness. In Sanders's language, the text offers us 'mirrors for identity'.[30] For women, the problem is in what is reflected back.

The mirrored image is primarily stories about men's experience of faith. The result is that women are forced to find a reflection by identifying with men, or to not find a reflection at all, or to see themselves only as women are seen by men.[31] This is not to say that it is impossible for women to find themselves addressed by Scripture. Sharon Ringe has articulated this very well:

> Although as a woman I surely find myself addressed most directly and immediately by those portions of the biblical traditions having particularly to do with women, because of the tropic quality of biblical language I nevertheless find my story told elsewhere in the canon as well.[32]

It is a limitation, however. I suspect that the reason many feminist biblical interpreters have focused their work on recovering the stories about women in the Bible is precisely because they are 'addressed more directly and immediately' by those stories. I know that I find myself very engaged by the stories of Tamar in Genesis 38 and of the women in Exodus 1–2. These stories are about women who act outside of normal conventions in order to further God's work. It seems to me that this reflects what feminist biblical interpretation is about: working outside of scholarly conventions in order to further God's work.

Yet it can even be problematic to recover stories about women. It can be argued that these stories do not really provide access to women's experience of faith because they are written by men about women. Thus, the experience is already interpreted through patriarchal eyes.

29. Sanders, *Sacred Story to Sacred Text*, pp. 16-18.

30. Sanders, *Canon and Community*, p. 72.

31. C. Heyward, *Our Passion for Justice* (New York: Pilgrim, 1984), pp. 168-69.

32. S. Ringe, 'Luke 9:28-36: The Beginning of an Exodus', *Semeia* 28 (1983), p. 97.

Furthermore, because of this filtered interpretation the few stories about women usually portray them in a negative light. A radical understanding of this might suggest that women can never find their faith experiences reflected in Scripture.

A second issue that is problematic from a feminist perspective is the problem of the patriarchal bias of the Bible. I mentioned above that canonical criticism offers a possible solution to this problem. However, from a feminist perspective it is not clear that this solution will in fact work. While there are some norms of the biblical world which are relatively easy not to absolutize, is it possible to avoid the norm of patriarchy? This question is important because patriarchy is not just an incidental norm or idiom from one of the cultures that influenced the Bible. Rather, it is an underlying presupposition in all of the cultures.

This is one of the critical questions for feminist biblical interpreters and feminist theologians. It points to the heart of the matter: whether the Bible is life-affirming or life-denying for women. The centrality of this issue is expressed by the spectrum of responses. At the extreme ends are those who categorically reject the Bible and those who uncritically accept the Bible.[33] The majority of feminist biblical interpreters find themselves somewhere in the middle. They acknowledge two seemingly contradictory facts:

> On the one hand, the Bible is written in androcentric language, has its origin in the patriarchal cultures of antiquity, and throughout its history has inculcated androcentric and patriarchal oppression. On the other hand, the Bible has also served to inspire and authorize women and other non-persons in their struggles against patriarchal oppression.[34]

Those who fall within this middle position employ a variety of strategies to address this conundrum, some of which are more critical of the patriarchal bias than others.[35] It seems clear that this is an issue with which feminist biblical interpreters will continue to wrestle. It is also clear that the feminist critique of the patriarchal worldview is a challenge to the

33. Postbiblical feminists such as Mary Daly and advocates of Goddess worship such as Carol Christ represent those who reject the Bible. More conservative, evangelical women represent those who thoroughly accept the Bible.

34. Schüssler Fiorenza, *But She Said*, p. 21.

35. See the taxonomies listed in n. 1 for various descriptions of these strategies and those who are advocates of the various positions. Feminists who employ strategies such as structuralism or reader-response theory tend to be more critical of the patriarchal construction of the Bible.

adequacy of relying only on a plurality of voices within the Bible to correct or defend against the absolutizing of cultural norms.

The issue of confronting a patriarchal worldview leads to a third issue for feminist interpreters: the process of canonization itself. A feminist perspective questions who was involved in this process of repetition and selectivity.

Much recent work has focused on the social processes involved in canonization. It is clear that there were multiple parties and competing voices involved in the process of canonization. Within the Scriptures themselves, we can see this in the competing voices of Ezra/Nehemiah and Ruth, Esther and Jonah over how Israel should include foreigners in the religious community, or in the pro- and anti-monarchic voices in 1 Samuel 8–10. Most recently, ideological criticism has begun to point to competing ideologies within the Bible.[36] In addition to a reinterpretation of polemical passages in the canon, there is archaeological evidence, such as the inscriptions from Kuntillet 'Ajrud, which suggests that worship of the goddess Asherah was a part of official, orthodox Israelite practice.[37] Other literature, such as the Pseudepigrapha and the sectarian texts from Qumran, indicates that there were additional writings that were also considered authoritative and that different communities had different authoritative traditions.[38] This makes clear that in the process of canonization some voices and texts were ultimately excluded from the authoritative tradition.

Sanders acknowledges this multiplicity of, and competition among,

36. D. Jobling and T. Pippin (eds.), *Ideological Criticism of Biblical Texts* (*Semeia* 59, 1992).

37. Z. Meshel, 'Did YHWH Have a Consort? The New Religious Inscriptions from the Sinai', *BARev* 5 (1979), pp. 24-35; W.G. Dever, 'Asherah, Consort of Yahweh? New Evidence from Kuntillet 'Ajrud', *BASOR* 255 (1984), pp. 21-37; J. Day, 'Asherah in the Hebrew Bible and Northwest Semitic Literature', *JBL* 105 (1986), pp. 385-408; D.N. Freedman, 'Yahweh of Samaria and his Asherah', *BA* 50 (1987), pp. 241-49; S.M. Olyan, *Asherah and the Cult of Yahweh in Israel* (SBLMS, 23; Atlanta: Scholars Press, 1988); B. Margalit, 'The Meaning and Significance of Asherah', *VT* 40 (1990), pp. 264-97; R. Hestrin, 'Understanding Asherah: Exploring Semitic Iconography', *BARev* 17 (1991), pp. 50-59; W.G. Dever, 'Women's Popular Religion: Suppressed in the Bible, Now Revealed by Archaeology', *BARev* 17 (1991), pp. 64-65; S. Ackerman, 'The Queen Mother and the Cult in Ancient Israel', *JBL* 112 (1993), pp. 385-401.

38. Sanders, *Canon and Community*, pp. 34-35. In particular see the essay by D.M. Carr in this volume.

voices and even recognizes that what was canonized was not the total of what was available. However, Sanders goes on to make the following assertions: (1) that the canon was shaped by the faithful leaders *and* followers; (2) that because of this no party, denomination, or hierarchy in Jerusalem or elsewhere would have had the power to foist off on to the people a literature which held little meaning or value for them; (3) that the decisions as to what to include and what to leave out were not made with forethought or malice.[39]

From a feminist perspective these caveats to the canonical process are insufficient for the following reason. It is clear from social analysis that the process of selectivity was at times an intentional process undertaken by those who had the power to exclude.[40] Sheila Briggs has called attention to the nature of 'canon' as a hegemonic term based on exclusivity, not inclusivity.[41] The canon is hegemonic insofar as it functions to exclude texts from what is authoritative where in other situations they may have been included. Insofar as canon is based upon a principle of exclusivity there needs to be included in canonical criticism a critical component which asks *who* was involved in the process of canonization and *whose* interests and existential needs were being served.

I believe that this critical component has emerged within canonical criticism.[42] In particular, Gottwald has done an excellent job of pointing to where sociological analysis and canonical criticism can dance together as partners. However, the work to date has focused primarily on political, theological and ideological tensions. This means that another aspect of social analysis is missing: the tensions within the communities of gender. I have not yet seen it acknowledged among canonical critics that those primarily making the decision, those whose identity and ethos were

39. *Canon and Community*, pp. 33, 38.

40. D.R. MacDonald, *The Legend and the Apostle: The Battle for Paul in Story and Canon* (Philadelphia: Westminster Press, 1983); Schüssler Fiorenza, *In Memory of Her*, pp. 53-56.

41. S. Briggs, 'The Politics of Identity and the Politics of Interpretation', paper prepared for the conference 'Gender, Race, Class: Implications for Interpreting Religious Texts', Princeton Theological Seminary, May 1988.

42. J. Blenkinsopp, *Prophecy and Canon: A Contribution to the Study of Jewish Origins* (University of Notre Dame Center for the Study of Judaism and Christianity in Antiquity, 3; Notre Dame, IN: University of Notre Dame Press, 1977); N.K. Gottwald, 'Social Matrix and Canonical Shape', *TTod* 42 (1985), pp. 307-21; G.T. Sheppard, 'Canonization: Hearing the Voice of the Same God through Historically Dissimilar Traditions', *Int* 36 (1982), pp. 21-33.

being canonized, were the community of male Israelites. Whether it was done maliciously or not, one of the functional results of canonical hegemony is that women's experiences of God are virtually excluded from Scripture or included only when valued negatively.[43]

These three issues, the canon's inadequacy as a 'mirror for identity' for women, the canon's patriarchal bias, and the exclusive character of the process of canonization, are areas in which a feminist perspective challenges canonical criticism. There is one area in which canonical criticism challenges feminist interpreters. Most feminist biblical interpreters have focused exclusively on texts that treat women. One of the things that canonical criticism affirms is that the *whole* canon belongs to the community of faith. Sanders has been critical of the historical-critical method insofar as it looks for what was 'original' and then deems all that is secondary 'spurious'. One of the great gifts of canonical criticism has been to say that even what is 'secondary' is authoritative and life-giving.[44] This calls feminist biblical interpretation to another task. This task is to read from a feminist perspective all of the canon and not only those parts that deal with women.[45]

For example, what might it look like to read wisdom literature from a feminist perspective? One of the aspects of wisdom that Sanders points to is the hermeneutic process by which Israel adapted and resignified wisdom from its neighbors through depolytheizing, monotheizing, 'Yahwizing' and 'Israelitizing'.[46] This is a biblical perspective which feminist biblical interpreters might affirm as they have theologized, Judaized and Christianized what secular psychologists, anthropologists, sociologists and literary critics have told us about women. In addition, wisdom's search for the divine order based upon reflection on experience might speak to feminist concerns. While feminists do not need to absolutize the order that is recorded in the book of Proverbs, wisdom's

43. P. Bird, 'The Role of Women in the Israelite Cultus', in P.D. Miller, Jr, *et al.* (eds.), *Ancient Israelite Religion* (Philadelphia: Fortress Press, 1987), pp. 397-419; S. Ackerman, 'And the Women Knead Dough: The Worship of the Queen of Heaven in Sixth-Century Judah', in Day (ed.), *Gender and Difference*, pp. 109-24.

44. Sanders, *Canon and Community*, pp. 38-41.

45. Schüssler Fiorenza (*Bread Not Stone*, pp. 39-41; *In Memory of Her*, pp. 32-34) advocates a similar position in her insistence that *all* biblical texts be evaluated as to how they either perpetuate the oppression of women or articulate the liberating experiences of the people of God.

46. Sanders, *Canon and Community*, p 56; *idem*, *Sacred Story to Sacred Text*, p. 21.

process of examining experience and discerning what is of God in that experience is precisely the task that feminist biblical interpreters and theologians have been about. On a more negative side, feminist biblical interpreters should be critical of wisdom's view of retribution and therefore its lack of a concern for justice. Such a critical examination of all the biblical traditions is a way in which canonical criticism challenges feminist biblical interpreters.

In summary, I have examined in this section ways in which canonical criticism and feminist biblical interpretation offer challenges to each other. A feminist perspective challenges canonical criticism in its understanding of how the canon shows us truths about ourselves as a 'mirror for identity', its need to be critical of the inherent patriarchal bias of the canon and the issue of exclusion in the process of canonization. Canonical criticism challenges feminist biblical interpreters to apply their methodologies to all of the canon. I will now turn to envisioning what the future might hold for these dance partners.

3. *Future Dance Steps*

Like chapter IV in *Canon and Community*, this last section might also be titled 'Work to Do'. One issue will be whether canonical criticism and feminist biblical interpretation are able to resolve the tensions listed above. There is nothing inherent in the analysis of the canonical process that prohibits the inclusion of how factors such as gender did or did not play a role in the process of canonization. The issues of the extent to which women are able to find mirrors for identity in Scripture and the extent to which Scripture's patriarchal bias inhibits that will probably continue to be areas of tension. It is also not clear whether there are theological and philosophical presuppositions on both sides that would prohibit or enhance the possibility of resolution of these tensions. Finally, feminist biblical interpreters are beginning to move away from an almost exclusive focus on texts concerning women. With more women entering the field of biblical studies and with men increasingly sensitized to issues of gender, I expect that feminist interpretations of other parts of the canon will continue to increase.

Another future direction is to continue to seek places of connection or tension between canonical criticism and feminist approaches. As an example we may consider the notion of canonical hermeneutics. By canonical hermeneutics, Sanders means the hermeneutics by which biblical traditions were adapted, represented and resignified. The two canonical hermeneutic modes which Sanders has identified are the *prophetic* and the *constitutive*. These arise respectively out of the view of God as Creator of all things and peoples, and God as Redeemer in Israel and Christ.[47] Sanders's understanding of the prophetic hermeneutic is helpful from a feminist perspective. The notion of God as Creator primarily stresses the freedom of God. This freedom is God's freedom continually to do a 'new thing'. In particular, this view of God serves as a prophetic critique of any settled theological position because God is free to critique her own creations and institutions.

Sanders considers these hermeneutics to be as canonical as the text itself. He then raises the question whether there should emerge a permissible hermeneutic *range* that indicates what is hermeneutically fair, according to the *canonical process*.[48] What might be 'hermeneutically fair, according to the canonical process' raises at least one question from a feminist perspective. The question is whether it is sufficient to limit hermeneutics to those located within the canonical process. Feminist biblical hermeneutics has primarily been a hermeneutic of suspicion. This is a 'non-canonical' hermeneutic. It may be that from a feminist perspective other 'non-canonical' hermeneutics need to be added in order to render the canon adaptable for the life of the community of women.[49]

Another place for future dialogue will be the impact of canonical criticism as a method within the community of women. One of the great gifts of canonical criticism is that it makes the Bible available to communities of faith. One of Sanders's concerns is to 'unchain the Bible from the scholar's desk'. I hope that I have made clear that I believe that canonical criticism is a way to make the Bible available also to the community of women. Yet in bibliographies on canonical criticism, that community is not represented. Canonical criticism has not been adopted by feminist biblical interpreters in any kind of thorough way. This essay has primarily been based upon isolated citations to Sanders's work by a wide range of feminist interpreters. It is my hope that more feminist biblical interpreters will incorporate canonical criticism and that canonical critics will incorporate feminist methodology! Perhaps one day we can

47. Sanders, *Sacred Story to Sacred Text*, pp. 89-105; *idem*, 'Canon (OT)', pp. 848-50.

48. Sanders, *Canon and Community*, pp. 61-62.

49. Schüssler Fiorenza (*But She Said*, pp. 144-56) especially is critical of feminist positions that locate their key hermeneutical principle within the canon.

add 'feminist canonical criticism' to the repertoire of methodologies.

I would like to close with an example of the method of canonical criticism and feminist hermeneutics dancing together. The 'text' is the book of Ezekiel. Like other prophets Ezekiel announces God's judgment upon Israel for its sins. But there are several distinctive aspects to Ezekiel's message. First, unlike Hosea and Jeremiah, Ezekiel claims that from its very inception Israel has been sinful (chs. 16 and 23). Secondly, unlike other prophets there is no opportunity for repentance in Ezekiel. Repentance will not avert the coming disaster. Judgment is sure. Thirdly, unlike Isaiah and Jeremiah there is no remnant theology in Ezekiel. There will be no 'stump' that is left (ch. 15). Perhaps the clearest example of this is Ezek. 37.1-14 where Israel is compared to a valley of very dry bones. Israel is completely dead.

This death can be interpreted in a number of ways. Primarily, it can be seen as the end of all that had held Israel's identity. This death includes the end of the institutions of temple and king. But it was also the death of the theology and ideology that had upheld these institutions. In this judgment God destroyed all the old ways, and even removed Israel's heart of stone (36.26).

The hope that is given in chs. 33–38 assures Israel that God will indeed give them a new identity. God will give them a heart of flesh. As God had once breathed life into Adam, God will now breathe life into a new Israel. They will have a new shepherd and a new temple. But Ezekiel's message is that before God would give them this new identity they first had to die to who they were before God. The old ways would not do.

The 'context' is the end of the twentieth century. By 'dynamic analogy' the contemporary situation is very much like that of Ezekiel's day. Women and other marginalized persons are the prophets who have come to announce God's judgment. 'Sin' is the religious and cultural institutions and ideologies that perpetuate oppression and marginalization based upon sex, race, class, religion, ability or sexual orientation. Some of these prophets claim that this sin has existed from the birth of human religion and culture. While it is true that changes and progress have been made, perhaps as with Ezekiel it is too late. There is no longer an opportunity for repentance and for God to withhold the punishment. Judgment is sure. God's punishment for this sin will be no less than the 'death' of the institutions and ideologies that perpetuate oppression. The destruction of this world order will be complete; no remnant will survive. But after this old worldview is a very dry bone, we are offered the hope of resurrection. In that day, God will give us a new heart and new leaders and new structures that promote the full humanity and the full participation of all of God's people.[50]

50. I would like to thank Judith Applegate, Anne Marie Hunter and Sandra Olewine, part of the community of women, both for their critical and helpful comments on a draft of this essay and for their friendship and encouragement.

Stained Glass Window, Kaleidoscope or Catalyst: The Implications of Difference in Readings of the Hagar and Sarah Stories

Richard D. Weis

Introduction[1]

'What difference does difference make in feminist hermeneutics?'[2] One construal of the question would see difference as foundational to feminist

1. Although James A. Sanders's name has not been associated with feminist hermeneutics, this essay's presence in a volume honoring him recalls that his work in comparative midrash and canonical criticism has been concerned, among other things, to bring into focus both the multivalent character of biblical texts and the historical reality of diverse interpretations of individual texts—suggesting a revaluing of difference in interpretation. Moreover, by calling attention to (reading) communities as the source of the diverse adaptations of a given canonical text, Sanders points to the social locations of those communities as important contributing factors in generating meaning(s) from texts ('Each generation reads its authoritative tradition *in the light of its own place in life*, its own questions, its own necessary hermeneutics' [emphasis added]: J.A. Sanders, 'Adaptable for Life: The Nature and Function of Canon', in F.M. Cross, W.E. Lemke and P.D. Miller, Jr [eds.], *Magnalia Dei: The Mighty Acts of God. Essays on the Bible and Archaeology in Memory of G.E. Wright* [Garden City, NY: Doubleday, 1976], p. 551) even though his own work does not particularly explore this dimension of the process of finding meaning within biblical texts.

2. This question, posed as the theme of the 1994 sessions of the Feminist Theological Hermeneutics of the Bible Group of the Society of Biblical Literature, embraces the point made by womanist, *mujerista* and Jewish feminist interpreters, among others, that the multiplicity of other reading communities to which feminist readers belong, and the resulting differences in the 'places' from which individual feminist readers read, matter enormously, and cannot be glossed over. Renita Weems makes the point quite eloquently in her essay 'Reading *Her Way* through the Struggle: African American Women and the Bible', in C.H. Felder (ed.), *Stony the Road We Trod* (Minneapolis: Fortress Press, 1991), pp. 67-71. See also b. hooks, *Ain't I a Woman* (Boston: South End, 1981), pp. 119-58, and *Feminist Theory:*

hermeneutics, the difference in the experience and constructions of reality associated with gender. From this basis feminist hermeneutics has opened new options in biblical interpretation, challenging the way the universalizing claims attached to particular interpretations (rooted in the experiences and interests of European and European–American male academics and/or clergy) render different experiences and understandings invisible or marginal. In another construal the question would ask for an exploration of the effect that the membership of feminist readers in diverse reading communities has or should have on feminist theological hermeneutics.[3] It is in this second manner that this essay seeks to pursue the question.

Since I think that we learn about the nature of interpretation best by watching people in the act of interpreting, this essay joins in that exploration by means of a comparative examination of interpretations of the Hagar and Sarah stories in Genesis 16 and 21. Specifically I will compare six published readings of these texts: a sermon by Katie Geneva Cannon, and essays by Sharon Pace Jeansonne, Elsa Tamez, Phyllis Trible, Renita Weems and Delores Williams.[4] All of these interpretations

From Margin to Center (Boston: South End, 1984). An earlier draft of this essay was read in a session of the Feminist Theological Hermeneutics of the Bible Group of the Society of Biblical Literature at its meeting in Chicago in 1994. I wish to express my appreciation to all who raised questions and points of conversation in that context. Similarly I wish to express my gratitude to New Brunswick Theological Seminary for a sabbatical in the fall of 1994 when this project, among others, was undertaken.

3. Defining a feminist after Katherine Sakenfeld, 'A feminist, broadly speaking, is one who seeks justice and equality for all people and who is especially concerned for the fate of women—all women—in the midst of "all people"' (K.D. Sakenfeld, 'Feminist Perspectives on Bible and Theology', *Int* 42 [1988], p. 5) and feminist interpretation after Phyllis Bird, 'For me, the essential signs or ingredients of feminist interpretation are *systemic analysis* of gender relations and a *critique* of relationships, norms and expectations that limit or subordinate women's thought, action and expression' (P. Bird, 'What Makes a Feminist Reading Feminist?' [paper presented in the Feminist Theological Hermeneutics of the Bible Group of the Society of Biblical Literature, November 18, 1993, Washington, DC], p. 4).

4. K.G. Cannon, 'On Remembering Who We Are', in E.P. Mitchell (ed.), *Those Preachin' Women* (Valley Forge, PA: Judson, 1985), pp. 43-50; S.P. Jeansonne, *The Women of Genesis* (Minneapolis: Fortress Press, 1990); E. Tamez, 'The Woman Who Complicated the History of Salvation', in J.S. Pobee and B. von Wartenburg-Potter (eds.), *New Eyes for Reading* (Bloomington: Meyer-Stone, 1987), pp. 5-17; P. Trible, *Texts of Terror* (OBT, 13; Philadelphia: Fortress Press, 1984);

may be said to be feminist in a broad sense.[5] Five of these interpreters explicitly identify themselves as either a feminist or a womanist.[6] The interpretations are all substantive and worthy readings that consider the text to have meaning for the readers' present. The methods of interpretation used by these scholars are roughly similar, partaking in varying combinations of literary and historical-critical approaches. Thus variations among the readings are less likely to be due simply to the strictures of method.[7] Four of the six interpretations explicitly articulate substantial connections to the interpreter's social locations. I trust that the interpreters are well known, and so the presence within their numbers of a degree of difference in social location is apparent.[8]

My examination has three parts: a comparison and consideration of the six readings as a whole, a comparison and analysis of how the readings realize the dialogue between Hagar and the messenger of YHWH at the well in the wilderness (16.8-9), and a drawing out of the implications for feminist theological hermeneutics.[9]

R.J. Weems, *Just a Sister Away* (San Diego: LuraMedia, 1988); D.S. Williams, *Sisters in the Wilderness* (Maryknoll, NY: Orbis Books, 1993).

5. See the definitions cited in n. 2.

6. Remembering Phyllis Bird's comment that 'what makes a feminist reading is a feminist reader' (Bird, 'What Makes a Feminist Reading Feminist?', p. 2).

7. The notable reading of these texts by Savina Teubal (S.J. Teubal, *Hagar the Egyptian: The Lost Traditions of the Matriarchs* [San Francisco: Harper & Row, 1990]) was excluded exactly on these grounds, that in significant ways its differences are due to differences of method. These differences of method and their results are quite valuable, but their inclusion here would risk blurring the focus on social location.

8. Two are European Americans living in the United States, three are African Americans living in the United States, and one is a Costa Rican. Four are professional biblical scholars, one is an ethicist, and one a constructive theologian. Three teach at free-standing ecumenical seminaries, one teaches at a Catholic university, another at a secular university, and the sixth at a university divinity school affiliated with a single denomination. The group is relatively homogeneous in regard to class location, being well-educated academics. When we focus on the social location of the readings, rather than the readers, somewhat more class diversity may be present in the sample. One of these readings is a sermon addressed to a congregation of lay people, another is specifically addressed to church women whether lay or clergy, the original vehicle of publication for a third suggests it was aimed at a wide audience, and the other three may be said to be aimed at the theologically literate reading public.

9. My own social location can be signaled by my identity as a middle-class, European American, heterosexual male academic who teaches Hebrew Bible in a free-standing Protestant denominational seminary. A significant aspect of my location for

Difference Among the Six Readings In General

Because each of these six readings of the texts about Hagar and Sarah has its own integrity as a story, I begin by asking after the basic stories these six readers find in these texts. Necessarily I will do this in summary fashion, even at some risk of being reductionistic. Without making claims about the intentions of the readers, or any claims of certainty, I will suggest some possible relations between differences bound up with social location, and differences among the readings.

For Cannon these texts contain a story of human character—furnished by a positive model, Hagar, and two negative models, Sarah and Abraham, who exemplify human character traits and attitudes that either open or close a person to the divine, to new life, and to healthy human relations.[10] This reading, which to some extent stands apart from the others in emphasizing character over plot, is a useful example of the importance of the particular location of an individual *reading* alongside the role of the *reader's* own location.[11] The emphasis on character, for example, may well come from the reading's identity as a sermon. Indeed, the various traits and attitudes lifted up in it are often *topoi* within Protestant preaching. Hagar's African identity is made explicit at the outset, and the African American congregation's identification with her is reinforced. Both of these aspects are rooted in a long-standing tradition

the views expressed in this essay is the gender, ethnic, denominational and age diversity of the student body at the school where I teach: 50% male, 50% female; 45% European American, 42% African American, 11% Asian and Asian American, 2% Hispanic American; 90% between 30 and 70 years of age; representing over 20 denominations with six having major and nearly equal representation. While continually discovering the ways in which I have learned too well how to oppress, I attempt to inhabit this location out of a commitment to expose the falsity of the claims to universality made for the experience, perspectives and discourse of persons of my social location, and to create structures and discourses that respect, value and learn from difference. A particular commitment to feminist interpretation comes from my attempts to keep solidarity with women in their experience of the injustice of patriarchal domination, and from my experience of the inadequacy of patriarchal definitions of humanness and world not only for others, but also for myself.

10. Cannon, 'On Remembering Who We Are', pp. 46-50.

11. This is also Weems's observation: 'how one reads or interprets the Bible depends in large part on which interpretative community one identifies with at any given time' ('Reading *Her Way* through the Struggle', p. 67).

of reading these texts in the African American community.[12]

For Weems this is a story of the failure of two women to establish a much-needed solidarity with each other across differences of race and class in resistance to patriarchal oppression.[13] She grounds this story, which she finds in the texts, in the experience of African American and other minority women in the United States, experience that has been widely told and analyzed in womanist reflection.[14]

The readings of Cannon and Weems have two significant aspects in common. Most immediately apparent is their shared focus on the human characters in the texts to the relative neglect of the divine character. While both necessarily refer to the deity in the course of their readings, God's role in the story is pushed into the background by comparison with the other four readings. This follows from Cannon's focus on character and Weems's focus on the missed opportunity for human solidarity. I think it is also related to the second aspect these readings share, namely, a concern for what a colleague of mine calls decolonizing the mind. In Weems's reading this will become most apparent when we look at her telling of the messenger's command to Hagar to return and submit to Sarai. In Cannon's reading this becomes visible in the qualities that she commends and censures. Those she censures involve acquiescence or mimicry of the system of racist domination the congregation experiences, and the qualities she commends point the congregation toward finding their true identity, toward a valid self-knowledge and toward an openness to others that would lead to communal solidarity across inner-communal differences. This concern for combating the way oppressive systems colonize the mind as well as the body, while certainly an important facet of feminist thinking in general, is also a particular concern in the African American community within which Cannon and Weems are located.[15]

12. Weems, 'Reading *Her Way* through the Struggle', p. 76.

13. Weems, *Just a Sister Away*, pp. 12, 15-18.

14. See, for example, hooks, *Ain't I a Woman*, pp. 15-86, 119-58; K.G. Cannon, 'The Emergence of Black Feminist Consciousness', in L. Russell (ed.), *Feminist Biblical Interpretation* (Philadelphia: Westminster Press, 1985), pp. 30-40; J. Grant, *White Women's Christ and Black Women's Jesus: Feminist Christology and Womanist Response* (AAR Academy Series, 64; Atlanta: Scholars Press, 1989), pp. 195-205; and Williams, *Sisters in the Wilderness*, pp. 34-139.

15. See, for example, C.T. Gilkes, 'The "Loves" and "Troubles" of African-American Women's Bodies: The Womanist Challenge to Cultural Humiliation and Community Ambivalence', in E.M. Townes (ed.), *A Troubling In My Soul*

This concern for internalized oppression correlates with a theme in Williams's reading that emphasizes how the marginalized—as a crucial element of their liberation—create an alternative culture for themselves, drawing on pre-oppression (in this instance, African) roots. Williams also explicitly stresses Hagar's African identity in a fashion similar to Cannon. These two concerns do not surface as prominently, if at all, in the other readings I am considering, so it is reasonable to hypothesize that they are related to the location of these three readers and readings within the African American community.

For Tamez this is a story of liberating human initiative—the initiative of the marginalized by which they claim a place for themselves in the center of a history from which they would otherwise be excluded, and of how God validates that initiative, indeed collaborates in the liberation of the marginalized.[16] This reading mirrors descriptions of the liberation struggle in Latin America as the poor becoming subjects of their own history rather than objects manipulated by others, or as the poor claiming a place in history from which they had previously been excluded as actors.

For Williams this is also a story of human initiative whereby the marginalized liberate themselves from the culture, structures and persons that oppress them.[17] In contrast, however, to Tamez for whom liberation means the poor *entering* history, for Williams liberation means the poor *leaving* an oppressive society to create an alternative world. Unlike Tamez, Williams does not see God playing a liberating role in that story. Instead she sees God assisting Hagar in obtaining the resources needed to survive as she continues with her struggle toward liberation. This is in line with a women-centered tradition of theological reflection and appropriation that Williams identifies alongside the well-known liberation tradition in African American theological reflection. She calls this tradition 'the survival/quality-of-life tradition of African American biblical appropriation' and finds it to be associated especially with the Hagar texts.[18] Tamez, on

(Maryknoll, NY: Orbis Books 1993), pp. 232-49; b. hooks, *Black Looks: Race and Representation* (Boston: South End, 1992); P.L. Hunter, 'Women's Power—Women's Passion: And God Said, "That's Good"', in Townes (ed.), *A Troubling In My Soul*, pp. 194-96; Weems, 'Reading *Her Way* through the Struggle', pp. 65-66; and Williams, *Sisters in the Wilderness*, pp. 84-88.

16. Tamez, 'The Woman Who Complicated', pp. 9, 16-17.

17. Williams, *Sisters in the Wilderness*, pp. 22-26.

18. Williams, *Sisters in the Wilderness*, pp. 4-6.

the other hand, indicates that the liberation theology of recent Latin American reflection is a formative frame for her interpretation. Once again we may ask if the readers' social locations do not enable these readings.

Jeansonne tells the story as a surrogate mother relationship gone sour in which Sarah's struggle to have a child leads her—out of fear and desperation—cruelly to victimize Hagar. God responds to both women, even though Hagar is a foreigner, in ultimately positive and vindicating ways (albeit not entirely unambiguously).[19] This reading would appear to bear particular relation to Jeansonne's location as a middle-class, educated European American. The cases of surrogate motherhood that have received attention in the news media during the last decade have featured couples from that location. While Williams reads the story in the light of various surrogacy roles that African American women have been forced to assume, Jeansonne's reading does not seem to echo that so much as the well-publicized surrogate mother cases.[20]

For Trible these texts can be said to contain a story of a failure of solidarity in a way similar to Weems's reading, but they are also just as much, and perhaps primarily, a story of how God collaborates with the oppressor to thwart the attempts of the oppressed to achieve liberation.[21] I cannot point to anything that I have been able to document, but I persist in thinking, on the basis of experience with my students, that this picture of a God who sides with the oppressor is far more thinkable in the current European American context than, for instance, in the current African American context, and thus is another reading enabled by the reader's social location.

Six different, even opposing, stories—the Genesis texts about Hagar and Sarah contain all these stories and more.[22] The role of social location in this abundance of stories seems to be as the source of familiar stories of women's lives that then serve as organizing principles for the reader's assembling of the textual data into a coherent story.[23] However, not just

19. Jeansonne, *Women of Genesis*, pp. 20, 28, 44-45, 49, 52.

20. Jeansonne, *Women of Genesis*, pp. 19-20, 44; and Williams, *Sisters in the Wilderness*, pp. 60-83.

21. Trible, *Texts of Terror*, pp. 16, 22, 25, 28.

22. Note also the list of stories contained in the text in Weems, 'Reading *Her Way* through the Struggle', p. 75.

23. For an in-depth discussion of this connection see C. Heilbrun, *Writing a Woman's Life* (New York and London: W.W. Norton, 1988).

any story from the reader's or reading's location will serve; to organize the textual data effectively the story must have some resonance, some metaphoric connection, with the text. At the same time, each telling of Hagar's and Sarah's story or stories cannot be reduced to the story from the reader's location, for even as this latter story organizes their reading, the texts (re)shape it.

Difference Among the Readings Under Close Examination

The Categories of Examination

As we move to examining specific textual phenomena and the readings that arise from them, I would like to introduce some categories of analysis, drawing in part on Wolfgang Iser's reader-response theory.[24]

In exploring the nature of the reading process Iser focuses on those aspects of a text's construction that call for the reader to engage in some activity of completing the text in order for a coherent reading to be derived from it. He groups many of these aspects under the heading of indeterminacy. This refers to those places where a text leaves something unresolved, indeterminate, which the reader must necessarily resolve in order to obtain a coherent and satisfying reading of the text.[25]

The possibilities for indeterminacy are manifold. For our purposes, three categories will suffice as illustrations: first, instances of an unresolved conflict or tension in the text; secondly, instances where the reader must determine the significance or referent for a term; thirdly, instances where the text invites the reader to fill in a silence in the text.[26]

In Iser's approach to the reading process the category of indeterminacy focuses chiefly on the behavior of readers as reactors to textual phenomena. However, readers engage texts more broadly. Thus as a supplement to the category of indeterminacy I would like to introduce the notions of filtering—a metaphor for the process of selecting what in a text is attended to or accorded importance (for which foregrounding

24. W. Iser, 'Indeterminacy and the Reader's Response in Prose Fiction' in J.H. Miller (ed.), *Aspects of Narrative* (New York: Columbia University Press, 1971), pp. 1-45; *idem*, *The Implied Reader* (Baltimore: Johns Hopkins University Press), pp. 274-94; *idem*, *Prospecting: From Reader Response to Literary Anthropology* (Baltimore: Johns Hopkins University Press, 1989).

25. Iser, *Implied Reader*, pp. 282-87.

26. Iser, *Prospecting*, pp. 7, 10-13, 34-35; *idem*, *Implied Reader*, pp. 279-81, 288. Other significant categories of indeterminacy could include instances of ambiguity (exemplified by the question of how to understand Hagar's reaction to her pregnancy).

and backgrounding also serve as metaphors), and mapping—a metaphor for the process of assigning meaning to textual phenomena based on some frame of reference.[27] The backgrounding of the role of God in the stories Cannon and Weems find in these texts is an example of filtering. Weems's reading of the texts as a story of a missed opportunity for solidarity across boundaries of race and class arises in part because she maps the texts to a frame of reference derived from the experience of African American women.

The Examination in Particular

These phenomena—indeterminacy, filtering and mapping—appear in the readings of the conversation at the well in the wilderness between Hagar and the מלאך יהוה, during which Hagar is commanded to return and submit to her mistress. The scope of Cannon's reading does not lead her to treat this aspect of the text, but the five remaining readings offer plenty of material for fruitful reflection.

We will watch how the readers treat five textual elements: *first*, the significance of the messenger's address to Hagar as שפחת שרי (reprising the term used by the narrator [v. 1] and Sarai [v. 2] to describe Hagar's status); *secondly*, the significance of Hagar's characterization of Sarai as גברתי; *thirdly*, the meaning of Hagar's failure to respond to the second question the messenger asks ('Where are you going?'); *fourthly*, the kind of location designated by the term מדבר; and *fifthly*, the resolution of the tension between the messenger's command to return and submit, and portrayals of God as on the side of the oppressed.

Interpretation of the first four textual elements is not prominent in Jeansonne's reading. She simply notes that the messenger addresses Hagar as 'servant of Sarai', but ascribes no explicit significance to that naming. She interprets Hagar's statement that she is fleeing her mistress as expressive of Hagar's suffering and as specifying the source of that suffering. She does not focus specifically on Hagar's characterization of Sarai or her failure to answer the second question. Jeansonne presumably maps the wilderness in terms of ecology (that is, as a physical place with a particular ecosystem), but actually describes it in the language of fertility as 'barren territory', and the well as a 'life-giving source'.[28] The character of the wilderness is not resolved in ch. 16, nor does it really

27. See T.W. Overholt, *Channels of Prophecy* (Minneapolis: Fortress Press, 1989), p. 18.

28. Jeansonne, *Women of Genesis*, p. 45.

figure in this part of Jeansonne's reading.

Jeansonne connects the command to submit (והתעני) to the word the narrator uses in v. 6 to describe Sarai's treatment of Hagar (ותענה), and understands this to mean that 'the *narrator* thus indicates that Hagar's pain at the hands of Sarai will not be abated' (my emphasis). For all that she describes this command as 'disquieting' or 'painful news', Jeansonne's reading ultimately resolves the tension in favor of portraying the deity as favorable toward Hagar. The harsh wording of the command is ascribed to the narrator—distancing God from the oppression. The annunciation that follows is read as balancing out the oppressiveness of the command since 'the narrator indicates that God assuages Hagar's suffering by promising that her offspring will be a great nation'.[29] The resolution, at least to the degree expressed in the reading, is a rather minimalist one, however, when compared with the other four.

Tamez's reading takes no account of the terms the messenger and Hagar use to describe her status in relation to Sarai. They betoken neither validation of the structures that imprison Hagar from without, nor expression of the mentality that imprisons within. They are simply filtered out of the reading entirely. Tamez does elaborate the significance of Hagar's response to the messenger's questions. Her answer to the first question, that she is fleeing Sarai her mistress, 'In a valiant, honest way...expresses her rejection of slavery, her past life, the ill-treatment at the hands of her mistress.' Her failure to answer the second question shows that she is 'disoriented' and simply fled without time to plan.[30] The wilderness in ch. 16 is mapped in climatological and ecological terms as 'the desert', and is read unambiguously as a place of danger and death.[31]

Tamez agrees that the messenger's command to return and submit to oppression would appear to put God on the side of the oppressor, but this is not the way she ultimately reads the meaning of these words. Crucial for her reading are several elements. She maps the texts as a whole against two frames of reference: the exodus story of liberation as the decisive picture of how God deals with the oppressed, and the struggle of the marginalized in Latin America to take control of their history and claim a place for themselves.[32] On that basis she reads the texts in a way

29. Jeansonne, *Women of Genesis*, pp. 45-46.
30. Tamez, 'The Woman Who Complicated', p. 14.
31. Tamez, 'The Woman Who Complicated', pp. 10, 14-15.
32. Tamez, 'The Woman Who Complicated', pp. 5, 9.

that gives great weight to the theophany, to God's promises to Hagar and to God's blessing of Ishmael. These are read as accepting Hagar's initiative and affirming her place in salvation history. Emblematic of the way in which the verses that follow the messenger's command (vv. 10-13) become the center of the story for Tamez is her mapping to Exod. 3.7 of the reference (Gen. 16.11) that God had noticed Hagar's affliction. This leads Tamez to perceive God's attention to Hagar's situation as a positive expression of the divine stance towards Hagar.[33] In this story the messenger's command is then an anomaly to be explained rather than a significant force in the story.[34] The meaning of the command is to provide Hagar with the ability to ensure the life of her yet-to-be-born son, which would have been at risk in the wilderness as Tamez construes it, and to ensure that the ritual and legal necessities to guarantee his inheritance and place in salvation history are fulfilled.[35]

Weems's reading contains nothing about the messenger's naming of Hagar as שפחת שרי, but makes much of Hagar's answers to the questions as the explanation for the messenger's command to return and submit. Two factors in Hagar's response are seen as determinative: her description of Sarai as 'my mistress' is read as expressive of Hagar's self-definition as a slave, and the absence of an answer to the messenger's question about where she is going is read as her inability to answer because her past still defines her.[36] The messenger's command is necessitated then by the fact that 'Hagar's body was free, but her mind remained in bonds. What Sarai thought of Hagar had become what Hagar thought of herself: she was property.' Thus 'the angel had no other choice, but to send the runaway slave back to the reality in which she had defined herself'.[37] The real story here, in Weems's telling, is not God's action, whether for good or for ill, but Hagar's incomplete progress toward liberation. In this reading the filtering out of the messenger's identification of Hagar (an expression of external structures) goes hand in hand with the mapping of Hagar's self-identification as expressive of internal self-awareness and definition. The wilderness and the way its

33. Tamez, 'The Woman Who Complicated', pp. 13-16.

34. 'Understood in this manner [as God siding with the oppressor], it simply doesn't go with the text. God's plans are not for Hagar to return to oppression' (Tamez, 'The Woman Who Complicated', p. 14).

35. Tamez, 'The Woman Who Complicated', pp. 14-15.

36. Weems, *Just a Sister Away*, p. 13.

37. Weems, *Just a Sister Away*, p. 13.

character and condition impact the action are also heavily backgrounded.

By contrast, the story Williams tells for this portion of text notices the messenger's address to Hagar and construes it to mean that YHWH 'still identifies Hagar as Sarai's property', but wishes to hear how Hagar defines herself with reference to both past and future direction.[38] Hagar's response to the two questions is understood to speak of neither past nor future, but only the present, and in words that suggest 'that Hagar still sees herself as property'.[39] The wilderness is a sociological category, characterized by a lack of the supportive social structures of family and clan, as much as it is an ecological category, characterized by scarcity of resources. It is fundamentally a place of danger, 'where survival seem[s] doomed', yet there are latent in it resources for survival and the possibilities of new social arrangements.[40]

As Tamez does, Williams acknowledges that the messenger's command to return and submit makes God appear to support slavery. She also finds a more positive meaning in the command. However, she does not map the command in terms of a liberation frame of reference. Instead she maps it in terms of the tradition of God as the supporter or guarantor of survival and quality of life, as the One who 'makes a way out of no way'. Alongside this she calls attention to the high infant mortality rates in the ancient Near East, and concludes that the meaning of the command is that 'God apparently wants Hagar to secure her and her child's well-being by using the resources Abram has to offer'. In other words, the sending back of Hagar is an interim measure to secure the survival of Hagar and Ishmael until they can effect their own liberation.[41]

Williams, Jeansonne, Tamez and Weems tell different stories of this dialogue between Hagar and the messenger of YHWH. Nevertheless each in her own way reads the text so that God is not taking the side of the oppressor, but in some way remains on the side of the oppressed. The story Trible tells of this dialogue is quite different. For her the command to return and submit is 'a divine word of terror to an abused, yet courageous woman'.[42] Several things contribute to this story. Mapping Hagar's flight into the wilderness to Israel's exodus into the

38. Williams, *Sisters in the Wilderness*, p. 20.

39. Williams, *Sisters in the Wilderness*, p. 21.

40. Williams, *Sisters in the Wilderness*, pp. 20, 26, 29-32, 108-109. The quotation is found on p. 109.

41. Williams, *Sisters in the Wilderness*, pp. 21-22.

42. Trible, *Texts of Terror*, pp. 15-16.

wilderness, and foregrounding the presence of water and the well's proximity to Egypt and home, the wilderness in Trible's story is a place of freedom and new life for Hagar. The language about status in the interchange between Hagar and the messenger is systematically read, not as expressive of Hagar's self-understanding, but as signaling external structures of power. Thus, although the messenger addresses Hagar by name, the epithets שפחת שרי for Hagar and גברתי for Sarai indicate the continuing force of the old structures of power and oppression so that 'Exodus from oppression has not secured freedom for Hagar'. It is Hagar's emphatic אנכי in 16.8, echoing and opposing Sarai's אנכי in 16.6, that signals her mentality, continuing resistance. Supporting the structures of oppression are: first, a parallel Trible finds between מלאך יהוה and שפחת שרי which she constructs as signaling that 'to be "of Sarai" is to be "of the Lord"', and secondly, the repetition in the messenger's command in 16.9, והתעני תחת ידיה, of the language of Abram's giving Hagar into Sarai's power (יד) and of Sarai's oppressive use of that power. Trible's mapping of this text to the exodus also contributes to the story she tells. In Exod. 3.7 God is said to 'see' the 'oppression' (עני) of 'a slave people', and to intend to come 'to deliver them *out of the hand*' of their oppressors. In Genesis Hagar describes herself as having been 'seen' by God. The messenger says that God has noticed her oppression (עני, 16.11), but she is not delivered out of the hand of her oppressor. Instead she is commanded to return there, truly a terrifying story.

Trible's striking reading of this dialogue between Hagar and the messenger is, I think, made possible by social location. Trible sees the wilderness as a place in which Hagar can survive. Hagar has options for life besides the conditions from which she flees, and so to send her back is to collaborate in maintaining her oppression. Of course, this is based on things clearly stated in the text, but those same things were in the text for the other readers. In one reading the wilderness has no effective place (Weems's), in another its possibilities are ambiguous at best (Jeansonne's), and in two others it is a place where Hagar will not be able to survive at this point and so she has no real options outside of Abram's and Sarai's household (Tamez's and Williams's). The well on the road to Shur, and the way it changes the significance of the wilderness, is foregrounded prominently in Trible's reading, and effectively pushed into the background in the other readings, whatever they say about it. The possibility that this foregrounding is related to the social location of the reader as a well-educated European American woman, living in a major metropolitan area in a period of (relatively) expanded options for women merits consideration. The story of the world as a place of greater opportunity for women does not create the story of the wilderness of Shur as a place of opportunity for Hagar, but it enables the reader to rearrange the data of the text so that this story, latent in the text, becomes visible.

Similarly, Weems's reading, which is notable for filtering out the wilderness and the messenger's address as factors in the story, seems enabled by the reader's social location. In resolving the tension produced by the command to return and submit through saying that Hagar's mental bondage meant the messenger had no choice, we see the previously mentioned concern for the liberation of the mind from the indoctrination of the oppressor. If the issue is whether Hagar is free in her mind, it makes little difference whether the wilderness represented an option for her or not. Thus this textual element is legitimately backgrounded in Weems's reading. The filtering out of the messenger's description of Hagar as שפחת שרי is likewise valid in terms of the socially derived story that is organizing Hagar's story for Weems at this point. In the story Weems draws on here it matters less how others name a person than how that individual names herself.[43] Thus Hagar's language in answer is crucial; the language of the messenger's address is peripheral. Again, however, this should not be seen as some element from the social location of the reader imposing a story on the text, but rather as the story current in the social location making visible something that is latent in the text. The stories of women's experience accounted conceivable in the social location of the reader serve to filter and map into a coherent story the data of the text, especially at points of indeterminacy.

With both Tamez and Williams the aspects of their social locations that we saw at work in the total stories they told seem to be shaping their reading of this part of the text. The differences between the readings of these two verses (16.8-9) offered by Weems and Williams ought to warn us against any simplistic notions of how difference in social location contributes to readings. When one looks at the broad sociological categories that we bandy about when we speak of social location—gender, race,

43. See also the analysis in the sermon by John Porter, 'Nobody Knows Our Names', in W.B. Hoard (ed.), *Outstanding Black Sermons* (Valley Forge, PA: Judson, 1979), II, pp. 81-88.

class, religious tradition, and the like—there seems to be little to distinguish in their social locations, and yet their readings are not the same.

We may get a better idea of the complexity of the impact of social location from the reading of this dialogue by a former MDiv student of mine, the Revd Girdie Washington. Ms Washington identifies herself as a womanist theologian, and is quite well versed in womanist theology and biblical interpretation. She reads the command of the messenger as God siding with the oppressor, and this text as a text of terror. She specifically affirmed the reading of Trible as the most satisfying one to her, and criticized the reading of Tamez—and by extension the one of Williams—as accepting the middle-class myth promulgated by patriarchy that women are weak and defenseless creatures in need of male assistance and protection in order to survive. She based her critique and reading on her experience that many single women, pregnant or with young children, do find the means to survive in the wilderness. In this reading the wilderness is mapped in sociological and economic terms as something like urban slums. Now the stories on which Washington bases her reading of the wilderness as a place where survival is possible are surely not unknown to Tamez and Williams, yet they do not shape their readings to the degree that they shape Washington's. Like Williams Washington is African American, well educated, middle class, nurtured in the black church and yet struggling with its sexism, and—if I am not mistaken—even of roughly the same generation. The difference may lie in the fact that Washington is a social worker in a public school system in New Jersey, who day in and day out works with children at risk—the children of mothers cast out into the wilderness and surviving.

I would argue that here we see at work a process of foregrounding and backgrounding going on within a reader's total social location. Washington's particular involvement with single-parent families in the wilderness of poverty makes one set of stories of women's experience that she and Williams both know relatively more prominent for her when she reads this text than for Williams. Thus she and Williams read different stories about Hagar and the messenger.

Implications

The complexity of the reading process is such that we cannot make definitive conclusions on the basis of this examination of difference in readings of the Hagar and Sarah stories. However, we may reasonably propose some of the implications that can be drawn from our consideration of those readings. In elaborating these implications, I intend ultimately to focus on the basic paradigms or root metaphors according to which interpreters deploy methods, rather than on any particular method or set of methodological strictures. I also suggest that these implications, while drawn for, and in the context of a discussion of, feminist biblical interpretation, are equally relevant for biblical interpretation in general.

As we have seen, the experience, perceptions and visions of the world, as well as the networks of relationships and group memberships, associated with and composing a reader's social location provide the fund of stories from which the reader draws the story or stories by which she or he organizes a reading of a biblical text.[44] The stories of experience, the perceptions and visions of the world available in the reader's social location fulfill this organizing function by serving as filters and maps for assigning importance and meaning to the phenomena of the text, especially at points of indeterminacy. This is not an incidental phenomenon, but is a central and indispensable process in the generation of meaning from a text.

Social location is a highly complex phenomenon, consisting of a reader's membership in multiple, often overlapping communities and groups. Elements of a reader's social location are foregrounded or backgrounded in relation to a text by a variety of influences: the audience for whom a reading is produced, other aspects of the context of a reading's production, the particular configuration of associations and involvements present in the reader's life at the moment of reading.[45] Indeed, the result is something that can be highly individualized so that it is not possible to create any sort of calculus of social location that then would suggest that this or that particular social location will necessarily produce this or that reading.

In the light of these preceding points we must say that when readers read biblical texts, they are reading themselves and their societal con-

44. A multi-faceted consideration of the relation between social location and interpretation may be found in F.F. Segovia and M.A. Tolbert (eds.), *Reading From This Place*. I. *Social Location and Biblical Interpretation in the United States* (Minneapolis: Fortress Press, 1995). See also D. Smith-Christopher (ed.), *Text and Experience: Towards a Cultural Exegesis of the Bible* (The Biblical Seminar, 35; Sheffield: Sheffield Academic Press, 1995).

45. Weems, 'Reading *Her Way* through the Struggle', pp. 67-68. A notable and self-reflective example of this phenomenon is found in L.J. Clark, 'Wrestling with Jacob's Angel', *USQR* 33 (1977), pp. 35-38.

texts just as much as they are reading the text. This holds true whether this is acknowledged or not. (As a case in point I cite Trible's or Jeansonne's interpretations which say little explicitly about their social location, yet are shaped by it as much as any other.) Thus every statement about the meaning of a text is also a statement about the reader's experience, perceptions and vision of the world.[46] The only variable is the degree to which this reality is acknowledged and open for discussion. In fact, I would contend that among highly competent readers the major, if not only, source of difference in textual meaning is difference in the resources drawn from the social location in the process of constructing meaning from the text.

David Couzens Hoy formulates this nicely when he says, 'this continual reinterpretation of the past goes hand in hand with the continual reinterpretation by the present of itself'.[47] This is true even when we claim to engage in historical reconstruction. As Annette Kolodny puts it,

> What we gain when we read the 'classics', then, is neither Homer's Greece nor George Eliot's England [and we might add nor J's and P's Canaan] *as they knew it*, but, rather, an approximation of an already fictively imputed past made available, through our interpretive strategies, for present concerns.[48]

These observations have further implications for our understanding of texts and meaning. It is still often assumed that each text has a single meaning, conceived either as that which its author intended or as that which its words say. In this conception the goal of interpretation is the recovery of that one meaning, and a diversity of readings of a single text is a problem, emblematic of the limitations of the readers. In this paradigm

46. This is even clearer when we contrast the interpretations examined in this essay with those of most male exegetes, who tend to push Hagar and Sarah into the background of the stories and to move Abraham and Ishmael (!) into the foreground (see, for example, W. Brueggemann, *Genesis* [Interpretation; Atlanta: John Knox, 1982], pp. 150-53, 177, 182-85).

47. D.C. Hoy, 'Hermeneutic Circularity, Indeterminacy and Incommensurability', *New Literary History* 10 (Fall, 1978), pp. 166-67, quoted in A. Kolodny, 'Dancing through the Minefield', in E. Showalter (ed.), *The New Feminist Criticism* (New York: Pantheon, 1985), p. 152. See also F.F. Segovia, 'Introduction: "And They Began to Speak in Other Tongues": Competing Modes of Discourse in Contemporary Biblical Criticism', in *idem* and Tolbert (eds.), *Reading From This Place*, pp. 28-32, and G.A. Yee, 'The Author/Text/Reader and Power', in *Reading From This Place*, pp. 115-16.

48. Kolodny, 'Dancing through the Minefield', p. 153.

of deploying interpretive methods difference is an obstacle to be overcome by better data or superior argument. For example, the competing understandings among Tamez, Trible, Weems and Williams as to whether and in which way the story of Hagar and Sarah is a story of liberation must be adjudicated to determine which one is 'correct'. Moreover, in this paradigm that adjudication must take place in terms simply of the data of the text and other textual grounds, submerging the issue of the character and conditions of liberation in the context(s) of the readers.

If we were to name a root metaphor for this model of texts and meaning it might be the stained glass window, and the task of interpretation is to draw—as accurately and precisely as possible—that window. Conversation among interpreters in this model is oriented toward determining which one reading most nearly approximates the one, true meaning. That interpretation is accorded the authority that—in this model—is attached to the biblical author or text. Our observations, however, show that what is going on underneath the surface is the authorization of one experience, perception and vision of the world to the exclusion of others, because the reading of self and world goes on in parallel with the reading of the text, but is never allowed to come to expression. Here the hiddenness of the parallel 'reinterpretation of the present' behind the 'reinterpretation of the past' cloaks a power play. The struggle to achieve a correct understanding of the text is a struggle to claim the authority of the text for legitimating a particular social regime of relation and control.

Our findings instead validate the increasingly common view that a text contains, or is capable of generating, many meanings, as many meanings as there are readers. The derivation of meaning from a text is the result of a collaboration between reader and text, and the different perspectives of readers necessarily lead to different readings—at least for literary texts. In this conception of the interpretive project a diversity of readings from one text is both a natural and positive outcome. Annette Kolodny again puts the matter helpfully:

> Any text we deem worthy of our critical attention is usually, after all, a locus of many and varied kinds of (personal, thematic, stylistic, structural, rhetorical) relationships...if feminists openly acknowledge ourselves as pluralists, then we do not give up the search for patterns...what we give up is simply the arrogance of claiming our work is either exhaustive or definitive.[49]

49. Kolodny, 'Dancing through the Minefield', p. 161.

Within this perspective, however, I think there are at least two possible paradigms.

One paradigm could be said to operate out of a root metaphor of the text as kaleidoscope, where the pieces of colored glass—instead of being arranged in a fixed pattern—can be continuously rearranged by a turn of the tube containing them. The text is still the object of our attentions, the provider of the meaning we seek. With the turn of the kaleidoscope by each new interpreter, a new pattern emerges from the brightly colored bits of text. The goal of the interpretive project becomes the accumulation of interesting readings from which we may pick and choose what appeals to us, or by which we may hope to catalog the possibilities of meaning in the text. The conversation among interpreters is still about how we read the text, rather than how we read ourselves and our world(s). This conversation is a considerable advance over that under the stained glass window model since it is characterized by tolerance and appreciation for divergent readings, which are now seen as enriching rather than problematic. Authority still resides in the text, but operates more flexibly and dynamically. In this paradigm difference is no longer an obstacle to be overcome in the quest for a unified meaning, but a source of variety to be acknowledged and celebrated, or at least tolerated.

While a distinct improvement over the paradigm of a single, unified meaning, this paradigm is not without problems. The emphasis on conversation about the reading(s) of the text (the image seen in the kaleidoscope) tends to suppress or minimize the parallel readings of self and world. The emphasis on tolerance tends to militate against an encounter among readings, leaving the possible relationships among them unexplored. To the degree that these tendencies are operative in an interpretive situation this model will result in a conversation where the experience, perceptions and visions of the world of other readers, while not overpowered, are not really encountered or taken account of in any direct way. Instead they are marginalized as 'adjective theology', leaving the existing structures of domination intact. In this paradigm Tamez, Trible, Weems and Williams would not be expected to agree as to whether and in what way the story of Hagar and Sarah is a story of liberation. On the other hand, the issue of the character and conditions of liberation in the context(s) of the reader(s) can easily remain submerged.

I propose that this study points us toward a paradigm that is signaled by a different root metaphor for the role of the text in interpretation. Specifically, I would propose the metaphor of the text as catalyst. In chemical terms a catalyst is a substance that facilitates a reaction between two other substances without itself being consumed in that reaction. The catalyst enables the reaction to take place under conditions in which it would not ordinarily go forward. The reaction can go forward, and produce a new substance from the combination of the two reactants because the catalyst supplies reaction sites that orient the molecules or atoms of the reactants in such a way that their combination becomes possible.

Proceeding from this metaphor, the role of the text in interpretation shifts from being the source of meaning to the site of struggle and the catalyst of conversation. The text itself is not ultimately the object of conversation, but by bringing into play certain experiences, perceptions and visions of the world on the part of its readers, it makes those experiences, perceptions and visions available for conversation and encounter with each other. Inspiration and authority lie not with the author or text, but with the potential community of readers—a position not without roots in theological tradition and communal practice. The interpretive conversation among readers makes the reading of self and world as explicit as the reading of the text. In this paradigm difference is the entry point to a conversation that leads to a more profoundly critical understanding of the context(s) of the readers. The discussion among Tamez, Trible, Weems and Williams in this instance is also concerned with their different readings of the text, but these serve as the starting point for the discussion of the differences that generated the readings so that the conversation becomes explicitly about the character and conditions of true liberation, resulting in a clearer understanding of the actions needed to bring about liberation.

The encounter of the different readings of the text then yields not so much a fuller reading of the text, but a fuller reading of the ways in which the social locations of the readers are linked by larger societal constructs, which can then be brought to expression and examined. By making visible the different readings of self and world that contribute to the different readings of the text, the interpretive conversation makes possible the exploration of the way those different readings of self and world are implicated in each other. It becomes the scene for the building across differences of a community that is founded in the discovery of affinities and connections, rather than in the obliteration or 'saming' of difference.[50]

50. Cf. L. Troch, 'A Method of Conscientization: Feminist Bible Study in the Netherlands', in E. Schüssler Fiorenza (ed.), *Searching the Scriptures*. I. *A Feminist Introduction* (New York: Crossroad, 1993), pp. 351-64. The language of 'affinities' and 'saming' is borrowed from M.M. Fulkerson, *Changing the Subject: Women's Discourses and Feminist Theology* (Minneapolis: Fortress Press, 1994), pp. 377-93.

BIBLIOGRAPHY OF JAMES A. SANDERS

1955 *Suffering as Divine Discipline in the Old Testament and Post-Biblical Judaism*. Special issue of *Colgate Rochester Divinity School Bulletin* 28 (Rochester, NY: Colgate Rochester Divinity School, 1995).

Review of *Jeremiah*, by E.A. Leslie, *Colgate Rochester Divinity School Bulletin* 27 (March 1955), p. 6.

Review of *The Rediscovery of the Bible*, by W. Neil, *Colgate Rochester Divinity School Bulletin* 28 (October 1955), B.

Review of *From Faith to Faith: Essays on Old Testament Literature*, by B.D. Napier, *Colgate Rochester Divinity School Bulletin* 28 (December 1955), B.

1956 'Thy God Reigneth', *motive* 16 (February 1956), pp. 28-31.

Review of *The Interpreter's Bible*. V. *Ecclesiastes, Song of Songs, Isaiah, Jeremiah*, ed. G.A. Buttrick, *JBR* 24 (1956), pp. 200-202.

Review of *The Old Testament Since the Reformation*, by E.G. Kraeling, *Colgate Rochester Divinity School Bulletin* 28 (June 1956), B.

Review of *Everyday Life in Old Testament Times*, by E.W. Heaton, *Colgate Rochester Divinity School Bulletin* 29 (December 1956), B.

1957 'Facts', *Colgate Rochester Divinity School Bulletin* 29 (1957), pp. 30-33.

Review of *Tools for Bible Study*, ed. B.H. Kelly and D.G. Miller, *Colgate Rochester Divinity School Bulletin* 29 (March 1957), B.

Review of *The Prophets*, by J.A. Bewer, *Colgate Rochester Divinity School Bulletin* 29 (March 1957), B.

Review of *Prophecy and Religion*, by H.H. Rowley, *Colgate Rochester Divinity School Bulletin* 29 (March 1957), B.

1958 'It is Finished', *Colgate Rochester Divinity School Bulletin* 30 (1958), pp. 70-74.

Review of *Prophetic Faith in Isaiah*, by S. Blank, *JBL* 77 (1958), p. 379.

Review of *The Authority of Scripture*, by J.K.S. Reid, *Colgate Rochester Divinity School Bulletin* 30 (March 1958), B.

Review of *The History of Israel*, by M. Noth, *Colgate Rochester Divinity School Bulletin* 30 (June 1958), B.

Review of *Theology of the Old Testament*, by E. Jacob, *Colgate Rochester Divinity School Bulletin* 31 (October 1958), B.

Review of *Old Testament Theology*, by L. Köhler, *Colgate Rochester Divinity School Bulletin* 31 (December 1958), B.

1959 Review of *The Root Sûbh in the Old Testament*, by W. Holladay, *JBL* 78 (1959), p. 262.

'Habakkuk in Qumran, Paul and the Old Testament', *JR* 39 (1959), pp. 232-44.

'It is Finished', *The Pulpit* 30 (1959), pp. 81-83.

Review of *Man, Morals and History: A Study of the Historical Process*, by C.C. McCown, *Colgate Rochester Divinity School Bulletin* 31 (March 1959), B.

Review of *A Light to the Nations*, by N.K. Gottwald, *Colgate Rochester Divinity School Bulletin* 32 (December 1959), B.

1960 Review of *Biblical Exegesis in the Qumran Texts*, by F.F. Bruce, *JBL* 79 (1960), p. 193.

Review of *Mystery on the Mount*, by T. Reik, *JBL* 79 (1960), p. 394.

Review of *The Dead Sea Community: Its Origin and Teachings*, by K. Schubert, *Colgate Rochester Divinity School Bulletin* 32 (May 1960), B.

Review of *God and History in the Old Testament*, by H.H. Guthrie, *Colgate Rochester Divinity School Bulletin* 33 (December 1960), B.

1961 *The Old Testament in the Cross* (New York: Harper, 1961).

Review of *Isaïe*. I. *1–39* (*Connaître la Bible*, 1), ed. and trans. J. Steinmann, *JBL* 80 (1961), pp. 202-203.

Review of *The Prophets of Israel*, by C. Kuhl, *JBL* 80 (1961), p. 198.

'The Grace of God in the Prophets', *Foundations* 4 (1961), pp. 262-65, 363-65.

Review of *The Old Testament: Its Origins and Composition*, by C. Kuhl, *Colgate Rochester Divinity School Bulletin* 34 (October 1961), B.

1962 'The Grace of God in the Prophets (Part III)', *Foundations* 5 (1962), pp. 74-77.

'The Scroll of Psalms (11QPss) from Cave 11: A Preliminary Report', *BASOR* 165 (February 1962), pp. 11-15.

'Dispersion', 'Enemy', 'Exile', and some twenty other entries, in *IDB*.

1963 'Psalm 151 in 11QPss', *ZAW* 75 (1963), pp. 73-86.

'God is God', *Foundations* 6 (1963), pp. 343-61.

Review of *The Psalms: A Commentary*, by A. Weiser, *JBL* 82 (1963), p. 127.

'They Belong Together', *Colgate Rochester Divinity School Bulletin* 35 (June 1963), pp. 12-15.

1964 'Two Non-Canonical Psalms in $11QPs^{a}$', *ZAW* (1964), pp. 57-75.

Review of *Salvation History: A Bible Interpretation*, by E.C. Rust, *Foundations* 7 (1964), pp. 89-90.

'Responsum', *ZAW* 76 (1964), p. 200.

'To Tell the Truth', *Christian Century* 81 (10 June 1964), pp. 763-66.

'The Sound of the Trumpet', *Colgate Rochester Divinity School Bulletin* 36 (1964), pp. 90-97.

Review of *Men of God: Studies in Old Testament History and Prophecy*, by H.H. Rowley, *Colgate Rochester Divinity School Bulletin* 36 (May 1964), B.

Review of *History, Archaeology and Christian Humanism*, by W.F. Albright, *Colgate Rochester Divinity School Bulletin* 36 (May 1964), B.

1965 'Pre-Masoretic Psalter Texts', *CBQ* 27 (1965), pp. 114-23.
'The Banquet of the Dispossessed', *USQR* 20 (1965), pp. 355-63.
'Nazoraios in Matt. 2:23', *JBL* 84 (1965), pp. 169-72.
The Psalms Scroll of Qumran Cave 11 (11QPs^{a}) (DJD, 4; Oxford: Clarendon Press, 1965).
Review of *History, Sacred and Profane*, by A. Richardson, *JBR* 33 (1965), pp. 176-77.
Review of *The Method and Message of Jewish Apocalyptic*, by D.S. Russell, *Colgate Rochester Divinity School Bulletin* 37 (March 1965), p. 3.

1966 'The Vitality of the Old Testament: Three Theses', *USQR* 21 (1966), pp. 161-84.
'Variorum in 11QPs^{a}', *HTR* 59 (1966), pp. 83-94.
'Promise and Providence', *USQR* 21 (1966), pp. 295-303.
'The Psalter at the Time of Christ', *The Bible Today* 22 (1966), pp. 1462-69.
Review of *The Old Testament: An Introduction*, by O. Eissfeldt, *USQR* 21 (1966), p. 347.
Review of *The Old Testament World*, by M. Noth, *USQR* 21 (1966), pp. 476-78.
Review of *Psalms I (1–50)*, by M. Dahood, *USQR* 21 (1966), pp. 478-81.
'The Old Testament and the Death of God', *Pulpit Digest* 46 (January 1966), pp. 9-16.

1967 *The Dead Sea Psalms Scroll* (Ithaca: Cornell University Press, 1967).
With Dora Sanders, 'Ten Commandments in Marriage', *Faith at Work* 80 (1967), p. 18.
'Urbis et Orbis: Jerusalem Today', *Christian Century* 84 (1967), pp. 967-70.
'Palestinian Manuscripts 1947–1967', *JBL* 86 (1967), pp. 431-40.
Review of *Gottesfurcht bei Jesus Sirach*, by J. Haspecker, *JBL* 86 (1967), pp. 480-81.
Review of *Old and New in Interpretation*, by J. Barr, *USQR* 22 (1967), pp. 147-50.
Review of *Deuteronomy: A Commentary*, by G. von Rad, *USQR* 22 (1967), pp. 269-72.
'Biblical Faith and the Death of God Movement', in J.L. Ice and J.J. Carey (eds.), *The Death of God Debate* (Philadelphia: Westminster Press, 1967), pp. 122-32.
'To Tell the Truth', in C.W. Christian and G.R. Wittig (eds.), *Radical Theology: Phase Two* (Philadelphia: Lippincott, 1967), pp. 71-80.

1968 Review of *Hesed in the Bible*, by N. Glueck, *Central Conference of American Rabbis Journal* 15 (January 1968), p. 96.
'Museum Exhibit Tells the Masada Story', *Christian Century* 85 (1968), pp. 89-90.
'Cave 11 Surprises and the Question of Canon', *McCQ* 21 (1968), pp. 284-98.

The New History: Joseph, Our Brother (Valley Forge, PA: American Baptist Convention, 1968. Pamphlet.

Review of *Theology of the Old Testament*, II, by W. Eichrodt, *USQR* 23 (1968), pp. 201-203.

Review of *The Religion of Ancient Israel*, by T.C. Vriezen, *USQR* 23 (1968), p. 407.

'Teaching and Learning: The Old Testament at Union', *The Tower* (Fall 1968), pp. 3-5.

'The Sovereign God', in E.K. Garber and J.M. Crossett (eds.), *Liberal and Conservative: Issues for College Students* (Glenview: Scott, Foresman, 1968), pp. 75-82.

1969 'Dissenting Deities and Philippians 2:1-11', *JBL* 88 (1969), pp. 279-90.

'The Best One-Volume Commentary', Review of the *Jerome Biblical Commentary*, ed. R.E. Brown, J.A. Fitzmyer and R.E. Murphy, *Int* 23 (1969), pp. 468-73.

'Outside the Camp', *USQR* 24 (1969), pp. 239-46.

Review of *The Exempla of the Rabbis*, ed. M. Gaster, with introduction by W.G. Braude, *USQR* 24 (1969), pp. 442-43.

Review of *Jacob Ben Chayyim Ibn Adonijah's Introduction to the Rabbinic Bible* and *The Massoreth Ha-Massoreth of Elias Levita*, ed. C.D. Ginsburg, with prolegomenon by N. Snaith, *USQR* 24 (1969), pp. 446-47.

'Cave 11 Surprises and the Question of Canon', in D.N. Freedman and J.C. Greenfield (eds.), *New Directions in Biblical Archaeology* (Garden City, NY: Doubleday, 1969), pp. 101-16.

1970 'In the Same Night', *USQR* 25 (1970), pp. 333-41.

Editor. *Near Eastern Archaeology in the Twentieth Century: Essays in Honor of Nelson Glueck* (Garden City, NY: Doubleday, 1970).

'This is for a Celebration', Foreword to *Near Eastern Archaeology in the Twentieth Century: Essays in Honor of Nelson Glueck* (Garden City, NY: Doubleday, 1970).

'Models of God's Government', Review of *The Old Testament and Theology*, by G.E. Wright, *Int* 24 (1970), pp. 359-68.

'The New English Bible: A Comparison', *Christian Century* 87 (1970), pp. 326-28.

Review of *The Old Testament and Theology*, by G.E. Wright, *USQR* 25 (1970), pp. 392-94.

'Mirror for Identity', *Thesis Theological Cassettes* 1 no. 10 (1970).

Translator. 'II Kings', in *New American Bible* (Paterson: St Anthony Guild, 1970).

1971 Review of *The Dead Sea Isaiah Scroll: A Literary Analysis*, by J.R. Rosenbloom, *USQR* 26 (1971), pp. 195-97.

Review of *Biblical Theology in Crisis*, by B.S. Childs, *USQR* 26 (1971), pp. 299-304.

Review of *The Kingdom of God in the Synoptic Tradition*, by R.H. Hiers, *TS* 32 (1971), pp. 303-304.

'What Happened at Nazareth?', Thesis Theological Cassettes 2 no. 10 (1971).

'Text Criticism and the NJV Torah', *JAAR* 39 (1971), pp. 193-97.

Introduction to 'A Propos a Definition of Midrash' by R. Le Déaut, *Int* 25 (1971), pp. 259-61.

'The Sirach 51 Acrostic', in A. Caquot and M. Philonenko (eds.), *Hommages à André Dupont-Sommer* (Paris: Librairie d'Amérique et d'Orient Adrien-Maisonneuve, 1971), pp. 429-38.

1972 *Torah and Canon* (Philadelphia: Fortress Press, 1972). Translated into French as *Identité de la Bible* (Paris: Cerf, 1975), and into Japanese (Tokyo: Kyo-Bun-Kwan, 1984).

'Jeremiah and the Future of Theological Scholarship', *ANQ* 13 (1972), pp. 113-45.

Edited with D.N. Freedman and F.M. Cross, *Scrolls from Qumran Cave 1: The Great Isaiah Scroll, The Order of the Community, The Pesher to Habakkuk*: From photographs of J.C. Trever (Jerusalem: Albright Institute of Archaeological Research and Shrine of the Book, 1972) (Color, and black and white photographs).

Review of *Amos of Tekoa*, by H.P. Routtenberg, *Jewish Social Studies* 33 (1972), pp. 319-20.

'Cave 11 Surprises and the Question of Canon', in R. Weis and E. Tov (eds.), *Nosah ha-miqra᾽ be-qumran* (Jerusalem: Hebrew University, 1972), pp. 104-13.

1973 'Palestinian Manuscripts 1947–1972', *JJS* 24 (1973), pp. 74-83.

'An Apostle to the Gentiles', *Conservative Judaism* 28 (1973), pp. 61-63.

'The Dead Sea Scrolls—A Quarter Century of Study', *BA* 36 (1973), pp. 109-48.

'Invitation to the Dispossessed', *Thesis Theological Cassettes* 4 no. 6 (July 1973).

With D. Barthélemy, *et al. Preliminary Report on the Pentateuch* (London: United Bible Societies, 1973).

1974 'Cave 11 Surprises and the Question of Canon', in S.Z. Leiman (ed.), *The Canon and Masorah of the Hebrew Bible* (New York: Ktav, 1974), pp. 37-51.

Edited with D.N. Freedman and F.M. Cross. *Scrolls from Qumran Cave 1: The Great Isaiah Scroll, The Order of the Community, The Pesher to Habakkuk*: From photographs of J.C. Trever (Jerusalem: Albright Institute of Archaeological Research and Shrine of the Book, 1974) (Black and white photographs).

'The Old Testament in 11Q Melchizedek', *JANESCU* 5 (1973), pp. 373-82.

'Reopening Old Questions about Scripture', Review of *The Bible in the Modern World*, by J. Barr, *Int* 28 (1974), pp. 321-30.

'The Ethic of Election in Luke's Great Banquet Parable', in J.L. Crenshaw and J.T. Willis (eds.), *Essays in Old Testament Ethics (J. Philip Hyatt, In Memoriam)* (New York: Ktav, 1974), pp. 245-71.

Epistle to the Hebrews: A Brief Comment. n.p.: Alba House, 1974. Audiocassette.

'Mysterium Salutis', in J.V. Allmen (ed.), *Year-Book 1972/73* (Jerusalem: Ecumenical Institute, 1974), pp. 103-27.

'The Qumran Psalms Scroll (11QPs^a) Reviewed', in M. Black and W. Smalley (eds.), *On Language, Culture and Religion in Honor of Eugene Nida* (The Hague: Mouton, 1974), pp. 79-99.

1975 Review of *Finding the Old Testament in the New*, by H.M. Shires, *USQR* 30 (1975), pp. 241-46.

'From Isaiah 61 to Luke 4', in J. Neusner (ed.), *Christianity, Judaism and Other Greco-Roman Cults: Studies for Morton Smith at Sixty* (Leiden: Brill, 1975), pp. 75-106.

'Torah and Christ', *Int* 29 (1975), pp. 372-90.

'Palestinian Manuscripts 1947–1972', in F.M. Cross and S. Talmon (eds.), *Qumran and the History of the Biblical Text* (Cambridge, MA: Harvard University Press, 1975), pp. 401-13.

1976 With S. Skiles. Review of *Biblical Exegesis in the Apostolic Period*, by R.N. Longenecker, *Int* 30 (1976), pp. 212-13.

With D. Barthélemy, *et al. Preliminary and Interim Report on the Hebrew Old Testament Text Project*. I. *Pentateuch* (Stuttgart: United Bible Societies, 2nd, rev. edn, 1976).

With D. Barthélemy, *et al. Preliminary and Interim Report on the Hebrew Old Testament Text Project*. II. *Historical Books* (Stuttgart: United Bible Societies, 1976).

Review of *The Dead Sea Scrolls: Major Publications and Tools for Study*, by J.A. Fitzmyer, *RelSRev* 2 (1976), p. 29.

Review of *Qumran and the History of the Biblical Text*, ed. F.M. Cross and S. Talmon, *RelSRev* 2 (1976), p. 29.

Review of *Book of Exodus*, by B.S. Childs, *JBL* 95 (1976), pp. 286-90.

'Adaptable for Life: The Nature and Function of Canon', in F.M. Cross, W.E. Lemke and P.D. Miller, Jr (eds.), *Magnalia Dei: The Mighty Acts of God. Essays on the Bible and Archaeology in Memory of G.E. Wright* (Garden City, NY: Doubleday, 1976), pp. 531-60.

'The Integrity of God', *Concern* (December 1976), pp. 9-10.

'Hermeneutics', *IDBSup*, pp. 402-407.

'Torah', *IDBSup*, pp. 909-11.

1977 'The Bible as the Church's Book', *Thesis Theological Cassettes* 8, no. 2 (1977).

Review of *The Samaritan Problem*, by J. Bowman, *RelSRev* 3 (1977), p. 60.

'The Promise is for All', *Concern* (June 1977) whole issue.

'Biblical Criticism and the Bible as Canon', *USQR* 32 (1977), pp. 157-65.

'Hermeneutics of True and False Prophecy', in G.W. Coats and B.O. Long (eds.), *Canon and Authority: Essays in Old Testament Religion and Authority* (Philadelphia: Fortress Press, 1977), pp. 21-41.

'Torah and Paul', in J. Jervell and W.A. Meeks (eds.), *God's Christ and His People: Studies in Honour of Nils Alstrup Dahl* (Oslo: Universitetsforlaget, 1977), pp. 132-40.

Review of *The Canonization of Hebrew Scripture*, by S.Z. Leiman, *JBL* 96 (1977), pp. 590-91.

Review of *The Liberating Word*, ed. L.M. Russell, *USQR* 32 (1977), pp. 186-88.

With Dominique Barthélemy *et al. Preliminary and Interim Report on the Hebrew Old Testament Text Project*. III. *Poetical Books* (Stuttgart: United Bible Societies, 1977).

Translator, 'Psalms 151', in *The Oxford Annotated Apocrypha* (New York: Oxford University Press, 1977).

1978 'Comparative Wisdom: L'Oeuvre Terrien', in J.G. Gammie *et al.* (eds.), *Israelite Wisdom: Theological and Literary Essays in Honor of Samuel Terrien* (Missoula: Scholars Press, 1978), pp. 3-14.

With W. Lowndes Lipscomb, 'Wisdom at Qumran', in J.G. Gammie *et al.* (eds.), *Israelite Wisdom: Theological and Literary Essays in Honor of Samuel Terrien* (Missoula: Scholars Press, 1978), pp. 277-85.

'The Gospels and the Canonical Process: A Response to Lou H. Silberman', in W.O. Walker, Jr (ed.), *The Relationship among the Gospels: An Interdisciplinary Dialogue* (San Antonio: Trinity University Press, 1978), pp. 219-36.

Review of *The Books of Enoch: Aramaic Fragments of Qumrân Cave 4*, ed. J.T. Milik and M. Black, *JBL* 97 (1978), pp. 446-47.

Review of *The Birth of the Messiah: A Commentary on the Infancy Narratives in Matthew and Luke*, by R.E. Brown, *USQR* 33 (1978), pp. 193-96.

Review of *Prophecy and Canon: A Contribution to the Study of Jewish Origins*, by J. Blenkinsopp, *CBQ* 40 (1978), pp. 598-600.

'History and Archeology of the Qumran Community', Review of *Qumrân: L'Establissement essénien des bords de la Mer Morte: histoire et archéologie du site*, by E.-M. Laperrousaz, *BASOR* 231 (1978), pp. 79-80.

'Isaiah 55:1-9', *Int* 32 (1978), pp. 291-95.

1979 *God Has a Story Too: Sermons in Context* (Philadelphia: Fortress Press, 1979).

'Text and Canon: Concepts and Method', *JBL* 98 (1979), pp. 5-29. (Presidential address delivered 19 November 1978 at the annual meeting of the Society of Biblical Literature.)

Review of *Biblia Hebraica Stuttgartensia*, ed. K. Elliger and W. Rudolph, *JBL* 98 (1979), pp. 417-19.

With D. Barthélemy *et al. Preliminary and Interim Report on the Hebrew Old Testament Text Project*. IV. *Prophetical Books I* (New York: United Bible Societies, 1979).

1980 'Canonical Context and Canonical Criticism', *HBT* 2 (1980), pp. 173-97.

With D. Barthélemy *et al. Preliminary and Interim Report on the Hebrew Old Testament Text Project*. V. *Prophetical Books II* (New York: United Bible Societies, 1980).

1981 'Text and Canon: Old Testament and New', in P. Casetti *et al.* (eds.), *Mélanges Dominique Barthélemy: Etudes bibliques* (OBO, 38;

Fribourg: Editions Universitaires; Göttingen: Vandenhoeck & Ruprecht, 1981), pp. 373-94.
'Response to Lemcio', *BTB* 11 (1981), pp. 122-24.
'The Bible as Canon', *Christian Century* 98 (1981), pp. 1250-55.
Luke—The Theological Historian (Nashville: United Methodist Communications, 1981). Seven videocassettes.
'The Bible as the Church's Book', *Thesis Theological Cassettes* 12, no. 5 (1981).

1982 'Isaiah in Luke', *Int* 36 (1982), pp. 144-55.
'The Conversion of Paul', in *A Living Witness to Oikodome: Essays in Honor of Ronald E. Osborn* (Impact, 9; Claremont: Disciples Seminary Foundation, 1982), pp. 71-93.
With Dominique Barthélemy *et al. Critique textuelle de l'Ancien Testament*. I. *Josué, Juges, Ruth, Samuel, Rois, Chroniques, Esdras, Néhémie, Esther* (OBO, 50.1; Fribourg: Editions Universitaires; Göttingen: Vandenhoeck & Ruprecht, 1982).
True and False Prophecy (Nashville: United Methodist Communications, 1982). Six videocassettes.

1983 'Canon and Calendar: An Alternative Lectionary Proposal', in D.T. Hessel (ed.), *Social Themes of the Christian Year: A Commentary on the Lectionary* (Philadelphia: Geneva, 1983), pp. 257-63.
Review of *The Hymns of Qumran: Translation and Commentary*, by B.P. Kittel, *JBL* 102 (1983), pp. 330-32.

1984 *Canon and Community: A Guide to Canonical Criticism* (Guides to Biblical Scholarship; Philadelphia: Fortress Press, 1984).
Editor. 'Jacob Neusner Issue', *BTB* 14 (1984), pp. 81-125.
'Presenting the Issue', *BTB* 14 (1984), pp. 82-83.
'Canonical Criticism: An Introduction', in O. Wermelinger *et al.* (eds.), *Le Canon de l'Ancien Testament: sa formation et son histoire* (Geneva: Labor & Fides, 1984), pp. 341-62.
Review of *The Creative Word: Canon as a Model for Biblical Education*, by W. Brueggemann, *JBL* 103 (1984), pp. 435-36.
Review of *The Book of Isaiah*. II. *Chapters 22–44*, ed. M.H. Goshen-Gottstein, *JBL* 103 (1984), pp. 448-49.
Review of *The Damascus Covenant: An Interpretation of the 'Damascus Document'*, by P.R. Davies, *JAOS* 104 (1984), pp. 773-74.
'A Multivalent Text: Psalm 151:3-4 Revisited', *HAR* 8 (1984), pp. 167-84.

1985 Review of *Sectarian Laws in the Dead Sea Scrolls: Courts, Testimony and the Penal Code*, by L. Schiffman, *JAOS* 105 (1985), pp. 146-47.
Review of *Dawn of Qumran: The Sectarian Torah and the Teacher of Righteousness*, by B.Z. Wacholder, *JAOS* 105 (1985), pp. 147-48.
'Canonical Hermeneutics in the Light of Biblical, Literary and Historical Criticism', *Proceedings of the Catholic Theological Society of America* 40 (1985), pp. 54-63.
Review of *Holy Scripture: Canon, Authority, Criticism*, by J. Barr, *JBL* 104 (1985), pp. 501-502.

The Bible as Canon (Nashville: EcuFilm/UMCom, 1985). Six videocassettes.

Biblical Reflections (Nashville: EcuFilm/UMCom, 1985). Four videocassettes.

1986 'The Bible and the Believing Communities', in D.G. Miller (ed.), *The Hermeneutical Quest: Essays in Honor of James Luther Mays on his Sixty-Fifth Birthday* (Allison Park, PA: Pickwick Publications, 1986), pp. 145-57.

With D. Barthélemy *et al. Critique textuelle de l'Ancien Testament.* II. *Isaïe, Jérémie, Lamentations* (OBO, 50.2; Fribourg: Editions Universitaires; Göttingen: Vandenhoeck & Ruprecht, 1986).

1987 'First Testament and Second', *BTB* 17 (1987), pp. 47-49.

Review of *Biblical Interpretation in Ancient Israel*, by M. Fishbane, *CBQ* 49 (1987), pp. 302-305.

Review of *The Old Testament Canon of the New Testament Church*, by R. Beckwith, *TTod* 44 (1987), pp. 131-34.

From Sacred Story to Sacred Text: Canon as Paradigm (Philadelphia: Fortress Press, 1987).

'Isaiah in Luke', in J.L. Mays and P.J. Achtemeier (eds.), *Interpreting the Prophets* (Philadelphia: Fortress Press, 1987), pp. 75-85. First published in *Int* 36 (1982), pp. 144-55.

Review of *The Editing of the Hebrew Psalter*, by G.H. Wilson, *JBL* 106 (1987), p. 321.

'The Bible and the Believing Community', *Biblical Literacy Today* 1.4 (Summer 1987), pp. 4-6.

'The Challenge of Fundamentalism: One God and World Peace', *Impact* 19 (1987), pp. 12-30.

'Extravagant Love', *New Blackfriars* 68 (June 1987), pp. 278-84.

'A New Testament Hermeneutic Fabric: Psalm 118 in the Entrance Narrative', in C.A. Evans and W.F. Stinespring (eds.), *Early Jewish and Christian Exegesis* (Atlanta: Scholars Press, 1987), pp. 177-90.

1988 'Annunciations', *Scripture in Church* 18 (1988), pp. 115-20.

'Fundamentalism and the Church: Theological Crisis for Mainline Protestants', *BTB* 18 (1988), pp. 43-49.

'The Strangeness of the Bible', *USQR* 42 (1988), pp. 33-37.

'The Mainline Churches and Theology', *Religion: Journal of the Kansas School of Religion* 25.3 (1988), pp. 1-5.

1989 'Sanders Bible Ministry Project' (Claremont, CA: SpiritQuest Production and Distribution, 1989). Six videocassettes.

Review of *The Narrative Unity of Luke–Acts*, I, by R.C. Tannehill, *Pacific Theological Review* 22 (1989), pp. 79-81.

Review of *Actualization and Interpretation in the Old Testament*, by J.W. Groves, *CBQ* 51 (1989), pp. 329-31.

'Response to Elliot N. Dorff', in J. Hick and E. Meltzer (eds.), *Three Faiths—One God* (London: Macmillan, 1989), pp. 30-34.

'The Heart of the Christian Faith For Me', in J. Hick and E. Meltzer (eds.), *Three Faiths—One God* (London: Macmillan, 1989), pp. 185-86.

'Rejoicing in the Gifts: A Sermon at the Intersection of Shavuot, Pentecost, and Baccalaureate', *Journal for Preachers* 12.4 (1989), pp. 2-6.

'Deuteronomy', in B.W. Anderson (ed.), *The Books of the Bible*. I. *The Old Testament/The Hebrew Bible* (New York: Scribner's, 1989), pp. 89-102.

1990 Member of translation committee, *New Revised Standard Version*. National Council of Churches.

'Extravagant Love', *Scripture in Church* 20.77 (1990), pp. 97-103.

' "Nor do I . . .": A Canonical Reading of the Challenge to Jesus in John 8', in R.T. Fortna and B.R. Gaventa (eds.), *The Conversation Continues: Studies in Paul and John in Honor of J. Louis Martyn* (Nashville: Abingdon Press, 1990), pp. 337-47.

'Hebrew Bible and Old Testament: Textual Criticism in Service of Biblical Studies', in R. Brooks and J.J. Collins (eds.), *Hebrew Bible or Old Testament? Studying the Bible in Judaism and Christianity* (Notre Dame, IN: University of Notre Dame Press, 1990), pp. 41-68.

1991 Introductions and annotations to Baruch, The Letter of Jeremiah, the 'additions' (Prayer of Azariah, Song of the Three Young Men, Susanna, Bel and the Dragon) to the Greek Book of Daniel, The Prayer of Manasseh, Psalm 151, in *The New Oxford Annotated Bible with the Apocrypha/Deuterocanonical Books*, ed. B.M. Metzger and R.E. Murphy (New York: Oxford University Press, 1991).

Review of *The Garments of Torah: Essays in Biblical Hermeneutics*, by M. Fishbane, *TTod* 47 (1991), pp. 433-35.

'Stability and Fluidity in Text and Canon', in G.J. Norton and S. Pisano (eds.), *Tradition of the Text: Studies offered to Dominique Barthélemy in Celebration of his 70th Birthday* (OBO, 109; Freiburg: Universitätsverlag; Göttingen: Vandenhoeck & Ruprecht, 1991), pp. 203-17.

'Understanding the Development of the Biblical Text', in H. Shanks (eds.), *The Dead Sea Scrolls After Forty Years* (Washington, DC: Biblical Archaeological Society, 1991), pp. 57-73.

'The Integrity of Biblical Pluralism', in J.P. Rosenblatt and J.C. Sitterson, Jr (eds.), *'Not in Heaven': Coherence and Complexity in Biblical Narrative* (Bloomington: Indiana University Press, 1991), pp. 154-69.

'Canon as Shape and Function', in J. Reumann (ed.), *The Promise and Practice of Biblical Theology* (Minneapolis: Fortress Press, 1991), pp. 87-97.

Review of *Deuteronomy*, by P.D. Miller, Jr, *TTod* 48 (1991), pp. 366-70.

'Dead Sea Scrolls Access: A New Reality', *The Folio: The Newsletter of the Ancient Biblical Manuscript Center for Preservation and Research* 11.3 (Fall, 1991), pp. 1-4.

'Scripture, Canon of the', in A.S. Atiya (ed.), *The Coptic Encyclopedia* (New York: Macmillan, 1991), pp. 2108-12.

Review of *Mikra*, ed. M.J. Mulder, *JAOS* 111 (1991), pp. 374-76.

1992 'Communities and Canon', in M.J. Suggs, K.D. Sakenfeld and J.R. Mueller (eds.), *The Oxford Study Bible: Revised English Bible with the Apocrypha* (New York: Oxford University Press, 1992), pp. 91-100.

'The Dead Sea Scrolls and Biblical Studies', in M. Fishbane and E. Tov with W.W. Fields (eds.), *Sha'arei Talmon: Studies in the Bible, Qumran, and the Ancient Near East Presented to Shemaryahu Talmon* (Winona Lake: Eisenbrauns, 1992), pp. 323-36.

'Qumran Update: What Can Happen in a Year?', *BA* 55 (1992), pp. 37-42.

With D. Barthélemy, *Critique textuelle de l'Ancien Testament*. III. *Ezéchiel, Daniel et les 12 Prophètes* (OBO, 50.3; Fribourg: Editions universitaires; Göttingen: Vandenhoeck & Ruprecht, 1992).

'Canon', in *ABD*, I, pp. 837-52.

'Sins, Debts and Jubilee Release', in R.P. Carroll (ed.), *Text as Pretext: Essays in Honour of Robert Davidson* (JSOTSup, 138; Sheffield: JSOT Press, 1992), pp. 273-81.

Preface to R.W. Wall and E.E. Lemcio (eds.), *The New Testament as Canon: A Reader in Canonical Criticism* (JSNTSup, 76; Sheffield: JSOT Press, 1992), pp. 7-11.

1993 Edited with C.A. Evans, *Paul and the Scriptures of Israel* (JSNTSup, 83; Studies in Scripture in Early Judaism and Christianity, 1; Sheffield: JSOT Press, 1993).

'Paul and Theological History', in J.A. Sanders and C.A. Evans (eds.), *Paul and the Scriptures of Israel* (Sheffield: JSOT Press, 1993), pp. 52-57.

'Habakkuk in Qumran, Paul and the Old Testament', in J.A. Sanders and C.A. Evans (eds.), *Paul and the Scriptures of Israel* (Sheffield: JSOT Press, 1993), pp. 98-117. (A revision of 'Habakkuk in Qumran, Paul and the Old Testament', *JR* 39 [1959], pp. 232-44).

'Response to Joseph A. Fitzmyer', in H.C. Kee (ed.), *The Bible in the Twenty-First Century: Symposium Papers* (New York: American Bible Society, 1993), pp. 26-29.

Foreword to C.A. Evans and D.A. Hagner (eds.), *Anti-Semitism and Early Christianity: Issues of Polemic and Faith* (Minneapolis: Fortress Press, 1993).

'Psalm 154 Revisited', in G. Braulik, W. Gross and S. McEvenue (eds.), *Biblische Theologie und gesellschaftlicher Wandel: für Norbert Lohfink S.J.* (Freiburg: Herder, 1993), pp. 296-306.

With C.A. Evans, *Luke and Scripture: The Function of Sacred Tradition in Luke–Acts* (Minneapolis: Fortress Press, 1993).

Introductions and annotations to 'Prayer of Manasseh' and 'Psalm 151', in *The HarperCollins Study Bible: New Revised Standard Version with the Apocrypha/Deuterocanonical Books*, ed. W.A. Meeks (New York: HarperCollins, 1993), pp. 1746-48, 1749-51.

'Introduction: Why the Pseudepigrapha?', in J.H. Charlesworth and C.A. Evans (eds.), *The Pseudepigrapha and Early Biblical Interpretation* (Sheffield: JSOT Press, 1993), pp. 13-19.

'Masorah and Masoretic Text', in B.M. Metzger and M.D. Coogan (eds.), *The Oxford Companion to the Bible* (New York: Oxford University Press, 1993), pp. 500-501.

1994 'Nazoraios in Matthew 2:23', in C.A. Evans and W.R. Stegner (eds.), *The Gospels and the Scriptures of Israel* (JSNTSup, 104; Studies in Scripture in Early Judaism and Christianity, 3; Sheffield: JSOT Press, 1994), pp. 116-28.

1995 'Hermeneutics', in W. Willimon and R. Lischer (eds.), *A Concise Encyclopedia of Preaching* (Louisville, KY: Westminster/John Knox Press, 1995), pp. 175-82.

'Scripture as Canon for Post-Modern Times', *BTB* 25 (1995), pp. 56-63.

Review of *Jesus, Qumran and the Vatican*, by O. Betz and R. Riesner, *Int* 49 (1995), pp. 300-302.

Forthcoming Translations, introductions and annotations to Psalms 151, 154, 155, Sirach 51.13ff., 'Plea for Deliverance', 'Hymn to the Creator', 'Apostrophe to Zion', 'Eschatological Hymn', 'Apostrophe to Judah', 'David's Compositions', in J. Charlesworth (ed.), *Princeton Theological Seminary Dead Sea Scrolls Project.*

'The Task of Text Criticism', in the Rolf Knierim *Festschrift*, ed. H.T.C. Sun and K. Eades.

'Identity and Dialogue', in the Lou H. Silberman *Festschrift*, ed. W.G. Dever and J.E. Wright (Atlanta: Scholars Press, in press).

'Intertextuality and Dialogue', in a volume on interfaith dialogue, ed. J.H. Charlesworth (Philadelphia: American Interfaith Institute, forthcoming).

'Scripture as Canon in Post-Modern Terms', in J. Gorak (ed.), *Reflections on the Cultural Revolution: Canons and Disciplinary Change* (Garland Press, forthcoming).

'Hermeneutics of Text Criticism', *Textus* 18.

'Hermeneutics of Translation', in *The Next Step: Removing Anti-Semitism from the Pulpit* (Philadelphia: American Interfaith Institute, forthcoming).

INDEXES

INDEX OF REFERENCES

OLD TESTAMENT

APOCRYPHA

NEW TESTAMENT

INDEX OF AUTHORS